REEL
FOOD

REEL
FOOD

ESSAYS ON FOOD AND FILM

EDITED BY ANNE L. BOWER

ROUTLEDGE
NEW YORK AND LONDON

Published in 2004 by
Routledge
Taylor & Francis Group
270 Madison Avenue
New York, NY 10016
www.routledge-ny.com

Published in Great Britain by
Routledge
Taylor & Francis Group
2 Park Square
Milton Park, Abingdon
Oxon OX14 4RN
www.routledge.co.uk

10   9   8   7   6   5   4   3   2   1

Library of Congress Cataloging-in-Publication Data
   Reel food : essays on food and film / edited by Anne L. Bower.
      p. cm.
   Includes bibliographical references and index.
   ISBN 0-415-97110-1 (hbk. : alk. paper) — ISBN 0-415-97111-X (pbk. : alk. paper)
   1. Food in motion pictures. I. Bower, Anne.
   PN1995.9.F65R44 2004
   791.43'6559—dc22

                                               2004001358

Acknowledgments

Most book projects on which I've worked have been painfully slow—full of stops and starts, uncertainty, and distractions. Not *Reel Food*. From that first moment at three o'clock in the morning when I woke up wondering if anyone had put together a book of essays exploring the variety of ways food is used in movies, everything about this project has come together almost magically.

The magic began with the rush of responses my call for proposals for essays elicited and continued with great cooperation from the authors whose proposals I selected—they all completed their articles in the four-month time period I allowed. Then came quick and enthusiastic interest in the book proposal expressed by Matt Byrnie, the editor I've worked with at Routledge, followed by revision work we all had to undertake. And once again, the essayists kept to our tight schedule. E-mails have flown back and forth, making the process easier, of course. I am not going to thank the Internet, but instead just the scholars—my new food and film colleagues from so many parts of the world—who read my urgent messages and replied so quickly. Thank you, thank you, thank you.

My own editing and arranging work plus the work on my introduction has been spurred along by colleagues closer to home who have given me suggestions, fed me, and calmed my nerves. Here I want in particular to thank Thomas Piontek, my "writing buddy," whose clear eye and sense of language have once again been so very helpful, and Guillermo Arango, whose vast knowledge of films I tapped over and over again.

Anne L. Bower
Ohio State University–Marion

Table of Contents

Focus on Gender—The Body, the Spirit

Making Movies, Making Meals

1

Watching Food: The Production of Food, Film, and Values

ANNE L. BOWER

Whenever I told friends I was working on a book about food and film, they instantly tossed out the names of movies that occurred to them, usually ones in which a main character is a professional cook, like Stanley Tucci and Scott Campbell's *Big Night* (1995), Gabriel Axel's *Babette's Feast* (*Babette's gaestehud* 1987), or Claire Denni's *Chocolat* (1989), or those in which food formulates a dominant symbol system, as in Marco Ferreri's *Blow-Out* (*La Grante Bouffe*, *1973*). As our conversations continued, it was clear that few of them realized how often filmmakers in *all* film genres turn to food to communicate important aspects of characters' emotions, along with their personal and cultural identities; nor did my friends necessarily perceive the intricate ways in which ethnic, religious, sexual, and philosophical aspects of narratives are communicated through food. So I'd find myself giving them examples from the essays in this collection; or I'd turn to some recent movie they wouldn't think had that much to do with food. Take, for instance, Stephen Daldry's *The Hours* (2002), a movie one certainly wouldn't put in the "food film" category.[1] Not only does food underscore thematic points in the film, but the movie's three protagonists—Virginia Woolf, Laura Brown, and Clarissa Vaughan (known to her former lover and now dear but dying friend Richard as "Mrs. Dalloway")—are in part characterized by their interactions with food.

As depicted in *The Hours*, Woolf (played by Nicole Kidman) has servants who prepare all the household's food—we see them chopping bloody meat, mixing pastry dough, and performing other kitchen work. The effete Woolf, however, is portrayed in this film as distant from and uncomfortable with both the servants and their work. At times she rejects food in particular, skipping a meal so she can concentrate on writing her novel *Mrs. Dalloway*. We could say her separation from food indicates both her dedication to her art (the "high art" of literature would have been, in her early-twentieth-century world, quite opposed to the "low art" of food preparation), but also her tenuous hold on life.[2]

Laura, the suburban 1950s housewife (portrayed by Julianne Moore), spends a great deal of her day making a birthday cake for her husband—a cake that must be perfect. In fact, she has so much difficulty fulfilling this domestic role that she throws the first cake away as imperfect and makes a second. It seems that this cake, presented at day's end to the husband back from a busy day in the city, is a summation of her being—pretty, iced, ready to be consumed. We know that she is much more than her cake, but Laura hasn't yet found a way to put *that* on the table.

Clarissa (Meryl Streep), who works as an editor, is preparing a party for her former lover, Richard, a man dying of AIDS, who has just been awarded a grand literary prize. While much of the food for the party is prepared by others, Clarissa insists on making a special crab dish herself; it is one of Richard's favorites. For this woman, as opposed to Virginia Woolf and Laura Brown, creating and sharing fine food is an enjoyable and even artistic activity. In a critical scene in her kitchen, we see her cooking and talking with an old friend of Richard's; this scene is one in which food-related activity advances psychological realism. As they chat, she acts organized and efficient, skillfully cracking eggshells and using her bare hands to separate yolks and whites, as if she's perfectly fine. Streep's acting here demonstrates that the character is repressing a variety of feelings: love and sorrow for her dying friend, jealousy that Richard rejected her as a lover in favor of the man with whom she is chatting, and more. But then, viewers see her shell crack too—her body folding, her breath uneven, her feelings spilling out, raw and formless like the eggs. Much later in the film, after Richard has committed suicide, there's a moment when the camera focuses on food sliding off platters into a garbage can as Clarissa, her lover Sally, and her daughter clean up the banquet that was abandoned. Beautiful, expensive, celebratory food becomes slop, indicating the sense of waste and loss Clarissa feels at this point—losing Richard, the love they'd shared, and perhaps even a part of herself.

In *The Hours*, the filmmaker draws on the tradition of using food and drink as "symbols of life and sensuality."[3] In this film, as in many others that are not centrally about food, we can see that food is still "an essential element," one that, being so very ordinary, "the audience experiences rather than understands."[4] By looking at films like *The Hours*, where food is an important element but not the focus of the movie, alongside "food films," where the narrative does focus on food itself, this volume offers readers the opportunity to study the many ways that food and food-related activities create meaning within movies.

Food has been part of film since films began, yet only recently have we given extended attention to the many and sometimes startling ways that food functions in movies. Food, I contend, is part of the semiotic process of film-making, and *Reel Food* provides new insights into this complex signifying system, involving what is eaten, not eaten, thrown away, preserved, chopped, baked, shared, hoarded, cooked from scratch, taken from a can, or stolen. Twenty years ago, Teresa de Lauretis helped us understand that "cinema is directly implicated in the production and reproduction of meanings, values, and ideology in both sociality and subjectivity" and therefore "should be better understood as a signifying practice, a work of semiosis: a work that produces effects of meaning and perception, self-images and subject positions for all those involved, makers and viewers."[5] Cinema critics and scholars have studied this semiosis in terms of clothes, setting, mise-en-scène, lighting, music, acting, cinematography, and many other elements. What about the recurrent use of food?

Why is it that until recently food's role in movies has been given so little attention, even though it has such powerful representational, metaphoric, and even narrative power? After all, as Gaye Poole, the author of one of the few works to look at this subject makes clear: "It is possible to 'say' things with food—resentment, love, compensation, anger, rebellion, withdrawal. This makes it a perfect conveyor of subtext; messages which are often implicit rather than explicit, but surprisingly varied, strong, and sometimes violent or subversive."[6] And it's not as though this kind of symbolic imagery is something we haven't seen in other visual art forms.

For eons painters have used food images and interactions involving food to tell us about ourselves and our values. How many depictions of Bacchus show him surrounded by grapes and other luscious fruits, signaling pleasures of consumption, orality, the powerful joys of the flesh? How many still lifes indicate—by the selection of foods and tableware, and the inclusion, at times, of elements such as insects or decay—a variety of values, from upper-class status (the ability to import exotic items and afford crystal or fine china), to mortality (a fly upon a luscious peach)? Visual artists use food partly because it is such a common element of their world.

In film, too, this very commonness is part of what allows food to function so evocatively, drawing us into a film's characters, action, and setting. Food is part of the way that, for over a century now, movies have been telling us who we are, constructing our economic and political aspirations; our sense of sexual, national, and ethnic identity; filling our minds with ideas about love and romance, innocence and depravity, adventure, bravery, cruelty, hope, and despair. E. Ann Kaplan reminds us that "in the postindustrial, high-tech age, subjects are constructed through all-invasive commodity relations; they are, that is, constructed preeminently as consumers." She also stresses that "we live in a culture overtaken by machines of the visual. . . . "[7] As we view a movie, then, we consume at many levels simultaneously. "Cinema itself is a kind of consumption," asserts film studies professor Ian Christie, that we are fed "in bite-sized chunks."[8] We consume the film itself, having paid the price of admission (and perhaps bought something to eat and drink from the concession stand), and often consume through it all kinds of values, ideals, and ideas.

While postmodern theory makes us aware of the commodification of personal and group identification, of culture and history, filmmakers, just like other visual artists, began playing with images that highlight consumption and commodification long before we called ourselves postmodern. Thus, while one might think of food in film as a newly emphasized aspect of cinema, upon investigation it turns out this would be a mistaken assumption. In fact, one of the very first movies made by Auguste and Louis Jean Lumière back in 1895 depicted a baby eating lunch.[9] Perhaps in this short film, the Lumières wanted to show something ordinary and reassuring (the domestic scene, the baby, the food) to both interject their new technology into the home and to balance the newness of that technology with the reassuring familiarity of what they depicted.

For many of us, new technologies are unsettling. Part of how we become more comfortable with and accepting of a quickly changing world (not only the technologies themselves, but their impacts on our lives—from changing weather patterns to communications styles to employment systems), is through the representations various media offer us. Consciously or unconsciously, we use cinema, for instance, to familiarize ourselves with strange and new elements of society. As Leo Charney and Vanessa R. Schwartz explain, taking a historical view, "with the advent of a chaotic and diffuse urban culture, the 'real' could increasingly be grasped only through its representations."[10] While they focus on cinematic and other art forms from the late nineteenth and early twentieth centuries, their comment remains useful in explaining one reason why movies of the past and present have such force in our lives. Part of the "real" we grasp is in food imagery, even though this aspect of movies has often been overlooked.

Another writer, Vivian C. Sobchack, looks at how the "excessive violence we see on the screen, the carelessness and devaluation of mere human flesh, is both a recognition of the high-tech, powerful, and uncontrollable subjects we (men, mostly) have become through technology—and an expression of the increasing frustration and rage at what seems a lack of agency and effectiveness as we have become increasingly controlled by and subject to technology."[11] Some food films can be taken as a kind of reaction against such waste and anomie, for they present food's preparation and consumption as reassuring signifiers of cultural continuity. In other movies we see cannibalism, food fights, or food disorders as signs of the very disruptions Sobchack describes. But whether food is coded negatively or positively, whether it plays a major or a minor role, it is often a major ingredient in the cinematic experience.

While *Reel Food* is not organized chronologically and does not intend to give readers a historic review of movies and food, it does include a number of essays that take us back fifty or more years, so that we can see how a variety of earlier filmmakers used food. For example, Eric Reinholtz discusses class and consumerist ideologies in Buster Keaton's silent films, and Blair Davis checks out the "civilizing role of food" in 1930s horror films. Thinking about the way films of the 1950s helped construct the very idea of modern Malaysia, Tim Barnard takes us into an area of cinema that will be new to many of us, yet beautifully illustrates the powerful role that food in movies has played in constructing a national identity, in this case reconciling the "modern" and the "traditional" aspects of a changing society.

In movies of the past and present, viewers' group and/or individual identities are acted upon, reinforced, or perhaps reformed based on national, generational, gender, or other ideologies. Movie characters perform behaviors on the big screen that we will cheer or boo, imitate or avoid. And a surprisingly large part of what allows our (dis)identifications is mediated through food, its sensuality pulling us into film scenes.[12] For example, Americans' Southern, African American, or Mexican cultural ties may be renewed or questioned by the foods served up in movies like Jon Avnet's *Fried Green Tomatoes* (1991), George Tillman, Jr.'s *Soul Food* (1997), and María Ripoll's *Tortilla Soup* (2001); the visceral reactions these movies produce affect viewers' emotional and intellectual reactions to the cultural issues highlighted by the characters and their conflicts. Even among viewers who don't share the ethnic or regional roots important to these films, many will find themselves experiencing a nostalgia for the kind of family or group solidarity that comes through the sharing of foodways.

Reel Food includes essays that focus explicitly on food and foodways, such as the three just mentioned, and thus permits us to explore the emerging "food film" genre. In any film genre, as Will Rockett explains, there is a recurring pattern of "story and situation (syntax or structure) and characters and iconography (semantic elements) [that] appear repeatedly throughout the body of films that make up a genre, doing so often enough to constitute dramatic conventions; this generates audience expectations that encourage their attendance." To be culturally literate means to share in the conventions of particular genres, as with those who go to vampire movies and already understand the references—vampires live on human blood, sunlight is destructive to them, they can be destroyed via a stake through the heart.[13] But even as a genre emerges, so do variations—and genres go through "cycles leading from innovation to emulation to exhaustion."[14] At the present moment, I would say the food film genre is in the emulation stage; whether it can maintain itself through variation and invention or whether it will soon exhaust itself remains to be seen.

What are the conventions within the emerging "food film" genre? To begin with, food, as mentioned above, has to play a star role, whether the leading characters are cooks (professional or domestic) or not. This means that often the camera will focus in on food preparation and presentation so that in closeups or panning shots, food fills the screen. The restaurant kitchen, the dining room and/or kitchen of a home, tables within a restaurant, a shop in which food is made and/or sold, will usually be central settings. And the film's narrative line will consistently depict characters negotiating questions of identity, power, culture, class, spirituality, or relationship through food. "Food genre" films discussed in *Reel Food* include the aforementioned *Big Night*, *Babette's Feast*, *Chocolat*, *Soul Food*, and *Tortilla Soup*, as well as Alfonso Arau's *Como Agua para Chocolate* (*Like Water for Chocolate*, 1993) and Juzo Itami's *Tampopo* (1987). What is and what isn't within the genre of "food film" is, of course, somewhat subjective, with each viewer deciding individually that a film's use of food is so dominant and pervasive as to put it within this classification rather than just in the class of films using food as but one of many elements contributing to a movie's setting, characterization, plot, or theme. Is Jean-Pierre Jeunet and Marc Caro's *Delicatessen* (1991), in which cannibalism is such a central issue, solidly within the genre or not? Is Peter Greenaway's *The Cook, the Thief, His Wife and Her Lover* (1990)—where again cannibalism and other forms of repulsive consumption are central—part of the genre? Some viewers will say yes and others no. Does a film's meaning reside within the food, or elsewhere? Again, different viewers will answer the question differently. Thus, while genres create and—one hopes—satisfy expectations (and also, of course, inform marketing decisions), and while defining and understanding genres assists exploration of cultural and historic trends as well as contributing to our understanding of aesthetic innovation, overreliance on strict genre definitions may be limiting.[15]

For instance, I would not place Martin Scorsese's film version of *The Age of Innocence* (1993) within the food film genre, but I do see it as a movie that makes effective use of food symbolism as part of the setting and character conflicts. In this movie, eight dining scenes are "venue[s] for negotiating conflict between control and resistence," in which all items on the table, from the foods themselves to the silverware, glassware, and china indicate "social standing and power within the group."[16] So even though this film doesn't fit the generic definition I use for a "food film," it clearly depends heavily on food's symbolic power in communicating class structure and social status.

Whether films fall into the food film genre or simply make effective use of food as a communicative element, we see that both what is and what isn't eaten have meaning—defining characters as purists, compromisers, gluttons, ghouls; as rejectors or acceptors of some cultural element (from aging to ethnicity, from class to gender identification, and so forth). Food as stand-in for or accomplice to sex is also something we easily "read" in films, as is a large meal as a sign of connection and communion, whether within a family, a religious community, a carnival, or a journey. Food, we also understand, can script traditional roles (the mother in the kitchen), or indicate dysfunction (food spoiled, badly cooked, poisoned, poorly chosen, vomited, or simply refused). Food can tell us about characters' abject poverty or egregious consumption, about their health or dissipation.

Many of the movies discussed in *Reel Food* would never be considered "food films" by any viewer—movies such as Tod Brownings *Dracula* (1931), Richard Fleischer's *Soylent Green* (1973), Alfred Hitchcock's *Notorious* (1946), and Quentin Tarantino's *Pulp Fiction* (1994). In their "readings" of these films (sometimes stimulated by considerations of food films as a genre), contributors to the collection help us see that the semiotic uses of food are even more multivalent and powerful than a concentration on "food films" alone would allow us to understand. They provide a variety of critical approaches to the film/food intersection, and while this book doesn't pretend to cover every issue, every genre, and every period of film, the many contributions model diverse theoretical approaches that will stimulate readers to see all kinds of films in new ways. By providing many different perspectives from different disciplines and cultures—discussing films from various national cinemas—this volume increases our understanding of how movies shape our sense of the world and our place in it.

Indeed, the essays in *Reel Food* make clear that the consumption of food can stand for consumption of *any* aspect of culture—whether cultural traditions, cultural hybridity, the hyperconsumerism of our postmodern Western world, or some aspect of gender conflict or definition. Food in films can allow filmmakers to comment on the very role of the filmmaker as a creator of culture. In order to present these ideas in a bit more depth, I'll briefly explore two food films that use the same story to present very different ideas about cultural formation and transformation: Ang Lee's *Eat Drink Man Woman* and María Ripoll's *Tortilla Soup*.[17]

Lee's *Eat Drink Man Woman* (1994) fills the screen with images of food preparation. An amazing amount of the film is given over to shots of hands—we're to assume they're those of master chef Chu—manipulating food into traditional Chinese dishes. Within the Chu household, chickens are caught, fish pulled from water barrels and killed, vegetables are selected; we see chopping, slicing, frying, stuffing, steaming, smoking, and other preparation methods. We watch as steamed food is unmolded onto a plate attractively, a whole boiled chicken is squeezed into a tureen, bits of stuffing are delicately enfolded within thin dough for dumplings, bits of pork and sauce are tossed in a wok, and more. The camera pans across racks of cleavers and knives, shelves of herbs, spices, and marinades. At the restaurant where Chu still occasionally works, we see a huge kitchen, with many white-hatted chefs in production. We also see Chu—the superman of the kitchen despite his deteriorating taste buds—enter the restaurant kitchen with a flourish to rescue banquets gone awry. Throughout this movie, food preparation dominates over scenes of actual eating, and one comes to realize that what is actually being prepared is more than food—it is traditional Chinese culture itself.

Chef Chu is a traditionalist in his cooking, and filmmaker Lee's representation is very much about maintaining traditional values of heterosexual family life as well as of the culinary arts, even when modern life places obstacles in the way. Though two of Chu's daughters take unusual paths to wards family life, they do write with men of their choice. Widower Chu also remarries but the youthfulness of his new wife surprises his daughters. The third daughter, who also has a (heterosexual) love interest, is a successful businesswoman, but has suppressed the longing to follow her father's culinary career path. He has dissuaded her from professional cooking, perhaps hoping to save her from a life of hard work, perhaps believing that only a man can be a chef. Although he has always been hypercritical of her, she is swayed partly by filial loyalty to turn down a job promotion that would have taken her out of the country. At the film's end we see this daughter—always the one in most conflict with her father—prepare an extensive and elaborate meal for him, using recipes traditional to Chinese cuisine and to the family's norms. At the beginning of this meal, he tastes the soup, says it is delicious, but then criticizes it for containing too much ginger. Then it dawns on him that he is actually *tasting* the soup; his daughter's cooking has magically restored his sense of taste. The father's recognition of his daughter's culinary power makes him honor her as his daughter and brings her a sense of fulfillment as she feels his recognition, respect, and love. However, this new understanding between father and daughter does not lead to anything further that we see on screen. As expert a cook as she is, we have no indication at the film's end that this young woman will challenge her father's role as a professional chef or in any way challenge his role as patriarch of the family.

Like the master chef at the heart of his movie, Lee, the movie's Taiwanese director, combines many ingredients to create a feast that emphasizes tradition. He splices scenes together, moving rapidly among the daughters' situations, Chu's work at home and at the restaurant, family meals with their sumptuous spreads and arguments, and long shots of traffic moving through wide streets and busy intersections, indicating modernity, change, and time passing. And though some of Lee's other movies have broken away from traditionalist values, this movie hardly questions the morals and values of its central character. The language of the movie is Chinese, all the characters are Chinese, and almost all of the food is traditional Chinese, prepared and cooked in traditional ways, using typical Chinese implements, serving dishes, and tableware. The film, then, can be understood as a production that honors and represents Lee's cultural heritage.

The 2001 film *Tortilla Soup*, based very closely on *Eat Drink Man Woman*, uses the same story to different effect. In this case, director Ripoll incorporates a number of the traditional values that we find in Lee's film—the need to stick with family, the ritual of Sunday dinner as a locus of both family joy and conflict, the absolute loyalty to heterosexuality, and the creativity of a complex cuisine that is very much an art. However, Ripoll overturns traditions when it comes to matters of national cuisine and cultural homogeneity.

In *Tortilla Soup* the many shots of food preparation have the same sensory beauty, precision, and artistry as in *Eat Drink Man Woman*, though obviously the food itself is very different. It is clearly a deliberate choice that the first food shots feature peppers, tomatoes, avocados, and napal cactus, foods that most any viewer will recognize as coming from the Americas and as foods central to Mexican cookery. Like his cinematic predecessor Chu, *Tortilla Soup's* male protagonist Martin is a traditionalist in his foodways, using his outdoor grill, his knives, traditional containers, baskets, and so forth to create and present Mexican dishes that are part of his heritage. But Martin and his family are in the United States and speak a mixture of Spanish and English, and this mixing or fusing of culture—while resisted by the father figure—is shown to be forceful, inevitable, and even desirable. It is the movie's end that most powerfully brings out its difference from *Eat Drink Man Woman* relative to many aspects of cultural formation.

Once again, the daughter with a business career (who has, in this case, overtly expressed her desire to be a professional cook) has foregone a business promotion to remain close to home and has decided to cook a meal for her hypercritical father. However, as she serves the food, Carmen announces right away that this is *her* version of a traditional chicken dish. Martin's reaction is to praise his daughter extravagantly, emotion bringing on the very mixture of Spanish and English we saw him scorn early in the movie. "*Exquisito!* You're good; you're very good!" he tells her. Then he suddenly realizes that he is tasting and smelling—that Carmen's cooking has given him back these senses. In this movie, the *daughter's version* of a standard recipe represents a necessary renewal of culture through artistic variation and generational change.

Ripoll takes cultural change into economic and gender role areas as well. The movie's last scene depicts Carmen, now turned restaurant owner and chef, at her establishment, Nuevo Latino. She is the proprietorial chef, bossing a kitchen full of workers, then emerging to mingle with her guests and in particular, with her own family—they are all at a long table to which she brings plates of lobster. When her father stands to begin questioning her preparation of the seafood, she forces him to sit and laughingly tells him to try the dish first and then offer his criticism. The final image shows Martin, who has married for the second time, with his pregnant young wife and her daughter, along with other family members celebrating the wife's announcement that the child she carries is a girl—impling that the next generations of women will play major roles in determining the future of this family and this culture. By giving us mixtures of foods and languages, along with showing major changes for female characters, filmmaker Ripoll indicates that, in her view, a culture must embrace change in order to thrive.[18]

I've presented this short analysis of two movies as an appetizer to the banquet that awaits readers of *Reel Food* and as a brief demonstration of food's ability to serve as a "remarkably concentrated signifier"—a powerful semiotic system that effectively communicates ideas about cultural formation and identity.[19] What the essays in this book make clear, moreover, is that a focus on food gives us startling new insights into a wide variety of films, whether the essay is written by someone from the United States or Spain, by a historian or a literary scholar, or whether the movies analyzed are from the 1930s or the present day. I suspect that having ingested some of these essays, most readers will find they have a new language, a new system with which to view movies of all kinds.

In much of *Reel Food*, a cultural studies perspective informs the work at hand. This approach airs questions about genre and gender, ethnicity, "high" culture versus popular and mass culture, nation building, migration, changing economic and social patterns, pluralistic societies, and even spiritual values. As Kaplan points out, cultural studies scholars "have precisely appreciated popular culture's ability to bring forth what is repressed and what cannot be said"—that is, the released voices of "certain ideological, minority, and female voices/positions/subjectivities." She further notes that "put another way, popular culture often manifests the breaking through of the semiotic—the preoedipal, prelinguistic terrain theorized by Julia Kristeva as closely linked to primary processes."[20] While Kaplan does not discuss food as a part of popular culture that has this nonlinguistic capacity, I do think that movie viewers respond so readily to food imagery because of food's primacy in our lives; it is a primacy that precedes literacy but then becomes part of our symbol-making, symbol-decoding capacity.

Reel Food's first section, "Cooking up Cultural Values," contains seven essays that consider the many ways that food has been used to represent and formulate national and ethnic identity within movies. Both well-known and little-known movies come under investigation, from 1950s movies produced in Malaysia to an Asian/African director's comedies, from the Japanese *Tampopo* to the Mexican *Como agua para chocolate* and American films about cultural negotiations such as Tim Reid's *Once upon a Time When We Were Colored* (1996) and the films of Woody Allen. The essayists included in this section come from the fields of theater, philosophy, English literature, history, and sociology, and draw on their disciplines to not only elaborate on their understanding of the movies but to show how understanding the movies contributes to their fields, enlarging the study of history and sociology, for instance.

The second section, "Focus on Gender—The Body, the Spirit" presents five very different explorations of food's symbolic power to shape film representations of gender issues, including sexual power, eating disorders, gender equity, female spirituality, and more. This section includes both documentaries and feature films, as well as a variety of feminist approaches to film analysis. The aforementioned *Chocolat, Babette's Feast,* and *Like Water for Chocolate,* as well as Yi-mou Zhang's *Raise the Red Lantern* (1991), Herbert J. Biberman's *Salt of the Earth* (1953), Jutta Brückner's *The Hunger Years* (1979), Todd Haynes's *Superstar: The Karen Carpenter Story* (1987), and Chul-Soo Park's *301/302* (1997), were created by directors from a number of different cultures and represent women of different classes and occupations. Yet the kinds of problems the characters share, concerning the sexuality, subjugation, freedom and power of the body, and spiritual solutions offered by some of the characters to ameliorate isolation or misunderstanding are the critical issues in this section. Once again, the essayists come from distinct disciplines—interdisciplinary studies, women's studies, nutrition and food studies, American studies, anthropology, and foreign languages—and bring the insights of their fields to their writing.

Reel Food's final section, "Making Movies, Making Meals," turns readers' attentions primarily to movies most viewers would not classify within the food film genre. Nonetheless, two movies analyzed here are frequently included in that genre: *Delicatessen* and *The Cook, the Thief, His Wife and Her Lover.* These two films turn the food film genre on its head, dealing as they do in cannibalism and other forms of horrifying or disgusting eating. But in both, food procurement, presentation, and eating itself are central, and in Greenaway's film, where a central character is a cook and the setting a restaurant, the deliberate play with generic boundaries adds to the film's power.

This group of essays investigates the amazing range of films in which food performs key roles, often in unorthodox or even shocking ways. The majority of contributors to this section come from the fields of literature, communication, and film studies, but popular culture and history are also represented; these writers emphasize how a film is made, how the story is told, and what food is doing in the films. As these essays make clear, horror, science fiction, gangster movies, and slapstick comedies all deploy food to create aspects of their narratives, symbols, characterizations, and visual motifs. In addition, food's sensuality and theatricality (a meal can be quite a production), along with our assumptions about what is and what is not to be eaten, mean that food in films can produce in viewers very strong, visceral reactions.

After all of these movies—what about the popcorn? *Reel Food* concludes with an essay that asks that very question—James Lyons's exploration of what we eat while viewing movies. He is interested in what moviegoing means and who moviegoers are. One way to approach these questions is to consider the physical location of the movie theater and the cultural connotations of particular foodstuffs served at different kinds of theaters.

Taking movies seriously as art, as literature, as cultural "work" has for many been a fairly recent phenomenon; film studies courses only entered university curricula about twenty-five years ago. Food as a cultural construct entered the academy even later, though it had been part of agricultural, home economics (human ecology), and industrial studies earlier and had been a topic also in anthropology and some sociology courses. "Food studies" as a separate (though highly interdisciplinary) field is of very recent vintage. It is thus not surprising that the putting together of food and film as a subject of investigation has only occurred recently. My hope is that the essays in *Reel Food*, presented in an array of writing styles and drawing on a wide variety of scholarly specialities, will provide readers with many models for looking at and understanding how food functions in and contributes to film. Clearly, when food appears in a film it is loaded with much more than calories.[21]

Notes

1. *The Hours*, directed by Stephen Daldry. Miramax/Paramount, 2002. Based on the novel, *The Hours*, by Michael Cunningham, screenwriter: David Hare (with Meryl Streep, Julianne Moore, and Nicole Kidman).
2. Whether or not the real Woolf had this relationship to food is not the point. In fact, characters in her novels are sometimes quite intimately involved with food. In the novel *Mrs. Dalloway* (1925), the eponymous protagonist is very involved in planning a large party, and all aspects of domestic life are important to Mrs. Ramsey in *To the Lighthouse* (1927).
3. Ronald D. LeBlanc, "Love and Death and Food: Woody Allen's Comic Use of Gastronomy," in *Perspectives on Woody Allen*, ed. Renée Curry (New York: G. K. Hall, 1996), 147.
4. Jane F. Ferry, *Food in Film: A Culinary Performance of Communication* (New York: Routledge, 2003), 2, 7.
5. Teresa de Lauretis, *Alice Doesn't: Feminism, Semiotics, Cinema* (Bloomington: Indiana University Press, 1984), 38.
6. Gaye Poole, *Reel Meals, Set Meals: Food in Film and Theatre* (Sydney: Currency Press, 1999), 3.
7. E. Ann Kaplan, "Popular Culture, Politics, and the Canon: Cultural Literacy in the Postmodern Age," in *Cultural Power/Cultural Literacy: Selected Papers from the Fourteenth Annual Florida State University Conference on Literature and Film*, ed. Bonnie Braendlin (Tallahassee: Florida State University Press, 1991), 26–27.
8. Ian Christie, qtd. in Susan Wolk and María José Sevilla, "Food on the Silver Screen," online at http://www.londonfoodfilmfiesta.co.uk/Filmma~1/Foodon~1.htm (accessed 14 September 2003).
9. Poole, *Reel Meals*, 13.
10. Leo Charney and Vanessa R. Schwartz, Introduction to *Cinema and the Invention of Modern Life*, ed. Leo Charney and Vanessa R. Schwartz (Berkeley and Los Angeles: University of California Press, 1995), 7.
11. Vivian C. Sobchack, "The Postmorbid Condition," in *Signs of Life in the USA: Readings on Popular Culture for Writers*, 4th ed., ed. Sonia Maasik and Jack Solomon (Boston: Bedford/ St. Martin's Press, 2003), 379.
12. While various postmodern theories have usefully questioned the idea of a "unitary" identity; while most readers of this volume will be comfortable with notions of fragmented and/ or many-layered notions of identity; and while some movies have explored identity in complicated and evocative ways, the powerful sensory experience of moviegoing, with such strong visual, aural, aesthetic, emotional, and intellectual content, often encourages us to have rather direct and at least temporarily uncritical "identifications" with what's depicted in a movie.
13. Will Rockett, "Jason Dreams of Freddy: Genre, Supertext, and the Production of Meaning through Pop-Cultural Literacy," in Braendlin, ed., *Cultural Power*, 179–80, 182.
14. Robert Sklar, *Film: An International History of the Medium* (Englewood Cliffs, N.J.: Prentice Hall with Harry N. Abrams, 1993), 116.
15. Cecilia Novero's (unpublished) presentation at the American Comparative Literature Association conference (4 April 2003), "From Food as Dialectical Image to Food as Icon of Consumption: Food in European Film and the Culture Industry," has helped me a great deal to think about the conventions within the genre of food films. In her own work on the food film genre, Novero sees three developmental stages in which (1) food is seen as excess, disruption, or encodes some dialectical tension, as in the movies of Luis Buñuel and in Jutta Brückner's *Years of Hunger* (1987); (2) food moves from images to "central motif" as in Marco Ferreri's *Blow Out*; and (3) the film food genre emerges solidly, as in Greenaway's

The Cook, the Thief, His Wife and Her Lover (a "film food" but one that is unusual in its insistent questioning of who eats what, why, and how). Novero is also concerned with the "nice" image many recent food films present, which actually hides the situation of food labor (domestic or commercial).

16. Ferry, *Food in Film*, 13.

17. *Eat Drink Man Woman*, directed by Ang Lee, screenplay by Hui-Ling Wang, Ang Lee, and James Schamus, Samuel Goldwyn Company, 1994 (with Sihung Lung, Kuei-Mei Yang, Chien-Lien Wu, Yu-Wen Wang, and Winston Chao). *Tortilla Soup* directed by María Ripoll, screenplay by Ramon Menendez, Tom Musca, and Vera Blasi (with credit also to the screenplay writers for *Eat, Drink, Man Woman*) Samuel Goldwyn Films, 2001 (with Hector Elizando, Jacqueline Obradors, Tamara Mello, Elizabeth Peña, Raquel Welch).

18. Other small bits of multiculturalism also enliven this movie. One daughter has a Brazilian boyfriend, so we hear a bit of Portugese and see the family include an additional ethnicity. And when Martin has to rescue a burned dessert prepared at the restaurant he used to co-own, he gives his creation a French name: *Belle Mélange*. (It should be noted that French cuisine had considerable influence on Mexican cooking, and not only because of French rule from 1864 to 1867.) I do not want to imply that only Ripoll's film accepts notions of change. While Lee's film is clearly more traditionalist, it does include plot and visual elements (although no food elements) that indicate social changes. Chef Wu's surprising marriage to his *young* neighbor (rather than to a woman his own age) her pregnancy with his child; his acceptance of his youngest daughter becoming pregnant before marrying her lover; the fact that one daughter has been a highly successful business woman; and the constant visual intercuts of busy traffic all indicate that change and growth are bound to occur.

19. Poole, *Reel Meals*, 3.

20. Kaplan, "Popular Culture," 20, 19.

21. I'm aware of an increasing number of opportunities for work on food and film: journals like the *Massachusetts Review*, *Food and Foodways*, and *Gastronomica*, and conferences such as those held by the Popular Culture Association, American Culture Association, and the American Comparative Literature Association, to name but a small sampling, that feature special sections on food and film, allow those of us working in this field to exchange ideas more readily.

1
Cooking Up Cultural Values

2

Feel Good Reel Food: A Taste of the Cultural Kedgeree in Gurinder Chadha's *What's Cooking?*

DEBNITA CHAKRAVARTI

Do we eat to live or live to eat? Either way, this profound metaphysical question emphasizes the close ties between food and life. The primary human activity of eating has fascinated filmmakers for years, and in attempting to capture life in all its nuanced variety, they could often do no better than portray the associated activities of acquiring, cooking, apportioning, and serving food. Since the first "food film" was made by the brothers Auguste and Louis Jean Lumière in December 1895 (titled *Déjéuner de bébé*, or *Baby's Lunch*, it was a record of Auguste feeding his infant daughter), directors have been keen to explore cinematic possibilities of food and its many connotations. As Gaye Poole notes, "Food and drink in films frequently act as striking metaphors for the 'big,' meaning-of-life questions. . . . Food as nourishment is a central concern, though the kind of nourishment it stands for, whether physical, figurative, or a combination of both, varies."[1] Philosophers and anthropologists, as well as gastronomes, have outlined the significance of food in deciphering cultural patterns, notable among them being Claude Lévi-Strauss in *The Raw and the Cooked* (1964), which studied food as a civilizing parameter for humans. The impact of food at the personal, familial, social, and universal level has been the subject of study for centuries, and the relatively recent art of cinema has proved particularly alive to exploring food—as fact and fantasy, as physical entity and powerful symbol—in uniquely creative ways.

That food often serves as shorthand for matters affective and emotional—for interpersonal passions and politics—is a well-established fact.

Food is employed as an eloquent indicator for attitudes and constituents of characters, a perfect conveyor of subtexts that often lie too deep for the spoken word. A very basic example should suffice here by way of introduction. In Chris Columbus's *Harry Potter and the Sorcerer's Stone* (2001), the first film in the popular series, Harry fries eggs for the Dursley family while they sit at the breakfast table, a striking visual reminder of the fact that Harry is the outsider in his aunt's family. Not only is he outside their family unit, he is also a wizard in this family of "muggles," which is Potter-speak for nonmagic people. In contrast, the sumptuous feasts at Hogwarts School symbolize a different way of life in which Harry not only belongs to the magic community by eating at the huge table but is often the center of mealtime attention, usually enjoying awe and praise along with his drumsticks and pumpkin pies. Food, an obvious element of physical fulfillment, can become a form of castigation when restricted. His uncle always threatens to cut off his provisions if he misbehaves (tries "anything funny" at the zoo, for example). His unintended "misbehavior" in the second film (*Harry Potter and the Chamber of Secrets*, dir. Chris Columbus, 2002), thanks to Dobby the house elf, occurs when the huge iced cake—embodying the all-important dinner party for his uncle's business associates in all its carefully prepared-for perfection—splats down on Mrs. Mason, an important guest. And if food fiascoes end relationships, the exchange of edibles also begins them; Harry finds his first friend in Ron Weasley, with whom he shares an array of confectionery on the train to Hogwarts, marking the commencement of a gratifying friendship.

In this essay I will look at a film that may arguably be considered one of the most thorough cinematic engagements with food in recent years—Gurinder Chadha's *What's Cooking?* (2000). In all three of her major releases—*Bhaji on the Beach* (1993), *What's Cooking?* and *Bend it like Beckham* (2002)—Chadha shows a consistent interest in food, but *What's Cooking?* affords the fullest study of food as cinematic metaphor. The film is consistent in its synecdochal use of food for family life. It brings the stray manifestations of food as a cultural signifier in the director's other films into sharper focus.

The film opens cleverly with a shot of three generations of a white, all-American family gathered around a Thanksgiving turkey. As the camera zooms out, we discover it to be a poster, an advertisement for a brand of turkey, hanging on the side of a Los Angeles metro bus. The camera enters the bus to reveal a driver and passengers of vastly varied nationalities. During the film's title sequence, the bus then takes us on a tour through the various ethnic neighborhoods of the city (Jewish, Japanese, Indian, African American, Russian, Mexican, etc.). This multicultural tour of the city is a fitting introduction to the subsequent narrative, which focuses on four middle-class families in L.A.'s Fairfax district—the African American Williamses, the Jewish Seeligs, the Mexican Avilas, and the Vietnamese Nguyens. One loses little time in realizing that these families bear little resemblance to the picture-perfect fiction of harmony introduced by the advertisement in the opening shot. The following sequence of children putting on a school show on the theme of universal love and peace also emphasizes the childish simplicity of such an uncomplicated worldview by its juxtaposition with political and domestic unrest outside. The film traces a trajectory from a superficial, all-too-easy fabrication of domestic cheerfulness to a more difficult but more profound and complex sense of community or kinship at the end.

When these four families from diverse cultural backgrounds celebrate Thanksgiving, the most traditional of American holidays, they are forced to confront their respective problems. The film explodes the myth of Thanksgiving dinner as the font of glib harmony, exposing it as the site of familial conflict and cultural aporias instead. The tensions at each dinner table will sputter, secrets will be spilled, and interpersonal conflicts will boil over before the families can truly proffer thanks for their togetherness at the end of this comic drama. It will be necessary here to briefly outline the structure of each family and their respective problems in order to analyze the use of food in each instance.

Herb and Ruth Seeling (Maury Chaykin and Lainie Kazan) welcome their lesbian daughter Rachel (Kyra Sedgwick) and her lover Carla (Julianna Margulies) for the holidays. They have always wanted their daughter to be happy, but had always expected that happiness to consist of a respectable husband and the stipulated train of cherubic children. They feel that they have erred in her upbringing, and suffer from a niggling guilt about her lesbianism. "We must have done something wrong," a weeping Ruth tells her husband. Preparations for the big meal take place amid a certain feeling of being ill-at-ease, where both the parents as well as the lovers establish tenuous codes for being around each other. A particularly tense moment is when Rachel's mother goes in to serve the lovers breakfast in bed, complete with cappuccinos from her newly acquired coffee machine. Rachel's father had shown them into a twin bedroom the night before with the two beds carefully placed apart. The mother finds them lying together in joined beds—Rachel having refused to let Carla move the beds back (in response to Mrs Seelig's wakeup call) in her attempt to present her choice of partner as well as her sexuality to her parents on clear terms. Her mother's offering the couple breakfast in bed is a marker of parental acceptance, albeit an uneasy and grudging one. The parents accepting this life choice themselves is, however, very different from declaring it to the world; Herb and Ruth are clearly still not comfortable with their daughter's sexual orientation. But Rachel's inquisitive Aunt Bea (Estelle Harris) and her husband are coming to dinner, and no one knows what questions to expect.

Like Carla at the Seelig household, new people also show up at the Avila family table. Gina Avila (Isidra Vega), the daughter, brings home her Vietnamese boyfriend Jimmy (Gary Nguyen), who is the eldest son of the Nguyens. Gina's family tries to be friendly to the stranger, but cultural stereotypes are hard to avoid, as we see with the relatives' stereotypical references to

Oriental action heroes like Jackie Chan and Bruce Lee whenever they need to break an awkward silence with Jimmy Nguyen. In a comic moment, the Mexican matrons discuss Jimmy, who is helping in the kitchen, under the assumption that he does not follow their language, and are shocked into nervous laughter when Jimmy suddenly completes the conversation in fluent Spanish. In partaking of their language along with their food, Jimmy is perhaps the most optimistic instance of the film's cultural crossings. Like the daughter in this household, the mother, Elizabeth Avila (Mercedes Ruehl), has also asked her boyfriend Daniel (A. Martinez) to join the family (for dessert). Therefore, Elizabeth is less than pleased when her son Anthony (Douglas Spain) invites her estranged husband Javier (Victor Rivers) to dinner after a chance meeting at the supermarket. Javier had left Elizabeth and the children for an affair with Elizabeth's cousin Rosa, but is now alone and keen to come back. The dinner seems set to test whether it will be as easy for Javier to return to his family as it had been for him to abandon it.

While in the two families discussed above strangers are present at celebratory gatherings, the two remaining families of the film miss a member each at the special dinner. In the Nguyen family, the eldest son Jimmy, on whom the family—especially his mother Trinh (Joan Chen)—pins its hope, will not be present for the holiday. He has called to plead academic pressure, but is actually right across the road with his girlfriend Gina Avila at her family's Thanksgiving dinner. This can be seen as the second-generation immigrant's fascination with another culture, accelerated to a certain extent by an impatience with his own, which he understands only partially. Jimmy's sister Jenny makes such a fascination clear when she sees Vietnamese chili paste going into the turkey and complains, "Why do you want to make the turkey taste like everything else we eat?" Her grandmother replies, "Why do you want everything to taste like McDonald's?" (In another film by an Indian director, Piyush Dinker Pandya's *American Desi* [1999], the young Indian character has a similar revulsion for his own spicy cuisine.)

As we see with the Nguyens, generation gaps become wider when the grandparents have lived their lives in their distant homeland, the young ones have never been to their country of origin, and the parents struggle to hold the family together, trying to survive in an alien culture while attempting to bring up their children according to their value system. The second Nguyen son smuggles a gun into his bedroom, and his sister Jenny discovers it (much to her chagrin), but she cannot communicate her fears to her parents, who find a condom among her clothes, see her with her white American boyfriend, and feel she is compromising the honor of the family. The children's acculturation and the immigrant parents' fears collide, much as in Chadha's more recent film *Bend It like Beckham* and her earlier *Bhaji on the Beach*. Characterization has always been Chadha's forte, and the Vietnamese family in L.A. provides as rewarding a study of life at a point of cultural adjustment as does the Indian community in England in *Bend It like Beckham*. The parents hold on to familiar conventions in an alien land with a desperation that can only arise from fear—the fear of the racial and cultural "other." Besieged by a way of life not their own, they are forever apprehensive of losing their children to forces they do not comprehend and cannot control. They have an urge to belong—not to the community at large, but to other families like themselves, a displaced hunger for acceptance that all emigrants have. The children of these families encounter their own share of problems. Caught between cultures, they cannot reconcile home and the larger world around them. The matriarch in *Bhaji on the Beach* declares, "This country has cost us our children"; Trinh Nguyen echoes the same dismay when she feels her daughter Jenny is sexually active. "What's happening to my children in this country?" she asks, and later replies to her own question, "We don't know anything about our children."

Over at the Williams house we find most of the earlier themes from the previous families repeated. While there are hints in the Vietnamese household that Trinh has to make special efforts to keep her resident in-laws content, the generational stress is more apparent in this African American home, where Audrey (Alfre Woodard) loses her patience with her critical mother-in-law Grace (Ann Weldon), who is visiting them for Thanksgiving. Grace finds her culinary ideas less than welcome within Audrey's carefully planned, cosmopolitan menu. Audrey's son Michael (Eric K. George) is a college dropout who refuses to attend Thanksgiving at home as he does not get along with his father; this shocks his grandmother, who cannot imagine the day without the presence of the entire family. Like Trinh, Audrey has a rebellious teenager on her hands. And as in the Avila household, the husband, Ron (Dennis Haybert), is guilty of an extramarital affair. Audrey and Ron Williams want to keep their own family's ruptures secret from Ron's mother and from the white friends who have joined them for the Thanksgiving feast. The friends' teenage daughter—a politically radical vegetarian—is an unwilling attendant at the dinner, proving that it is not only immigrants who find their growing children alienated from themselves.

Tradition becomes a seminal issue in the context of each family's ritual American celebration. Even as the customary turkeys are stuffed, roasted, and basted, each family reiterates familiar conventions and values, and resists confrontation with frightening changes. The Seeligs struggle to cope with their daughter's "unnatural" decision. The Avilas sit down for dinner with a member of an unfamiliar culture (Jimmy) under the unspoken tension of having the prodigal patriarch Javier back at the head of the table along with the presence of Elizabeth's new boyfriend. The Nguyens find their established beliefs being challenged by their children. The Williamses feel Michael's absence, and matriarch Grace finds her regular macaroni and cheese rejected in favor of Audrey's shitake mushroom stuffing. "I may be wrong, but something doesn't seem quite right," she says soon after she arrives at in L.A., and viewers realize that not only are there troubles in the Williams family, where Ron and Audrey are writhing in a fragile marriage while Michael sees his father as an antagonist, but the trouble is spread across the four families, and the first three quarters of the film delineate the individual anxieties in careful detail. As the title suggests, there is something cooking, things are building up to a head, and the film hurtles relentlessly toward a crisis in each of the four households.

The narrative expertly interlocks the four separate plots, and does so in many ways. Jimmy Nguyen is Gina Avila's boyfriend. Elizabeth Avila is the teacher of the youngest Nguyen son, Joey. The Nguyens own a video store frequented by the Avilas. Joey goes to the same school as the younger Williams daughter, and we see both Trinh Nguyen and Audrey Williams at the school play where their youngsters are performing. But the greatest connection among the four families is primarily through the food that they acquire, prepare, and consume on this day of celebration. Anthony, the eldest Avila son, buys a turkey from the same supermarket where Audrey Williams is shopping with her daughter. Once the provisions, dominated by the massive fowl, are brought home, the camera begins its dizzying dance from kitchen to kitchen. All through the film, even as they busy themselves with the chopping and churning, the frying and the filleting, the sauces and the sautés, the characters are busy trying to find a recipe for life.

The film celebrates the sheer physicality and enjoyment of food, but simultaneously equates its preparation, serving, and consumption with the general business of constructing modes of existence and testing them for viability in a less than perfect world. Most important conversations and actions take place in the kitchen and dining room, where meals are readied and served, consumed or abandoned, accompanying domestic delight or discord. It is interesting how food in films—often the same fare—can be put to very different uses, and can present different, even contradictory connotations. The symbolic uses that may be made of food can cover a broad spectrum. In Nagesh Kukunoor's *Hyderabad Blues* (1998) a young girl tries to woo the protagonist into marriage, as he is her passport to the United States. She tries to consolidate her claim on him by bringing him sweet delicacies, which her mother emphasizes she has prepared "with her own hands." Similar fare, used as a bribe again, but for a more chillingly devious purpose altogether, can be seen in the more recent *Monsoon Wedding* (Mira Nair, 2001); the pedophile patriarch lures the young girl with fresh sweetmeats (the same confection mentioned in the previous film) in a household that is too busy with wedding preparations to notice her absence.

Chadha realizes that because the preparation of food requires thought, labor, attention, time, and often love, it becomes the perfect vehicle for emotional manifestations. Feelings are kneaded into food; passions find shape in culinary creations. Through its footage of food, *What's Cooking?* evokes life in all its cultural variety, but ultimately reveals the essentially integrating bedrock of human nature. The American dramatist Thornton Wilder, in *The Long Christmas Dinner* (1931), presents an analysis of continuity and change as played out by the annual ritual of the festive dinner. Chadha likewise uses the

Thanksgiving meal as a seminal dramatic moment heightening conflicts in the lives of her characters. Beginning with the day before Thanksgiving and concluding on the evening of the big feast, *What's Cooking?* encapsulates the lives of its characters for the viewer along with all the problems that have troubled them up to this moment of resolution.

If eating is in itself the most primary human action, then eating together as a group becomes a ritual device to structure communal existence. Alan Saunders notes that "we usually learn more about characters when they meet across the dinner table than when their bodies sweatily conjoin in intercourse . . . what goes on over meals is in itself so revealing. . . ."[2] Eating together often serves in films to distill broader areas of action and interaction into the limited focal zones of plates and bowls; the dining table can be an effective battlefield with the cutlery flashing angrily, or it might be the only place where people drown their differences in the clink of glasses. Whatever the case, films have always used communal feasting as well as the common family dinner to telling effect. And it follows that eating together on a special occasion, perhaps an annual event that brings people together—often members of the same family—who have not seen each other for a long time, serves as a pivot in numerous films. If collective repasts denote a stabilized and cohesive social pattern, then that pattern can be symbolically ruptured if a meal is interrupted, abandoned, rejected, or disturbed in any way. Given the tension that permeates the film by the time that all four families sit down to their respective dinners, it seems no surprise that none of the four meals in *What's Cooking?* go according to plan.

Around each table, things come to a head. Dinners are disturbed, and feasts literally and metaphorically fall apart, during the many open and covert disturbances brewing in four families. At the Seeligs, the dinner starts well, but Aunt Bea soon singles Rachel out to barrage her with advice about getting married and having children "before it's too late." She finally wears down Rachel's patience, despite desperate attempts by Herb and Ruth to change the subject, drawing out Rachel's confession that she is a lesbian and that Carla is more than just her roommate. But Herb and Ruth are in for a further surprise before they get over the shock of having this fact made public. Rachel is pregnant from a gay donor, her sister-in-law's brother, who is also present at the dinner. Aunt Bea now has a new question, this time about the unborn baby's religion, as the "father" is not Jewish and neither is Carla.

At the Avilas, Javier turns up at the family meal expecting his place at the table (and in his household) to still be empty. But Elizabeth has a stranger by her side, and Javier finds that hard to digest, leading to violent outbursts during dessert. Violence rears up in a more frighteningly physical form in the Nguyen kitchen where the turkey burns beyond recognition. The chaos of the fire alarm turns frantic as the gun is revealed to the family, and in the ensuing confusion the young Joey picks up the gun and plays with it, inadvertently firing a bullet.

At the Williams house, the dinner literally falls apart when the table breaks in the middle, and Audrey's carefully laid-out fare lies scattered in disarray even as her life seems to shatter. Her son Michael shows up at the last minute, and over a hastily reinstated meal declares that he has been involved in political violence, against the principles of his father. Ronald's extramarital affair is revealed, and Audrey suffers from a near breakdown in a skillfully rendered scene that signals her precarious mental state through her cutting up and gobbling down slice after slice of pie as skeletons keep emerging from the family cupboard. Caught up in an ego clash between her husband and son, humiliated by her husband's infidelity, and pressured to keep up appearances before her demanding mother-in-law, Audrey dissolves under duress. In a film largely about food, this moment stands out in its urgency and anguish, and will be remembered as one of the most effective screen uses of food to delineate extreme passion.

Like all of Chadha's films, *What's Cooking?* is concerned with the place of the woman in the familial and social structure. Chadha often hints at the fact that because women are largely responsible for family meals and because the meals are symbolic of familial well-being, women of the household are key in determining the family's happiness, comfort, and security. Provision becomes an instrument of female power, and this film explores its functioning. The displacement of cultural tensions into gastronomic calamities is related to women's social/familial roles and their conventional responsibilities for domestic repose and repasts. Chadha's women not only prepare the food, they often decide who gets to sit at the table to partake of it. Elizabeth Avila proves resistant to her husband Javier's request to return to the family, in spite of the family's—especially the male members'—wish to have him back. She has decided her future for herself. In rejecting a husband who had once rejected her, she asserts her identity as an individual who does not exist merely to comply with her husband's whims. Audrey Williams makes a place at the table for her son despite her husband's displeasure, and in the process brings them to a resolution—if a somewhat uneasy one—at the end. Unlike Elizabeth, she chooses to forgive her repentant husband and agrees to work toward a new start. Rachel Seelig sits at her parents' table to participate in the traditional meal, but does not swallow her words with the turkey. She refuses to conceal her life, and lays her decisions on the table along with the food. Lesbianism, male infidelity, and the single woman's search for self-definition provide table talk in the film.

Chadha's earlier film, *Bhaji on the Beach*, is (as its trailer claims) about "friendship, fun and food." It deals with a group of Asian women taking a day off from their ceaseless chores as cooks and caretakers of the family to go for a picnic on the beach in Blackpool, England. During the course of the day there are several disagreements, hard words are exchanged, meals are disturbed, and drinks are spilled. Only at the end do the women of different ages and backgrounds unite in a common understanding. This female bonding comes to the forefront in *What's Cooking?* as well. The disruptions often bring the women together in an act of solidarity, united by a common understanding of feminine issues. Grace reprimands her son for his unfaithfulness to Audrey and recognizes her daughter-in-law's strength in trying to keep the family together despite all odds. A telling instance of this mutual respect between Audrey and Grace occurs when Grace accepts Audrey's new meal ideas, and Audrey in turn allows her to serve her regular macaroni and cheese to her grandson. In accepting each other's dishes, the two women demonstrate an understanding that is never expressed in words. When Elizabeth rejects her husband's plea to come back to her, she finds support from both her teenage daughter and her mother in the face of initial protest from her son.

Bend It Like Beckham, Chadha's next movie, while engaged in furious footballing does not neglect the writer-director's concerns about cuisine. The film holds out the idea of food as one of the last bastions of tradition against an all-invasive cultural otherness, an important cultural capital. Faced with inevitable, incomprehensible changes to her way of life, Mrs. Bhamra (Shaheen Khan) insists that Jess (her daughter and the film's protagonist, played by Parminder K. Nagra) learn to cook a full-course North Indian meal even though she is all set to become a champion football player. In bequeathing this seminal skill to her daughter, Jess's mother can find comfort in the feeling that she has not failed in her maternal duties. Similarly, the protagonist's mother in Kukunoor's *Hyderabad Blues* insists on piling his plate with home-cooked fare during every meal while he is home on vacation; there appears a kind of urgency to make her American-based son imbibe as much as possible of his familial/cultural values in the short span of time that he is at home. In a rapidly shifting world, food is often one of the last fundamentals of normalcy and familiarity. In *What's Cooking?* the festive dinner thus becomes an important occasion.

Undercooked or overdone, bland or blazing, leftovers are carefully gathered, and reworked as best they can be at the end of the film. What viewers are left with is a sense of necessary compromises in cultural values, new and different tastes of life. Cultural fusions are difficult, as Chadha knows and shows (to the delight of her viewers, many of whom, like the cinematic characters, have also been rendered rootless by the shifting sands of global capital and international commerce). "Border crossings and diaspora are at the center of Kenya-born, Punjabi-parented Asian/African filmmaker Gurinder Chadha,"[3] notes Gwendolyn Aubrey Foster, as they are with Chadha's contemporary, Mira Nair, who is "a cineaste of uncompromising feminist postcolonial subjectivity" whose "work explores the nomadic space of postmodern feminism."[4] Interestingly, Nair's *Mississippi Masala* (1992) also draws emphatically on a food metaphor in its title—*masala* (meaning "spice" in Hindi) juxtaposed alliteratively with the very American *Mississippi*—foregrounds the culture collision that forms the film's theme. In an interview, Nair said that being a brown person, between black and white, she could move between the two worlds because she was neither;[5] all her films prove that Chadha possesses the same ease of mobility, the same chameleon "negative capability" of being able to imaginatively inhabit differing worlds. Like Nair, Chadha grasps the immigrant subjectivity complete in all its elation and angst. She operates from a postcolonial feminist rhetorical space and has developed her own voice in the increasingly growing plethora of exile discourses.

What's Cooking?—as this essay has attempted to prove—stands relevantly poised at the new millennium with its intelligent inroads into the problematic of cultural conflicts. The film maps itself over the emerging cinematic genre of postcolonial cultural crossings, especially against recent examples like Damien O'Donnell's *East is East* (1999), Nair's *Monsoon Wedding*, and others. For Chadha, as for many of her contemporaries, the new world order is inevitably and irrevocably a mixed one. And her constant and consistent connection between matters cultural and culinary underscores the hybridization of contemporary metropolitan life.

Notes

1. Gaye Poole, Preface to *Reel Meals, Set Meals: Food in Film and Theatre* (Sydney: Currency Press, 2001), xi.
2. Alan Saunders, Foreword to Poole, *Reel Meals*, 5.
3. Gwendolyn Audrey Foster, *Women Filmmakers of the African and Asian Diaspora: Decolonizing the Gaze, Locating Subjectivity* (Carbondale: Southern Illinois University Press, 1997), 132.
4. Ibid. 111.
5. Ibid.

3

Food, Play, Business, and the Image of Japan in Itami Juzo's *Tampopo*

MICHAEL ASHKENAZI

This essay examines the image of "Japaneseness" created by the director Itami Juzo as he looks at Japan through the lens of food in his 1985 film *Tampopo*.[1] The film, which chronicles the (re)construction of the character Tampopo's noodle restaurant, hybridizes "traditional" and "modern" aspects of Japan. Through multiple images of food and food consumption, through a narrative structure that owes much to traditional Japanese theater, and through sly digs at the Japanese establishment, Itami touches on, and illuminates, much of how Japan views itself.

Two main aspects of the film are examined here. The first is the nature of the foods shown, prepared, and consumed. Itami chose those foods with great care, and each instance of food refers to multiple layers of social reality within Japanese culture (with some subtle satirical digs). My essay attempts to advance an answer to the question of why certain foods are featured. A second aspect to be dealt with here is the interplay of social relations and status that all scholars and native Japanese agree are critical for understanding Japanese society. Virtually all important relationships and social issues are expressed in the film through individuals' relationships to food rather than directly. Among the social issues are sex and violence, and the breakdown of Japan's traditional isolationist position: in some ways, Itami prophesies the rise of the multicultural Japan of the twenty-first century. Though Itami the satirist often exuberantly overshadows Itami the social realist and Itami the filmmaker, the film's unusual nonlinear structure, the images it evokes, and its peculiarly sober view of Japan offer particularly useful insights into the relationship between the Japanese and their food.

A brief summary of the plot is useful, though it must be noted that the plot is often interrupted by asides—sketches of Japanese life that bear little relationship to the main story except that they reflect on the common theme of food. As in Japanese Kabuki and Noh drama, these asides embellish the theme rather than the main story. These asides are briefly noted in a separate paragraph below.

A milk-tanker driver, Goro (Tsutomu Yamazaki), and his assistant, Gan (Ken Watanabe), are struck by pangs of hunger—Gan has been reading a book describing the "art of noodle eating"—and stop at a rundown noodle restaurant run by the depressed widow Tampopo (Nobuko Miyamoto), who is fancied by Pisken (Rikiya Yasuoka), a builder. After an exchange of words, Goro is attacked by Pisken and his men. Waking up in Tampopo's kitchen after a beating, he critiques Tampopo's noodles. Because of his masterful critique, she begs him to be her sensei (master teacher), and teach her to make proper noodles. Goro's training regimen, known as seishin (spiritual training: a form of training for personnel in large Japanese corporations) includes not only speed and quality trials, but physical education. Tampopo and Goro then start a lengthy process of observing their competitors, with Goro critiquing each shop: a shop full of wasteful motion and inattention to customers is contrasted with a shop run by two old men in perfect harmony with their customers and their food. A young *Sapporo ramen* (a type of popular noodle) cook shows attention to customers. Goro introduces Tampopo to a group of homeless men, whose leader, a former professor, is an expert on noodles, and he joins the Tampopo support team. Goro and Tampopo have a brief romantic evening. Following a fistfight between Pisken and Goro the two men become friends, and the builder Pisken joins the team, remodeling Tampopo's restaurant as well as giving Tampopo herself a makeover. Tampopo, who is having difficulty with the soup base for the noodles, steals a secret recipe from a Chinese noodle shop. Eating with her friends at a *nihonsoba* (buckwheat noodle) shop, she saves the life of a wealthy old man who is choking on some food, and he offers her the assistance of Shuhei, his chauffeur and cook, who helps her steal the secret of perfect noodle dough from another Chinese shop. Finally, Pisken teaches her the secret of his family's special garnish, and the new Tampopo noodle shop is born. A long queue forms outside the prosperous shop, and the various helpers depart in silence.

The film actually opens with two asides; other asides are interwoven throughout the narative. First, a *yakuza* (organized crime) boss (Koji Yakusho), his mistress (Fukumi Kuroda), and his henchmen (carrying a luxurious picnic) attend a film, and the *yakuza* boss addresses us, the viewers. The film then moves to a scene of a young man being taught to eat noodles by an old noodle master. The *yakuza* boss and his mistress appear from time to time throughout the film in a continuous series of food consumption and erotic activity. In other asides, a group of senior businessmen are confounded by a Western menu, just as a class in etiquette training for young women is disrupted by a Westerner enjoying a plate of spaghetti. An old lady walks into a luxury convenience store late at night; she handles and damages the products, which results in her being chased by the clerk. A thief is hustled by a con man in a restaurant and then arrested by a detective, but the camera abandons them to follow a husband rushing to the bedside of his dying wife. In her last dying act, she cooks food for her family. A man with a toothache hallucinates about Chinese dumplings, then offers an ice cream to a child whose parents are attempting to maintain an organic lifestyle. In the penultimate scene, the *yakuza* is shot, but before dying he talks to his mistress about some special sausages he has never tried. Whether in the film's main storyline or in the various asides, the setting is almost wholly within an urban landscape, making this Japanese film remarkable for the fact that there is not a cherry blossom nor a pretty temple, shrine, or perfect volcano to be seen: Itami's Japan is a thoroughly modern and cosmopolitan one.

The Foods

A large number of meals and items of food are consumed throughout the film. However, within the broad spectrum of Japanese cuisine, which encompasses many types of food,[2] Itami has chosen to show only a few of the foods that Japanese people consume. An intriguing question that arises is, therefore, "Why those foods?" It is obviously possible to reply that Itami simply liked those foods, but Japanese culture has exhibited a fondness for visual and verbal puns and for extracting meaning from the juxtaposition of items and activities, and it is therefore likely that these foods were chosen with special care. However, the implications and even symbolic meanings of these foods cannot be understood without some understanding of the underlying cultural contexts.

Noodles

The major food in this film is noodles, and this would appear to be paradoxical. "Everyone" knows that the Japanese staple is rice, yet rice appears only twice in the film, in very specific contexts. In fact, the Japanese eat a wide array of noodles. These can roughly be divided into three classes: indigenous Japanese noodles; noodles of Chinese origin; and European noodles, such as spaghetti.

Japanese-style noodles come in two major classes (there are others that we can afford to ignore here). Both soba (thin buckwheat noodles) and udon (usually thick wheat noodles) are consumed in or with a broth based on traditional Japanese dashi (bonito and seaweed stock). Various garnishes—fried tofu, mochi rice cake, duck meat, fish of various types, leeks and/or other vegetables, and many other ingredients—are added.

There are also a large variety of Chinese-origin noodle dishes. These are usually crinkled egg-flour noodles that are most often, as in the film, served in a pork- or other meat-based stock with vegetables, often referred to as ramen (Japanese rendition of the Chinese lo-mien) or as chûka soba (Chinese soba). Like Japanese noodles, they are served in a bowl of stock, and garnished according to choice. One particular variant of Chinese-style noodles— *Sapporo ramen*, named for Sapporo, the capital of Hokkaido, Japan's north-ernmost island—should be kept in mind.

Spaghetti has been tremendously popular in Japan, as elsewhere. It is usu-ally served on a plate with the usual Italian-style sauces, though oddities such as spaghetti sandwiches (confined, to the best of my knowledge, to Japan and Scotland) and fried spaghetti are available.

Japanese-style and Chinese-style noodles can be clearly distinguished. First, most dedicated noodle shops, of which there are a great number, will serve either one or the other, and will be clearly identified as such. Japanese noodle shops, usually referred to as *sobaya*, will have Japanese décor, and usually sport a blue or a white *noren* (a small banner suspended over the shop entrance to announce it is open). Chinese noodle shops will have a white *noren* with red characters, and probably a Greek-key design. Their interiors often include some evocation of China as well.

The presentation of Chinese and Japanese noodle dishes is also clearly identified, even in shops that sell both. Chinese noodles come in white porce-lain bowls, often with a motif of flowers or a classic Greek-key design around the rim. Japanese soba comes in earthenware bowls, often in colors of black or brown, with little or no decoration. The use of specific utensils for specific foods is well documented in Japanese food culture,[3] and so it is not surprising to find that a specific garnish-noodle combination will appear in a specific type (color, shape, glaze) of bowl for Japanese noodles. Finally, European noo-dles will appear, of course, on a European-style plate with fork and spoon.

For those with a statistical bent, let me note that noodles are consumed in eleven scenes in *Tampopo*. One noodle dish is Japanese and one is European; all the rest are Chinese, with one instance of a *Sapporo ramen*, clearly identi-fied by the headband and long hair of the cook (emulating the Ainu natives of Hokkaido, and thus signifying Sapporo) and a small figurine of a bear.

Certainly the choice of noodles as the focus of the film is not accidental. Noodles are a "minor" food in Japanese cuisine and do not have the sacerdotal and formal context of rice. However, they are quintessentially popular, con-sumed in standing-only bars as well as noodle specialty shops, and can also be a gourmet food. Thus the issue of class, in its Japanese guise, emerges through this most humble and common of Japanese dishes.

Japanese Foods

Interestingly enough, there are only two instances involving the consumption of indigenous Japanese foods in the entire film. That having been said, it must also be noted that the Japanese have been inveterate borrowers of foreign culture virtually since the formation of Japanese culture in the fourth or fifth century CE. The original diet of the inhabitants of the islands—millet, iris bulbs, and shellfish—was modified by borrowings from the Chinese and the Koreans. Rice replaced millet as a staple. A formal dining arrangement evolved over centuries, as did the standard structure of the Japanese meal, *ichiju sansai* (one soup, three side dishes, and rice as an unstated given).[4]

Significantly, "native" Japanese foods are shown in only two scenes. On the morning after meeting Tampopo, while recovering from the beating he received at the hand of Pisken and his men, the truck driver Goro and his sidekick Gan are served a traditional breakfast: rice, seaweed, and raw egg beaten into *natto* (fermented beans). In this scene, Itami places the action in context. The film takes place in eastern Japan, where *natto* would be very accepted; western Japanese from the Kansai (Osaka-Kyoto) area and farther westward are as horrified by the strong smell and unctuous texture of *natto* as are most foreigners. Tampopo is a traditional woman (she makes her own pickles, which most housewives no longer do, but which was a measure of a housewife's domestic skills in the past), and her household is a traditional one (with a Japanese breakfast rather than today's more common toast and coffee).

The second scene that shows Japanese foods takes place at a Japanese noodle shop, decorated in conventional Japanese style, with both tables and tatami mat seating. An old man is brought in by his wife, who then departs in her chauffeur-driven Rolls Royce. He orders *kamo-nan[ban] soba* (soba noodles in stock garnished with slices of duck and leeks); *tempura soba* (soba noodles in stock garnished with battered deep-fried prawn) and *oshiruko* (a thick sweet soup—almost a porridge—of azuki beans garnished with balls of *mochi* (pounded glutinous rice cakes). It has to be said that these foods may have been chosen simply because Itami likes them; however, Itami cannot have been ignorant of the fact that all three of these Japanese dishes have foreign referents. Foods labeled *nanban* (meaning "foreign" or "barbarian" style) are those introduced initially by the Portuguese and Spanish, who had great influence on Japan in the sixteenth century. The same is true of tempura, the deep fried delicacies that are today a mainstay of Japanese haute-cuisine; the word tempura, some scholars believe, is derived from the Portuguese term tempera (with egg). And *oshiruko* is part of the class of *okashi*, confectionery, which, while it is usually called *wagashi* (Japanese sweets) to distinguish it from *yogashi* (cakes and other Western confectionery), was introduced into Japan from China.

Japanese foods displayed in the film are thus true to type as an eclectic mixture of influences and foodstuffs that the Japanese have made uniquely their own. In effect, these foods celebrate the diversity within homogeneity that is the true expression of Japanese culture.

Non-Japanese Foods

In Japanese cuisine, as in the film, foreign influences have been formative in the creation of a unique cultural expression. I have argued elsewhere, following Ivan Morris, that Japanese food, as well as much else of its material culture, must be seen in terms of a process of importation followed by a process of digestion; I have labeled this process "Japanization."[5] Foreign influences are absorbed, then transformed and fitted into the Japanese scheme of things socially, behaviorally, and aesthetically. Thus, the fact that most of the foods (in about thirty-two different food scenes throughout the film) are of non-Japanese derivation is unimportant. These are Japanese foods because that is what the Japanese eat, and, in fact, the entire culture of Japan is composed of objects, actions, and ideas of non-Japanese origin that the Japanese have modified to their taste (in both senses of the word). Two cultural influences predominate, and both are present in the film: East Asian and European. (Interestingly, Itami did not display American fast food or American cuisine, perhaps because, insofar as the former goes, he felt there were boundaries of taste he did not want to overstep.)

Excepting noodles, which have been dealt with above, there are some other instances of Chinese foods being consumed. In the film, there appears to be a thread running through the choice of Chinese foods, which is also common to the appearance of another food culture—that of Korea. The thread here is the contrast between elite and common fare. In regard to the Chinese food, in a scene unrelated to the rest of the story line, we see a tout discussing a business proposition with an elderly, unworldly man who we learn is a professor from Tokyo University (Japan's most prestigious and powerful institute of learning). They are in an expensive Chinese restaurant, and while he listens to the pitch the professor engulfs a large number of pieces of Peking duck wrapped in pancakes—one of the crowning achievements of Northern Chinese cuisine. The professor agrees to give his lifetime savings to the tout for investment. The tout hurries off to get things arranged, and we discover two things: the tout is a con man, and the "professor" is actually a small-time thief who has picked the con man's overstuffed wallet. The professor is then and there collared by a detective, and as the two leave the restaurant they are almost run over by a man running by who is hurrying home to his dying wife. Before the wife dies, as an act of delaying the inevitable and of expressing his grief and perhaps love, the husband urges her to cook a meal. She quickly prepares some *chahan*, fried leftover rice with vegetables—a staple of inexpensive Chinese noodle shops and of everyday home fare.

In both scenes, the origin of the food is Chinese, but through juxtaposition, an expensive delicacy is directly related to an everyday home food. This domestication of the foreign is also apparent in the consumption of Korean food. In the scene following the housewife's death, Goro and Tampopo go out for dinner at a Korean restaurant, and Tampopo plays the part of the traditional woman, wrapping morsels of grilled meat in lettuce leaves and offering them to her companion. This is also the only scene in which Tampopo and Goro discuss their personal lives. Thus, again, the foreign exotic is domesticated and made a part of uchi, the intimate realm of Japanese life.

The European foods displayed in *Tampopo* are also the foods of the powerful as well as the powerless: all of the Western foods appear in the paradigms of social power that interest Itami. The central figure here is that of the *yakuza* boss. He is dressed stylishly when he addresses the audience at the beginning of the film, much as an actor in Kabuki theater might address an audience. While he dreams of traditional foods, imagining delicacies on his deathbed, what he actually consumes is Western food, along with his other pleasures, films and sex. And, unsurprisingly, for a country where the criminal underworld is well integrated into business culture, while he is entertaining his girlfriend with food and sex, a group of managers and businesspeople gather in a French restaurant in the same hotel.

The businessmen are, with one exception, ignorant of Western food culture and stuck in a group mentality, but the reverse is true of the common people, as is shown via members of a homeless gang, who are at the other end of the social scale. In a discussion aimed at Tampopo (who is positioned at the camera's point of view), they discuss and critique the various foods and wine they have gathered from the garbage bins of elite restaurants. Itami is obviously casting a sly eye on the foibles of his countrymen. In yet another scene featuring Western food (spaghetti), a middle-aged manners-school teacher has brought her class to a restaurant to teach these young Japanese women the secrets of Western etiquette. "Unlike the Japanese, who make a slurping noise when eating noodles, Westerners never slurp. It's all done very quietly," the matron says to her attentive class. Their efforts to consume spaghetti in the approved "Western" style are disrupted by the sight of a Westerner happily slurping away at his spaghetti, a sly smile on his face. It should be added that Itami hid a joke within a joke here: the foreigner consuming spaghetti is in real life a well-known Tokyo restaurateur, one of the first to open a Cordon Bleu restaurant there. Itami, whose sympathies are often with the powerless, seems to be indicating here that while the elite in Japan are often prisoners of the social forms they control, the powerless are free to choose from many cultural paradigms, and do so with gusto.

Class and Quality in Japanese Food

Like any other cuisine (the term here following Jack Goody[6]), Japanese food establishments can be placed on a scale of quality and of class. By class is meant, simply, price: higher class establishments cost more, for the producer and consumer alike. Quality is a far more difficult issue. The Japanese tend to be fastidious, highly aware consumers.[7] The idea of providing quality services and goods permeates Japanese society for a variety of social and historical reasons.[8] The thread of quality, of the need to be a proper consumer— enlightened, open, demanding—runs through the film. To improve the quality of her noodles, Tampopo takes a series of lessons from individuals occupying very different stations in life: from Goro the driver, from the homeless professor, from Chinese cooks, from Shuhei the chauffeur. And, in line with Japanese management and business views,[9] improving the product by attention to every tiny detail is impossible without *seishin*: the process of improving the person, both physically and mentally, that is intrinsic to most Japanese manpower management theory.[10] Significantly, quality is not related, in Japanese social theory, to class in the Marxian or British sense. It is related rather to the concept of self-cultivation, of providing oneself with a skill that, whatever one's class, is practiced to the utmost: the secret, many say, of Japanese economic success.

Practice as a consumer and practice as a producer are directly related in the Japanese view, and Itami takes no exception to that view. Tampopo is expected, and expects herself, to work hard and to use whatever tools are necessary to improve her lot in life. And though, as she says to a competitor, those who eat noodles are all amateurs, in the Japanese view, amateurs are experts who do not choose to become pros, to make money from their expertise. Indeed, in modern Japanese culture the concept of *gurume* has become a significant linguistic icon. A *gurume* is not merely someone who enjoys food. A *gurume* (of course, derived from the French word gourmet) is someone who knows food—who understands its *honne*, or essence.

During the years of Japan's greatest economic success, from the 1970s to the early 1990s, *gurume* activities—restaurants, talk shows, food shows, food tours—were plentiful. The object was not merely to entertain oneself, nor, for that matter, solely to engage in conspicuous consumption, which the Japanese did to a great degree. It was also related to the concept of *seishin*. In this view, a *gurume* is someone with an understanding and appreciation of culture as it emerges in food: in effect, a modern consumer, aware of the balances between price and quality, tradition and change.[11] Itami, though never the traditionalist, accepts this cultural construct as a given. Modern Japan is not the cherry-blossom and Mt. Fuji Japan of the past. Neither of these icons appears in the film, nor do traditional clothes, temples, or any of the other items that signify Japan to the West. Itami's Japan is instead the Japan of its people, whose cultural principles have now left the old material culture behind while maintaining the inner culture of Japanese-ness within the new context of modern life.

The Social Relationships

Japanese society has been characterized as being hierarchic, group oriented, obsessed with cleanliness and formality, dedicated to providing good education, and strongly oriented toward the family.[12] All of these are true to a degree, and all, of course, are not absolutes. The Japan that until the 1970s was conservative and scored high on all of the aforementioned qualities is beginning to change. There is less formality in Japanese life today than there was in the middle of the twentieth century. There is evidence that the Japanese are not as group oriented as many scholars once seemed to think.[13] The incidence of divorce and other marital strains is rising.[14] Nonetheless, Japanese society is far more rigid than is the norm in European or American societies. It is useful, therefore, to look at the social relations Itami portrays in *Tampopo*.

It should be said at the outset that these social relationships are all portrayed through the lens of the protagonists' relationships to food. And while some of these relationships are familiar to non-Japanese people, some of them have particular Japanese twists to them that ought to be examined more closely.

Japanese culture, as noted above, has borrowed many of its features from China; these imports include elements of the Confucian sociopolitical philosophy. Within the Confucian system, pride of place is given to a set of five hierarchical relationships, those of parent and child; ruler and ruled; husband and wife; teacher and student; and friend and friend. This view of interpersonal dealings has had great impact on Japanese social relations.

In the modern world, however, things are not simple, as Itami demonstrates. The child-parent relationship is still important (and the only intact one in the film). Even here, Itami cannot resist a dig at this presumably secure aspect of society: a young child bearing a handwritten note from a parent obsessed with natural foods is seduced into partaking of an ice cream. The seducer himself is obsessed by food to the point that he has allowed a tooth to rot in his head while he has fantasies of consuming Chinese delicacies.

Looking at family relationships, it becomes apparent that there is no single "standard" husband + wife + children relationship in the entire film. The closest one comes to such a family group is in the scene of a dying woman whose husband cannot find any other way of expressing his grief or helping his dying spouse than by ordering her to cook one final meal, then consuming it with his children as an expression of devotion. In Itami's view, the husband-wife relationship is virtually nonexistent in its Confucian and conservative qualities. One couple we see is an infirm and compulsive old man and his wealth-besotted younger wife who deals with him like her favorite lapdog. And the two main protagonists exist outside marriage: Tampopo is a widowed woman and Goro is a divorced man. It is not, apparently, that Itami has anything against marriage or the family (he apparently had a happy and lengthy marriage to the actress Miyamoto Nobuko, the star of *Tampopo* and of his other films). It is rather that, unlike Japanese conservatives, Itami is ready to state that the Japanese family system is not the be-all and end-all of Japanese society. Marriages and families are necessary—they exist—but absence of the normative arrangements is not a destroyer of Japanese society. Nor is marriage the necessary inner location in which sex takes place.

Like many other societies, the Japanese are obsessed with sex, and, like many other societies, often find that sex is a difficult and culture-ridden process. There are two clear sexual contrasts that Itami gleefully explores. One is the relationship between the food-obsessed *yakuza* boss and his girlfriend; the other is the relationship between Tampopo and Goro, her truck-driver mentor. The *yakuza* boss and his companion consummate their relationship joyously in two scenes in the film, in which sexuality is expressed by the erotic use of various foods—whipped cream, *ebi-odori* (a bowl of live "dancing prawn" in strong liquor), and a raw egg passed from mouth to mouth by the lovers to enhance sex, until the crushed yolk expresses their climax. The second sexual liaison is expressed in much more repressed terms—Goro's shy brushing of his hair in the bath, using Tampopo's hair brush, and her own nervous handling of underpants she folds and leaves for him to use.

Japanese have expressed their sexuality in ways that may seem odd, even bizarre to members of other cultures who have other cultural tastes.[15] A historic pedophilic preference for prepubescent women is well recorded,[16] and Itami cocks a judicious eye at it, as the *yakuza* boss lustfully consumes a raw oyster spotted with blood from the hands of a prepubescent *ama* (diving girl). (In fact, most *ama* are in their forties and fifties.[17]) The blood on the shellfish actually comes from the man's lips: an inversion of roles that Itami clearly relishes. The erotic symbolism of eggs is well documented in Japan as well.[18] And the same is true of the ebi-odori: The death throes of the fish on the mistress's belly are not only erotic, but they also evoke that very Japanese thrill of death in association with sex.[19]

Stepping outside the relationships of family members and lovers, it seems that the Confucian virtues are somewhat upheld. There are two relationships that Itami deals with sympathetically and at length: the relationship between pupil and master, and the relationship younger people have with the aged.

Any student of the martial arts or viewer of martial arts films will be familiar with the want-to-be-a-disciple scene. The sincere student mortifies himself before the master until accepted as a student.[20] This is precisely what Tampopo does when Goro shows her he is a master of noodles. And, indeed, he takes her on as his *deshi* (disciple). The concept is so important (and yet, even for Itami, slightly ridiculous) that one of the opening scenes of the film—again, detached from the main storyline—shows an elderly "noodles professor" instructing an eager young disciple in the mysteries of eating noodles. The "way," as many Japanese sages have noted gravely, can indeed be found in many things, and this includes, apparently, noodles. Whether this is a reaffirmation of the Zen desire for both obscurity and simplicity, or whether the director was merely delivering a sly dig at the portentiousness (and pretentiousness) of "Oriental philosophy" can be left, in traditional Zen fashion, to the decision of the viewer.

And the role of the teacher, Itami continues, is to make a student greater than oneself. At the end of the film, with Tampopo established as a master of her craft, the teachers (Goro and others), masters all, fade unnoticed into the background. In effect, Tampopo's real teacher has been the totality of the Japanese culture.

Like any other modern society, Japan has a problem with its aging population. Birthrates have been shrinking since World War II, and yet the Japanese population has remained virtually constant. The "graying" of the Japanese population is causing a great deal of concern to the authorities.[21] The Japanese, who enjoy strong family ties, with a Confucian concern for the aged, are unable to cope. Itami demonstrates the problem in a characteristic way. An elderly woman enters a posh convenience store late at night. She scurries down the aisles, squeezing the fresh, luscious, ripe foods until they are as careworn and used as she is herself—a peach, a piece of camembert, and various pastries receive her attention. The young male store clerk, obviously baffled by this behavior, rushes after her, trying to stop the vandalism, and, in the process, provides the old lady with at least a modicum of human contact.

There are other old people in the film, each of whom has to make his or her own adaptation to inevitable circumstances. One old man is the mentor of a band of homeless people. Another, the professor of noodles, instructs an awestruck young man in the proper way of consuming them. The elderly thief cons a con man for a good meal of Peking duck. Two venerable noodle chefs calmly, and without a wasted motion, move the pots around on a stove, displaying the perfection of art that comes only from years of practice. The aged, in Itami's world, may be hard to deal with, but they have incomparable skills and experience to offer. They have achieved a mastery of style only possible, in the Japanese view (which Itami seems to support), after decades of singleminded practice.

Style in All Things

The idea of perfect style has been a hallmark of Japanese culture for more than a millennium. Elegance and style—in life as in death—have been considered more important, in many ways, than actual success. Early Japanese writing, such as that in The *Pillow Book* of Sei Shonagon and the *Tale of Genji*, was obsessed with the idea of finding the perfect style in dress and deportment.[22] Style was important in death as well as in life, and there are numerous myths and legends about heroes—male and female, and indeed entire clans such as the Taira—dying in style.[23] The same is true of Japanese food, in which the presentation is at least as important as the taste and consistency,[24] and where elements of presentation are matter for lengthy and dedicated training.[25]

The transformation from Lailai (the original name of Tampopo's noodle shop) to Tampopo is an important stylistic change in two ways. Both Tampopo the person and Tampopo the place are refurbished. The dowdy, down-home Japanese decor is replaced with a modern, bright, stainless steel and white-surface style of modernity and the West. That those who have caused the transformation—Goro and the rest of his gang—feel uncomfortable about it is almost a given. They do not fit anymore, though their values and style will be transmitted in the new form. Only the young driving assistant, Gan, understands and approves of the transformation: it is part of his world, and of Tampopo's son's world: the modern Japan of today.

But style also has another side. This is the inner style of doing things, the style embodied in the Zen practitioner; and as Itami shows in one of the most evocative scenes in the film, all Japanese have style. Tampopo, accompanied by her son and guided by Goro, visits the homeless. Groups of homeless can be found in many warm underground passages and subway stations in Japan. Most people ignore them, averting their eyes as they pass. But these people, Itami argues, are as Japanese as any other. In this scene, the homeless—scavengers of restaurant garbage bins—are completely capable of discussing the qualities of superior vintage and commenting adversely on the choice of cuts from one restaurant while praising those from another. One of them offers to cook for Tampopo's son (who is not tempted by any of the fancy French dishes the derelicts have assembled), promising him a homely dish familiar to millions of Japanese children: *omeraisu*.

In a wordless choreography, accompanied by a tune on a honky-tonk piano, the homeless man and the young man sneak into a neighboring restaurant. With quick, deft, balletic motions the derelict quick-fries some cooked rice with ketchup. Placing this on a plate, he expertly beats the eggs, fries a perfectly cooked omelet, tips it over the rice, slicing open the egg so that the softer insides glisten in the light and the egg covers the rice. He then garnishes the top with some more ketchup: voila, a perfect *omeraisu*, and a no less important demonstration of "Japaneseness": perfect style.

"Japaneseness," or *Nihonjin-ron*, is a much-debated issue in Japanese society. For centuries the Japanese have argued that their culture is unique, unapproachable, and not understandable by others.[26] While Harumi Befu and others have argued that not all Japanese hold this view, and while this view is clearly the derivative of political and elite thinking,[27] it does filter down into common thinking. While Itami is clearly satirizing most Japanese pretensions, here and in his other films, it also seems clear that at least in the matter of style, he agrees with the supporters of *Nihonjin-ron*: style is everything, and even those who are down-and-out in Japanese society have it, and (at least in the film) can flaunt it.

The Food, the Film, and the Satirist

It is difficult to do justice to a film as complex as *Tampopo* in a short essay. In highlighting some of the film's features, it is possible only to scratch the surface of Itami's intentions and of the richness of this film, let alone his entire oeuvre. Itami's premature death, whether from suicide or murder, leaves unanswered the questions that many of us would have liked to ask the director himself.

Clearly, Itami is critical of his fellow Japanese; at the same time he is also just as clearly proud of them. The penultimate scene of the film shows the diverse collection of clients who frequent Tampopo's refurbished noodle shop:

white- and blue-collar workers, housewives and teenagers, foreigners, some with their babies, some working men with hard hats. Itami seems to be rather heavyhanded here in utilizing a symbolic ending, saying, apparently, "Look at us, we Japanese. The entire world comes to learn from us. And what we have done has not been done by the politicians and leaders, it is rather the anonymous common people, who do their work, and then, like Goro, the homeless (and nameless) professor, Pisken, the chauffeur, and many others, vanish into the mass of the populace." And whether or not he intended that particular message, this is the impression that comes through.

But Itami the satirist cannot end on a mawkish note. In the final scene, completely unrelated to any scene that has come before, but directly related to the theme of the film, he shows a mother breastfeeding her baby. The baby's expression says it all, and very smugly: no matter what our style, we're all obsessed with food.

Notes

1. *Tampopo* directed by Itami Jûzo. 1985.
2. Michael Ashkenazi and Jeanne Jacob, *The Essence of Japanese Cuisine: An Essay on Food and Culture* (Richmond, United Kingdom: Curzon Press, 2000).
3. Ibid.
4. Naomichi Ishige, "(Table) Manners Makyth the Man," *UNESCO Courier*, May 1987, pp. 18–21.
5. Michael Ashkenazi, "Japanization, Internationalization and Aesthetics in the Japanese Meal," in *Rethinking Japan*, eds. Adriana Boscaro Franco Gatti, and Massimo Raveri, (London: Paul Norbury, 1989); Ivan Morris, ed. and trans, *The Pillow Book* of Sei Shonagon (New York: Columbia University Press, 1967).
6. Jack Goody, *Cooking, Cuisine and Class* (Cambridge: Cambridge University Press, 1982).
7. The nature of modern Japanese consumerism has been discussed in, among others, Michael Ashkenazi and John Clammer, eds., *Consumption and Material Culture in Contemporary Japan* (London: Kegan Paul, 2000); Brian Moeran and Lisa Skov, "Mount Fuji and the Cherry Blossoms: A View from Afar" in Pamela Asquith and Arne Kalland, eds., *Japanese Images of Nature: Cultural Perspectives* (Richmond, United Kingdom: Curzon Press, 1997).
8. Robert J. Smith, *Japanese Society* (Cambridge: Cambridge University Press, 1983).
9. Masaaki Imai, Kaizen (Ky'zen), *The Key to Japan's Competitive Success* (New York: Random House, 1986).
10. Thomas P. Rohlen, "'Spiritual Education' in a Japanese Bank," *American Anthropologist* 75 (1973): 1542–62.
11. For a discussion of consumer knowledge in Japan, see John Clammer, *Contemporary Urban Japan: A Sociology of Consumption* (Oxford: Blackwell, 1997).
12. Chie Nakane, *Japanese Society* (Berkeley and Los Angeles: University of California Press, 1970); Smith, *Japanese Society*; Joy Hendry, "Humidity, Hygiene; or Ritual Care: Some Thought on Wrapping as Social Phenomenon," in *Unwrapping Japan*, eds. Eyal Ben-Ari, James Valentine, and Brian Moeran. (Manchester: Manchester University Press, 1990); Joy Hendry, *Wrapping Culture: Politeness, Presentation, and Power in Japan and Other Societies* (Oxford: Oxford University Press, 1993); Michio Nagai, *Higher Education in Japan*, trans. Jerry Dusenbury (Tokyo: University of Tokyo Press, 1971).
13. Ruth Benedict, *The Chrysanthemum and the Sword* (Boston: Houghton Mifflin, 1946) is the classic example. See Harumi Befu, "A Critique of the Group Model of Japanese Society," in *Social Analysis*, nos. 5–6 (1980): 29–43, for a summary of the weaknesses of the group theory in Japanese society.
14. Wim Lunsing, "Prostitution, Dating, Mating and Marriage: Love, Sex and Materialism in Japan," in Ashkenazi and Clammer, eds., *Consumption and Material Culture in Contemporary Japan*.

15. See, for example, Nicholas Bornoff, *Pink Samurai: The Pursuit and Politics of Sex in Japanese Society* (London: Grafton, 1992), and *Moa Ripôto: Nihon no Joseitachi ga Hajimete Jibuntachi no Kotoba de Sei wo Katatta* [*Further Report: Japanese Women tell for the First Time in their Own Words about Sex*] (Tokyo: Shûeisha, 1983).

16. Bornoff, *Pink Samurai*.

17. See Dolores P. Martinez, "Tourism and the Ama: The Search for a real Japan," in Ben-Ari et al., eds., *Unwrapping Japan*.

18. Liza Crihfield Dalby, *Geisha* (New York: Vintage, 1983).

19. On the Japanese fetishistic admixture of eroticism and death see, for example, Brian Moeran, "The Beauty of Violence: Jidaigeki, Yakuza and 'Eroduction' Films in Japanese Cinema," in *The Anthropology of Violence*, ed. David Riches (Oxford: Basil Blackwell, 1986), and the Oshima Nagisa film *Ai no Corrida* (*In the Realm of the Senses*; 1976).

20. The film *Karate Kid* (directed by John G. Avildsen, 1984) shows one Americanized example of this long tradition.

21. John Creighton Campbell, *How Policies Change: The Japanese Government and the Aging Society* (Princeton, N.J.: Princeton University Press, 1992).

22. Morris, ed., *Pillow Book*; Murasaki Shikibu, *The Tale of Genji*, trans. Royall Tyler (New York: Viking, 2001).

23. See, for example, the vast spread of Japanese romantic literature such as Helen Craig McCullough, trans., *The Taiheiki* (New York: Columbia University Press, 1959); Helen Craig McCullough, trans., *Yoshitsune: A Fifteenth-Century Japanese Chronicle* [Gikeiki] (Stanford, Calif.: Stanford University Press, 1966); and Helen Craig McCullough, trans., *The Tale of the Heike* (Stanford, Calif.: Stanford University Press, 1988).

24. Yoshio Tsuchiya, *A Feast for the Eyes: The Japanese Art of Food Arrangement* (Tokyo: Kodansha, 1985).

25. Tsuneo Tanaka, *Hôchô Nyumon* [*Introduction to the Kitchen Knife*] (Tokyo: Shibata Shôten, 1976).

26. Claims of this sort by Japanese intellectuals are legion, but the idea has also spilled over into foreign scholastic discourse; see, for example, Ruth Benedict, *The Chrysanthemum and the Sword* (Boston: Houghton Mifflin, 1946); Nakane, *Japanese Society*; Edwin O. Reischauer, *The Japanese* (Tokyo: Charles E. Tuttle, 1978).

27. Harumi Befu, *Hegemony of Homogeneity: An Anthropological Analysis of Nihonjinron* (Melbourne: Trans Pacific Press Japanese Society Series, 2001); Peter N. Dale, *The Myth of Japanese Uniqueness* (New York: St. Martin's Press, 1986).

4

Il Timpano —"To Eat Good Food Is to Be Close to God": The Italian-American Reconciliation of Stanley Tucci and Campbell Scott's *Big Night*

MARGARET COYLE

I first saw the movie *Big Night* during a blizzard in 1998. The snow began coming down hard at dusk, covering the streets of my midsized Maryland town. My then husband and I decided to go to our local video store and rent a movie to occupy us during the cold winter evening. We chose the videotape of Stanley Tucci and Campbell Scott's *Big Night* (1996), which had an interesting back cover that promised a good cast. Furthermore, we fancied ourselves to be budding gourmets, utterly fascinated by the art of the Italian table, though we were really beginners in culinary technique. Anticipating the "treat for food lovers"[1] that the back cover advertised and lulled by promises of culinary comfort, we were assured that the film would be the perfect companion to a glass of wine and a plate of grilled bruschetta while cuddling on the couch under a warm blanket.

By the end of the movie, we were both ravenous, absolutely starved for good Italian food: food made with care and passion, and thorough attention to detail and artistry, as the character of Primo (Tony Shalhoub) demonstrates so aptly in the film. *Big Night* had awakened our sense of hunger, need, and infatuation with "real" Italian cooking. Inspired by the way the movie fed the soul and the mind, now we needed a similar (literal) filling of the belly. Knowing that the blizzard had shut down all restaurants within walking distance, we poured more wine and began to cook. We pulled some shrimp out of the freezer, and Marcella Hazan's *Essentials of Classic Italian Cooking* off the shelf. With the ingredients we had on hand, we were going to try to reproduce the seafood risotto that was featured during the feast of the film, where the guests are served three risottos; seafood, parmesan, and pesto, plated in the shape of the Italian flag. A little over an hour later, we demolished the results happily with crusty bread, a good salad, and a dry pinot grigio as the winter winds blew outside.

But the dish that made the biggest impression—the culinary star of the film and its structural metaphor for Italian culture and food as nourishment for the soul—was the pasta course *Il Timpano*, the specialty dish that Primo prepares for the party. As cowriter/codirector/actor Tucci notes in the forward to *Cucina & Famiglia*, the cookbook cowritten by his mother Joan Tropiano Tucci and Gianni Scappin that features the family recipe *timpano* alla *Big Night*, "Food, above politics, art, or personal matters, is the subject to which we return over and over again. Possibly because we derive nourishment from it not only physically but also spiritually, the creation of a great meal is perhaps the ultimate artistic endeavor. . . . I feel it necessary to explore and celebrate from whom and where I come."[2] Food tells us who we are, where we have come from, and connects our past, present, and future. It sustains us with more than nutritional value alone, or *can* when we are aware of it and allow it to feed our spirit. The film makes a critical observation about food as a form of expression—crucially important to our everyday lives—combining artistic creativity, spirit, and sensual delight.

Big Night captures the collision of society and morals of old world Italy and the new world of America. Primo (Tony Shalhoub) and Secundo (Tucci) are the Italian American Pilaggi brothers in 1957 New Jersey, trying to save their failing restaurant by sponsoring a party for jazz singer Louie Prima. Their culturally educated palate is in dispute with American tastes and expectations of what Italian food should be (tomato sauces and garlic, meatballs and grated cheese). The neighboring restaurant owner Pascal (Ian Holme) flaunts a flourishing business because he caters to American tastes. The various Americans depicted in the film further illustrate the distancing of Primo and Secundo from mainstream "American" cuisine and culture. The brothers cannot easily let go of the "truths" their palate dictates to them, though Secundo tries to transform himself into an American by adopting American ideas about what is important.

Timpano exemplifies the Italian tradition of eating, that which takes effort, time, passion, and is meant to be shared with loved ones and family. It consists of a homemade pasta crust that lines a deep bowl; it is filled with other foods, prepared separately, including meats, cheeses, hard-boiled eggs, pasta, and sauce, layered in a lasagna-like fashion. The dish is topped with another layer of pasta, weighted down and baked until done. This particular recipe, a Tucci family secret until the publishing of *Cucina & Famiglia*, is the main structural image of the film. As Tucci notes, "*Timpano* [is] the centerpiece of the meal in

Big Night. . . . Structurally and creatively, it gave us the strong focus for the meal and had repercussions we never anticipated. During the first screenings we were amazed by the audience's reaction to this dish. They were exactly those of the characters in the film—audible gasps of awe and wonder."[3] *Timpano* seems the quintessential Italian dish, for it takes time to prepare, tastes wonderful, and is reserved for festive occasions when family and friends gather around the table to share their lives. It is a labor of love.

The Americans in the film are stunned and impressed by the dish, but sense in themselves somehow the inability to reproduce it for themselves. The food sense of Americans is seen as more than just "different" from that of Italians; rather, it appears as the defining rupture between the two nationalities. Food nourishes Italians and Americans alike, but only Italians see it as an artistic and implicit expression of themselves and their national/personal identity. Americans are far more likely to define food as necessary to sustain life, but not as self. For Italians, "*Chi mangia bene sta molto vicino a dio*—To eat good food is to be close to God," Primo says, whereas the business-oriented world of America cannot understand or support godliness or the joy that results from a perfect culinary form of self-expression, and instead embraces consumerism.

The irreconcilable rift between two styles of living is the issue at the heart of the film, with cuisine being the prime example of how different cultures express their attitudes toward the everyday expectations of a good life. If the Pilaggi brothers can possibly succeed on the Jersey shore, they must adapt their cooking to American cultural expectations. However, by doing so, they lose their self-respect and diminish the privilege that innate knowledge of traditional culture and culinary expertise bestows upon them. If they sell out, they lose out. *Big Night* is layered, like the timpano, with depictions and deeply held beliefs about life and food of Americans and Italians alike, and challenges the very essence of identity and cultural traditions for each nationality—disparate elements mixed up in a single vessel.

The characters of the film are multidimensional as well—complexly layered, much like the dish itself. Primo, the chef who believes in the traditional way of cooking, is juxtaposed to Pascal, the self-proclaimed "businessman" who has sold out his heritage to give the public what it wants. Primo's brother, Secundo, who tries to adapt to the American way of doing business, is caught in the middle, neither American nor Italian, fish nor fowl nor good red herring, wanting the best of all worlds but able to stand fully in neither. The other Italian Americans—Pascal's "lady friend" Gabriella (Isabella Rossellini); the barber Alberto Pisano (Pasquale Cajano);[4] and the waiter/busboy Christiano (Marc Anthony)—understand implicitly the lure of tradition, whether or not they abide by it. However, the other Americans—Bob the Cadillac salesman (coauthor/codirector Campbell Scott); Phyllis, Secundo's girlfriend (Minnie Driver); Ann the flower lady (Alison Janney); the restaurant customers; and the feast guests—do not understand Italian culture, and though they may enjoy it, for them it still holds a foreign mystique, being "other" than what they are. One wonders who is marginalized in this view of the world: Americans or Italians. This film illustrates the various ways that Italians approach culinary perfection, and the ways that American culture wishes to appropriate it and change it to suit a corrupted palate. It illustrates the elemental differences between American and Italian ways of life.

This uneasy mixture of ingredients (American and Italian culture, love, cooking, business, family, and food) explicates a simple theme, much like the old adage, "Most of the world eats to live, but Italians live to eat."[5] In the worldview of this movie, to be Italian is to love the experience of food as a form unto itself, in the planning, the creating, and the eating; to be American is to lack the experience and knowledge of complexity yet to want "it all" in its glory. By the end of the film, Secundo and Primo determine that their Italian traditions are better suited for them than the brash American style, and return to the basic truth of food and ritual as a way of life.

Il Timpano: Italian Cuisine as Opposed to Italian-American Cuisine

Primo and Secundo peering into the oven at the baking *timpano*:
>   Secundo: What do you think?
>   Primo: More time.
>   Secundo: How long?
>   Primo: Until it's done.[6]

According to Dean Richards, "Italians have been enjoying *Timpano*—if only once or twice per year—in one form or another since the Renaissance. Nearly every region of Italy includes some kind of savory pie in their cuisine: from *Torta Pasqualina* in Emilia Romagna, to *Capelli d'Angeli al Forno* in Tuscany, to *Timballo di Maccheroni* in Abruzzi and Calabria."[7] Italian cooking is primarily a regional cuisine and cannot really be defined as a national cuisine, for every region has its own special foods and recipes.[8] It stands to reason that there are as many *timpano* recipes as there are regions in Italy. *Timpano* (eardrum or kettledrum), or *timbale* (after the French, for "drum") as it is also known, is believed "to have entered the lexicon of Italian cooking from Morocco through Sicily."[9] Even cooks from the same region or town may have slightly different ways of preparing the dish, and so there is no consensus on the perfect recipe.[10] The dish itself, a complicated affair, is prepared mostly for special occasions, combining many different ingredients depending on the regional tradition the cook comes from.

Americans have a less regional and more cautious approach to their culinary tradition. "The cuisines that were most successful in infiltrating American kitchens were those that resemble the cooking of England. . . . There even seems to be a tendency [when cooking foreign foods] to invent instead an American dish with a foreign name and a vague resemblance to a foreign creation," noted Waverley Root and Richard de Rochemont in 1976.[11] Although Americans appreciate the taste of foreign foods, they have often appropriated it into their own cuisine and changed it to suit their taste. The American palate is more likely to accept generalized versions of authentic cuisine, homogenized and simplified to suit a blander palate. American cooking of the 1950s largely remained English in nature, featuring plain and unseasoned preparations like roasts, looking with suspicion on difference, change, and exotic spices. In a very real sense, the Italian-American "food choice" of spaghetti with tomato sauce and meatballs is much more authentic for many Americans than is a *timpano* or risotto.

In general, American food has suffered from being a commodity, reduced to the lowest common denominator and sold en masse to consumers. To give an example from John and Karen Hess's *Taste of America*, "Pop sociologist Vance Packard laments: 'This is what our country is about—blandness and standardization.' . . . [We] must give the multitudes exactly what they want." An old advertisement claimed that Howard Johnson's was "the taste of America,"[12] which was meant that each restaurant standardized taste, and in doing so eliminated originality and singularity. In giving the customer exactly what he or she wants, the cuisine becomes less authentic. Many restaurants simplify their cooking to adapt to their customers' tastes and create a standard products, and this is the "cuisine" that Americans have practiced and propagated within their own homes. That is not to say that the foreign cuisine is not delicious, but that it is "other than American" and is therefore eaten in moderation. The excess of Italian dishes like the *timpano* is somehow suspicious to our taste. Note the Hesses, writing in the 1970s, "Our Italian restaurants are even less Italian. A second and third generation of cooks and clients are drowning a great culinary tradition in a red tide of canned tomato sauce on limp factory pasta."[13] In Italy the variation of the food is important; in America it seems to be consistency and sameness that is paramount.

The Tucci family, whose traditional recipe for a *timpano* is the one prepared in the film and will be used as the basis for this article, is from the Calabria region of Italy, in the south near Sicily; this is the homeland of Stanley Tucci's paternal and maternal families. The recipe was brought over to America in 1904 by Apollonia Pisani, Tucci's great grandmother, from "Serra San Bruno, a small hill town in Calabria."[14] The Calabria version of the dish is called *Timballo di Maccheroni* due to the inclusion of macaroni among the strata of the *timpano* as well as the pasta-dough crust.[15] As Tucci noted in a 1996 interview, "You can't get *Timpano* anywhere; it's a secret family recipe. . . . It's not a common thing. It's from a small town in Italy. It's my father's mother's family's recipe. It is so fucking good."[16] The recipe was not published after the release of the movie despite audience demands for the traditional family recipe. It was finally made public in 1999 when *Cucina & Famiglia* was published. This cookbook gives the history and origin of the recipes included within, and celebrates the Italian traditions of good food and family.

In fact, the cookbook honors the history of Italian cooking, where recipes are handed down from generation to generation, where evolution of the recipe happens based on traditional tastes, and food itself is lauded as a meaningful connection to one's past and one's culture. It could reasonably be said that each Italian cook has her own way of creating a dish. Recipes written down on paper are a relatively new invention. Each generation learns from the one preceding it, and leaves its own indelible stamp on the product according to personal taste and choice. The Tucci *timpano* recipe gives tips for procuring the correct type of drum pan for the baking of the dish, as well as preparation hints, and even the importance of *not* opening the door of the oven often to check the progress of the dish, since this will affect the final taste.[17] The recipe itself can be found in the cookbook *Cucina & Famiglia*; it is also available online at http://recipes.alastra.com/pasta/timpano03.html.

In many ways, the idea of a tried and true recipe is an Americanism, for it connotes trying to standardize the dish in order to make it continually the same. Italian cookery relies on a cultural standard, but there is room within it for experimentation and enjoyment within that tradition. Italian cooking, as exemplified by the *timpano*, relies on tradition *and* improvisation, personal palate, and relish of taste. As Stanley Tucci notes in the foreword to *Cucina & Famiglia*, "I've always felt that *Big Night* was partly about the respect for one's heritage and the pursuit of truth in one's art. To me, this cookbook embodies those themes."[18] Italian cooking takes as much time as it needs to take in order to raise a meal above good to great.

An example of this concern for the best and inherent standards of Italian cooking is the moment in the movie when Primo first begins to understand the financial problem he and his brother are caught in. He feels that Louie Prima should come to their restaurant "just for the food." Secundo takes him aside and explains the vital importance of the dinner, and that it is their last chance for success. "I don't think we can do what we came here to do the way we want to do it," Secundo says, meaning that they need to adapt to a false standard in order to succeed economically. Primo does not reply, but we see him internalizing this truth for the first time, understanding that his standards of perfection and his exacting principles dictated by tradition and art are costing them their livelihood. He is, however, incapable of lowering his expectations.

The next scene, in the kitchen, shows Primo raising his own standards to cope with the importance of the meal; this is his way of understanding the need for success. No longer is the meal for Louie Prima a bit of crass commercialism; now it suddenly becomes important as a lifesaving mechanism. It demands the best that he can prepare, and so it demands the *timpano*. He tells Phyllis and Christiano to get the white enamel pans (also recommended by the Tucci family in *Cucina & Famiglia* as imperative for making a good *timpano* that does not stick). Secundo, knowing what the appearance of the enamel pans means, protests against making a *timpano*, and Phyllis asks what it is. Primo tells her it is pasta with a special crust shaped like a drum and "in it all the most important things in the world" are placed. Primo, in the only way he knows, decides to celebrate the feast for the jazz singer with the most difficult and involved food he can prepare, a dish that is quintessentially Italian–the best dish he knows how to make.

One can see why Secundo protests making the *timpano*. The dish is time consuming and demands an involved preparation. It is reserved for special occasions, for it serves anywhere from ten to sixteen people. It is a dish that was primarily meant as a pasta course, though it can also be served as a main course. It is not usually found in restaurants due to its complexity, and was unfamiliar to Americans until the premiere of the movie *Big Night*.[19] The food stylist for the film, Deborah Disabatino, said she felt like an architect when constructing a timpano, and "[s]he did not know, until a crew screening of the movie, that the movie included a full-screen shot of the *Timpano* actually being sliced. The slice and pull, whether it's a pie or a pizza, is the stylist's nightmare, she explains, because there's no room for error. What if the rough layers collapsed on camera and turned into a saucy mess? 'I lost a lot of sleep over that,' she says, even though her fellow crew members cheered when they saw it for the first time."[20]

The Tucci family requested that Disabatino not share the traditional recipe with her clients and students, and this is a request she honored. Finally though, it was unveiled to a clamoring public upon publication of *Cucina & Famiglia*: "Though many *Big Night Timpano* recipes have been printed in various magazines and newspapers since the film's release, they are imposters. This is the one true recipe for our *Timpano*. Good Luck and Buon Appetito!"[21] The complicated structure, time-consuming preparation, and magnificent taste of the *timpano* stands as indicative of Italian cuisine, and as a standard for Italian cooking that Americans admire.

The Crust: Heritage and Country Holds It All Together

Secundo to Bob, the Cadillac salesman:

In Italy, there is nothing but history.

Timpano crust can be made of many things—pastry, pasta, and even rice in one version of the dish. But in the timpano of *Big Night*, the crust is made out of pasta dough. A mixture of flour, eggs, salt, and olive oil is kneaded and then rolled out and fitted into a buttered, oiled *timpano* pan. Pasta is considered the quintessential Italian food, and incidentally the one food that Americans have seized upon and made inclusive of all Italian food; it speaks to us of heritage and culture.

Primo, the holder of art and heritage, is a chef of the Italian tradition. His standards are exacting and he is a genius in the kitchen; he is also knowledge-able about the rules and etiquette attached to the tradition. Secundo dreams of success in America because of Primo's talent in the kitchen. Primo, however, merely wants to cook the best that he possibly can; you get the sense from the film that he needs to cook, and that it really does not matter where. Perhaps America is not the best place for him, for his customers are incapable of appreciating his work. Primo cannot compromise his training and his beliefs, for he is a keeper of his heritage, but Secundo is caught between the need for success and capturing the American Dream, and the need to remain true to the traditions and palate of his Italian ancestry. Italy has long traditions and a firmly entrenched, self-regulating history. America seemingly cares little about this knowledge; it just wants the experience without the learning. Americans want to import the tradition without taking the time to form it for themselves.

In one of the opening scenes of the movie, Secundo is serving an American couple their dinner. The woman, smoking a cigarette at the table, is obviously hungry and says of the slowness of the service that she thinks the server went "all the way to Italy to get it." She becomes confused when she looks at her seafood risotto and sees no scallops or shrimp. She calls "Monsieur?" in an attempt to get Secundo's attention as he is grating cheese over her husband's pasta.[22] She wants to know where the seafood is, for she is ignorant of the preparation for risotto, where all ingredients are chopped small for a smooth consistency. Dissatisfied with Secundo's explanation, she then orders a side dish of spaghetti. Secundo attempts to explain that, traditionally, you do not serve two starches together, and then that they do not serve meatballs with spaghetti, for sometimes "spaghetti likes to be alone." However, these customers think that the prototypical Italian-American dish of the 1950s, spaghetti with meatballs, must be on the menu somewhere. They insist, and Secundo goes back to face the temperamental Primo with the news of a need for compromise. Primo wonders angrily if he should make the "criminal" woman some mashed potatoes, and demands to speak to her. In a fit of pique, Secundo throws open the dining room door and Primo comes forward, staring down at the woman, but then backs off. "She is a philistine," he says. "She no understand anyway." Secundo returns to the dining room, as ever the perfect host, while Primo, fuming, begins to prepare the woman's spaghetti, but then stops and hurls the pan at the wall instead.

Secundo knows that serving pasta and rice together is not acceptable. In strict accordance with tradition, no Italian would ever think of such a combination.[23] In this first and possibly best example of the clash between cultures, the commodity of food becomes a medium of cultural exchange. The Americans push to have their conditions accepted, little realizing that by overlaying their taste on top of the regional food they alter it. Primo resists this, as an attempt to stay true to his heritage. Secundo, on the other hand, falters and tries to be a good businessman, to sell to his customers what they want, but he cannot quite toss aside his innate knowledge. When he suggests to Primo they stop serving risotto since it is an expensive dish to prepare and takes up too much of the chef's time, Primo sarcastically suggests they take it off the menu and "Instead we could put . . . I was thinking . . . what they call it . . . hot dog. . . . I think people would like those." In this throwaway reference to the instability and crassness of American cuisine, Primo thumbs his nose at the new cuisine, and confirms his desire to remain true to his art. Secundo knows he must subvert tradition in order to attain success. Primo is convinced that Americans can learn to like the true Italian cuisine given enough time and exposure—that they will discover their taste if only encouraged. Secundo replies, "Well, I don't have time for them to learn. This is a restaurant, not a fucking school."

The pasta crust holds the *timpano* together and shapes it into a whole. Italian culture does the same thing for its cuisine: it is overriding, despite the many different regions and areas that compose the country. The rules and the standards by which the cuisine is formed have taken many centuries to develop and are based on generations of cooks testing and applying the rules to their recipes, and Primo comes out of this tradition. But Americans cannot understand it, since they did not take part in the formation of it; they can only grab and enjoy what they think to be "culture." Primo the chef wants to give it to them undiluted, whereas Pascal the businessman is willing to give Americans whatever they want, bastardizing the name of Italian cooking.

Ragu Sauce and Ziti: Art Takes Time, But Is Business Art?

Pascal lecturing Secundo in his office:

> Give to people what they want; later you can give them what you want.

In the film, Primo makes the macaroni and the meat sauce for the *timpano* from scratch. The main problem with a *timpano*, or at least the reason that many people hesitate to make it, is that several of the component layers take time to prepare before the dish is assembled. The Tucci family recipe for *timpano* calls for "Ragu Tucci" and boxed ziti to be prepared, though in the film Primo rolls and forms his own pasta, a multistep process. The family ragu, for which the recipe can be found in *Cucina & Famiglia*,[24] takes about three hours to prepare before the *timpano* can be constructed. It uses pork spareribs and stewing beef in a tomato-based sauce. This very important step cannot be overlooked. Tradition must be adhered to. You may make a *timpano* with a sauce that takes less time, or even with a commercially prepared sauce, but in the final evaluation, it will not truly be a timpano.

Big Night has strong views on the incompatibility of art and business. Primo lovingly prepares each component of the *timpano*, and for him this is the ultimate expression of his abilities and the duty he owes his art. It is how he expresses his sense of truth. However, as Secundo often points out, they lose time, money, and business with this attention to detail. Pascal, on the other hand, will serve what his customers want. Here is the very real chasm between the artist and the businessman. Pascal throws away the traditional preparations and instead gives to the customer what he expects. The dish is not important by itself, but instead is a means to an end, procuring financial success and making customers happy. The film shows us, in a comparative shot, the darkened front of the Pilaggi brothers restaurant, which has closed early due to lack of customers, as opposed to the manic gaiety displayed by Pascal's customers, beautiful people dressed up and having a party. Primo says of Pascal's menu that the "man should be in prison for the food he serves" and

Secundo replies, looking wistfully at the line of customers laughing and waiting in front of Pascal's, "People love it." This exchange illustrates the basic differences between the two restaurants. Art may feed the soul of the creator, and the minds of those who have the ability to appreciate it, but it does not work for everyone. The businessman, however, knows how to sell to the lowest common denominator. If you please people and give them what they think they want, you have succeeded. Primo is the creative artist, Pascal the charlatan.

In a later scene, Secundo goes to ask for Pascal's help, but it is revealed that Pascal wants to make use of Primo's talents in his own restaurant. Pascal hatches a plot supposedly to help the Pilaggi brothers—that they will serve a big meal to jazz singer Louie Prima and Pascal will help. However, Pascal would really like to ruin the brothers, for he wants both men to work for him as a way of increasing his business. Pascal admires the artistry of Primo, but instead would have him sell it out for the sake of pleasing the customers. Pascal believes you should "bite your teeth into the ass of life, drag it to you." Art is nice, but success does not come from holding to unreachable standards; rather, he believes it comes from pleasing people. As Pascal says to Secundo in one of his most characteristically indicative speeches in the film, "A guy goes out to eat in the evening, after work, a long day at the office, whatever. He don't want on his plate anything he has to look at and think, "What the fuck is this?" No, right, what he want is 'Hey! A steak! I like Steak!' You know, 'Mmm, I'm happy.' You see what I mean? I mean, don't get me wrong. I think your brother is good. Shit, he may be the best I have ever seen. Give to people what they want; later you can give them what *you* want."

There is no room for tradition in Pascal's worldview. His restaurant happily propagates the myth of Italian American food. The important thing is making people happy, for Pascal believes in the American way of businessmen: "Work hard and sell your product and you will succeed." There is no honor in his actions; he has succumbed to American consumerism and tactics. In a later scene, Secundo sees Pascal and an associate setting fire to a man in a chef's uniform, brutally putting the "squeeze" on another competitor. Pascal has sold out the tradition that formed him.

Upon tasting the *timpano* at the dinner party, Pascal breaks down and slams his hand on the table top, surprising the others at the table. He cries out with great emotion, "Goddammit, I should kill you. This is so fucking good, I should kill you." He then embraces Primo, as the startled guests laugh and continue to enjoy the food. Sadly, Pascal has the ability to appreciate the artistry of Primo; he just does not believe that it is as important as making a living. In holding money and pleasing the customer above the traditional and the established, Pascal has become American.

Salami and Cheese: Magic and Tradition in Simplicity

Primo to Secundo in front of the restaurant:
    I do not grow the flowers. I like to pick the right one.

The Tucci's traditional *timpano* calls for Genoa salami, provolone cheese cubes, and grated Romano cheese. This inclusion of basic meats and cheeses indicates the southern Italian origin of this particular recipe (salami instead of prosciutto, provolone in place of mozzarella, Romano and not Parmagiano Reggiano),[25] and also reveals the fundamental nature of the ingredients. You do not need expensive or exotic ingredients to go into the creation of this dish. Sometimes the simplicity and goodness of the fillers make the meal. In many ways, the salami and the cheese are a treat—unpretentious and basic goodness—that adds depth and variation to the course. Alone they make a meal of their own. They testify to the ability of Italian cuisine to make use of all the ingredients available. Sometimes simplicity creates its own magic.

The two characters that run the risk of fading into the background of the film are perhaps some of the most interesting to examine within this framework. The basic qualitities and inherent straightforwardness they bring to the film helps provide it with a depth, as opposed to the other characters. Christiano the waiter and Ann the flower lady both function as a kind of background against which to view the other characters. Their essential qualities of "being there" as an audience to the drama being played out, yet integral to the plot on their own, makes them analogous to the meat and cheese included in the dish. Christiano is often present, but seldom speaks. His role is that of the next generation, the future of Italian cooking. He allows us to view the action through his eyes. He serves while others dance; he cleans pots and pans while Primo cooks. He offers his jacket in a beautiful gesture to the distraught Phyllis; he has no clue who Louie Prima is. He dances and sings while sweeping the floor. His inherent thoughtfulness, quietness, and attention to tradition and goodness provide more depth to the Italian perspective. One cannot call him a main character, for we do not get to know him well enough. Instead he helps to support and fill out the picture, much as the plain cured meat exists as a bolster to other foods. His quixotic personality, deserving a more detailed exploration at a later date, reflects the essence of Italian culture that exists in the film. His apprenticeship is about to be cut short, but you get the sense he understands the magic of good food and simple preparation. He will follow the example of Primo, rather than Pascal, when he achieves his majority.

Ann the flower lady, though an American, plays Primo's love interest in the film. She displays an attention to detail and an appreciation for the "rightness" of actions and things, an old fashioned belief missing in so many of the other Americans. In her quiet way, she is as much of an artist as Primo is. She is shy, but gives Primo his due as an artist and is attracted to what she sees in the man. She has the most traditional values of all the American characters; she reads about the pioneers, she berates people for not doing their jobs, she wears a corsage to the dinner, and she submits to Primo's tutelage and wooing in the kitchen. He shows her how to make a quick Florentine sauce, seduces her with the mention of cream sauces, and offers to take her to Bologna someday, to try that region's lasagna. Primo says, "After you eat [it] you have to kill yourself, you can't live." Ann quietly agrees with him and takes a bite of his sauce. Her face is transformed by the taste, feeling the magic in its simplicity, and she exclaims "Oh . . . my . . . God!" Her smile shows her delight in his gift. Primo accepts her homage, saying, "Is good . . . ehh . . . you like? 'Oh my God' is right. Now you know to eat good food is to be close to God; to have knowledge of God is the bread of angels. I am never sure what that means, but is true anyway." Ann agrees, and their fates are joined at that moment. Her easy comfort and the ease of her company is what Primo likes; she blends well with him. She is the only American character privy to the brothers fighting on the beach near the end of the film. Her quiet understanding and her inclusion in this private Italian moment show that, indeed, Americans can be worth the teaching and can learn—that magic and custom can be a part of the American tradition. Perhaps Ann has made the transition from American to Italian in a culinary sense; perhaps her relationship with Primo continues on past the end of the film. Ann quietly fills out the picture with her goodness, and balances the other women of the film, who are less likely to exist quietly.

Hard-Boiled Eggs: Women

Gabriella and Phyllis outside the restaurant, during the party:

> Gabriella: Maybe I should go out west, find a cowboy with a horse, the whole thing. Yeah, I want one. Strong. Silent. Like a statue. Cool. Always there.
>
> Phyllis: Cowboys are consistent.

Central to the Tucci *timpano* recipe, and also to Southern Italian cooking, is the inclusion of hard-boiled eggs, to give the recipe some "filling" and also as a symbol of rejuvenation. As two of the layers of the *timpano*, eggs are quartered and quartered again to give the dish more substance. In Italian cuisine eggs symbolize religion, prosperity, and rebirth, as well as the ability of woman to procreate. Eggs, a necessity to subsistence peasant food, help provide protein and solidity for a meal when meat is hard to come by. Hard-boiled eggs keep longer and give the eater the sense of filling up the belly, without the heaviness associated with meats. In American culture, *hard-boiled* refers to a person who has become a superrealist—hard-hearted and altogether knowing about the seamier side of life.

The two main women in the film, the Italian Gabriella and the American Phyllis, are both love interests of Secundo, and are women emblematic of the 1950s. Each symbolizes the culture from which she sprang; Gabriella is fashionable, exotically beautiful, and submissive, yet knows how to haggle and bargain and use each person to her advantage, while Phyllis is "untouched" and seemingly naive while still displaying knowledge of how things happen in the world. Both women are selfish and self-serving, used to manipulating men with sex and a woman's power. These women demonstrate the female perspective on male-female relationships: Gabriella the mistress and Phyllis the girlfriend, perpetuating the past traditions and paving the way for the marital future, good sex and proper marriage. Both, however, have control of their relationships in uniquely feminine ways. Each, though seemingly weak, manipulates to get what she wants yet is unable to force men to adhere to her beliefs. Neither of these women is soft and pliant—both are individuals formed by their cultural identification, and harsh realists when it comes to male-female relationships.

When they have a scene together during the party, we see them only making small talk about travel and men, albeit with a very specific subtext. This scene points out their similarities as women, but their cultural differences as well. Neither of them is happy within her relationship, and each actually feels superior to men. The younger Phyllis has as of yet no real knowledge of men and only wants a consistent man. However, the more mature Gabriella wants a man who is strong and silent (read: neither Pascal nor Secundo). She can teach her rival a thing or two about men, for she has experienced them already. Phyllis is a younger, more naive Gabriella, bound to make the same mistakes in love and relationships that Gabriella has. They have more in common than just Secundo.

Gabriella is Pascal's wife and business partner, and she is also Secundo's mistress. She has absorbed some of Pascal's business tactics, but wields them with a softer, more manipulative knowledge. She is sharp and wily, beautiful but enigmatic, and somehow has a weary knowledge of how the world works yet retains her "goodness" at the same time. She is as jaded as Pascal; yet she seems weary rather than corrupted. She admits, after a rendezvous with Secundo, that she is with Pascal for his money, regardless of his age, for she likes her material possessions more than she needs love. However, she bargains with the liquor salesman on behalf of Secundo in order to get him cheap booze for his party. She knows the routine of the restaurant business for she works as Pascal's hostess and overseer of the dining room. Despite her obvious talents, she is pushed aside and is unable to impact the action directly, essentialized as a submissive woman of the 1950s. When Pascal and Secundo are talking in front of the restaurant, Gabriella contradicts Pascal by suggesting that Secundo does not want to go home. Pascal dispels the moment of tension as he tells her to go in and take care of business, and she obeys without a word, deferring to him. She allows herself to be used, yet manipulates at the same time. She is privy to Pascal's plan to ruin the Pilaggi brothers' business, yet does not tell her lover. It is only at the end of the evening when they are leaving, after she has been discovered with Secundo by Phyllis, that she preempts Pascal's disclosure and informs Primo that Louie Prima is not coming. She tempers this hard truth with a smile and says to Primo, in all honesty and charm, "Thank you for the best meal I will probably ever have." However, she still leaves with Pascal, choosing to take money and status over love. She has seen much of the world, and one gets the feeling that in her past there was a young girl like Phyllis, learning firsthand about men and how to use them for her own ends.

Phyllis, in contract, is a virgin and is looking to marry Secundo. While she is inexperienced, she has more common sense than Secundo expects. She is more callow and less subtle than Gabriella, and this can be attributed to her youth and also her nationality. In many respects, however, Phyllis and Gabriella have similar outlooks on life and relationships. When Phyllis and Secundo are making out in the car, and he stops because he does not want to have sex, she gets frustrated with his squeamishness and says, "We've done other things. What's the problem?" Then, when he makes a statement that she will not understand finances (by implication because she is a woman), Phyllis rolls her eyes at him and tells him she understands money, for she works at a bank. Phyllis has the forthright nature of her nationality. She is very straightforward and tries to mold Secundo to her needs, blind to differences. When he vacillates about the future of their relationship, she comes right out and asks whether or not he wants to marry her. She is interested in helping Secundo succeed, and tries her best to subjugate her own desires to support his needs as a "proper" woman should. However, her puppylike loyalty seems performed as she occasionally lets her real personality peek through this good girlfriend act. She is smarter than she seems, and much more brash than her innocent demeanor suggests. Her chief assets to Secundo, it seems, are her "innocence," which is actually something of a performance, and her status as an American girl. Not used to alcohol, she gets drunk at the party and vomits. She drunkenly talks to Gabriella about her disappointment: "You know how they getcha, these people, men, boys? They make you think they have secrets to tell, they have nothing to tell, and then they talk . . . and they keep talking and what do they say?" Gabriella knows the answer—they say nothing. Phyllis agrees with her. Phyllis is on the road to the same place in life that Gabriella already occupies. When she discovers Secundo and Gabriella in a lover's embrace, she dives into the ocean to cleanse herself, and then walks away from Secundo, learning from this event that men are duplicitous. This marks the beginning of her hardness and an end to innocence. She will not put up with Secundo's cheating. On her way home, Christiano stops and gives her his jacket, and she leans over and kisses him fully on the lips, beginning again the search to find a man who will be consistent. Sadly, she has learned to trade her sexual attraction as a reward for decent behavior. She may lack subtlety, but she does have passion and enthusiasm for life.

Meatballs: The Average Guy

Alberto the barber, in his shop, to Primo:

> I am like monkey. Don't see, don't hear, don't speak.

Secundo to Bob the Cadillac salesman:

> This year you buy next year's car; next year, next year's come out already.

One of the basics of Italian cookery appears as an ingredient in *timpano*—meatballs. In this recipe, bread, beef, parsley, cheese, and garlic are mixed together, formed into small balls, and then fried before being added as a layer within the *timpano*.[26] Meatballs take on a mystique for Americans, and become a standard alongside pasta in their expression of Italian cookery. They exist as a filler food like meatloaf, a way to stretch ground meat to feed a larger family. Colloquially in American slang, *meatball* is an expression for someone who is dull or ordinary, stupid and without wit. It also means a man who walks through life as an average guy; a meatball is no one special and no one important. (It would be interesting to discover if the term derived from a colloquialism indicating Italian immigrants, but so far I have found no record of that.) In *Big Night*, we have two examples of the average guy from each culture: Alberto the barber as the prototypical Italian who adheres to his own cultural dictates and Old World traditions, and Bob the Cadillac salesman, who stands for the average American guy pursuing the American dream and consumerism. Not surprisingly, Primo is friendly with Alberto, and sees him as something of a father figure, while Secundo meets and is drawn to Bob, due to his blatant appreciation for popular culture and the so-called finer things in life.

Alberto is an Italian immigrant. He runs his barbershop traditionally, with porcelain shaving cream containers and a straight razor, and is a confidante and friend to Primo. He does things the right way and the old way, more attuned to the culture he left behind than the one he finds himself in. Whenever Primo has a problem, he turns to Alberto for advice and succor. They spend time together and interact in the barbershop, a traditionally male-centered environment. In our first view of Alberto, Primo is scolding him for talking about Ann the flower lady with Secundo. Alberto routinely denies mentioning Ann, but we come to understand that he indeed talked about her to Secundo. Actually, Alberto wants to bring the two of them together. We get the sense that Alberto is scheming and trying to manipulate events so that Primo gets the chance for happiness. He functions as a matchmaker within this film, constantly on the lookout for ways to get Primo and Ann together. His solution to Primo's worries is to relax and drink some grappa, and then to change the subject to the food that Primo has brought to him. Alberto is very traditional in his outlook on life. He further serves as confidante to Primo's worries about America and whether or not he should return to the old country, even watching Primo on the telephone talking to his uncle in Italy. When Primo is angered by Pascal's restaurant, he honestly shares his opinion of the food with Alberto: "Do you know what goes on in that man's restaurant every night? Rape! Rape, that is what goes on in that place every night—the rape of cuisine." Primo feels safe sharing his true feelings with Alberto, using him as a pressure valve. As a type, Alberto stands as indicative of the Old World of Italy, caring about people, tradition, and life rather than material possessions.

Bob, on the other hand, is very much the flashy American. He sells Cadillacs, the prototypical American cars of the 1950s. They are big, expensive and eye-catching, use a lot of gas, and create a strong statement and presence. Bob's demeanor, as well, is modern and of the New World. He is sitting in a car (a 1958 Series 60 Fleetwood Cadillac) when Secundo first meets him, and starts to smooth talk Secundo into making a purchase. The two hit it off and begin to talk about the differences between Italy and America. Secundo wants what Bob has, next year's car and the material possessions. But Bob does not have the Italian love of family and tradition. Bob tells Secundo that he hates his younger brother: "I hate his guts. He's cheap." Secundo expresses the traditional Italian concern for family and says, "but he is your brother." Bob doesn't share Secundo's attitude and replies: "Yeah, he is my brother. I hate cheap people." To Bob, the biggest sin is being cheap, not liking the finer things in life. Family does not rank as something that is important. Secundo, though surprised, accepts this. Bob, in trying to explain the expectations of American consumer society says to Secundo about new cars, "I got two kids. They see their friend with a new toy, they gotta have it." In the great 1950s tradition of keeping up with the neighbors, Bob advocates getting things because someone else has them. He lusts after the 1958 Caddie when this year's model should do him just fine. For Bob, a man is judged by what he has and how he looks, rather than by what is inside. When Bob attends the dinner, he dances feverishly with women and tries to sell cars over the meal, turning the feast into a business dinner. He is only doing what comes naturally to him. Our last shot of him is when he is driving two "American" girls home in the middle of the night after a good party, one passed out in the back seat of the convertible luxury car. Bob stands as indicative of the average guy values in America, with fast cars, opportunities galore, a smooth-talking manner, and the company of beautiful women. He enjoys a good time.

Serving *Il Timpano* at the Table: Business and Art Performed

Italian man to sobbing blond American woman after the meal:
>   Man: What's the matter?
>   Woman: My mother was such a terrible cook.

The presentation of the *timpano* at the table is the strongest food image in *Big Night*. Primo and Secundo kiss it and pat it lovingly like a child before carrying it into the dining room. The guests react with gasps of delight and eyerolls of culinary ecstasy after tasting it. It stands as the foreign image of love and cultural tradition. The feast continues after the presentation of the *timpano*, with fish, a roast suckling pig, many different dishes of vegetables and sides including asparagus, greens, baked tomatoes, stuffed mushrooms, artichokes, and much more. The excess of the Italian table and the feast prepared is enjoyed and eaten by the guests, in frenzy. It brings them together for a moment they will never forget. Afterward they have trouble leaving, for they are drawn to this warmth and ritual that is so lacking in their own existence. The brothers provide them with a taste of Italian culture, and bring both nationalities together for the dinner.

The feast operates as a turning point for Primo, Secundo, and Pascal. Pascal's duplicity and shady business dealings have completely ruined the Pilaggi brothers. This performance of bad faith leaves their friendship in ruins. Primo remains the artist, happy to perform his magic for the true believers; Pascal remains the charlatan and consummate businessman, whereas Secundo must renounce his hopes for success and the American dream. The cost of doing business in the American way is too much, and he resigns himself to a return to family, tradition, and cultural truths.

In the final confrontation between the brothers, witnessed by all of the Italians and Ann, Primo informs Secundo that "You have rotted . . . this place is eating us alive." Eating, usually so enjoyable, means in this instance a painful decay. The emotional cost of doing business in America is ruining the family and the traditions of the brothers. Secundo has ingested these new ideas and they have made him unfit for Italian life. Being eaten equals destruction and death. Primo convinces Secundo that they must return to the Italian way of living by saying, "If I sacrifice my work, it dies. It's better that I die." Secundo finally understands that there are more important things than success in life, that although financial success may be enticing and seducing, family and tradition endure. He watches Bob drive off in a convertible, allowing his dreams to recede as well.

The next confrontation is with Pascal, who is playing the piano in the dining room. Pascal dreamed once of artistic success with his music, but felt that money and security were more important. Secundo confronts Pascal's shady business ethics and reminds him there is a higher order than money, that artistic truth is more important in the final evaluation. "You will never have my brother. He live in a world above you. What he have and what he is, is rare. You . . . are nothing." American ideals are empty; they consume the soul rather than feed the spirit. Pascal's response shows us Secundo's entrapment between worlds and principles, as he says, "I am a businessman. I am anything I need to be at any time. Tell me, what exactly are you?" Secundo must decide who he is, and he does in the final, much talked about, enigmatic scene in the film that shows us the rapprochement of the brothers. Secundo, without dialogue and in a single shot, cooks and serves a *frittata* as Christiano gets plates and bread for the meal. Primo enters the kitchen and Secundo serves him breakfast. Christiano wanders off and slowly Secundo puts his arm around Primo's shoulder. Primo continues to eat, but then embraces his brother back. The shot establishes itself with the two eating breakfast together silently.

"In Italy we don't care about the presentation so much; we care about what we eat. Italian food satisfies you," Marcella Hazan once commented in an interview.[27] *Big Night* establishes itself as a performance of culture and tradition. There are no ambiguities about its message; you must live well and eat well, and you must feed the soul what it needs, or else you have failed. The beliefs and standards of Italian culture are inherent in the way that Stanley Tucci talks about food. The messages are imbedded in *Big Night*, and within the glorious layers of the majestic *timpano*. The true Italians are rich because they adhere to a standard of cuisine, whereas others are morally and emotionally bankrupt if they sell out and simply create (or become) a consumer product. They may succeed, but in doing so they lose their souls. *Big Night* teaches us the truism of Italian culture: *"Dimmi con chi vai chi ti diro chi sei*—Tell me who you go with and I'll tell you who you are."

Notes

1. Back Cover, *Big Night*, directed by Stanley Tucci and Campbell Scott, 109 min., Columbia/Tri-Star, 1996, videocassette.
2. Stanley Tucci, foreword to Joan Tropiano Tucci and Gianni Scappin, *Cucina & Famiglia* (New York: William Morris, 1999), ix.
3. Stanley Tucci, in Tucci and Scappin, *Cuciuna & Famiglia*, 171–72.
4. Pisano is a Tucci family name, the name of the ancestor who first immigrated to America, bringing the family recipe for Timpano with her from Calabria. Alberto perhaps stands in for the traditional Italian figure, the past that stands guard over culture.
5. Stanley Tucci, foreword, ix.
6. All quotes herein are transcribed by the author from a videocasette of the film.
7. See *timpano di maccheroni* recipe at Dean Richards's Food Time website, http://wgnra-dio.com/dean/timpano.htm, accessed 1 July 2002.
8. According to Marcella Hazan, in an interview with Chris Sherman, (*Saint Petersburg* [Fla.] *Times*, 25 March 1999.), "'there is really no such thing as Italian cooking.'" Italy has a large variety of regional cuisines, going far beyond the misconception that southern italians use red tomato sauce and northerners use butter and cream. 'I love seeing notes in the newspaper that there is a new Tuscan restaurant serving Northern Italian specialties,' Victor Hazan said in the same interview; 'Tuscany is in Central Italy!' Marcella adds with equal exasperation, 'In Florence, they didn't even know how to twirl spaghetti on a fork until a hundred years ago. They ate soup, they didn't eat pasta.'"
9. Tucci and Scappin, *Cucina & Famiglia*, 170.
10. Stanley Tucci has related a Tucci family legend regarding the timpano: "Peekskill, N.Y., is where my family is from, which was very heavily Italian and Irish. There were stone quarries and stuff around there, and Italians worked there. It's right on the Hudson River. When my father was a kid, they used to take little day trips up to the state park, which is very pretty. They would bring this Timpano up, and they would have these huge family gatherings in this beautiful park. They were walking through the woods one day finding firewood, and there's another family, another Italian family, with their Timpano. It turns out they were from the same village that my father's mother was from. Nobody else had ever heard of this." Stanley Tucci, "Interview with Stanley Tucci" by Rob Wilson, 28 September 1996, online at http://reeltime.cln.com/movies/interview.asp?ID=34, accessed 31 July 2002.
11. Waverley Root and Richard de Rochemont, *Eating in America* (New York: William Morrow, 1976), 276.
12. John L. Hess and Karen Hess, *The Taste of America* (New York: Grossman, 1977), 198.
13. Ibid., 213–14.
14. Tucci and Scappin, *Cucina & Famiglia*, 170.
15. However, even in *timpano di maccheroni*, there are vast differences in ingredients and preparation. Different recipes may incorporate a pastry crust, chicken, peas, pigeon, eggplant, and other ingredients.
16. Tucci, interview with Rob Wilson.
17. Tucci and Scappin, *Cucina & Famiglia*, 171.
18. Tucci, foreword, x.
19. Tucci, interview with Rob Wilson.
20. Susan Houston, "The Towering Timpano," *Raleigh News-Record*, 22 March 2000.
21. Tucci and Scappin, *Cucina & Famiglia*, 172.
22. The customer should have called out "Signore." For Americans, the foreign elements of cuisine are interchangeable; all "other" cooking is foreign and so the same. Using the French term for "sir" only points to her ignorance. To add insult to injury, in an example of American excess, the husband makes Secundo grate cheese onto his serving three times.
23. In fact, one cook, Ornella Capra, mentions her daughter, who refuses to eat her *timpano* because it combines rice and pasta, and this is considered a sin by most Italian gastronomes. See http://www.ornellacucinaitaliana.com/pages/articles/timpano.html, accessed 1 July 2002.
24. Tucci and Scappin, *Cucina & Famiglia*, 126.

25. There is a deep nationalism that runs through Italian cuisine. One can tell the origin of the dish by the components of the recipe. "*Nostrano* (local/ours) lays claim to food, saying this is from our land, from our place in the world." It is looked upon with suspicion to use one region's ingredient or specialty in another region's cuisine. See Lynne Rossetto Kasper, *The Italian Country Table* (New York: Scribner's, 1999), 17.
26. Tucci and Scappin, *Cucina & Famiglia*, 201.
27. Hazan, interview with Chris Sherman.

5

Cooking Mexicanness: Shaping National Identity in Alfonso Arau's *Como agua para chocolate**

MIRIAM LÓPEZ-RODRÍGUEZ

In 1991, when Mexican film director Alfonso Arau decided to adapt the 1989 novel *Como agua para chocolate* (*Like Water for Chocolate*) as a film, he probably did not imagine it would become the most successful foreign film of the year. The novel had been written by his wife of that time, Laura Esquivel. Both book and film attracted a lot of critical attention—not always positive, but at least they were being talked about, prompting interest. That the film should be successful in Mexico was no surprise, since the book had also been extremely popular, but its international triumph was startling to many given the fact of its "Mexicanness." Why would foreign audiences be interested in a film about a Mexican woman cooking Mexican meals? Obviously they were, as the film earned "almost $20 million at the U.S. box office, [thus becoming] the first Latin American film—indeed, any foreign film—to have this kind of popular reception in the Hollywood-immersed North American market."[1]

Although Esquivel's book/script is rich enough in meaning to provide for an analysis from many different theoretical points of view (magic realism, contemporary Mexican literature, the border, war in women's writing, etc.), my interest in *Like Water for Chocolate* concerns feminist and postcolonial

---

*I would like to dedicate this essay to Dr. José Luis Maldonado Rivera of México City for introducing me to traditional Mexican food and its cultural implications; his comments have been an invaluable help in the writing of this paper. To Dr. Ruth Stoner I owe my gratitude for her proofreading and constant encouragement.

theoretical understanding of the way food is represented. My overall aim is to focus on the female characters' relationship with food and how the choice of dishes presented in this particular film helps define Mexican national identity through the connections that these recipes have with cultural traditions and their historical implications. With this purpose in mind I look at two aspects of the food in the movie: the choice of recipes with respect to their ethnic (Spanish versus Creole versus Indian), sociopolitical (upper versus working class), and historical (pre- and postrevolutionary) associations; and how the characters in the film are developed via these recipes. Different recipes have certain ideological implications that highlight characters' roles in the family and in the kitchen, their relationship with food (e.g., mere nourishment versus creativity and national pride), and their relationships with the other characters in the story.

To begin with, *Como agua para chocolate* tells the story of the Garza family and the family's servants during the Mexican Revolution (1910–1917). The ranch and the lives of those there are ruled by Mamá Elena, who decides the future of her three daughters—Gertrudis, Rosaura, and Tita—regardless of their own desires. Thus, the youngest child, Tita, is not allowed to marry Pedro because she is given the life role of caring for her mother. Esquivel's choice of names for these two characters, Mamá Elena and Tita, is significant: Elena is the matriarch, the one holding the power at the Garza ranch, and both the audience and the other characters in the film are reminded of that through her name, *Mamá* Elena. With regard to Tita, her name is a diminutive that may be short for Josefina, among other names, but it also means "auntie," which stresses the idea that she is destined by Mamá Elena to be an aunt but never a mother.

Condemned to see the man she loves married to her elder sister Rosaura, and relegated to a servant-like position as cook of the family, Tita finds her only refuge in the kitchen. And while the Mexican Revolution takes place in the background, on the Garza ranch another subtle revolt is taking place: like the greater one, this second revolution is an attack on tyranny, racism, and class consciousness. By the end of the film both groups of revolutionaries, in spite of the casualties left along the way, can see their causes victorious and united in the figure of Esperanza, Tita's niece.

This film's plot is structured around location and time, moving from 1895 to 1910 to 1934 and shifting across Rio Grande and Piedras Negras, Mexico, and Eagle Pass, Texas. In the novel, however, the story is presented, in part, as a cookbook that is divided into twelve sections, one for each month of the year on a timeline of more than twenty years, with twelve corresponding recipes: in January, *tortas de Navidad* (Christmas cakes); in February, *pastel Chabela de bodas* (Chabela wedding cake) and *capones* (capons); in March, *codornices en pétalos de rosa* (quail in rose-petal sauce); in April, *mole de guajolote con almendra y ajonjolí* (turkey in almond and sesame sauce); in May, *chorizo norteño* (northerner's spicy sausage); in June, *masa para hacer fósforos* (mixture for making matches); in July, *caldo de colita de res* (oxtail soup); in August, *champandongo* (a lasagne-like dish);[2] in September, hot chocolate and *rosca de Reyes* (Three Wise Men ring-shaped cake);[3] in October, *torrejas de nata* (fried fruit with whipped cream); in November, *frijoles gordos con chile a la teztucana* (broad beans in chili sauce, Teztucan style); and in December, *chiles en nogada* (chili peppers in walnut sauce). The film's shift away from structuring the plot around the monthly recipes could give one the idea that the film director has abandoned the book's emphasis on food, but that is not the case. Arau, in fact, compensates for that change by offering his audience beautiful close-ups of the food, and in fact, the food often gets more screen time than most of the actors. The loving way the camera focuses on food (the eggs carefully added to the wedding cake dough, the quail being served with the rose petals, the glistening oxtail broth, as just a few examples) makes clear to the film audience that food is a central character in this story.

Every one of these dishes has its historical and ethnic implications. For example, the Christmas cake could be considered a Christian tradition imported to Mexico by the Spanish clergy. However, this Mexican version of the recipe includes American ingredients such as chili.[4] This same Mexicanization of Spanish dishes can be found in other instances, as in the September recipe, in which the traditional ring-shaped cake is eaten with hot chocolate prepared not the Spanish way with milk, but the Nahuatl way with water. Mexicanization is also present in the names of the utensils and foods that have preserved their Nahuatl origin (*molcajete, tejolote, metate, jitomate, guajolote, elote*) instead of their Spanish equivalents.[5] One does see, in contrast, as evidence of Mexico's cultural mixture, that the characters have renounced the indigenous frugality of eating only to satisfy hunger in favor of the Spanish gusto and abundance that turns any meal into a social event to be shared with friends and relatives.

In February, Tita is ordered by her mother to cook the menu for Rosaura and Pedro's wedding reception. The main dish, chosen by Mamá Elena, is significantly enough "capons"—that is, castrated chickens. An unsexed meal for an unsexing event, since this wedding means the destruction of Pedro and Tita's dream of a life together.[6] Pedro could have "kidnapped" Tita and eloped with her, as his own father suggested, but lacking the courage he prefers to accept Mamá Elena's suggestion of marrying the older daughter Rosaura. In colloquial Spanish this lack of courage is referred to as lacking *cojones* ("balls"),[7] symbolized in the castrated chickens cooked especially for Pedro. In fact, several of the words used in Mexican slang to name the male sexual organ, such as *pájaro* ("bird") and *chorizo* ("sausage"), also refer to food.

The recipe for March is quail in rose petals, which, in my opinion, comes to define the relationship between Tita and Pedro.[8] To celebrate Tita's first year as head cook of the ranch Pedro buys her a bunch of pink roses, provoking the jealousy of his pregnant wife Rosaura and the anger of Mamá Elena. Having been ordered to get rid of the bouquet, Tita resourcefully uses it to create a delicious dish that will represent her passionate love for Pedro. This quasi-orgasmic meal has as its basic ingredients birds and roses, symbolic of Aphrodite, the goddess of love in Greek mythology. The original symbols are actually doves and red roses, so the change in Esquivel's story/screenplay to quail and pink roses may imply that this love is not as great or authentic as it should be—that is, on Pedro's side!

In April, Tita cooks *mole de guajolote con almendra y ajonjolí*, a dish that, like the one for December (*chiles en nogada*), has historical significance for Mexico. The *mole poblano* or *mole de guajolote* was created some time between 1680 and 1688 by Sor Andrea de la Asunción, a Dominic nun, to honor Antonio de la Cerda y Aragón, Viceroy of New Spain, during his stay in Puebla.[9] She combined the traditional elements of a Mexican sauce (chile, chocolate, pumpkin seeds, peanuts, and tomato) with Spanish ingredients such as raisins, almonds, and sesame seeds to elaborate a dark red sauce to accompany the turkey meat.[10] According to tradition this dish was forbidden to women during the colonial period due to its supposed aphrodisiac quality.[11] *Chiles en nogada* is another recipe created in Puebla to honor a particular man, in this case the revolutionary leader Agustín de Iturbide, who happened to spend the day of St. Augustine, his patron saint, in Puebla on his way back from Mexico City, where he had signed the Treaty of Córdoba (1821), which gave Mexico its independence from Spain. The dish re-creates the colors of Mexico's national flag, combining the green of the peppers with the white of the creamy sauce and the red of the pomegranate seeds sprinkled over it.

The preparation of a less complex dish, the *chorizo norteño*, brings viewers the only moment in the film in which Tita and her mother are seen cooking together. This does not, however, imply an emotional reconciliation, but quite the opposite. The scene shows Mamá Elena in all her cruelty: she breaks Tita's nose after hitting her with a wooden spoon simply because she is crying over her nephew Roberto's recent death. The battle in the kitchen mirrors the "real" battle of revolution going on in the country at this time. Even more important, we see that, in contrast to Tita, who uses cooking utensils to create love, in Mamá Elena's hands those same utensils are transformed into weapons. The *chorizos* the two women are making are another Spanish import to which Mexicans add their local touch of chile instead of the milder European paprika, reflecting another case of the Mexicanization of a European recipe. But the most important implication of this food item, a rude one if we remember the symbolic meaning of *chorizo* in Mexican slang, is its appearance in the film at exactly the moment when Pedro is ordered by Mamá Elena to move north with his wife and son to San Antonio, Texas; it is also the moment in which the northerner John Brown begins to feel attracted to Tita. Is Mamá Elena saying to Tita, "I have moved your 'sausage' north," or "Here comes a new 'sausage' from the north"?

The movie presents John as the only character who, in spite of his soft manners, dares to challenge the domination of Mamá Elena.[12] He refuses to commit Tita to a mental asylum and instead takes her to his home to look after her and help her recover from a nervous breakdown caused by the death of her beloved nephew. It is also John who gives Tita the special "recipe" for June, *masa para hacer fósforos*. It may be argued that this mixture for making matches is not a culinary recipe, but as a recipe it nonetheless plays an important part in the film, for it introduces three "ingredients": first, John's respect for Tita as a woman (he is eager to teach her his knowledge of basic chemistry without ever questioning her ability as a female to understand the process); second, John's respect for the domestic labor of women in general (instead of following the male tradition of diminishing woman's work, John presents a parallelism between the work of the cook and that of the alchemist, as both mix ingredients in certain quantities to obtain specific results; and third, John's honoring of his—and Mexico's—indigenous women (he was taught this match recipe by his Indian grandmother, Luz del Amanecer, which establishes a second parallelism between John and Tita, since both of them, white middle-class individuals, have acquired their knowledge from older illiterate Indian women).[13]

Finally, we come to the recipe for September, the *rosca de Reyes* that, as its name indicates, should be eaten on the morning of 6 January rather than in September. According to Christian tradition, the Three Wise Men or Three Kings started traveling in search of the Son of God on 25 December, following a shining star that took them to Bethlehem. Arriving there on the morning of 6 January (this period represents the twelve days of Christmas), they presented to the newborn Jesus gold, incense, and myrrh. Based on that legend, Spanish Catholics exchange Christmas presents and eat the Three Kings Cake on this morning. A possible explanation for Tita's preparing the cake in September instead of January is the fact that she mistakenly thinks she may be expecting Pedro's child; in light of that, the cake is a celebration of that imaginary birth.

Perhaps, before going any further with the analysis of the food in the film, some general information on Mexican cooking habits should be clarified: from a gastronomical point of view, the country divides itself into three areas: the north, the center, and the south. The northern cuisine typically contains a lot of meat in the daily diet together with wheat tortillas.[14] In the center and the south of the country, meat takes on a secondary position, dishes are almost always presented with corn tortillas (wheat tortillas are very rare), and dishes considered in the United States as quintessentially Mexican, such as the burrito, are unheard of.[15] The typical cuisine characteristic of the center of the country is quite varied, while much of the south dintinguishes itself through its Mayan origins.[16] Big cities have, logically, been more open to foreign influences while the countryside remains closer to its indigenous tradition. In general, one can say that Mexican food is, as mirrored in the country, a mixture in which the Indian elements coexist with those of the Spanish and the Creole. This cohabitation has not always been easy, but as Esquivel shows us, it has enriched all: she presents cooking, both in the film and the novel, not as a war among races or cultures but as a way to combine the best of each.

Having considered some of the historical, ethnic, and ideological implications of Esquivel's choice of recipes, I would like now to focus on a feminist reading of the relationship between food and the female characters in the film. First of all, from a scholarly point of view, food has become an important topic in the field of cultural materialism, especially among feminist critics, as it brings to the forefront those elements of life that were traditionally overlooked because they belonged to the domestic sphere and not to the public, broader, male—and therefore "more important"—sphere. Being denied the right to speak freely by patriarchy and tradition, women throughout history have resorted to expressing their feelings through the daily activities and crafts associated with housewifery. They learned to use cooking, quilting, gardening, and the like as *texts* that tell the uninitiated—mostly other women—what they could not communicate in any other way. In this sense, the chosen activity has four functions: production of a useful item (food, garment, etc.); release of internal tensions; expression of creativity; and connection to other women. In regard to the last point, we can understand Tita's relationship with food and with people such as the Indian servants Nacha and Chencha, her friend John Brown, and her niece Esperanza as a kind of extended or loose quilting bee, offering her a refuge from her mother's tyranny and a sense of community, solidarity, and sisterhood that—in the words of Cecelia Lawless—provide Tita with "a means of self-definition and survival."[17]

Regarding the relationship of the central women characters to food and cooking we can establish two well-differentiated groups: on one side we have Mamá Elena and Rosaura, and on the other Nacha and Tita. Each pair of women share common characteristics that clearly mark them as either "the "good girls" or "the bad girls." Neither of the two negative characters, Mamá Elena and Rosaura, can breastfeed her children, making the assistance of a "positive" woman, Nacha or Tita, necessary for the babies' survival. When Tita is born, her father has just died, and the shock of this unexpected death makes Mamá Elena incapable of breastfeeding. Tita is passed over to Nacha, who raises her on milk, Indian teas, and cornmeal mush. Years later, when Roberto, and later Esperanza, are born, Rosaura has no milk, either. Tita follows Nacha's example to make sure her nephew and niece grow healthy in body and soul. The negative-versus-positive female concept is dramatically portrayed when Mamá Elena orders Pedro and Rosaura to move north in order to separate her son-in-law from Tita. Away from his aunt and left to the care of his cold-hearted mother, little Roberto dies, indicating Rosaura's inability to be a loving and nurturing woman.

Esquivel makes it clear that the concepts of motherhood and nurturing do not necessarily go together, that giving birth does not automatically turn a woman into a nurturing, loving mother. Both Nacha and Tita have been denied the right to be mothers by Mamá Elena, but no one, not even domineering Elena, can kill the mother in each of them.[18]

A second characteristic shared by both the "negative" women is their attitude toward food: while all the other characters, male and female, enjoy cooking and/or eating, Elena and Rosaura do not. Mamá Elena always has some complaint to make about Tita's cooking: it does not follow the recipe, it is either too spicy or not spicy enough, it is poisoned, and so on. And Rosaura as a child enfuriates Nacha with her squeamishness at mealtime and by expressing her disgust at seeing Tita eat traditional Nahuatl delicacies such as armadillo and maguey worms.[19] As an adult, Rosaura is consistently plagued by digestive problems, and she suffers from stomach aches and relentless "wind." Perhaps this is Esquivel's scatological way of symbolizing that this woman—personification of the most intolerant patriarchy and tradition—cannot *digest* the postrevolutionary multicultural Mexico exemplified in Tita's cooking.

It is because of their negative relationship with food that these two "bad" women finally die. Mamá Elena, convinced that Tita is poisoning her meals in order to get rid of her and marry John Brown, takes a massive dose of an emetic, which causes her ironically symbolic death. Rosaura's death is not so clearly explained, leaving it to the audience to decide whether she dies of some form of stomach cancer (which might explain her digestive disorders) or whether there is some sort of magical punishment. In any case, the first death brings Rosaura and Pedro back to the ranch, reuniting the two original lovers, Pedro and Tita; the second death frees them to live their love without restrictions though, unfortunately for them, it does not last long because of Pedro's death while making love.[20]

The main protagonist of the film is obviously Tita de la Garza, the main "positive" woman, and her relationship with food is, of course, critical to her own existence and certainly the element that unifies the plot.[21] It is Mamá Elena's view of cooking as just another domestic chore and not as a creative activity that makes her relegate her younger daughter to the kitchen as a kind of exile. From a very young age, being relegated to the kitchen differentiates Tita from her older sisters, who are kept in the most "noble" rooms of the house. Being bound to the kitchen from the moment of her emblematic birth in this very same room, Tita is treated first by her mother and later by Rosaura as just another servant, as if to stress that her role will be to wait upon her mother and sister for the rest of her life.[22] Given Mamá Elena and Rosaura's concept of cooking, being condemned to the kitchen is, from their point of view, a punishment; but it is not so for Tita, who at first considers cooking to be a game that she plays with the Indian servant Nacha, and later finds it the only medium through which she can express herself, give herself a voice. Tita, having rejected her mother as a role model, turns the kitchen into "a zone of transformation. . . . In other words, although Tita finds herself in the traditional site of the kitchen, where women have been domestically relegated, she sets up her own territoriality."[23]

Traditionally, mothers have used the kitchen as a gathering place where daughters and daughters-in-law learned family recipes, shared the work, and talked freely, away from the male world. Cooking, like sewing and other "feminine" tasks, provided the perfect excuse to meet other female relatives and friends, exchange tips and gossip,and so forth, functioning very much like a modern therapy group. Neither Mamá Elena nor Rosaura, advocates of the most narrow-minded tradition, fulfill the traditional role of the mother as teacher, leaving it once more to the "positive" women, Nacha and Tita. It will be Nacha who turns the kitchen into a formative little haven for Tita and, in due time, Tita will do the same for Esperanza, each woman feeding not only the body but also the soul of her surrogate daughter. It is only the two childless women in the film who care to pass the family recipes from one generation to the next, becoming figurative mothers. Each passes her heritage differently: Nacha does it verbally, while Tita does it in writing, which reflects what some would see as the natural order of culture and language.[24]

For Tita, cooking is a small rebellion against her mother's tyranny, as it provides an outlet for the creativity Mamá Elena is always restraining. The first time Tita shows some creativity, while sewing a new dress, she is punished for not following her mother's instructions step by step, for not doing things the "proper" way. In contrast, Nacha and her cooking lessons foster Tita's initiatives, for the young girl is not simply duplicating old recipes but also transforming them and creating new ones. In March, one month after her death, the ghost of Nacha whispers to Tita a pre-Hispanic recipe for pheasant with rose petals, but since there are no pheasants on the ranch, Tita alters the recipe and the meal is prepared with quail. This scene also serves to indicate that Nacha's spirit, and therefore her Indian American culture, lives on through her recipes.[25]

From the beginning of the film, Tita is presented as a very sensual person, constantly aware of her senses. She is repeatedly portrayed tasting, seeing, smelling, touching, and hearing. It is only logical that she communicates through an activity that comprises all the senses. Given that "the house rules [do] not include dialogue," Tita takes her creativity one step further when she transforms food into a new language.[26] Learning to cook, she learns also to transfer to her dishes whatever she is experiencing at the time so that her meals become the medium through which she can comunicate to others her feelings while at the same time escaping her mother's close vigilance. In John Kraniauskas's words, "food now becomes a weapon in Tita's hands," transforming the kitchen, the orchard, and even the outhouse into her own little kingdom.[27]

This liberation through food and cooking is not limited to Tita alone, but also occurs for the people who eat her meals—all except, of course, her mother and Rosaura. In a house in which no expression of emotions is allowed, Tita's cooking causes uncontrollable outbursts of pleasure, sadness, and so forth. Mamá Elena may control the outward behavior of those on the ranch, but she certainly cannot control what they feel. Emotions are Tita's territory: she feels and she makes others feel. At Rosaura and Pedro's wedding, sadness takes possession of all the guests after eating the castrated chickens. Moments later, while eating the cake, they feel as sick as Tita did while having to prepare it. Unable to understand this magic, Mamá Elena accuses Tita of poisoning the food and beats her once the reception is over and the guests are gone. That night Nacha dies alone in her bedroom, leaving Tita as the ranch's main cook, which gives Tita a certain amount of power (however limited).

One year later, while preparing the quail in rose-petal sauce, Tita is thinking of her love for Pedro. This passion is magically transferred to the food, which acquires a quasi-orgasmic quality most clearly seen in Gertrudis, but also evident in dull Pedro as he confesses to his sister-in-law not having experienced such a pleasure ever before, which says a lot about his sex life with Rosaura. This scene, in which "a strange alchemichal process had dissolved [Tita's] entire being in the rose petal sauce . . . enter[ing] Pedro's body, hot, voluptuous, perfumed, totally sensuous," offers the audience an erotic instant in which Tita and Pedro turn a traditional sexual encounter upside down, as it is Tita who penetrates Pedro's body. As Esquivel herself explained in a 1990 interview with journalists Alejandro Semo and Juan José Giovannini, "cooking inverts the traditional sexual order. Man is the passive recipient, while woman is the active transmitter."[28]

The pleasure produced by food is expanded to the whole process of cooking on the next occasion necessitating a special recipe as Pedro, understanding that cooking is Tita's way of telling him what she cannot vocalize, feels aroused by the smells and noises coming from the kitchen where she is preparing the dishes for Roberto's baptism reception. Here food preparation acts as foreplay, awakening Pedro's senses for the later pleasure of eating that food. Seeing the effect her cooking has on Pedro, and realizing he can decode the hidden messages in it, Tita feels compelled to create more and more recipes that will keep alive the love that Mamá Elena and Rosaura had tried to kill. It is this need to create or re-create delicious dishes that moves Tita to put in writing all the recipes she has received from Nacha; that is how their cookbook is born.

As Anne Bower explains in "Bound Together: Recipes, Lives, Stories, and Readings," a communal cookbook—such as the one written by Tita with Nacha's recipes—should be valued "not just as a fun source of recipes but as a literary text whose authors constructed meaningful representations of themselves and their world. . . . Although women were often limited in access to recognized status-bearing discourse forms such as poetry and fiction, public speaking, and journalism, they expressed themselves through other print and nonprint materials."[29] In *Como agua para chocolate* Nacha and Luz del Amanecer, members of ethnic minorities, have been denied by the dominant white upper class the possibility of expressing their knowledge through any medium other than the recipes they cherish. By passing the recipes on to the next generation they are not only able to communicate some practical information but to preserve elements of an indigenous culture that would otherwise be lost. In this context it is important to underline how the two illiterate older Indian women pass their oral tradition to younger literate white persons, Tita and John Brown, who, proud of the mixed heritage of their countries, will write down the legacy received to make sure that a third generation (symbolized by Esperanza) can enjoy it too.

It is through the line of surrogate mothers–Nacha and Tita–that Esperanza, the embodiment of modern Mexico, receives a cookbook that symbolizes not only the loving relationship among women but also the preservation of Nahuatl heritage and its mixture with Spanish and Creole elements. Thus, the book Esperanza finds after returning from her honeymoon is much more than a simple compilation of recipes: it is the story of Nacha's and Tita's lives, an autobiography of those associated with the Garza ranch, a record of their small community. This cookbook is a story of Mexico, though not one written by generals, politicians, chroniclers, or other men, but written by humble, unknown women. It is the diary of an illiterate Indian woman who passes her knowledge on to a literate Creole girl who in her turn bequeaths it to Esperanza, the character born in the twentieth century whose name means "hope." It is possible to see this girl, fed on Indian and Spanish recipes, as a symbol of a mestizo Mexico. In prerevolutionary Mexico, Europe and European modes were the fashion, while everything with an Indian connotation was considered second class; throughout the film, however, Tita makes no distinctions between Indian and Spanish cultures or between the middle and the working classes. For her, *all* of this is Mexico. It is this combination of elements that constitutes the basics of her recipes and of real Mexicanness.

This refusal on Tita's side to divide human beings into tight compartments—on the basis of race, class, or educational level—brings us to the subtopic of limits. Throughout the film, the concepts of borders and frontiers appear again and again: the Garza ranch is situated in the north, near the Mexico–United States border; John Brown lives on the other side of this border (in Eagle Pass, Texas); the separation from little Roberto and Pedro (sent by Mamá Elena to San Antonio, Texas) leads Tita to a mental breakdown that places her within the limits of madness; her interpretation of cookery as an artistic activity and not mere housework defies her mother's limits on what she can and cannot do. In the light of all this, Esperanza's marriage to John's son Alex implies breaking the limits imposed by Mamá Elena, once more indicating that the younger generation accepts no meaningless barriers.

We see the breaking down of borders also in the social and political implications of the recipes chosen by Laura Esquivel/Tita de la Garza for this particular cookbook—many of which show up in the film adaptation. First, all the recipes are basically mestizas (half-breeds), as they are either pre-Hispanic with some Spanish/Creole influence or Spanish with an Indian-American touch. It is hard to classify any dish as purely Indian or Spanish given that

Mexican cooking, just like its culture, language, and population, is a constant mixture of elements from both sides of the Atlantic.

Second, and continuing with the concept of breaking down borders and barriers to produce new mixtures, Tita cooks both simple working-class dishes, such as November's *frijoles gordos con chile a la teztucana*, and more elaborate expensive meals such as the quail. Her creativity makes her turn any combination of ingredients into a delicious experience that goes beyond mere nourishment while at the same time creating a definition of national identity and inadvertently breaking the strict code of behavior women had to conform to.

In the third place, Esquivel is clear about her notion of what the healthy relationship between women and food should be: "good" women enjoy talking about food, cooking it, and eating it; "bad" women do not. For the positive characters, cookery goes beyond mere nourishment, serving as a source of creativity and fostering a sense of community and national identity; for the "negative" women, eating is just another physical function that implies no pleasure.

My fourth and final point concerning breaking barriers is that Esquivel's fictional cookbook is clearly postrevolutionary. It prides itself on the interbreeding mentioned above, which presents an obvious contrast with the ideology prevailing during Porfirio Díaz's regime (1877–1911), which praised everything foreign as an indication of progress.[30] With regard to food, the French were supposed to be the masters of "high cuisine"; this made middle-class Mexicans celebrate their special events in Frenchified hotels and restaurants while the upper class paid small fortunes to "import" their own cooks, substituting European men for their previous Indian American female cooks. This follows the maxim that whenever a man chooses to work in a traditionally female task this job stops being considered a mere domestic chore to gain an "artistic" quality: cooks become chefs, seamstresses become couturiers. However, Esquivel renounces all this snobbery and chauvinism, making three illiterate Indian women (Nacha, Luz del Amanecer, and Chencha) the source of all knowledge while literate middle-class Creoles (Tita, John, and Esperanza) become the chosen custodians and transmitters, thereby breaking all race and class barriers to a degree uncommon even in present-day Mexico.

I find that the truly magical thing about the film version of *Like Water for Chocolate* is not its use of what is called magical realism, but the particular way in which author/screenwriter Esquivel conveys all of the narrative's important elements in the script through food images, and the way director Alfonso Arau translates them to the screen. Together Esquivel and Arau manage to bring viewers the concepts of mixing Indian-American and Spanish gastronomical traditions, blending working- and middle-class dishes, cooking as a source of creativity, and the concept of defining national identity through food. All this is accomplished through the use of food imagery. Thus the film becomes a tribute to Mexican cookery and to the women who have created and preserved it.

Notes

1. Harmony H. Wu, "Consuming Tacos and Enchiladas: Gender and the Nation in *Como agua para chocolate*," in *Visible Nations: Latin American Cinema and Video*, ed. Chon A. Noriega (Minneapolis: University of Minnesota Press, 2000), 183.
2. *Champandongo* alternates layers of minced meat and vegetables with corn flour tortillas, this being the main difference from Italian lasagna, which uses sheets of wheat-based pasta.
3. The Spanish Three Wise Men cake has also made its way to the United States in the form of the Mardi Gras king cake served in New Orleans, surprisingly similar not only in shape and taste but also in the inclusion in both of them of a small hidden trinket supposed to bring good luck to whomever finds it in his portion of the cake. The truth is that Spaniards have no tradition of baking any type of cake or pudding for Christmas except for the already mentioned "rosca de Reyes"; there is, however, a broad selection of Christmas delicacies such as *mantecados*, *polvorones*, and *turrones*, all of which have a Moorish origin!
4. I use the term *American* in the sense of "from the Americas," and not necessarily "from the United States."
5. European Spanish incorporated many Nahuatl words such as *tomate*, *aguacate*, and *cacahuete* ("tomato," "avocado," and "peanut," respectively); however, the words mentioned above (*molcajete*, *tejolote*, etc.) are totally unknown in Spain.
6. When castrating the first chicken Tita gets dizzy; she feels it is her mother who should be doing the castration as she seems to have a natural inclination for mutilation and punishment. See Laura Esquivel, *Como agua para chocolate* (México City: Planeta Mexicana, 1989), 34.
7. "Balls."
8. For an explanation of the importance of rose petals in Mexican culture and the connection with the myth of the Virgin of Guadalupe, see Barbara A. Tenenbaum, "Why Tita Didn´t Marry the Doctor; or Mexican History in *Like Water for Chocolate*," in *Based on a True Story: Latin American History at the Movies*, ed. Donald F. Stevens (Wilmington, Del.: Scholarly Resources, 1997).
9. See http://www.ramekins.com/mole/wheremole.html.
10. Sesame seeds, together with most other spices, were introduced into Spanish cooking by the Moors, who dominated Spain from 711 to 1492.
11. This is mentioned online at http://www.mexamerica.org; other interesting websites on Mexican cooking are http://www.azteca.net/aztec/nahuatl/indexsp.shtml; http://cocinamexicana.com.mx/historia/; Nacecocina.html, http:// elportaldemexico.com/arteculinario.html; http://www.mexflavours.com.mx; and http://www.mexconnect.com /mex_/recipes/foodindex.html.
12. John Brown´s name could be a symbolic reference to the average U.S. man or it could be a link to the revolutionary of the same name who led the attack on Harper's Ferry during the U.S. Civil War.
13. *Luz del Amanecer* translates as "Light of Dawn."
14. In European Spanish the word *tortilla* means "omelette," while in American Spanish it designates "unleavened bread."
15. For an analysis of the cultural and historical implications of eating corn tortillas versus wheat tortillas, see Jeffrey M. Pilcher, "Recipes for Patria: Cuisine, Gender, and Nation in Nineteenth-Century Mexico," in *Recipes for Reading: Community, Cookbooks, Stories, Histories*, ed. Anne L. Bower (Amherst: University of Massachusetts Press, 1997).
16. The rest of the country is Nahuatl.
17. Cecelia Lawless, "Cooking, Community, Culture: A Reading of *Like Water for Chocolate*," in Bower, ed., *Recipes*, 222.
18. Both are denied the right to get married and have children in order to dedicate their lives to the care of Mamá Elena. The younger servant Chencha eventually marries, but only after Mamá Elena's death.
19. Esquivel, *Como agua*, 36. The maguey is an American agave plant in which core worms grow; once cooked they can be eaten.
20. In a Romeo and Juliet–like scene, Tita poisons herself to die embracing her lover's body.
21. Chencha, Esperanza, and—in a certain way—Gertrudis are also positive females, but their roles in the development of the story are of lesser importance.
22. In her will, Mamá Elena leaves the ranch to Rosaura, thus making sure that Tita, penniless and beyond "marriable age," has no choice but to remain at her sister's service.
23. Lawless, "Cooking," 228.

24. For the connection between food and storytelling in the film, see Yael Halevi-Wise, "Storytelling in Laura Esquivel's *Como agua para chocolate*," in *The Other Mirror: Women's Narrative in Mexico, 1980–1995*, ed. Kristine Ibsen (Westport, Conn.: Greenwood Press, 1997).

25. The notion of creativity in the face of penury is seen again in November when the lack of food, due to war restrictions, makes Tita leave aside elaborate dishes and instead prepare humble broad beans.

26. Esquivel, *Como agua*, 17; my translation.

27. John Kraniauskas, "On *Como agua para chocolate*," in *Film/Literature/Heritage: A Sight and Sound Reader*, ed. Ginette Vincendeau (London: British Film Institute, 2001), 154.

28. Kristine Ibsen, "On Recipes, Reading, and Revolution: Postboom Parody in *Como agua para chocolate*," in Ibsen, ed., *The Other Mirror*, 120.

29. Anne Bower, "Bound Together: Recipes, Lives, Stories, and Readings," in Bower, ed., *Recipes*.

30. See Pilcher, "Recipes for Patria," 1–14.

6

Chickens, Cakes, and Kitchens: Food and Modernity in Malay Films of the 1950s and 1960s

TIMOTHY P. BARNARD

At the beginning of P. Ramlee's *Bujang Lapok* (*Ne'er-do-well Bachelors*, 1957), a Malay-language comedy describing the exploits and loves of three middle-aged men who must negotiate between their jobs in the modern city of Singapore and their idyllic life in the *kampung* (village), the main characters decide to cook at home rather than eating at a restaurant in the city. After purchasing a live chicken from a Chinese merchant they return to their kampung, where they are confronted by an elderly village man. He asks the three bachelors what they are doing with the chicken and mocks their conceit that they can cook. In the process he implies that cooking is something better left to the women in the village. The bachelors respond to the good-natured ribbing by asserting that they are capable of properly cooking and serving a chicken for dinner since they have cooking school "diplomas."

Temporarily perplexed by the idea that one could earn a degree in something as mundane as cooking, the elderly man is taken aback and agrees to slaughter the chicken for our *bujang lapok*. The viewer is then taken inside their boarding house, where the three men proceed to pluck the chicken, prepare the spices, and borrow a stove from their beautiful landlady. While cooking the bird, each man tastes the broth and proceeds to add more salt to the mix. When they believe it is thoroughly cooked, they then place the chicken, along with the broth, in a dish, on the floor next to a number of plates filled with rice and other vegetables and condiments that would be expected at a Malay meal. The three bachelors have also changed from their shabby clothes into nice pants and dress shirts, along with the *peci* or head covering a Malay (Muslim) man would wear to prayer or formal occasions. While sitting on the floor (Malay homes traditionally had little or no furniture), the men begin to eat, but discover that the chicken is like wood and the broth is unpalatable. Despite the outward markings of cooking a traditional Malay meal, along with its proper presentation, the incompetence of our three modern bachelors shines through. Food has been used to reflect the sorry state of their lives. Their attempts to portray themselves as competent, modern individuals able to provide themselves with the basic necessities of life has instead shown their need to find someone capable of taking care of them.

Malay Film in Society and History

The chicken scene from *Bujang Lapok* is one of the best known in Malay cinema. Although the movie was made almost half a century ago, Malay secondary school and university students in Singapore and Malaysia can refer to the film today in conversations, as well as quote lines from it, reflecting the power that Malay cinema holds over the community. An interesting aspect of this power is that the films that are continually watched to the point that they have entered Malay consciousness were made during the "golden era" of Malay cinema, the 1950s and 1960s. While Malay-language films continue to be made today, they must compete against fare imported from Hollywood and Bollywood that audiences perceive as more vibrant and modern. Despite the dearth of Malay-language films in the cinemas today, Singaporeans and Malaysians continually watch classic Malay films every week on local television stations, and they are available for sale at pirated videodisc shops in the region. These films have become family affairs, with three or four generations gathering around the television to enjoy flickering images of the past. In the process, the common theme of modernization in films of the 1950s and 1960s provides a template for how Malays can negotiate between a modern lifestyle while still honoring their traditions and the roles of men and women in this process. The old films still provide not only a view into the past, but a guide for social interaction and mores. And it is surprising how often food is a critical element in these films.

Before looking specifically at how food functions in certain of these Malay films, I think it necessary to give readers some background on cinema in Malaysia. As an historian, I've found it surprising that film has been so overlooked as a source for studying the Malay past. As Anthony Milner has pointed out,[1] Malay history has been limited by its reliance on the colonial record, which has not only created boundaries for scholars but also influenced the questions that are posed. Any insight other sources may provide into Malay history has been overlooked in the pursuit of dates and facts about colonial administrators and their policies. As archives and official depositories of the Malay past are limited by such sources and studies, where can a scholar of Malay social and cultural history find material? While there can be valuable information ascertained by "reading between the lines" of colonial records, and this has been done successfully in combination with other approaches,[2] there is another source that can provide a window into the past and reflect many of the changes society was undergoing: this source is Malay film, but it remains largely untapped.

The dismissal of Malay film as a source text for scholars is puzzling, since it evolved alongside an increasingly modern and urban society. Malay film was introduced to the Malay Peninsula and Singapore beginning in the 1930s when a handful of films were made. It only became a popular and productive medium for Malay artists after World War II, when two companies, Shaw Brothers' Malay Film Productions and Cathay Keris, began to produce films for distribution in their network of cinemas in Singapore and throughout the Malay Peninsula. The films were made in Singapore, the technological and economic hub of the region at the time, and featured multiethnic staffs: Chinese producers and technicians worked with Indian directors and artists who filmed Malay actors and singers. These films often featured the most popular songs of the time, were in the Malay language, and were mainly directed toward a Malay audience. From the beginning this system produced many stars that became icons of style, language, and mannerisms for the surrounding community. In many respects these films taught Malays how to act modern, while also glorifying the lifestyle of the traditional audience at which they were aimed.

One of the central icons in Malay film was the star and director of *Bujang Lapok*, P. Ramlee. Born on the island of Penang in 1929, Ramlee moved to Singapore in 1948 to work as a back-up singer for the Shaw Brothers' Malay Film Productions; he quickly rose through the organization due to his musical abilities and charisma. Beginning as a bit player in films such as B.S. Rajhan's *Nasib* (*Fate*, 1950), he quickly became the most admired actor in Malay films, which was clearly related to his role as a popular songwriter and singer. By 1955 Ramlee translated his growing power in the industry into an opportunity to direct films. This was a significant development, since there had been some opposition to Malay directors (directors were considered the key participant in the filmmaking process) from the Chinese studio owners. Almost all early Malay films were the product of Indian directors, who had been imported from the vibrant film industry in South Asia, and could be controlled by the studio bosses. While Indian directors had provided the industry with a stable base of fare, many in the Malay community believed they had overlooked some of the basic cultural norms that would have informed the stories being told and the manner in which Malays would have reacted in particular situations. In addition, the 1950s was a period of decolonization, and Malays were demanding a greater role in society, with many of those demands coming from the artistic community.[3]

The pedagogical role of Malay film was not lost on the filmmakers of the time. Ramlee took his new position as a director and writer seriously, since it occurred within the context of a rapidly changing society in which he played a prominent role. Among Malay intellectuals, one of the most important organizations promoting revolutionary ideals of the relationship between artists and society was ASAS 50 (*Angkatan Sasterawan* 50, or Generation of the Writers of the 1950s), which was mainly known for its literary production. Its members saw themselves as revolutionaries promoting modernity. Their critique of British rule and modernization, as well as "feudalistic" elements of Malay society, resulted in a period of artistic renaissance among the urban-based Malays of Singapore and Kuala Lumpur. These urban centers, particularly Singapore, played an important role in the ASAS 50 group's work because they were outside many of the restrictions that the colonial government had imposed due to a communist "emergency" in the peninsula.[4] The Singapore where the members of ASAS 50 lived, wrote, and performed was a vibrant port city in which Ramlee would have been the brightest and most influential Malay star. Ramlee's importance lay in his ability to reach beyond the literary circles that limited many of the members of this artistic group, which focused on the ideal that art should be for society and that their work should provide guidance to the people (*rakyat*).[5] This guidance was not to focus simply on the traditional subjects of religion and race, but also on the belief that people should take control over their destiny or fate (*nasib*).[6] One prominent member of the ASAS 50, Asraf Wahab, even wrote, "Leadership can only be given to them if the writer can give real pictures of their situation and of the 'causes' which create the situation."[7] The connection between Ramlee and the ASAS 50 went beyond a shared artistic vision. Ramlee published his own film magazine, *Bintang* (*Star*), which shared an office building with the ASAS 50. The connection was even stronger, since the editor of the *Bintang*, Fatimah Murad, was also the wife of Asraf, the leading ideologue of ASAS 50.[8]

In the vibrant context of a society that was going through decolonization, rapidly modernizing, and dealing with a variety of issues that revolved around race, citizenship, communism, and whether Singapore and Malaya should be part of a united country, Ramlee made his films. Under such influences, and guided by the ideals of ASAS 50, he included commentary on many of these issues. He also made a concerted attempt to portray life as realistically as possible, within the dramatic or comedic parameters that limited the story. Ramlee's film *Penarek Becha* (*The Trishaw Driver*, 1955) can serve as an example of his attempts to infuse social commentary that represented the ideals of the ASAS 50 into his films. *Penarek Becha* tells the tale of a trishaw driver named Amran, played by Ramlee himself, who helps a rich young woman named Azizah, played by Sa'adiah, when she is being harassed by a group of spoiled urban youths. To repay him for his kindness, Azizah hires Amran as transportation to her daily lessons at a school named *Harapan Wanita* (A Woman's Hope). Seeing the nobility of his character, Azizah falls in love with Amran. In the meantime, the leader of the young men who harassed Azizah, named Ghazali, endears himself to Azizah's rich and snobbish father, who is horrified that his daughter has fallen in love with a poor man. After a series of confrontations between Ghazali and Amran, the father understands that Amran has noble intentions and allows the young man to marry his daughter and oversee his business interests. Within the context of a simple drama, Ramlee is able to raise a number of issues that reflect the goals of ASAS 50. For example, Azizah continually urges Amran not to leave everything in the hands of God, claiming she has "lost patience" and that he must work his way out of poverty. She also emphasizes to Amran, and the audience, that he should not consider himself inferior in a society that may look down upon his profession. While she promotes these radical ideas, Azizah is always presented as a modern woman who also is able to honor the traditions of her past.[9]

The supposed dichotomy between modernity and tradition, and how Malays had to deal with these issues on a daily basis, was a relevant topic of the time for many artists. As one writer living during the period noted, "The 50s were the climax of a collective awakening of Malay society and this awakening was really the result of an awareness of the world around them."[10]

While viewing these films, with their attempts at developing an understanding for mass audiences of the joys and dangers of modernity, it is striking how often food is used to convey certain notions and ideas about characters and their situations. It is not that the food is Western; the important issue with regard to food is that it is *not* from the *kampung*. "Modern food" is cooked using new devices, such as stoves; or it is men who are doing the cooking. It is a new world, and the metaphoric role of food in this world allowed Ramlee to use it for either dramatic tension or comedic relief. In the process, the importance of women in their traditional role as cook or supervisor of the proper Malay meal, as long as it is modern, was also reinforced. In the chicken scene from *Bujang Lapok*, for example, the facade of modernity is undermined, as we see that a cooking diploma will not allow the three bachelors to live independently. They need a woman who knows how to cook in order to live a fulfilling life. It is from an analysis of the role of food and how it is prepared that greater insight into Malay understandings of modernity and its influence on gender can be better understood.

Traditions, Modernity and the Power of Women

The 1950s were a period in which modernity was the rage throughout Malaysia, and it was often placed squarely on the shoulders of women. Women were to modernize themselves and their kitchens, and thus lead the nation forward into a new era. Popular Malay magazines, such as the Singapore-produced *Fashio·*, had columns that promoted household tips to assist in the development of these goals. In addition to explaining modern cleaning products and appliances, the magazine provided suggestion on how to maintain a modern kitchen, such as how to keep fruit fresh, as well as recipes for Western dishes such as chicken macaroni. Several issues even had photographs of women posing with Western-style wedding cakes they had baked themselves.[11] In all instances, Western food and kitchen habits were equated with the modern. While the traditional position of women was linked to their mastery of the kitchen, they now must also be modern and thus be knowledgeable in the food styles of the West.

The link between food as a symbol of both the traditional and modern, and the need for women to gain a mastery over it, is conveyed in *Penarek Becha*. At the home economics school named A Woman's Hope, where Azizah spends her days, she learns the rudiments of becoming a post–World War II house-wife.[12] The school not only has modern machines at which students can learn how to sew, but also contains appliances and accessories such as stoves and mixing bowls so that the young women can learn to fulfill their new roles in society. The first shot involving the school is a close-up of the institution's name on a cake that one of the students has just taken out of an oven. The owner of the school, whom the camera follows, compliments the woman who has just finished baking it, and then goes over to the women working over mixing bowls. She then says that the skills they are developing "will be useful when you are all married." The foods that they are taught to prepare, however, are not traditional rice-based dishes, which would presumably be taught in the home. At a modern school such as A Woman's Hope, women are taught how to make foods such as cakes and pies in kitchens that are stocked with modern appliances. While women are expected to maintain their traditional roles as wives and cooks, they will be conduits for modernity through their mastery of the tools of the kitchen and the food they can produce.[13]

Films such as *Penarek Becha*, as well as popular magazines of the time, con-veyed images of women that posited that they would be more desirable if they could master modern cooking styles and appliances. Such modern practices, however, were also fraught with danger since they could mean a distancing from the traditions that had sustained the community. These problems are portrayed in scenes that takes place at the dining table in *Penarek Becha*.[14] The dining table, a piece of furniture that conveys modernity in a society that nor-mally eats from communal dishes placed on the floor, is the first clue as to how distant Azizah's rich family is from their traditions. When Azizah pro-poses during breakfast that her father hire Amran to transport her to A Woman's Hope and he refuses due to his dislike for the poor as well as his stin-giness, an argument ensues. As her mother slices her eggs with a knife and fork, and her father sips his coffee, Azizah berates her father for his snobbish-ness. The scene is one of extreme discomfort in Malay culture. Azizah has raised her voice and is defying her father. They are sitting in chairs around a table; they are eating a Western-style meal, not rice, for breakfast. The prob-lems this family faces are even conveyed through the utensils they use. Malay meals traditionally were eaten using only the hands; the acceptable utensils today are a fork and a spoon. A knife, however, is a weapon; the use of a knife in this secne conveys ideas of how distant such a family is from the traditions of the Malay community. This family scene conveys all of the dangers of modernity: the individuals portrayed have forgotten their Malay traditions. The material success of this modern family thus brings little comfort and has left them distanced from the basic values of society. The dangers of the modern lifestyle, symbolized by their ease with modern food, have torn the family apart. Greed and selfishness have taken the place of the communal values that are promoted in the romanticized *kampung* of the 1950s.

While the overriding message in *Penarek Beca* is to value one's traditions and respect the contributions all members of society can make, many of these ideas are promoted through images that make food very dichotomous. Thus, if the meals eaten in Azizah's house are modern and dangerous, food consumption in the *kampung* is done under trying circumstances but ultimately reflects the communal values of caring for each other. This is conveyed earlier in the film when Amran first returns to his *kampung* after a less-than-successful day riding around Singapore. He has not made much money, so when he approaches his neighborhood food stall he requests only one packet of food. The stall owner, however, gives Amran two packets and tells him that he can pay for them another day. On his way home, Amran meets a beggar asking for food; Amran gives him one of the packets. Upon arriving at his mother's house, Amran insists that she eat the remaining packet because she is ill. She ultimately shares it with her son, and they sit next to each other to share their limited resources, eating their meal using their hands, which is in great contrast to the divisive nature of the dining table in the scenes of Azizah's family. The scene promotes the traditional communal values of the *kampung* since Amran shares his food with others, and ultimately his mother reinforces his decisions. This village food scene highlights both traditional values and the important approval of the mother figure.

The dangers of modern food consumption are also central to *Bujang Lapok*. In this film, Ramlee's character continually searches for a girlfriend in the modern city of Singapore. At different junctures he meets three women for dates at the same restaurant. Upon entering the restaurant with the first young woman he proceeds to a booth with curtains and high-backed seats that will allow for privacy. The couple sips Coca-Cola straight out of the bottle while flirting with each other. When Ramlee invites the woman for a walk in the park, she claims that she cannot go without her identity card, which she has left at home. Ramlee lends her some money so she can take a taxi home and retrieve the card. While he reaches for his wallet she surreptitiously puts candies in her bag. Of course, she does not return. The second date with another woman also ends in disaster when she sees a male friend and deserts Ramlee, taking her Western dish of food (there is no rice) to sit with the man. The third opportunity arises when Ramlee encounters a young girl crying outside the restaurant. When she explains that her much older sister was supposed to meet her there, Ramlee invites her inside for a meal while they wait. When the attractive older sister arrives, Ramlee invites her to eat "beefsteak," which will be served with mashed potatoes. The scene turns tragicomic, however, when

Ramlee is forced to buy this same meal for the nine other sisters who converge on the restaurant. Ramlee's ventures into the city have resulted in manipulation. While few other city scenes are shown in the film, those that take place in the modern restaurant clearly promote the belief that the city is filled with manipulative women. In addition, Ramlee's attempts to control food, either by purchasing it or through the earlier cooking of the chicken, have further emphasized the problems he is facing when dealing with a modern lifestyle.

The roles of women as supervisors of food and maintainers of tradition is conveyed further in another scene later in *Bujang Lapok*, when one of the bachelors, played by S. Shamsuddin, must participate in the traditional negotiations related to a marriage proposal. In this scene he is the only man in the room. Shamsuddin sits next to his fiancée, while his mother shares tea and Malay cakes with his future mother-in-law and his landlady, who oversees the negotiation of the bride-price. While all of the women in the room are jovial in the negotiation and share their tea and cakes, Shamsuddin cannot even hold a bowl of gelatine, a modern food, without it shaking comically out of control. When his fiancée forces him to put it down and suggests that he have a sip of tea, he cannot bring the cup to his mouth without it rattling against the saucer and spilling its contents. The women finally ask him to leave the room so they can complete the negotiations without distraction. At this point the imagery of food has conveyed the idea that women are in control over the traditions in the community, and men are unable to master not only its cooking but even its consumption. Food is clearly within the female sphere.

It seems food is a dangerous and ambivalent icon in Malay film, one that men are having difficulty in mastering. This idea is further emphasized in another comedy Ramlee made in the early 1960s called *Labu dan Labi* (*Labu and Labi*, 1962). The film focuses on the two male characters whose names make up the title, and brings together many of the themes revolving around gender, food, and modernity that have been emphasized in the previous films. Labu (Mohd Zain) and Labi (Ramlee) work for a rich man named Haji Bakhil who is famously stingy (*bakhil* in Malay means "miserly") and lives with his caring wife and beautiful daughter in a traditional Malay house on stilts, which has a modern kitchen and appliances. While Labi works for the family as their driver, Labu is their cook. He is someone who would have graduated from the kind of cooking school mentioned in *Bujang Lapok*. Labu cooks elaborate meals, but it is apparent from his attitude and the reaction of his employers that he is not very good at this profession. When Haji Bakhil's wife asks Labu if the evening meal has been prepared, he replies that it has been done since early in the morning. When she states her fears that it will be stale, Labu responds, "that is what Haji Bakhil likes." During all of these scenes, Labu wears a Western white chef's outfit, which Labi also dons when they serve the family their dinner. When Haji Bahkil ultimately interrupts the meal, angry after Labu flirts with his daughter, the distance between the goofy but lovable servants and the stern modern boss is made clear.

While Malay filmmakers used food as a metaphor for the tension between modernity and tradition, often with the presentation of a strict dichotomy between Western foods such as breads and cakes versus Malay staples like rice and vegetables, it is interesting to note that one film expressed a need to expand the metaphor to its limits through a discussion of how food represents civilization. In *Labu dan Labi*, Labu dreams that he is Tarzan (the film has several fantasy sequences in which the two servants dream about romancing their boss's daughter). In this scene, Labu must deal with a mischievous monkey who is an "animalification" of the greedy father, Haji Bakhil. As Labu is hungry he asks the monkey to get him food to eat. The monkey picks up some bananas and pineapples and hands them to Labu. He explains to the animal that he is tired of this food, and desires rice. After the monkey retrieves rice that has been cooked in the hut, Labu also explains that rice cannot be eaten plain but also must be accompanied by *belacan* (fermented fish paste), a Southeast Asian delicacy. Labu goes to the kitchen of his Tarzan hut, grabs a mortar and pestle, and places some fish in the mortar. He then begins to grind the ingredients while explaining that this will make the meal delicious. This simple, comic scene provides the viewer with an explanation of the proper Malay diet. But it emphasizes a dietary conflict that stands for larger cultural issues. When this basic and traditional diet of fish and rice is brought into the modern world, there is a conflict. Modernity complicates issues about how the Malay population could position its culture, how it could successfully adopt certain aspects of a changing world but hold on to its own cultural values. Part of this issue included the roles of women and men who became situated as vying for their social roles.

Conclusion

Malay film is rarely seen as anything but entertainment. However, as a source for the cultural history of postwar Malay social life it is a rich mine of material. In this article I have tried to explore how food was used to convey powerful ideas about the role of modernity in Malay life, and how men and women were positioned in these films within the notions of modernity. One of the key figures in this cultural production was P. Ramlee, the influential director, writer, actor, and singer who dominated Malay film during the 1950s and 1960s. Ramlee saw his films as having the power to change society during a period of decolonization and modernization when the positioning of the new citizens of Malaya between local traditions and modern society was a key issue. Influenced by the literary figures of his time, he believed that his films could help the poorer members of Malay society realize their worth, and show that being modern was not necessarily evil as long as traditions were not abandoned. One of the key methods used for this approach was his depiction of food and its presentation.

During this period, food in Malay film was dichotomized between the modern and the traditional. Modern foods, such as cakes and breads, were present in scenes in which conflict, or the possibility of it, arose. Actors would violate many of the cultural mores of Malay society, from shouting to denigrating those around them when consuming "modern" food. The modern (often Western) food simply reinforced the disagreeable actions they were taking. Even when shocking behavior was not displayed, the inability of men to master food preparation conveyed the dilemmas they faced when trying to balance between modernity and tradition. Men could not navigate the complicated nature of food; women were being trained to do so, and it would make them desirable if they used it to reinforce their traditional role as cooks in the household. Men were comic fodder when they tried to cook. Traditional food, however, was comforting. It conveyed the idealized beliefs about communal village life, such as the sharing of rice and condiments. Although such traditional fare might be unimpressive and basic, it made one human.

How were Malays to negotiate between the conflicting ideals of modernity and tradition in the 1950s and early 1960s? Perhaps Ramlee best conveyed his understandings of the delicate balance required in a scene in *Penarek Becha* in which Azizah and Amran first fall in love. It is a vacation day, so Azizah and her schoolmates have hired Amran and his friends to carry them to a beach, where the women will have a picnic. These students of modernity, learning how to be desirable candidates for the role of urban Malay housewives, unwrap and set out their picnic meal, which consists of cakes they have probably made as well as packets of rice. While setting out the meal, Azizah sings a love song, which attracts Amran who, accompanied by all of the men and women who sing backup or play musical instruments, begins to sing along. Despite the class differences between the two groups, the women have attracted the men over to their picnic site with its display of food and drink that is both modern and traditional. By overlooking their class differences, Azizah and Amran can reach a new understanding; this seems clearly symbolized by the food spread out before them. While embracing the benefits of modernity and the food it represents, Malays can also maintain their traditions.

Notes

1. A. C. Milner, "Colonial Records History: British Malaya," *Kajian Malaysia* 4, no. 2 (1986): 1–18. While I refer here to Malaysia, it should be noted that the nation of malaysia did not exist until 1962. Thus, none of the films I am discussing were made in "Malaysia." They were all made in Singapore, although Malaya was the larger entity.
2. See, for example, Cheah Boon Kheng, *The Peasant Robbers of Kedah, 1900–1929: Historical and Folk Perceptions* (Singapore: Oxford University Press, 1988).
3. M. Amin and Wahba, *Layar Perak dan Sejarahnya* (Shah Alam, Malaysia: Fajar Bakti, 1998), 17–28; Hamzah Hussin, *Memoir Hamzah Hussin: Dari Cathay Keris ke Merdeka Studio* (Bangi: University Kebangsaan Malaysia, 1998), 24–30. Malaya, consisting of various states in the Malay Peninsula, became independent in 1957, following a series of negotiations with the British government. In 1962 Singapore, along with two states in northern Borneo, joined Malaya to form the nation of Malaysia. In 1965 Singapore became independent. Since then Malaysia and Singapore have continued to remain closely linked economically, but tensions exist over such issues as water sharing.
4. Virginia Matheson Hooker, *Writing a New Society: Social Change through the Novel in Malay* (Honolulu: University of Hawaii Press, 2000), 182–88; T. N. Harper, *The End of Empire and the Making of Malaya* (Cambridge: Cambridge University Press, 1999), 302–6.

5. Craig A. Lockard, "Reflection of Change: Socio-political Commentary and Criticism in Malaysian Popular Music since 1950," *Crossroads* 6, no. 1 (1991): 23.

6. Hooker, *Writing a New Society*, 185.

7. Asraf Wahab, quoted in Hooker, *Writing a New Society*, 185. The original source is A. M. Thani, "Peranan dan Kesah Tokoh-Tokoh ASAS 50" in *Warisan ASAS 50* (Kuala Lumpur: Dewan Bahasa dan Pustaka, 1981), 3.

8. James Harding and Ahmad Sarji, *P. Ramlee: The Bright Star* (Subang Jaya, Malaysia: Pelanduk, 2002), 102–3.

9. The depiction of poor and rich in the film has been analyzed in Rohayati Paseng Barnard and Timothy P. Barnard, "The Ambivalence of P. Ramlee: *Penarek Beca* and *Bujang Lapok* in Perspective," *Asian Cinema* 13, no. 2 (2002): 9–23; see also William van der Heide, *Malaysian Cinema, Asian Film: Border Crossings and National Cultures* (Amsterdam: Amsterdam University Press, 2002), 170–76.

10. A.M. Thani, quoted in Hooker, *Writing a New Society*, 182.

11. Kartini Saparudin, "A Self More Refined: Representations of Women in Malay Magazines of the 1950s and 1960s." Honours thesis, National University of Singapore, 2002), 38.

12. Such schools were a common feature of 1950s Singapore. See Kartini, "A Self More Refined," 39–42.

13. The role of women in modernization during a period of decolonization is the subject of Kristin Ross, *Fast Cars, Clean Bodies: Decolonization and the Reordering of the French Culture* (Cambridge, Mass.: MIT Press, 1995). I would like to thank Richard Derdarian and Kartini Saparudin for bringing this book to my attention.

14. Van der Heide, *Malaysian Cinema, Asian Film*, 176.

7

"I'll Have Whatever She's Having": Jews, Food, and Film*

NATHAN ABRAMS

A number of films in the last few decades have famously used food in their narratives to celebrate particular cultures. There is a deliciously long list of films in which foods—marked as Jewish and kosher, Jewish but not kosher, or non-Jewish, are not simply glimpsed as part of a film's setting but also employed as important plot devices that explore cultural, ethnic, and religious issues. Woody Allen, for example, makes much use of the nature and function of food and dining in his films. His movies abound with memorable moments and food allusions: the Chinese food scene in *Manhattan* (1979); the crazy seder in *Sleeper* (1973); the split-screen families and their foods in *Annie Hall* (1977); the serious discussion at the seder in *Crimes and Misdemeanors* (1989); the jokes about kosher food and fasting during Yom Kippur in *Radio Days* (1987); New York's Carnegie Deli and the plates of kosher meat in *Broadway Danny Rose* (1984), and so on. Certainly, Allen's use of food in his films intrinsically connects that food to Jewish culture.

Surprisingly, very little has been written about the topic of Jewish cultural representation through food in films. I will attempt here to begin filling this gap by exploring the ways in which "Jewish," kosher, and *treyf* (explicitly non-kosher) foods are represented in film. My discussion will include observations on the ways in which Jews have been represented and stereotyped in visual

*I would like to thank Alex Gordon, David Desser, Gail Samuelson, and all those who responded to my queries on the various H-NET discussion lists; without their help this essay would not have been possible. I am also extremely grateful to Douglas Brode and Terry Barr, who have written extensively about food in the films of Woody Allen and Jewish dining scenes, respectively.

popular culture through food. Specifically, I'll look at the connections among food and Jewish motherhood, cultural traditions, history, identity, sex, and nostalgia. Finally, I will also examine cinematic representations of the Jewish family meal as the primary site of philosophical debate about the Jewish condition and Jewish identity.

Motherhood

Much of Jewish humor is food related, and many traditional jokes are concerned with Jewish mothers. Likewise, film often plays with the traditional stereotype of the Jewish mother, usually presented as an overeating, overcaring, and overbearing matriarchal figure who stuffs her children with far more than they can possibly digest. As the poet Isaac Rosenfeld has put it, "the hysterical mother who stuffs her infant with forced feedings (thereby laying in, all unwittingly, the foundation for ulcers, diabetes, and intestinal cancer with each spoonful she crams down the hatch) is motivated by a desire to give security to her child."[1] At the same time that they denigrate the mother figure, however, such jokes are laced with a reverence for mother's cooking. She is known as the *baleboosteh*, a Yiddish term for a praiseworthy mother.

The stereotypical image of a Jewish mother is represented by the mother of Buddy Young Jr. (Billy Crystal) in *Mr. Saturday Night* (dir. Billy Crystal, 1992). This woman goes through a daily ritual of pushing food on all of her relatives particularly her sons, with the admonition, 'Eat, eat.' During Buddy's opening monologue, a close-up montage of the delicious and filling foods she has lovingly worked hard to prepare by hand for her family over the years is shown: matzo balls, onions, tomatoes, corned beef, stuffed turkey, stuffed cabbage, latkes, challah, matzo-ball soup, and all kinds of desserts. Buddy describes his mother forcing food on her family, quipping, "My mother was trying to kill us with fat." The same kind of stereotype occurs on American television. The sitcom *The Nanny* (1993–99) lampoons the loving Jewish mother character, in this case Fran's (the nanny's) mother, who is also stereotypically obsessed with food and is usually seen in the kitchen or around food. Interestingly, though, in an unusual inversion of the stereotypical self-abnegating Jewish mother who just pushes food on her kids, Fran's mother cooks (and eats) more for herself than for her child.

Identity and Culture

Foodstuffs are intimately related to Jewish identity and culture in film. Although many of these products have long been assimilated into mainstream American culture, on film a corned beef or pastrami sandwich on rye bread, bagels and lox, gefilte fish, chicken soup, or matzo typically code the Jewish world semiotically. Chicken soup might now be considered a universal panacea, popularized even further by the best-selling book series *Chicken Soup for the Soul*, but it has long been identified with Jewish culture. In the television program *Northern Exposure* (1990–95) chicken fat is described as "Jewish mayonnaise," and in *The Apartment* (dir. Billy Wilder, 1960) the Jewish neighbor character nurses Fran Kubelik (Shirley MacLaine) back to health with chicken soup. Authentic chicken soup often features dumplings or balls made from matzo meal (hence the apocryphal question Marilyn Monroe asked when visiting Arthur Miller's parents, "What kind of animal is a matzo?"), and because of matzo's connection to Passover it is also considered a trope for Jewishness. In *Torch Song Trilogy* (dir. Paul Bogart, 1988), Arnold Beckhoff's mother goes into the kitchen looking for matzo meal. When Arnold (Harvey Fierstein) tells her which shelf it is on, she says, "He has matzo meal! I brought him up right," suggesting that his ownership of a Jewish food product overrides his "deviant" (by Jewish religious law)—and thus disappointing—(homo)sexuality.

In Robert Redford's *Quiz Show* (1994), the Reuben sandwich is semiotically deployed to code Jewishness. The Reuben—a grilled combination of corned beef, Swiss cheese, and sauerkraut (or coleslaw) on sourdough pumpernickel bread—is a clear signifier of ethnicity; its origins are specific to Jewish delicatessens in New York. One theory even attributed its invention to the movies themselves when, in 1914, Annette Seelos, the leading lady in a Charlie Chaplin film, first ate the sandwich (albeit with Virginia baked ham rather than corned beef). The link between film and food was cemented when the New York delicatessen Reuben's began naming sandwiches after actors.[2] In *Quiz Show*, Dick Goodwin (Rob Morrow), a Jew, orders the sandwich as the special of the day at the Athenaeum, the elitist Manhattan club. Aware of his outsider status as a Jew and the unwillingness of white Anglo-Saxon Protestant (WASP) America to accept his ethnicity, Goodwin remarks that the sandwich was named after Reuben Kay of Nebraska, before wryly observing about the club, "Unfortunately, they have the sandwich here, but they don't seem to have any Reubens." Here the Reuben sandwich serves to code both his Jewishness and his interloper status, standing among the patrician elite. Later, the distance is emphasized when he is invited to the Van Doren estate in rural Connecticut, where he feasts on distinctly nonethnic and genteel fare such as fresh corn on the cob and tomato salad. Goodwin is slowly seduced by the gentile world of the Van Dorens, and this is emphasized in a key sequence featuring an exchange between him and the other main Jewish protagonist, Herb Stempel (John Tuturro). Goodwin goes to the Stempels' apartment to interview Stempel about his charges that the quiz shows are rigged. The gulf between them is signified when Stempel offers Goodwin some ruggelach, "a Jewish delicacy." Stempel has to explain this because to him, Goodwin carries all the signifiers of assimilation; indeed, he seems to be the epitome of the successful and accepted American who has escaped the bounds of his ethnic culture. Goodwin has an important government job; he has straight white teeth, wears well-made suits, and carries a briefcase. Stempel believes that Goodwin has forgotten, if indeed he ever knew, his traditional Jewish roots. When Goodwin disdainfully declines, Stempel rebukes him with the words:

"You don't know what you're missing." Goodwin contemptuously replies that he "knows ruggelach" and the point is made that Goodwin is perfectly aware of his ethnic roots but prefers the splendor of genteel and gentile rural Connecticut fare more than thoroughly ethnic pastries served from a tin in the middle of Queens.

Perhaps the most distinctively Jewish foodstuff is gefilte fish. *Gefilte* literally means "stuffed," and this specialty is basically a poached fishball made from whitefish, pike, and/or carp with filler (bread crumbs or matzo meal), served on the Sabbath and holy days among German and Eastern European Jews. Gefilte fish carries the mark of Jewish authenticity. Its preparation (when not bought ready-made in a jar) requires skill and patience. *The Jewish Home Beautiful*, the guide for aspiring Jewish mothers, states, "If there is any one particular food that might lay claim to being the Jewish national dish, gefilte fish is that food." One company, Mother's, once advertised its product by connecting it to history and tradition. It was "old-fashioned" and the "real" thing, made in the "finest tradition," and carried with it all of the symbols of *kashrut* (being kosher) and Jewish authenticity, including Hebrew writing. Gefilte fish was often upheld as a method of prevention against assimilation, as represented by the consumption of Chinese food by Ashkenazi urban Americans, and summed up in the words, "Down with chop suey! Long live gefilte fish!"[3] Since Gefilte fish is clearly and visibly Jewish, it is readily used in film and television. In the American television sitcom *The Nanny*, the characters worry over whether gefilte fish should be served at a favorite aunt's funeral. In one episode of *The Goldbergs* (1949–54), the immensely popular television sitcom that attracted some forty million viewers per week at its peak, the heroine of the show, Molly Goldberg, was invited by a leading food manufacturer to produce some of her own gefilte fish in his test kitchen.[4]

In contrast to such foods as Reuben sandwiches and gefilte fish, Wonder Bread, mayonnaise, pork and/or ham, and lobsters signify the non-Jewish world. Wonder Bread stands for whiteness because of its uniformly white nature and its origins in the Midwest. Comedian Lenny Bruce once quipped, "Pumpernickel is Jewish and, as you know, white bread is very goyish," and Nora Ephron has commented on the socioethnic construction of mayonnaise, in particular Hellman's, as gentile.[5] In *Hannah and Her Sisters* (dir. Woody Allen, 1986), Mickey (Allen), newly (and temporarily) converted to Catholicism, unloads a grocery bag, withdrawing a loaf of Wonder Bread and a jar of Hellman's mayonnaise, clear and humorous signifiers to any Jewish audience of Mickey's conversion. Along those lines, in Susan Mogul's taped performance *The Last Jew in America* (1984), the heroine Barbara is trying to attract a Jewish mate by pretending to be a Christian. As a consequence, she goes out and buys Wonder Bread and removes not only the matzo from her pantry, but also the Chinese food. And, although not about Jewishness (but similarly positing a distinct ethnicity—Greek in this case—as against "Americanness"), the film *My Big Fat Greek Wedding* (dir. Joel Zwick, 2002) perpetuates the link between Wonder Bread and whiteness. As its Greek protagonist moves into the American mainstream, she swaps moussaka for Wonder Bread sandwiches, and is hence accepted by her white peers whereas hitherto her consumption of ethnic foods symbolized her distance from the American mainstream.

Jewish versus Non-Jewish

In addition to serving as a cultural identifier of Jewishness, in many films food also stands as a trope for the clash between the Jewish and non-Jewish worlds. A scene used humorously by Allen (and others) features a non-Jew ordering a corned beef/pastrami sandwich and asking to have it with mayonnaise on white bread, thus violating Jewish tradition and *kashrut* laws, both of which "prescribe" that corned beef be eaten on rye bread with mustard. At dinner in a Jewish delicatessen in *Annie Hall*, Annie (Diane Keaton) clearly feels out of place and, with no idea of how to order "properly" in a deli, orders a WASPish meal—pastrami on white bread "with mayonnaise, tomatoes, and let-tuce"—to Alvy's (Allen's) obvious disgust. A similar scene occurs in the (in)famous orgasm sequence in the famous (kosher) Katz's Deli on Manhat-tan's Lower East Side in *When Harry Met Sally* (dir. Rob Reiner, 1989), which begins with the eponymous gentile Sally (Meg Ryan) ordering a turkey sand-wich on white bread with mayonnaise, while the overtly Jewish Harry (Billy Crystal) eats salt beef on rye. Harry visibly winces as she orders, as does Alvy in *Annie Hall*; in each case the girlfriend's sandwich becomes emblematic of the cultural clash between the male Jewish protagonist and his non-Jewish female partner, and suggests the problems that lie ahead for the relationship. In a later scene in *Annie Hall*, Alvy's discomfort with Annie's family is expressed through food and dining, when the use of a split screen, juxtaposing both families' mealtimes, reinforces their differences, like "oil and water."

The same kind of coding of simple foods showed up in the television series *Eight is Enough* (1977–81). In one episode, one of the eight daughters befriends a Jewish doctor, and a waitress at the hospital coaches her on how to eat a deli sandwich with mustard, rather than mayonnaise, and not with a glass of milk. This change of eating pattern caused her father to think she was converting to Judaism.

Pork, since Jewish *kashrut* laws proscribe it, also frequently occurs as a sym-bol of the cultural clash between Jews and gentiles. Comedian Lenny Bruce articulated the culinary side of this Jewish self-definition: "Spam is goyish and rye bread is Jewish." Pork and ham stand as tropes for all that is non-Jewish or *treyf*. "Pork," as Rosenfeld puts it, "means the uncircumcised."[6] *Big Boy* (dir. Alan Crosland, 1930), starring Al Jolson, ends with him singing about coming home to his little cabin, which he describes with vivid details, extolling the smell of the ham his mother is preparing in the kitchen. After a slight pause Jolson says: "Ham? . . . Wait a minute! That ain't my house!" Of course, simply because something is forbidden doesn't mean it isn't eaten. Indeed, probably because they are forbidden, some Jews will choose such foodstuffs.

Often the consumption of forbidden foods symbolizes rebellion and/or the rejection of traditional ethnic roots. In *Mr. Saturday Night*, Buddy Young Jr. invites a beautiful woman in the audience (who will later become his wife) to part with her traditional Jewish parents and treats her to a roast pork dinner. In Boaz Yakin's *A Price above Rubies* (1998), the main character uses food to demonstrate her rebellion againt the Hasidic tradition by buying a nonkosher hot dog on the street in Manhattan and loving it. Later, the effect is compounded when her husband and their rabbi/therapist are shocked when they learn that she's been keeping kosher only at home. In *The Jazz Singer* (dir. Alan Crosland, 1927), Al Jolson pointedly eats nonkosher food: in the first scene after he has left his Orthodox family to pursue his jazz singing career, he sits in a restaurant practically dancing in his chair with delight as he digs in to bacon, juicy pork sausages, and eggs. There is even a quasi-pornographic close-up of the plate. In Allen's *Radio Days*, eating pork chops as well as clams (which one character breaks the fast to eat with his Jewish communist neighbors) stands for conversion to atheistic communism.

Religious food restrictions limit gastronomic exploration, but more important, they can curtail social and geographic mobility, which has led many people in real life to break away from such religious sanctions. Therefore it is not surprising to find that, in order to achieve higher social identification, Jews in film have eaten forbidden foods, as the conspicuous consumption of such food is an important indicator of status. Consequently, the consumption of such products becomes emblematic of attempts to assimilate, to move away from Jewish origins. The pork-eating scene in *The Jazz Singer* also serves to underscore the protagonist's accelerating assimilation. In *Annie Hall*, Alvy is eating Easter dinner at his partner's very WASPish parents. He compliments her grandmother, Grammy Ann, on her "dynamite ham," even though he has no idea what he is talking about. He is simply trying to fit in, since everyone else is complimenting her, too. The failure of this gesture is underlined by her imagining him dressed in the long black coat and hat of an Orthodox Jew, complete with mustache and beard. In *Europa, Europa* (dir. Agnieska Holland, 1991), set in the Holocaust era, the Jewish hero, who is posing as a gentile, is served ham at his girlfriend's house, coding the dilemmas of that period between *kashrut* and survival. Here ham is used to disguise his Jewishness. And a similar situation takes place in *Chariots of Fire* (dir. Hugh Hudson, 1981) when the Jewish character inadvertently confronts pork that has been ordered for him.

Along with assimilationism, certain foods considered *treyf* by Jews are items that, in addition, signal sophistication and the desire to gentrify. In the leading and influential Jewish journal *Commentary*, a full-page color 1970s advertisement for Bolla Italian wine depicts lobster, clearly encoding it (along with other *treyf* foodstuffs, including various shellfish) as the epitome of worldliness and cosmopolitanism. But even as a food like lobster is coded to signal assimilation and sophistication, it can become emblematic of the cultural gap between Jews and non-Jews. In *Annie Hall*, Alvy and Annie spontaneously laugh at crawling crustaceans on the kitchen floor as they awkwardly prepare a lobster dinner at a beach house in the Hamptons: "Maybe we should just call the police. Dial 911. It's the lobster squad." Alvy is fearful of the creatures, and when he realizes that one big lobster has crawled behind the refrigerator, Alvy jokes: "It'll turn up in our bed at night. Talk to him. You speak shellfish…Annie, there's a big lobster behind the refrigerator. I can't get it out. . . . Maybe if I put a little dish of butter sauce here with a nutcracker, it will run out the other side? . . . We should have gotten steaks, 'cause they don't have legs. They don't run around." As with a similar scene in the British film *Leon the Pig Farmer* (dir. Vadim Jean and Gary Sinyor, 1992), lobsters symbolize the inherent distance between the male Jewish protagonist and the non-Jewish figure of his erotic infatuation.

Food and Sex

The link between dietary and sexual prohibition in Judaism is often repeated throughout Jewish culture, and interpretations linking sex and *kashrut* food regulations have long been made. Indeed, since Adam and Eve ate the apple in the Garden of Eden, food and sex have been inextricably linked. Rosenfeld adumbrates the link: "When the Lord forbade Adam and Eve to eat of the Tree, He started something which has persisted throughout our history: the attachment of all sorts of forbidden meanings to food, and the use of food in a system of taboos which, though meant to regulate diet, have also had as their function—perhaps the primary one—the regulation of sexual conduct."[7] Meat and milk in Jewish law cannot be mixed and/or eaten together, for example, deriving from the enigmatic Biblical injunction against "seething a kid in its mother's milk." In a 1979 article in the *New York Review of Books*, "The Dietary Prohibitions of the Hebrews," Jean Soler argued that this biblical ban on cooking a kid in its mother's milk was linked to an incest taboo, wittily observing, "You shall not put a mother and her son into the same pot, any more than into the same bed."[8] Many films have connected food and *kashrut* with sexuality. This sanction has provided further grist for the popular culture mill. It is no coincidence, for example, that Alisa Lebow and Cynthia Madansky named their 1998 documentary about Jewish lesbians *Treyf*. Similarly, growing sexual awareness is signaled in *A Walk on the Moon* (dir. Tony Goldwyn, 1999), when a young Orthodox girl eats bacon for the first time.

The classic incident connecting food and sex in a Jewish setting is the orgasm scene in *When Harry Met Sally*. Harry and Sally are discussing sex over a meal in a kosher deli; Sally has just ordered a "*treyfed*" version of a typically Jewish sandwich (as discussed earlier). Harry confidently believes that his sexual prowess satisfies his female partners and brings them to orgasm, until Sally explains how "most women, at one time or another, have faked it." Harry doesn't believe that he has been fooled because he "knows":

Sally: Oh right. That's right. I forgot. You're a man.

Harry: What is that supposed to mean?
Sally: Nothing. It's just that all men are sure it never happens to them, and most women at one time or another have done it, so you do the math.
Harry: You don't think that I can tell the difference?
Sally: No.
Harry: Get outta here.

Sally then looks at Harry seductively, and begins to illustrate, in the middle of the busy restaurant, how easily women can convincingly fake an orgasm. With a loud and long display of pants, groans, gasps, hair rufflings, caresses, table poundings, and ecstatic releases, she yells "Yes, Yes, YES! YES! YES!" as she brings herself to fake orgasm. The entire restaurant is quieted down and attentive to her realistic act. When she is finished with her demonstration, she calmly composes herself, picks up her fork and resumes eating. The sequence ends with an older woman customer (Estelle Reiner, director Rob Reiner's mother) requesting, "I'll have whatever she's having," thus implying the erotic effect of non-kosher food upon Jews; the *treyf* version of the traditional Jewish sandwich being inherently preferable to Jews than the kosher one. Likewise, a similar sequence in *Annie Hall* suddenly cuts from Annie and Alvy eating to the couple in bed, having just finished making love.

As seafood is only kosher if it has fins and scales, all shellfish are forbidden. The symbolic or allegorical interpretation of the *kashrut* laws has it that fins and scales on a fish are signs of endurance and self-control; the lack of them can be construed to mean wild, impetuous abandon. Shellfish—in particular the king of shellfish, lobster—stands as a code for wantonness and excess. In the musical *Funny Girl* (dir. William Wyler, 1968), which depicts the life of Jewish comedienne Fannie Brice (Barbra Streisand) from her early days in the Jewish slums of New York's Lower East Side to the height of her career with the Ziegfeld Follies, her future husband, Nick Arnstein (Omar Sharif), introduces Fanny to lobster. The scene opens on a close-up of a restaurant table covered with lobster debris (shells, crackers, butter, etc.). The camera pulls back to Nick and Fanny. She has a napkin round her neck. He watches her benignly as she licks her fingers and wipes her hands. Nick says, "You don't know how proud I am to think that I am the man who introduced you to your first lobster," to which Fanny giggles and replies, "Among other things." The restaurant owner/cook in the background says to her, "Lady, if you're game for this one, he's on the house. Nobody in history ever had three." Fanny responds, "Start boiling the water!" Fanny directly equates the loss of her gastronomic virginity with the loss of her sexual virginity, and her appetite for both is seemingly insatiable. In *Portnoy's Complaint* (dir. Ernest Lehman, 1972), the protagonist's mother connects lobster with sexual temptation and urges restraint. But when the fifteen-year-old Alex Portnoy sucks on a lobster claw one night, within the hour "his cock is out and aimed at a shiksa on a Public Service bus." Along the same line, for Woody Allen, lobsters are the symbol of insatiable sexual attraction; they symbolize love affairs, as opposed to the more humdrum foods of marriage. In *A Midsummer's Night Sex Comedy* (1982), when his wife interrogates him about a previous relationship, Allen's character nervously replies, "I went out with her *once* . . . and had a couple of *lobsters . . . that's it!*"

Lobster's role as signifier of temptation also occurs in an episode of the television series *Seinfeld* (1990–98). Jerry Seinfeld, who plays himself in the series, is dating a Jewish girl who maintains a strictly kosher diet and refuses to eat the lobster that they catch out on Long Island when they—Jerry, George (Jason Alexander), Elaine (Julia Louis-Dreyfus), and Kramer (Michael Richards)—are spending the weekend at a friend's place. All evening the friends talk of how delicious and succulent the lobster is and the temptation proves too difficult to resist. In the middle of the night, Jerry's girlfriend creeps down to the kitchen to sneak some of the lobster without anyone else seeing. Kramer, guessing that this would happen, is guarding the refrigerator and refuses to let her eat it, essentially becoming the self-appointed guardian of her morals. The next day, however, in an act of revenge for an earlier transgression, George puts the leftover lobster in the scrambled eggs without her knowledge. On hearing of this, she feels defiled. Lobster here clearly signifies temptation and abandon. The girlfriend's attempts to avoid eating it symbolize her efforts to remain ritually pure. *Treyf* foods like lobster thus signify, in the words of Rosenfeld, "the whole world of forbidden sexuality, the sexuality of the *goyim*, and there all the delights are imagined to lie, with the *shiksas* and *shkotzim* who are unrestrained and not made kosher."[9]

Whether involving *treyf* foods or acceptable ones, one sees that connections between food and sex abound in films about Jews. In *Once upon a Time In America* (1984), Sergio Leone's epic about Jewish gangsters, a young gang member buys an ornate and nonkosher pastry in order to obtain sexual favors from the neighborhood sweetheart. As he waits outside her door, his desire for the pastry proves stronger than his lust for the girl: he begins licking the cream from his fingertips and ends up wolfing down the whole thing.

Allen's entire oeuvre is shot through with references to food and sex; indeed, the two become synonymous in his work. In *Annie Hall* he says, "We'll kiss now . . . then go eat." When he arrives at Diane Keaton's character's apartment in *Manhattan*, hoping to have sex, he asks, "Have you got anything to eat here?" Lunch, in particular, has sexual connotations: in *Manhattan* he tells his young date, "You'll have lunch—and attachments form," while in *The Purple Rose of Cairo* (1985) he suggests buying lunch as a prelude to sex.

The link between food and sex in film has further been explored through the use of certain settings as part of a film's mise-en-scène. Although not a Jewish invention, the delicatessen often symbolizes Jewish space; it is no coincidence that Katz's Deli is the site of the orgasm sequence in *When Harry Met Sally*. The prominence of Jewish summer resorts in the Catskills has continued the connection between kosher food and kosher dating since such places consciously linked Jewish traditions of matchmaking with kosher cuisine. The advertising for the most famous of them, Grossinger's, suggested that under this hotel's guidance, food was an opportunity for sociability and the means to endogamous marriage and reproduction. Indeed, Grossinger's enjoyed a high reputation as an ideal place to look for a mate. *Sweet Lorraine* (dir. Steve Gomer, 1987), *The Apprenticeship of Duddy Kravitz* (dir. Ted Kotcheff, 1974), *Dirty Dancing* (dir. Emile Ardolino, 1987), and *A Walk on the Moon* are all films situated at kosher resort hotels in which a protagonist is often either seeking love or is eligible marriage material. In such settings, food is frequently used to woo affections, as in *Dirty Dancing,* when the nerdy hotel owner's son takes the heroine, Baby (Jennifer Grey), into the hotel kitchen for a snack as part of his maladapted amatory efforts.

Key love scenes often take place in sites of food preparation or retailing. There is food in almost every Yiddish feature film: *Mamele* (dir. Joseph Green, 1938), for example, has such a scene at the end, when Khavtshi Samet (Molly Picon) is running off to get married; first she stops to check the chicken in the oven. In Joan Micklin Silver's *Crossing Delancey* (1988) the too-Jewish suitor is a kosher pickle salesman and wooing scenes take place in his store.

On a different note, it may even be argued that the movie and theater industries could not have functioned without Jewish delis. *Broadway Danny Rose* features the quintessential Jewish "kosher style" delicatessen, the Carnegie Deli on Fifty-Fifth Street and Seventh Avenue in New York. Its proximity to Broadway means that it has over the years been filled with regulars like actors Warren Beatty, Dustin Hoffman, and Burt Lancaster. Barbra Streisand, Kathleen Turner, Bruce Willis, and Dan Akyroyd are just a few of the stars that have lunched at Katz's. And when Johnny Depp met with his FBI contact in *Donnie Brasco* (dir. Mike Newell, 1997), it was at Katz's, as it was when Judge Reinhold went out to eat in *Off Beat* (dir. Michael Dinner, 1986). "We get a good deal of Jewish delicatessen in Hollywood," wrote Orson Welles. "Without pastrami sandwiches there could be no picture-making."[10]

Food and Nostalgia

Yet another function of Jewish foods in movies and television shows involves the expression of nostalgia for a somehow happier past. Here, "the Jewish *bagel* stands out like a golden vision of the bygone days when life was better, when things had substance, staying power, and an honest flavor of their own."[11] The bagel symbolizes the past not just because of its sixteenth-century origins but also because its preparation is difficult work that takes a good deal of time to learn. Until the invention of machine techniques, bagel making couldn't have been accomplished by just anyone—it required skill and patience. The skilled craft of making bagels by hand, which had defied the age of machine techniques, contrasted with the mass production of American bread—what Irving Pfefferblit has called "that tasteless, flavorless, bodiless miracle of modern science."[12] The bagels and lox, in *Down and Out in Beverly*

Hills (dir. Paul Mazursky, 1986), as well as the knishes and the jar of real kosher-from-Brooklyn and U-Bet chocolate syrup in *A Walk on the Moon*, all address concerns about holding onto traditions. Food in movies sometimes focuses on the issue of continuing or losing or changing Jewish cultural traditions and thus express a desire to preserve the past, as if in a sterilized jar.

The Dinner Table

Traditional Jewish culture focuses on the importance of family. After decades of ignoring such issues, in the 1960s Jewish American filmmakers began making movies that explored Jewish self-definition. A key part of this exploration was the depiction of eating as not only an important ritual for Jewish families but also a key signifier of their difference from the gentile world. Some Jewish American filmmakers looked back to remember the past nostalgically as a golden age, depicting family life with dashes of sentimentality, bitterness, longing, and, at times, ridicule. Thus, the Jewish family's partaking of food together, particularly on ritual occasions, has become a cherished filmic ritual.The Jewish Sabbath and Passover meals show up, in particular, as obvious cultural expressions. In *A Stranger among Us* (dir. Sidney Lumet, 1992) many explanations about food and other customs are given, including a detailed sequence about food preparation for the Sabbath. The various versions of *The Jazz Singer* films (1927, 1953, 1980) each have Passover seder scenes. In *Tevye* (dir. Maurice Schwartz, 1939) there is a scene during a Passover seder in which the daughter who intermarried is looking in on her family through a window and crying hysterically. There are several scenes in the *Revolt of Job* (dir. Imre Gyöngyössy, 1983), where food, around Jewish religious holidays, is eaten and discussed by the elderly Jewish couple and the Christian child they raise before the Holocaust. In the 1998 British film *The Governess* (dir. Sandra Goldbacher), a young woman, Rosina da Silva (Minnie Driver), passes herself off as the gentile Mary Blackchurch. As her Jewish identity is unknown to her employer, she celebrates Passover alone and the salt water included in her meal proves to be a fixative for photographic images. This ritual element, therefore, is an important part of the plot, which revolves around the invention of photography. In such films, what is stressed concerns the specific cultural aspects of the ritual meals.

Key filmic scenes are situated at the Jewish dinner table, a suitable location for the delivery of scenes worthy of the Socratic dialogue. Filmmakers clearly intend to show that important matters are discussed with the entire family present, and the entire family must be present for the evening and/or ritual meal. An extended family discusses morality, among other issues, over a meal in *A Price above Rubies*. In Allen's *Crimes and Misdemeanors* a Passover meal is the setting for debates about the nature of murder, ethics, and divine punishment; the character Judah Rosenthal flashes back to a Passover seder of his youth, during which he remembers his extended family arguing over complex moral issues like religion, Marxism, the Holocaust, and the "eyes of

God." While his father Sol insists that God's justice will ultimately rule, Judah's Aunt May believes that human beings can and will commit any crime they can get away with, and that they can even live peacefully with their crimes if they choose to. The seder scene is particularly important because the family is together, united around the observation of the traditional rituals. Even though the family members argue over complex moral issues and cannot reconcile their views, this is regarded as normal, for arguing is often presented as being a staple of the Jewish diet. In *My Favorite Year* (1982) directed and written by Richard Benjamin, the Jewish family meal offers a debate on the meaning of love and the importance of family. And, in *Avalon* (dir. Barry Levinson, 1990), the Jewish family meal includes commentary on Jewish culture and eating that reveals the legacy of immigration and the history of family assimilation into an American mainstream and the divesting of ethnic traits. Dining scene after dining scene in *Goodbye Columbus* (dir. Larry Peerce, 1969), the film based upon the story by Philip Roth, satirically portrays Jews and food (in particular, in the quasi-orgiastic wedding feast scene, as all the relatives stuff themselves at the big buffet), caricaturing Jewish food obsessions as a ridiculous abundance of food paired with greed. The movie *Wedding in Galilee* (dir. Michel Khleifi, 1987) illustrates a very different sort of clash of cultural identities between Israeli Jews and Palestinians. A Palestinian seeks Israeli permission to waive curfew in order to give his son a fine wedding, but the military governor's condition is that he and his officers attend, leading to a banquet full of tension. In *The Last Supper* (1995), a dark comedy directed by Stacy Title, a group of graduate students—one of whom is Jewish—use the dinner table to articulate their belief system and to convert nonbelievers. They invite a variety of politically inappropriate—sexist, racist, fundamentalist, politically conservative, and so on—individuals to supper to try to persuade them to change their ideas, but poison them and bury them in the back yard if they don't.

The dinner table also becomes the arena for articulating competing versions of Jewishness. For the Jewish characters, the conflicts with their ethnic and sexual selves are staged most pointedly at meals. In *The Last Supper* the Jewish character kills the first guest, a vicious anti-Semite, thereby reversing the stereotype of Jewish physical weakness. In *Kissing Jessica Stein* (dir. Charles Herman-Wurmfeld, 2001), the Jewish family dining scenes become an arena in which the Jewish daughter strives to assert her lesbian sexuality against the obvious wishes of her parents, who use these same mealtimes to try to match her with more suitable partners. Similar issues are dealt with in *What's Cooking?* (dir. Gurinder Chadha, 2000), where Herb and Ruth Seelig (Maury Chaykin and Lainie Kazan) are unwilling to discuss openly their grown lesbian daughter's relationship with her lover around the Thanksgiving dinner table. In both scenes, we witness an intergenerational clash, with daughters bringing home doubly "unsuitable" partners, both ethnically and sexually. In such dining scenes, it is usual for the gentile to be subject to parental interrogation, assessing whether she is fit/kosher enough to marry into the family. *Kosher* is also slang for "A-OK"; literally, it means "fitting and proper" in Hebrew (during the 1970s, advertisements for the Israeli national air carrier El Al would promise, "We don't take off until everything is Kosher").

The checking-out-the-gentile-at-the-Jewish-family-table formula is reversed to great effect in *Meet the Parents* (dir. Jay Roach, 2000), a comedy about a Jew, Greg Focker (Ben Stiller), who wants to marry a rich, WASPy blonde and accompanies her to visit her parents on the north shore of Long Island. In scenes reminiscent of *Quiz Show*, everything there conspires to remind him that he's a Jew of low status. The girlfriend's ex-CIA father Jack Byrnes (Robert De Niro) puts Greg under constant scrutiny and surveillance (he even has a series of hidden cameras rigged up to spy on the unwitting Stiller) and thus the seemingly simplest situations, like using the toilet, conceal hidden traps. The sequence around the dinner table is particularly important for establishing the cultural distance between the Jewish Focker and the WASP Byrnes family. Greg is asked by Jack to say grace at dinner. "Greg is Jewish," Jack is told. "I'm sure Jews bless their food," Jack smiles, and Greg launches into a tortured prayer that segues, to his own horror, into lyrics from *Godspell.* Mealtimes continue to be fraught with social danger. At breakfast, he is the last to arrive; still wearing his pajamas, he is the only person shown eating a bagel—a clear signifier of Jewishness—further widening the social gap between him and the Byrnes family.

Interestingly, Jewish families on film are often depicted celebrating the all-American and secular holidays of Thanksgiving and Independence Day rather than their own Jewish ritual holidays, suggesting their assimilation into the mainstream culture. In *Avalon*, the Thanksgiving meal serves as the pivotal point at which the extended Russian-Jewish Krichinsky family, now living in Baltimore, disintegrates into the separate, nuclear-family structure of the dominant culture. This also hints at the demise of the traditional Jewish, family-centered culture.

Conclusion

Food has become a means to explore Jewish identity visually, whether the food itself is "Jewish," kosher, or *treyf.* In this essay, I have tried to bring together a variety of films and topics as a step toward beefing up the study of visual victuals, giving some illustrative (and hopefully tasty) examples of the rich selection of films to be productively researched further from a variety of perspectives—social, cultural, religious, class, gender, and even sexual. Clearly, there is plenty of material for further exploration, and I hope that, in the future, the links among film, food, and Jewish social dynamics will be confronted. Even as we "consume" films, we can also "read" them, discovering much about both culture and filmmaking.

Notes

1. Isaac Rosenfeld, "Adam and Eve on Delancey Street," *Commentary,* no. 8 (1949): 386.
2. Alan Davidson, *The Penguin Companion to Food* (London: Penguin, 2002), 829.
3. Jenna Weissman Joselit, *The Wonders of America: Reinventing Jewish Culture 1880–1950* (New York: Hill and Wang, 1995), 215.
4. See Donald Weber, "Memory and Repression in Early Ethnic Television: The Example of Gertrude Berg and *The Goldbergs,*" in *The Other Fifties: Interrogating Midcentury American Icons,* ed. Joel Foreman (Urbana: University of Illinois Press, 1997), 159–61.
5. Lenny Bruce, quoted in William Novak and Moshe Waldoks, eds., *The Big Book of Jewish Humor* (New York: Harper and Row, 1981), 60; for Ephron, see Deborah Tannen, *Talking Voices: Repetition, Dialogue, and Imagery in Conversational Discourse* (Cambridge: Cambridge University Press, 1989), 156.
6. Rosenfeld, "Adam and Eve," 387.
7. Ibid., 385–86.
8. Jean Soler, "The Dietary Prohibitions of the Hebrews," *New York Review of Books,* 14 June 1979, online at http://www.columbia.edu/itc/religion/segal/v3201/soler.html; accessed 2 December 2003.
9. Rosenfeld, "Adam and Eve," 387.
10. Welles, Orson. "From Mars," *Commentary,* no. 2 (1946): 70.
11. Irving Pfefferblit, "The Bagel: On This Rock . . . ," *Commentary,* no. 11 (1951): 475.
12. Ibid.

Further Reading

Barr, Terry. "Eating Kosher, Staying Closer," *Journal of Popular Film and Television* 24, no. 3 (1996): 134–144.

Brode, Douglas. *Woody Allen: His Films and Career.* London: Columbus Books, 1985.

Cohen, Sarah Blacher, ed. *From Hester Street to Hollywood: The Jewish-American Stage and Screen.* Bloomington: Indiana University Press, 1983.

Davidson, Alan. *The Penguin Companion to Food.* London: Penguin, 2002.

Desser, David, and Lester Friedman. *American-Jewish Filmmakers.* Urbana: University of Illinois Press, 1993.

Friedman, Lester D. *The Jewish Image in American Film.* Secaucus, N.J.: Citadel Press, 1987.

Gabler, Neal. *An Empire of Their Own: How the Jews Invented Hollywood.* New York: Anchor Books, 1988.

Girgus, Sam. *The Films of Woody Allen.* New York: Cambridge University Press, 1993.

Greenberg, Betty D., and Althea O. Silverman. *The Jewish Home Beautiful,* 9th ed. New York: National Women's League of the United Synagogue of America, 1958.

Joselit, Jenna Weissman. *The Wonders of America: Reinventing Jewish Culture 1880–1950.* New York: Hill & Wang, 1995.

Nathan, Joan. *Jewish Cooking in America.* New York: Alfred A. Knopf, 1995.

Novak, William, and Moshe Waldoks, eds. *The Big Book of Jewish Humor.* New York: Harper and Row, 1981.

Paskin, Sylvia, ed. *When Joseph Met Molly: A Reader on Yiddish Film.* Nittingham: Five Leaves, 1999.

Pfefferblit, Irving "The Bagel: On This Rock..." *Commentary* 11 (April 1951).

Rogin, Michael. *Blackface, White Noise: Jewish Immigrants in the Hollywood Melting Pot.* Berkeley and Los Angeles: University of California Press, 1996.

Rosenfeld, Isaac. "Adam and Eve on Delancey Street," *Commentary* 8 (October 1949).

Soler, Jean. "The Dietary Prohibitions of the Hebrews," *The New York Review of Books* (June 14, 1979).

Tannen, Deborah. *Talking Voices: Repetition, dialogue, and imagery in conversational discourse* (Cambridge: Cambridge University Press, 1989).

Weber, Donald. "Memory and Repression in Early Ethnic Television: The Example of Gertrude Berg and *The Goldbergs,*" in *The Other Fifties: Interrogating Midcentury American Icons,* ed. Joel Foreman (Urbana and Chicago: University of Illinois Press, 1997).

Welles, Orson. "From Mars," *Commentary* 2 (July 1946).

Whitfield, Stephen J. *In Search of American Jewish Culture.* Hanover, N.H.: University Press of New England, 1999.

8

Food as Representative of Ethnicity and Culture in George Tillman Jr.'s *Soul Food,* María Ripoll's *Tortilla Soup,* and Tim Reid's *Once upon a Time When We Were Colored*

ROBIN BALTHROPE

Cooking can be described as a "labor of love," and a quick perusal of cooking experiences can prove the truth of this statement. Just think of the ways in which the process of cooking involves work—the physical tasks of cleaning and chopping foods, the possibility of injury from sharp knives or other instruments, the chance of burns from hot grease or ovens. Doing a turn in the kitchen can also involve emotional work, worrying over the quantity and/ or quality of your meal, feeling joy when everything turns out perfectly, and disappointment when the reverse occurs. There is also the work of buying and/or growing one's own food, as well as presenting the dishes one has slaved over. In these and other ways do the members of the families in *Soul Food* (dir. George Tillman Jr., 1997), *Tortilla Soup* (dir. María Ripoll, 2001), and *Once upon a Time When We Were Colored* (dir. Tim Reid, 1996) demonstrate their love for one another, laboring in (and out of) the kitchen to provide nourishment for both body and spirit.[1]

These films follow the Joseph, Naranjo, and Young families, whose support for each other takes many forms, including that of food. My particular interest is in the way these films use food to represent ethnicity and culture in African American and Latino families. Food plays an important role in all three movies, even though *Once upon a Time* is more limited in its use of scenes in which meals and/or eating relate to the story. *Once upon a Time* is a sentimental journey into a black man's childhood in post–World War II Mississippi, whereas *Soul Food* and *Tortilla Soup* are set in contemporary times. The movies all celebrate the power of families to sustain their members through life's sorrows as well as embrace life's joys, using food as a metaphor for many emotional experiences.[2]

There is no question that *Soul Food*, *Tortilla Soup*, and *Once upon a Time* place family meals in their broader contexts, showing meals that take place on Sundays, throughout the week, and on special occasions. We thus have numerous instances for observing African American and Latino food customs. Each film (all were commercial if not critical successes) participates in a broad exploration of how food exists within a culture, giving viewers meaningful glimpses into ethnic foodways; here I accept the definition of foodways as "the pattern of what is eaten, when, how, and what it means."[3] Part of my task in this essay will be to delve briefly into the history of various foods within these two heritages, and discuss how the 1960s and 1970s helped produce a more hospitable climate for ethnic foods so that films like *Soul Food* and *Tortilla Soup* could one day be made.[4] The fact that *Tortilla Soup* is a Latino version of director Ang Lee's *Eat Drink Man Woman* in no way diminishes the power behind the film, since it captures some of the very things that make Latino families strong, such as their emphasis on communications at meals (a custom ethnographers and other scholars have documented).[5]

The three cinematic families exhibited here all find strength from their shared meals, so that they are able to overcome any crisis. However, before looking at the dynamics through which food functions in these families, I will provide a short synopsis of each film.

Soul Food revolves around food's place in the Joseph family, for it begins with a wedding reception and ends with the three sisters gathering vegetables in the family garden. The head of the family, Big Mama (Irma P. Hall), has three daughters, Terri (Vanessa L. Williams), Maxine (Vivica A. Fox), and Robin, who is known by her nickname Bird (Nia Long). The narrator, however, is ten-year-old Ahmad (Brandon Hammond), Maxine's son, who shares a close relationship with his grandmother. Every Sunday the family meets at Big Mama's for a magnificent feast. Ahmad tries to keep the family together after Big Mama dies, by inventing a story so everyone will come to the house for dinner. Food thus becomes a major element of the film through the community and solace it provides the squabbling family members, serving as the glue that holds this northern urban clan together.

While African American cuisine is abundantly on display in *Soul Food*, Cliff Talbert's family and friends in *Once upon a Time* eat very simply most of the time. The audience sees life in the postwar South through Cliff's eyes. He idolizes his great-grandfather, Elder Young, known as Poppa (Al Freeman, Jr.), whose wise words about life and family help guide Cliff (at age five, played by

Charles Earl "Spuds" Taylor, Jr.; at age twelve by Willis Norwood, Jr.; and at sixteen by Damon Hines) in a sometimes hostile world. His extended family and community shower him with support and love, again sometimes in the form of food. Cliff also encounters a white woman who demonstrates concern for his well being, and food is important to his friendship with her.

Tortilla Soup, focused on a Latino family in Los Angeles, is a celebration of food and family in which the patriarch (a semiretired chef) tries to hold onto his grown daughters despite their efforts at independence. Here the family meals are truly spectacular repasts, to which others who are not family members are also treated; the family's discussions during these meals are engaging and often conflicted. Martin Naranjo (Hector Elizondo), his daughters Letitia (Elizabeth Peña), Carmen (Jacqueline Obradors), and Maribel (Tamara Mello), and friends share love over meals—often in a boisterous manner. The fact that so many emotional scenes erupt over the dinner table and are soon resolved strongly suggests that good food has the power to heal the many wounds families inflict on each other.

Having briefly introduced each film, it is now time to consider the ways in which food is used, first by dissecting the two minority cultures' foodways in terms of what is prepared, how it is prepared, when it is served, for whom it is served, and, most important, the meanings behind the foods. In both *Soul Food* and *Once upon a Time*, the cinematic African American families feast on traditional Southern foods such as fried chicken, catfish, ham, string beans, greens, corn on the cob, mashed potatoes and gravy, macaroni and cheese, cornbread, and desserts like the ubiquitous sweet potato pie. While Cliff and his relatives in *Once upon a Time* do not eat this way every day, his great aunt Punk (Phylicia Rashad) spreads out many of these foods for her visiting son Melvin (Leon); in contrast Big Mama and her progeny in *Soul Food* do share this kind of bounty every Sunday afternoon.

The term *soul food* has been in constant use since the 1960s, when the civil rights and black power movements thrust blacks and their heritage into the national spotlight. Soul food was credited with being authentic black food by some in the black community, while others took a more ambivalent stance about the foods that survived slavery and became synonymous with poor blacks prior to the 1960s.[6] This contested history makes Big Mama's comment to Bird all the more interesting when she states that, to her, "soul food cooking [is] cooking from the heart." This view equates soul food with the family, and the love that undergirds soul food cooking motivates Big Mama and countless other mothers to spend hours in the kitchen.

Foodways include food selection and preparation, and *Soul Food* spends a lot of time showcasing these acts, from the first kitchen scene where Terri, Maxine, and Bird compete for the title of "best chef" among the sisters to the final scene where Terri and others gather greens and other fresh vegetables. The cooking styles in favor here include frying, boiling, and baking, which are also found in *Once upon a Time*. These traditional African American techniques, along with instructions such as Big Mama's "four pinches of this," illustrate what culinary historian and cookbook author Vertamae Smart-Grosvenor has personally acknowledged, which is that "when I cook I never measure or weigh anything. I cook by vibration. I can tell by the look or smell of it. I just do it by vibration. Different strokes for different folks. Do your own thing your way."[7]

Smart-Grosvenor's statement may be somewhat tongue in cheek, but numerous other black cooks have expressed similar sentiments,[8] helping shed light on the propensity to creativity within the African American tradition. We know from history that many slaves received the worst scraps of food, and while they could sometimes augment such meager fare with garden produce, wild foods, and pillaged items, black cooks learned to create flavorful meals through the use of various spices and a little imagination. A cooking style developed that did not rely on written instructions, since slaves were denied literacy, and even after slavery was abolished, some blacks were unable to attend schools; a tradition was established of passing down cooking secrets orally.[9] The contest between grown women in *Soul Food* over who is the best cook is in part a tribute to Big Mama, who tries to instill in all three daughters how rewarding cooking can be even if the results are not always gratifying. Bird is the least skilled among the siblings, which is comically demonstrated midway through the film when her reclusive Uncle Pete (John M. Watson, Sr.) rejects the Sunday dinner she prepares when Big Mama is hospitalized.

There are few cooking scenes in *Once upon a Time*, since food is not as central to the film's plot; Punk is the one that the audience usually finds in the kitchen. The meals are more modest since there are only she and Cliff to cook for, but there are two extravagant repasts in the film—Melvin's homecoming meal and the church picnic. These are two extraordinary occasions that are impressive for both the table setting at the church as well as the quantities of food. Melvin's feast will be discussed a bit later in the essay, but a word about the church finery is in order. The church utilizes fine china and silver for its outdoor celebration, which it probably does to express to the community—black as well as white—its pride and accomplishment in surviving such a harsh environment.

Most of the meals in *Soul Food* are prepared for the family's traditional weekly gathering, yet the audience catches a glimpse of Terri and husband Miles (Michael Beach) at home, discussing work issues over an ordinary dinner of pasta, salad, and wine. The atmosphere at the couple's condo is in direct contrast to the raucous, good natured banter and love on display at Big Mama's house. The marriage between Terri and Miles is already on shaky ground at the start of the movie, which their simple meal and tense conversation at their home suggests. Big Mama chides Terri early on, advising her to pay more attention to Miles (her "husband number two," as Big Mama puts it), but from their exchanges over a small meal the audience gathers that Terri is unwilling to make compromises; she and Miles have serious differences about career and financial issues.

A scene near the end of the film in which Terri, Maxine, and Bird meet in a restaurant for lunch to discuss Terri's marriage and, more important, the sale of Big Mama's house, ends without anyone ordering lunch due to their inability to agree on any matters. That no food finds its way to their table, in light of Big Mama's sudden departure, supports the primary message that food symbolizes love. Its absence here indicates animosity and the unrelenting conflict two of the sisters—Terri and Maxine—carry over from childhood.

Before delving further into the meaning behind food scenes in these three films, I would like to spend some time on foodways in *Tortilla Soup* because the Mexican American heritage is highlighted, presenting a vibrant cuisine that melds indigenous and Spanish influences over several centuries in the Southwest.[10] Since the 1960s and 1970s, when the Chicano movement raised the nation's consciousness regarding Mexican American rights, more interest has been paid to Latino cuisine and cooking. The foods served in the Naranjo home and in Martin's restaurant reveal a love of fresh fruits and vegetables, among other ingredients. The very first image in the film is of hands picking vegetables, then grilling peppers and cactus. Fish is on the grill, bananas are frying, and there is other food preparation; as the camera pulls back, viewers discover the hands are those of Martin Naranjo—a man of prodigious culinary talents. Ordinary fare such as corn as well as more "exotic" but genuine Mexican fare such as octopus simultaneously grace the screen.

Not only does Martin cook for family and patrons, but he voluntarily furnishes a friend's daughter with "authentic" lunches of Mexican American cuisine in lieu of the meatloaf and other bland foods her own mother has prepared for her. Many of the cooking techniques found in African American culture are also utilized prominently in *Tortilla Soup*—namely, frying and baking. Yet the Mexican American heritage also introduces distinctive techniques such as roasting vegetables, and twists on ordinary practices like baking in parchment. Martin is quite proficient as a professional chef while middle daughter Carmen takes pride in her own cooking skills, making a meal for her boyfriend that earns his wonder at the vast amount of food she prepares for just the two of them. Her cooking, while spicier that Martin's, also draws rave reviews and rekindles her childhood fantasy of becoming a chef.

Beyond the level of basic nutrition, what we see in the foodways represented in these three movies is a fairly universal view of food as a representation of love. Anyone who has partaken of a special birthday meal or had a spouse serve an elaborate anniversary dinner can attest to the loving aura that food can create. Big Mama's sage words at the start of *Soul Food*, that "green beans, sweet potato pie, and Southern fried chicken would settle any disputes," bespeaks the power of food to smooth ruffled feathers and promote love or at least calmer sentiments among the combatants. Even the act of teaching someone to cook can become an act of love, wherein the teacher wants the pupil to bring happiness to others through food. This is certainly the kind of lesson that Big Mama offers her daughter Bird while helping her learn to make delicious meals.

Big Mama represents the countless mothers (and fathers and other family members) who prepare their children's favorite foods because they love them. Aunt Punk, whose son Melvin fled Mississippi for greater freedom in Detroit, reacts to his visit home by cooking enough for a small army even though only three people are present. The table is laden with fried chicken, mashed potatoes and gravy, cornbread, and sweet potato pie. She constantly fears that he hasn't been "eating good" and, much more to the point, thinks "it's a shame you don't have somebody up north cooking sweet potato pie for you." For Punk, a measure of love is that someone prepares your favorite dessert. Punk ultimately is satisfied when Melvin returns to Detroit with former girlfriend Alice, contentedly saying that "I guess I don't have to worry about who's gonna cook sweet potato pie for you in Detroit." Punk turns down Melvin's offer to move her north to stay near family, but at least she feels sure her son will be cared for.

Melvin is representative of most of the black men in *Once upon a Time* and *Soul Food* in that he does not cook for himself, but Poppa is one of the chefs at the church picnic in *Once upon a Time*. Men as well as women express their love through cooking, and Poppa deep fries some treats that Cliff and his friends cannot wait to eat. There are many hands preparing food, and some of the hands basting meats on the grill are very likely male hands. Grilling is something most men have at one time or another performed at home or at a park; it is traditionally viewed as a "masculine" activity, unlike baking or boiling.[11] Poppa is the only identifiably male cook at the picnic, and the only male in the Young family to cook.

Miles, in *Soul Food*, claims to have "slaved over" dinner in one scene, but the only things on the table are a big salad, glasses of wine, and a big bowl of pasta. We do not witness Miles's efforts in the kitchen as we do Poppa's at the picnic (in *Once upon a Time*), while Maxine's husband Kenny (Jeffrey D. Sams) is only in the kitchen to give a little help with the final dinner in *Soul Food*. Technically he assists Maxine and their daughter with dinner, but retreats quickly once a sister-in-law arrives. Ahmad also helps in the kitchen, but at ten years old he has to be warned not to put dishtowels on the stove near flames. The male cooks here are thus more like apprentice chefs, responsible for less important tasks or meals while the featured dinner remains in female hands.

Martin Naranjo in *Tortilla Soup* is different from the men in the two African American films since he is a professional chef—a largely white male occupation that has status and can earn substantial pay. He also cooks the meals at home for his three grown daughters. His meals are veritable cornucopias of colorful entrees and side dishes. Martin takes pleasure in having meals with his adult children, even though they do not always act according to his expectations. His love is of the stern variety, with constant urgings to avoid "Spanglish" at the table and admonishments to arrive home on time for dinner. Martin's insistence on English at the table contrasts sharply with the Mexican cuisine eaten with such relish there. And when he is working at the restaurant, Martin frequently speaks with a fellow chef in Spanish.

Martin, a widower for fifteen years, is master of the kitchen even though his sense of taste has started to fail—a fatal curse for a chef. He is also, although stern with his daughters, slowly becoming a pushover, providing his attractive neighbor's daughter Alice with special lunches for school. His softer side emerges again near the end of the film when he refers to his daughters as "three angels at the table." Food is central to Martin's life, so it is not surprising that he announces his marriage proposal to Alice's mother Yolanda (Constance Marie) at dinner. The news both surprises and thrills everyone there except Yolanda's divorced mother Hortensia (Raquel Welch), who has tried desperately to hook Martin for herself. The last gathering of the film, another family meal, brings good news about Martin and Yolanda's baby girl, due in a few months. This special occasion is heightened by the fact that Carmen's new restaurant is the site for this dinner. Carmen is finally able to live out her childhood dream of being a chef by turning her back on a business career in order to find happiness in the kitchen. Food is the vital connection among family members here and in the other films—a most ordinary part of life, but one that allows expression of individuals' devotion to one another.

Love is the most powerful emotion engendered by the preparation and eating of food, but it is symbolic of other feelings and ideas represented in these films. Food, along with table settings, can symbolize wealth or abundance. All of the families at some point personally partake of bounteous meals, with the Joseph family being the most extravagant in this area, entertaining guests at Bird's wedding with mountains of food and drink. The Sunday dinners in *Soul Food*, like the many dinners viewers see in *Tortilla Soup*, are usually lavish spectacles of food that the families are fortunate enough to afford—particularly since both families entertain friends at their meals. In *Soul Food* and *Tortilla Soup*, middle-class family members (chefs, businesswomen, and lawyers) enjoy a lifestyle that the Young clan in *Once upon a Time* can only dream of. Poppa and Mama Pearl's extended family includes field workers, maids, and teachers. But even with modest jobs and incomes, for special occasions all of a person's favorite foods are spread out in abundance for his or her enjoyment.

Presentation, however, can reveal as much about a family as can exactly what they consume. The Naranjo dining room table regularly displays fine china, wine glasses, and silver. The fancy table setting is befitting their elegant, upper-middle-class home, while the Joseph and Young families dine with more modest tableware. The church picnic discussed earlier in this essay utilizes the best dishes the church can afford to purchase, something viewers are to assume the church uses only for special events such as the celebration depicted in *Once upon a Time*.

A bourgeois meal trend found only in *Tortilla Soup* is starting off the meal with soup, such as squash flower soup or tortilla soup. None of the other cinematic families feature soup as a distinctive course of their meals, and when soup does appear on the menu it is featured by itself as the total meal. Cliff's lunch with Mrs. Maybry (Polly Bergen) in *Once upon a Time* is gumbo, bread, and lemonade, which is very modest fare for a woman who can afford to hire a maid. Perhaps Mrs. Maybry did not normally eat a big lunch during summer, or did not want to devote much time to her midday meal.

Not all of the meals in *Once upon a Time* are so modest, and the sense of security that a large meal can generate is another potent way that food becomes symbolic in these films. Cliff undoubtedly feels secure at the church picnic, with family and friends to share good food and other pleasures like games and conversation. There is a deep sense of community that the picnic celebrates, including a reminder to be proud to be American when the pastor reminds Cliff and his playmates to respect the flag, keeping it from dragging on the ground, because black men are dying in Korea. The picnic provides not just frivolity but a note of solemnity as well as a brief respite from the daily grind of life in a segregated society. Cliff's entire childhood is one of safety in the bosom of his family while blacks, including family members, face danger from whites who seek to maintain the status quo of discrimination.

In *Soul Food*, everyone from Ahmad to Big Mama finds stability in their weekly dinners, which have their roots in the experiences of Big Mama and her late husband, who attended church dinners in Mississippi. Security and tradition are literally served up each week, with stories passed down through the generations along with recipes and feuds. The dinner table, laden with good food and surrounded by loving family and friends, is the scene of good times—jokes and laughter shared by all, children and adults enjoying memories of past dinner and dreams of the future.

The Naranjo daughters feel secure enough at their family dinners to each announce momentous news to Martin and the others at the table. The first with news, Carmen, shocks her family by telling them she will move into her own condominium. This news upsets Martin, but not as much as her later announcement that she will move to Spain to run a start-up company. Her independence runs counter to his desire to keep his girls close to him. Yet Martin's reaction to news from youngest daughter Maribel at dinner one evening impels her to take drastic action. Maribel brings a new Brazilian boyfriend, André (Nikolai Kinski) home for dinner, then tells everyone that she plans to postpone college rather than go immediately, as Martin had wished. Martin gives the standard parental refrain, "As long as you're living under my roof . . . ," as a way to control Maribel; instead she promptly decides to move in with Andrew, much to his and Martin's surprise. (Up to this point, Andrew has tried to win Martin over by praising the meal, calling Martin an artist, despite Martin's insulting remarks about Brazilians.)

Usually silent at the other meals or the one to give the prayer, eldest daughter Letitia breaks the most surprising news of the film over dinner near the end of the movie. She has just married a man whom she has known only a short while. Orlando (Paul Rodriguez), a former catcher with the Los Angeles Dodgers and now a baseball coach at the middle school where Letitia teaches science, tries to win Martin's friendship by complimenting his cooking. Tortilla soup starts off the meal, which Orlando praises so highly that he declares it better than his mother's soup. The conversation further turns to food when Orlando invites Martin to a baseball game, offering to treat him to hot dogs. The horror on Martin's face vividly expresses his dismay at such pedestrian fare, so Martin volunteers to bring more "acceptable" refreshments. Yet food is not the major subject at the table that night; instead, discussion centers on Letitia and Orlando having already married, marriage, Orlando's feelings for his wife, and his ability to be a good husband to her. Only after Martin is satisfied that Letitia will be happy can he watch the couple ride away on Orlando's motorcycle.

Home may be the place where surprising, even shocking, news is eventually digested, but people need acceptance when they feel unwanted. The security of joining beloved family members for a delicious meal also fosters acceptance for individuals like cousin Faith (Gina Ravera) in *Soul Food*, who is a controversial member of the family whom Big Mama nonetheless welcomes to her Sunday table because she is family no matter what occurred previously. It is Terri who most loudly voices concern—even hostility—about Faith rejoining the family, so when Faith has an affair with Miles it seems that Terri's fears are realized. Yet Ahmad by fooling family members with a story about Big Mama's money, manages to gather everyone at Big Mama's house for dinner, including cousin Faith. She and almost everyone there feel uncomfortable in this situation, but at least the adults manage to act civilized long enough to talk through their problems and work together in a crisis—putting out the fire set off when Ahmad accidentally leaves a towel on the stove.

Akin to acceptance, friendship is a consequence of some of the meals prepared in these films, a value demonstrated in *Once upon a Time*. Punk shares her weekly pie (apple, cherry, or sweet potato) with Cleve (Richard Roundtree), a neighborhood iceman who eventually faces competition from white businessmen in 1962. Their talks are important to both because they give Cleve an opportunity to commiserate with a friendly soul, while Punk has another adult to talk with besides coworkers and family. Another instance of friendship over food in this film is the growing friendship between Cliff and the woman he works for, Mrs. Maybry. He performs chores around her house, and she takes an interest in his education. What makes this friendship so problematic is the fact that Mrs. Maybry is a middle-aged white woman who lives alone and is known in the black community as a crazy driver. Their shared lunch in Mrs. Maybry's kitchen upsets Cliff's cousin Annie (Anna Maria Horseford), who works as a maid for Mrs. Maybry. Much to Annie's chagrin, Cliff speaks up with Mrs. Maybry, telling her of his relatives' (real and fictive) advice to go as far as possible in school. The sense of equality between the two, even though he is a twelve-year-old child and she an adult, is heightened because they share not only food but their thoughts freely.

This incident takes place a few years before the famous Woolworth sit-ins in 1960, and it is important to remember that the scene depicted here occurs in a private as opposed to public place. Likewise, there are no physical repercussions for Cliff as there would be for the young men and women activists in the 1960s. Yet this scene is also instructive in that Mrs. Maybry's interest in Cliff's education soon leads her to complain about the local library's racist policy of not letting blacks check out books. She initially gives Cliff books from her own library, then begins to check out books for him. Thus, in her own surreptitious manner she helps undermine Jim Crowism in Glen Allan, Mississippi.

So many other symbolic uses of food abound in these films, but one of the more touching aspects of sharing food that they demonstrate is that food brings comfort or solace to someone hurt or grieving. The last meal the family shares in *Soul Food* brings a measure of comfort to everyone, even as they mourn the loss of their matriarch and even when they learn that a child has tricked them into appearing for dinner. Big Mama's earlier words about family coming together like a mighty fist clearly reverberate here, and the fire they suffer that day leads to a beneficial discovery—that there really had been a family fortune hidden somewhere in the house. Ironically, the family recluse, Uncle Pete, is the key to the recovery of the money Big Mama hid in his television.

A very traditional use of food to console people occurs after a death, during a mourning period or funeral reception. When Mama Pearl dies in *Once upon a Time,* after a long illness, friends bring food to Poppa's house, alerted to her death by the tolling of a bell, this being a close-knit black community. Food plays a different role in consoling someone in *Soul Food.* Uncle Pete reacts to his sister's death by confusing Maxine with her mother; he is lost in memories of their father catching catfish and killing pigs to make smoked sausages. He finds refuge in the past where life with his family was simple and the food flavorful as well as plentiful. Maxine soon decides to take care of Uncle Pete rather than put him in a nursing home (as Terri suggests), showing him the same consideration Big Mama did because he was family.

While the above examples link food to sad emotions in various family settings, a very positive use of food in an individualistic manner grants some of the cooks here the opportunity for self-actualization, even gratification. Big Mama's expertise in the kitchen is legendary, and her daughter Maxine is the next best cook in the family, if Ahmad is to be believed. Maxine has time to concentrate on cooking, as she did not "stay in the books" as Terri did, and is a stay-at-home wife and mother as Terri is not. Yet Big Mama worked outside the home when it was necessary, so that a job and cooking well are not seen as incompatible. In fact, if a person has a gift for cooking, then outside activities cannot detract from it; then again, no amount of practice can cultivate a gift if it is not innate. But all of the sisters strive to achieve the kind of culinary skills their mother possessed, which brought their minister Reverend Williams to dinner every Sunday for soul food.

The pride in cooking that family members display in *Soul Food* is duplicated by *Tortilla Soup*'s Martin and Carmen. One the established chef and the other the aspiring chef, they gain satisfaction from cooking Latino dishes for loved ones. They compare their cooking, Martin asserting that Carmen's is too spicy (he calls it "mongrel" food because it is a mingling of flavors and styles) whereas Martin's food is too tame for Carmen. Both express creativity in the kitchen, using food as the medium of expression for their talents. Martin is able to rescue overcooked restaurant food at a private party, turning it into a completely new dish with a French name. Carmen takes unusual ingredients to arrive at "Nuevo Latin" dishes (as she calls them) for her boyfriend, and later for patrons at her restaurant.

One last example of food's symbolism in all three of these films is the use of food as a reward or treat. Martin treats youngster Alice to wonderful Mexican foods for lunch in *Tortilla Soup* as he gets to know her mother Yolanda better. Ahmad, victorious in a big basketball game, prevails upon his mother in *Soul Food* to prepare a victory dinner with his favorite dishes. He anxiously anticipates greens, lima beans, neckbones, and fried chicken, planning to use this dinner (and a little white lie about Big Mama's money) to unite his warring family. While most problems are resolved for the Joseph family after this dinner, in *Once upon a Time*, Elder Young and Cliff's day in Greenville, where Cliff appreciates a special treat, is forever marred by a chance encounter. After Cliff starts to enjoy an ice cream cone, he hands it to Poppa to get a drink of water. Cliff then hears music and wants to see the "parade." As a boy of five he does not understand what he is witnessing, but his great-grandfather nearly squeezes Cliff's cone to death as they watch a Ku Klux Klan rally in the middle of town. Cliff innocently watches the proceedings while Poppa is disgusted by the spectacle. Meanwhile, the cone, crushed and melting in the sun, is a safe target for Poppa's anger, which he dare not express openly to the Klansman who questions him and frightens Cliff. Happily, however, Poppa promises Cliff another cone so he can reclaim some sense of normalcy after such an upsetting event.

There are doubtless many more uses of food in these three films that this essay cannot address in such a short space. The important thing to remember about food and its uses in *Soul Food*, *Tortilla Soup*, and *Once upon a Time When We Were Colored* is the powerful way food is shown to facilitate communication among family, friends, and community. It has been said that in sharing food and talk, people can become more connected.[12] Since both food and talk have graced the Joseph, Naranjo, and Young tables, not just their bodies but their minds and spirits have been fed. Food is indeed plentiful in these three films, but the audiences are fed as well with food for the soul that lingers on long after these cinematic feasts are concluded.

Notes

1. *Soul Food*, directed by George Tillman, Jr. Twentieth-Century Fox, 1997 (with Vanessa Williams, Irma P. Hall, Vivica Fox, Nia Long, and Brandon Hammond); *Once Upon a Time When We Were Colored*, based on the autobiographical novel by Clifton Taubert, directed by Tim Reid. Republic Studios, 1996 (with Al Freeman, Jr., Phylicia Rashad, Leon, Paula Kelly); *Tortilla Soup*, directed by María Ripoll. Samuel Goldwyn Films, 2001 (with Hector Elizando, Jacqueline Obradors, Tamara Mello, Elizabeth Pena, Rqquel Welch).

2. It would be difficult to list every book written on the black family, so I will mention a few of the more recent works. There are anthologies, such as Melvin E. Wilson, ed., *African American Family Life: Its Structural and Ecological Aspects* (San Francisco: Jossey-Bass, 1995), and Robert Joseph Taylor, James S. Jackson, and Linda M. Chatters, eds., *Family Life in Black America* (Thousand Oaks, Calif.: Sage, 1997); comprehensive studies such as Andrew Billingsley, *Climbing Jacob's Ladder: The Enduring Legacy of African American Families* (New York: Simon and Schuster, 1992); and "advice" books such as Joyce A. Ladner, *The Ties That Bind: Timeless Values for African American Families* (N.Y.: J. Wiley, 1998) Two recent works regarding the Latino family and masculinity as it relates to family life, respectively, are David T. Abelos, *The Latino Family and the Politics of Transformation* (Westport, Conn.: Praeger, 1993) and Alfredo Mirande, *Hombres y Machos: Masculinity and Latino Culture* (Boulder, Colo.: Westview Press, 1997).

3. Susan Kalcik, "Ethnic Foodways in America: Symbols and the Performance of Identity," in *Ethnic and Regional Foodways in the United States: The Performance of Group Identity*, ed. Linda Keller Brown and Kay Mussell (Knoxville: University of Tennessee Press, 1987), 37–65, 38. A seminal study of food and culture is K. C. Chang, ed., *Food in Chinese Culture: Anthropological and Historical Perspectives* (New Haven, Conn.: Yale University Press, 1977).

4. See note 9, below, for the impact of soul food on America. Regarding the Chicano cultural resurgence of the 1960s and 1970s, see, for example, Harvey Levenstein, *Paradox of Plenty: A Social History of Eating in Modern America* (Oxford: Oxford University Press, 1993), 218. Many Mexican cookbooks have been published within the last two decades, including Rick Bayless, D. G. Bayless, and J. M. Brownson, *Rick Bayless' Mexican Kitchen* (New York: Charles Scribner's Sons, 1997); Diana Kennedy, *The Art of Mexican Cooking* (New York: Bantam, 1989); and Maria Yzabul, Dolores Torres, and Shelton Wiseman, *The Mexican Gourmet* (San Diego: Thunder Bay Press, 1995).

5. Eric Aoki, "Mexican American Ethnicity in Biola, CA: An Ethnographic Account of Hard Work, Family, and Religion," *Howard Journal of Communications*, no. 11 (2000): 207–27; see also Kathleen J. Niska, "Mexican American Family Processes: Nurturing, Support, and Socialization," *Nursing Science Quarterly* 12, no. 2 (1999): 138–42, for another ethnographic study that documented the titled processes in Mexican American families. Abelos, *The Latino Family*, analyzes the Latino family's need to become more democratic, allowing for individual selfhood that can be stifled in the name of family unity.

6. Levenstein, *Paradox of Plenty*, 218; regarding black nationalism and soul food, see Jessica Harris, *Welcome Table: African American Heritage Cookbook* (New York: Fireside, 1990), 33, 261. A very different view of soul food's acceptance in the black community is detailed in Doris Witt, "Soul Food: Where the Chitterling Hits the (Primal) Pan," in *Eating Culture*, ed. Ron Scapp and Brian Seitz (Albany: State University of New York Press, 1998). Specifically, Witt theorizes that soul food's acceptance is more complicated than generally thought because of several issues: the long standing stigma of blackness with filth, which is applied to the sine qua non of soul food, chitterlings; the connection between soul food and poor blacks; and negative images of black women, especially during the 1960s, as domineering matriarchs, castrating bitches, and so on. In a different vein, books such as John Pinderhughes, *Family of the Spirit Cookbook: Recipes and Remembrances from African-American Kitchens* (New York: Simon and Schuster, 1990) caution against reading Southern cookbooks as strictly black cooking, as the author's Aunt Margie warns readers to remember that blacks and whites "all ate pretty much the same way." John Egerton stresses the same thing many times in his *Southern Food: At Home, on the Road, in History* (Chapel Hill: University of North Carolina Press, 1992).

7. Vertamae Smart-Grosvenor, "Introduction to Soul Food," online at http://www.northby-south.org/1999/food/neh/introduction.htm. See also Vertamae Smart-Grosvenor, *Vibration Cooking, or the Travel Notes of a Geechee Girl* (New York: Ballantine, 1970), for her personal story of her upbringing in South Carolina and her travels in the United States and Europe. Smart-Grosvenor also links various African traditions to the New World—greens in Brazil, okra in Bahia, southern United States hush puppies—in her forward to Ntozake Shange's *If I Can Cook, You Know God Can* (Boston: Beacon Press, 1998). Another of Smart-Grosvenor's cookbooks is *Vertamae Cooks in the Americas' Family Kitchen* (San Francisco: KQED Books, 1996). The famous black bibliophile, Arthur A. Schomburg, recognized black creativity when planning to write a book on transatlantic black culinary traditions during the 1920s. He noted the fact that there were no exact formulas in black cooking, and further, that "no matter how ingredients are measured they must be combined with a sort of magic [to] achieve the perfect blend." Schomburg, unpublished manuscript, Schomburg Papers, cited in Doris Witt, "'My Kitchen was the World': Vertamae Smart-Grosvenor's Geechee Diaspora," in *Kitchen Culture in America: Popular Representations of Food, Gender, and Race*, ed. Sherrie A. Inness (Philadelphia: University of Pennsylvania Press, 2001).
8. See Harris, *Welcome Table*, 235, on her first culinary invention at a young age and her subsequent love of cooking. Monique Y. Wells, in *Food for the Soul: A Texas Expatriate Nurtures Her Culinary Roots in Paris* (Seattle: Elton-Wolf, 2000), explains her need to be creative living in Paris because she needed to improvise for ingredients she could not get in France. Egerton, *Southern Food*, relates many stories of black cooks' creativity. Yet Egerton acknowledges, as do other writers, that white observers frequently denigrate blacks' cooking skills, equating their techniques with "voodoo"; see, for instance, Barbara Haber's concluding assessment on black cookbooks, that "[t]hese same books have also helped to eradicate the demeaning images, perpetuated for years by American popular culture, of black women cooks as ignorant or comical figures," in *From Hardtack to Home Fries: An Uncommon History of American Cooks and Meals* (New York: Free Press, 2002), 207.
9. A wonderful example of oral traditions keeping cooking styles alive is found in Josephine A. Beoku-Betts, "We Got Our Way of Cooking Things: Women, Food, and Preservation of Cultural Identity among the Gulluh," *Gender and Society*, no. 9 (1995): 535–55, 548–52.
10. Elaine N. McIntosh, *American Food Habits in Historical Perspective* (Westport, Conn.: Praeger, 1995), 152, 177–79, 195–97; see also the works cited in notes 2 and 3, above, on Chicano consciousness and its impact on new cuisine.
11. Gendered cooking is usefully discussed in Charles Camp, *American Foodways: What, When, Why, and How We Eat in America* (Little Rock: August House, 1989), 86. Allen Beardsworth and Teresa Keil, *Sociology on the Menu: An Invitation to the Study of Food and Society* (London: Routledge, 1997), also ventures into this area of gender and cooking.
12. Roger Abrahams, "Equal Opportunity Eating: A Structural Excursus on Things of the Mouth," in Brown and Mussell, eds., *Ethnic and Regional Foodways*, 19–36.

2
Focus on Gender—The Body, the Spirit

9

Gendering the Feast: Women, Spirituality, and Grace in Three Food Films

MARGARET H. MCFADDEN

Introduction

Three films—all of which began textual life as printed fiction—tell us much about the place of gender in any discussion of food and feasting. Since food studies, film studies, and even feminist film criticism have really just begun to ask relevant gender questions about that interdisciplinary borderland of "reel food," this article will contribute to the interrogation by looking at Lasse Hall-ström's *Chocolat* (2000), Alfonso Arau's *Like Water for Chocolate* (1993), and Gabriel Axel's *Babette's Feast* (1987).[1] All three, in very different ways, use women's gender difference in conjunction with discussions of spirituality and the theological concept of grace. This grace is bestowed freely through the women's gifts of food and feasting. Contemporary versions of the 1940s and 1950s genre of the "women's film," these films nevertheless universalize the possibility of grace.

Chocolat unfolds a morality tale about a single mother with Mayan Indian roots who wanders from town to town, spreading healing and understanding to sworn enemies in the form of gifts of chocolate. Vianne Rocher (Juliette Binoche), with her red shoes and colorful dresses, and young daughter Anouk, blows into the village of Lansquenet at the beginning of Lent, upsetting the staid Lenten denials of the Catholic community. *Like Water for Chocolate* uses the creation of monthly recipes to narrate the story of the love of Tita (Lumi Cavazos) and Pedro (Marco Leopardi) over the background of the Mexican Revolution. Each dish has spiritual significance in this tale of the absolute connections among food, love, and spirituality. *Babette's Feast* is a story about an ascetic Protestant community on the wild North Sea coast of Denmark. Martine (Birgitte Federspiel) and Philippa (Bodil Kjer) the two daughters of the pastor, are contrasted with the cosmopolitan French Catholic servant, Babette (Stéphane Audran). Babette comes into a fortune and then gives it all away with her creation of an artistic spiritual feast that transforms the community.

The relatively new interdisciplinary field of food studies combines anthropology, sociology, political science, cultural studies, pop culture, folklore, culinary history, ethnic studies, agriculture, sustainable development, nutrition, global studies, history, literature, and women's studies. But it is astonishing how few of the articles and books in food studies ask gender questions. In fact, one of the more successful assignments in my Women, History, and Food course is always the one in which I ask the students what they would do to "gender" one of our reading assignments. Seemingly obvious questions about who was growing what, or who was cooking what, or who was selling what—in slavery times in Jamaica, in mountainous Peru, in Mayan Mexico, in colonial Nigeria—seem often not to be asked. Both Nelson Foster and Linda S. Cordell's *Chilies to Chocolate: Food the Americas Gave the World* and Sidney Mintz's *Tasting Food, Tasting Freedom* are weakened by this omission. Even Carole Counihan and Penny Van Esterik's very useful anthology *Food and Culture*, while it reprints some classic articles that deal with gender (such as Caroline Walker Bynum on medieval religious women and Susan Bordo on anorexia nervosa), still keeps gender questions on the periphery.[2]

Film studies, as well, did not traditionally deal with questions of gender. In the past two decades, however, feminist film theory has become important in the second wave of the women's movement, with new books on feminist cinema being published at a great rate. But even such anthologies as Sue Thornham's *Feminist Film Theory: A Reader* (1999), and E. Ann Kaplan's *Feminism and Film* (2000) do not deal with food films at all and certainly not with the importance of gender in those films.[3] While food films seem to have proliferated in the past few years, criticism does not often deal with gender questions, even when the films reviewed are explicitly female oriented.[4]

Grace

Each of the films in question deals with grace differently. A way into the subject of women's connection to grace is to explore briefly the theological concept of grace. Grace is usually defined as unmerited divine love and favor given freely to humans by God; it is also that divine influence that operates in humans to regenerate or sanctify. Grace often comes as a surprise, humans understanding it only in retrospect. The English word *grace* comes from Old French *gratia* and is sometimes translated as "mercy," but "grace" is the more correct theological term. In the New Testament, the word used is the Greek *charis*, meaning "gift of spirit." The German mystic Johannes Tauler (*c.*1300–1361) called grace "an enjoyment granted from beyond."[5]

How to deal with the conflict between grace and free will consumed Catholic theology for hundreds of years. Heretics were burned, and works were banned on the basis of one's attitude toward grace. Luis de Molina (1535–1600), a Jesuit, spent his theological life working on an attempt to resolve this apparent contradiction. He posited a middle way, the *scientia media*, which is "the knowledge that God has of conditional future contingent events." Philosopher John A. Mourant notes that "in effect, Molina endeavored to preserve more fully the freedom of the individual without destroying the power of grace; the Thomists [after Thomas Aquinas] were more concerned with preserving the power of grace without destroying the freedom of the individual."[6]

Julian of Norwich (*c.*1342–*c.*1416), anchoress, mystic, and recluse whose revelations and visions have been so influential in the past century, is helpful in understanding a more gendered and feminine Catholic conception of grace. She speaks of Jesus as our true mother, the female part of the Holy Trinity, who "feed[s] us not with milk, but with himself, opening his side for us and claiming all our love."[7] According to Julian, Jesus as mother is able to reunite the self to its oneness with the divine—God the Father and God the Holy Spirit—through the Incarnation. Jesus is a mother in three ways: first, through the natural creation of the body; second, through redemption and salvation by grace; and third, in restoring the *imago Dei* in the soul, "how we are brought back by the motherhood of mercy and grace into our natural place, in which we were created by the motherhood of love, a mother's love which never leaves us."[8] Julian's oft-quoted, "All shall be well, and all shall be well, and all manner of things shall be well," when combined with her view of Jesus as Mother, comes close to a universal view of grace available to all without question. As in these religious definitions, the grace proffered by Babette in *Babette's Feast* and Vianne in *Chocolat*, and to a lesser extent Tita in *Like Water for Chocolate*, is given without conditions, and its acceptance changes the human community.

Martin Luther's Protestantism was founded on the rock of unconditioned grace. He proclaimed the Kingdom of Grace (*das Reich der Gnaden*) as he railed against reason as the "Devil's Whore" that keeps humans from receiving grace from the divine. As B. A. Gerrish explains, "The proclamation of an unconditioned grace—which demands nothing, save the acceptance of faith—can be greeted by reason only with incredulity. What needs to be 'sacrificed,' therefore, is not human rationality, without qualification, but rather the legalistic mentality of the natural man. As Luther put it, grace must 'take us out of ourselves,' and we must learn to 'rise above reason.'"[9] Thus, the miraculous feasts in all three films; these events are literally transcendent, as characters are surprised out of their old selves.

Spirituality and Grace for Women

Caroline Walker Bynum, in her massive *Holy Feast and Holy Fast: The Religious Significance of Food to Medieval Women*, as well as in her later work

Fragmentation and Redemption: Essays on Gender and the Human Body in Medieval Religion (1992), gives detailed evidence and analysis of the role of food in medieval women's lives, both saints and laywomen. The contextual material she gives, the numbers of religious paintings reproduced in the works, and the specifics from medieval documents, by both women and men (evidence from saints' lives, from medieval mystics' works, and from church records of miracles), paint a convincing picture of the gender specificity of the significance of food to women. The three films under discussion here can all be said to be modern exemplars of Bynum's evidence, both symbolically and literally.

Traditionally, women were intimately involved not just in asceticism and fasting, but with feasting as well. As Bynum notes, "Medieval food behavior was service of others as well as rending and sacrifice."[10] Both then and now, in many cultures, women cook and men eat. Food is important to women in traditional societies because it is the one resource that they control. In the Middle Ages, continues Bynum, "one of the strongest social links between male and female lay in the fact that wife or servant cooked what husband and lord provided and in the even more consequential fact that mother's womb and mother's milk guaranteed survival of the next generation. . . . This is not, of course, to say that women never ate or that only male children were nourished from the female body. It is, rather, to say that social arrangements and cultural symbols stereotyped reception of nurture as a male activity, provision of nurture as a female one" (277). This description of women's role from medieval times is certainly true of colonial Mexico (*Like Water for Chocolate*).

That contemporary dualism of Mexico was not found in the same way in the late Middle Ages, asserts Bynum, which was not a time of asceticism rooted in dualism, spirit opposed to body. The wild practices of religious people in the thirteenth to the fifteenth centuries were not "a world-denying, self-hating, decadent response of a society wracked by plague, famine, heresy, war, and ecclesiastical corruption. Rather, late medieval asceticism . . . was a profound expression of the doctrine of the Incarnation: the doctrine that Christ, by becoming human, saves *all* that the human being is" (294). Women religious in the Middle Ages did not see themselves in terms of the duality of male/female, spirit/flesh, or nurture/authority. These dualities were much less important to women than to men; women "saw themselves as human beings—fully spirit and fully flesh" (296). *Babette's Feast* seems to illustrate this more universal understanding of gender difference.

In our own era, these spiritual meanings of food have not been lost. Simone Weil, the great French war resister and mystic, wrote, "If I grow thin from labour in the fields, my flesh really becomes wheat. If that wheat is used for the host it becomes Christ's flesh. Anyone who labours with this intention should become a saint" (quoted in Bynum, 297). Weil died of self-starvation in 1943. In a very different way, the food writer M. F. K. Fisher begins *The Gastronomical Me* (1943) with a meditation on food writing, demonstrating her understanding of the connection between spirituality and food. She ends this section of her book with the assertion, "There is a communion of more than our bodies when bread is broken and wine drunk."[11]

So Babette Hersant enables the people at her dinner to accept grace, from General Loewenhielm (Jarl Kulle) whose best friend killed Babette's husband and son in the 1871 Paris Commune, to the elderly ascetic parishioners, divided by schisms. Babette, a good French Catholic, bestows the Protestant concept of grace (or at least a feminine, Julianic kind of grace) by means of her gift of the decadent seven-course meal: the Kingdom of Grace (Luther's *Reich der Gnaden*) has come to pass. Babette has free will, and her actions, as created in the short story by Isak Dinesen (Karen Blixen) and on film by director Axel, are not foreknown or determined. She did not know that General Loewenhielm, friend of the violent General Galliffet, would be a guest at her dinner. The general did not know that the former chef of Café Anglais in Paris would be there on the coast of Jutland in Denmark. Even after being served her specialty, *cailles en sarcophage* (quail in a pastry tomb), symbolically the body of the savior entombed, he does not seem to realize that this is *the* Babette. Babette Hersant ("herself a saint," from Old Frisian), like her namesake St. Barbara, has offered not only her food but herself, her soul and body (as the ritual of the eucharist says), to him and a community of people who had lived their lives by denying their bodily desires. St. Barbara is known as the patron saint in time of danger from storms and fire and as intercessor to guarantee that each petitioner will receive the last rites and the eucharist at death. She is also the only female saint pictured as carrying the sacramental wine chalice and wafer. Thus Babette arrives in a terrible storm, a refugee from the violence and fires of Paris, ready to serve the eucharistic feast, given freely for everyone. Philippa and Martine (named for the great Protestant theologians Philip Melancthon and Martin Luther) and the puritanical community of their pastor father (Pouel Kern), as well as the dissolute General Loewenhielm from the royal court, all partake. The general is more profoundly changed by the gift of Babette's feast than the others. He understands, finally, the true meaning of the pious platitudes he had mouthed at court. Through the abundance of the wine, poured out for him without end (Babette instructs the boy waiter to keep his wine glass full), he is transformed by grace to be in communion with Martine: "I shall dine with you in my soul every night."[12]

Grace in *Chocolat* is bestowed in quite different ways, as the religious conflict here is not between Protestants and Catholics, but between Catholics and pagans (either wiccans or ancient Aztecs and Mayans). As in *Babette's Feast* and *Like Water for Chocolate*, however, the one who functions as a Christ figure, bestowing grace freely, is a woman. Vianne, a non-Christian, is the representative of the good, while, in an ironic reversal, the villain in the story is the representative of the Church. Vianne bestows grace in a very Christian way by her acceptance of otherness—the poor, the gypsies, the downtrodden—almost as a gloss on Jesus' Beatitudes and the Parable of the Good Samaritan. Set in Lent, beginning with Carnival, Shrove Tuesday, and Ash Wednesday, and ending with Easter, the structure of both the book (by Joanne Harris) and the film is set around both the Christian and the pagan celebrations of new life. The film transforms the novel's dialogue between old and young priest about how to deal with witchcraft into a dialogue between the mayor (Alfred Molina) and the young priest (Hugh O'Conor) about non-Christian diversity.

In *Like Water for Chocolate*, set in the borderlands between Texas and Mexico at the time of the Mexican Revolution, Christianity is a backdrop. Tita's quail with rose petal sauce becomes the medium for grace: Tita's body and passion become the host by transubstantiation into her food, which is then eaten by Pedro and the others. The so-called magic realism of the film (and novel—the screenplay was written by the book's author, Laura Esquivel) is a modern-day version of the medieval saints' eucharistic visions. Symbolically, all the elements of miraculous (female) Christian saints are there to be read. Mexico's patron saint, the Virgin of Guadaloupe, is not specifically mentioned, but she is nonetheless there as are the elements of traditional Indio religion, invoked by the Indian household servants Nacha (Ada Carrasco) and Chencha (Pilar Aranda).

The Eucharistic Feast as Transformation

Feasting was as much a part of medieval Christian life as was fasting. Again, from Bynum: "The characteristic medieval meal was the feast, and it was more an aesthetic and social event than a gastronomic one. The feast was a banquet for all the senses; indeed, food was almost an excuse for indulging senses other than taste" (60). She continues her description of one of the sources of her information, noting, "Medieval cookbooks make it clear that visual effects were more important to a medieval diner than taste and that vivid colors (for example, green dye from spinach or leeks, or gold- and silver-leaf garnish) were often applied at the expense of flavor. . . . cookbooks provide detailed instructions on how to construct illusions or tricks for the eye, such as imitation meat concocted from fish, or roast fowl sewn back into its plumage in order to appear alive, or pies (like that in the nursery rhyme) with live birds baked inside" (60–61). Cinematography is, of course, all about illusion; the eye tricks of color, lighting, and camera angle give the food and its preparation the centrality each film calls for. All three films lovingly portray close-ups of food preparation: the plucking of the quails in *Babette's Feast*, the pomegranate garnish on the green chiles in *Like Water for Chocolate*, the hand grinding of cacao beans in *Chocolat*.

The profoundly Christian *Babette's Feast* comes close to saying that the Christ as female (in the person of Babette) as well as the female suffering servants (Philippa and Martine) make a difference to this community as women. In their spirituality and in the bestowing of grace (as in one of the final scenes in which the community joins hands in the moonlight and dances around the fountain), Philippa, Martine, and Babette are finally joined together. The third course entrée, cailles en sarcophage, suggests that the Christ is consumed, the god is eaten (a medieval way of referring to the eucharist), served by the feminine priest.

The feasting in *Like Water for Chocolate* (the Mexican metaphor for being at a boiling point) comes to conflagration in the passion of Tita and Pedro, who have been separated for so long and are finally consumed by their passion. The central image and metaphor of the title, that point at which a physical substance is transformed "into something liquid and consumable, brought about by time, heat, and pressure" is, according to critic Diane Long Hoeveler, like Homi Bhabha's concept of hybridity.[13] The novel and film suggest that "a new world for Mexican women will be born only under great pressure and over long periods of time." The story straddles both Old World and New World traditions. It is Mexican in the characters of Nacha and Chencha and the invocation of Aztec goddesses Coatlicue, in her twin guises of a benign Earth Mother or the horrific La Llorona who devours children (as shown in the character Mamá Elena, played by Regina Torné).[14] It is Greek in the portrayal of Tita as the fertility goddess Ceres and the Platonic suggestion of the soul finding its way back through the tunnel to the light of divine origin, and Christian in the invocation of bodily transcendence.

Tita becomes one with Pedro in the final ecstatic vision, just as she had in the feast of the quail in rose petal sauce. It is significant that in both *Babette's Feast* and *Like Water for Chocolate* the most important dish in the feast is quail—little birds often suggestive of Christ (as portrayed in traditional Christian Iconography). At the feast for the seventieth birthday of Armande (Judi Dench) in *Chocolat*, the pièce de résistance is *plateau de fruits de mer* (seafood platter in their shells), chosen so that the guests will need to take time to eat and socialize. On this final night of Armande's life (she is diabetic and has decided to die), everyone is at the table for over four hours. But Vianne also serves turkey with mole, the dark chocolate sauce spooned over the poultry in a clear reference to the rich grand dish of *Babette's Feast;* even the camera angle is the same in both films.

Many images suggest that women's bodies and their products—wombs, tears, blood, and milk—are what mediate between the earthly and the divine, between flesh and spirit. The virgin Tita breastfeeds her nephew Roberto when Rosauro has no milk, just as medieval women who had never given birth were able to do (and had visions of Mary and female saints doing the same; Christ is often imaged as lifting his wounded breast for suckling). These and other images used by Esquivel are reminiscent of traditional medieval Christianity, as evidenced by Bynum.[15] Tita nourishes spirit through the body, through her tears, milk, and, always, through food; her motto might be, "I cook, you eat, therefore I am." *Babette's Feast* (and this is true, too, in *Like Water for Chocolate*), by means of color, light, and sound, portrays a beatific vision, a realm beyond, a vision of the paradise so often invoked in this film by opera star Achille Papin (Jean-Philippe Lafont), General Loewenhielm, and finally Philippa. Vianne in *Chocolat* brings the community together in the grand festival on Easter afternoon. What we see in all three of these films is a visionary picture, similar to one of Julian of Norwich's "showings," an epiphany in which all creation is seen as new.

In *Chocolat* the sin of gluttony is manifested by the mayor (in the film version) and priest (in the novel), first in their minds and then in fact, as the good Catholic is revealed to be the perpetrator of the fire on the gypsies' houseboats and the destroyer of the chocolate figures in the shop—the Mayan god and the chocolate pyramid. Yet Vianne stands forgiving on that Easter morning, holding out a healing potion for the lustful and gluttonous mayor. Theologically, the film is less satisfying than the book, for in the latter, Vianne, as the representative of paganism, needs to travel elsewhere to bring her healing arts of chocolate to another community. The novel is truer to Vianne's character, as it shows that she cannot stay with the people in the village of Lansquenet, but, now pregnant with a kind of virgin birth, moves on to bring grace and salvation to a different village. The film portrays a more romantic ending, bringing Vianne and the gypsy, Roux, together once more and implying that her wandering is over. The specificity of her relationships with Roux, the battered wife, Joséphine, and Armande, as well as Anouk's place in this community and her feelings of inadequacy and shame at her mother's difference, all go to make the viewer wish for a "happy" ending. The film is unable to convey the details of Vianne's foreknowledge (but only suggests it as, she reads the future in melted chocolate), and thus the portrayal of Vianne as divine giver is compromised, even as the viewer is satisfied that Roux, Vianne, and Anouk have become a "real" family.

Gender, Food, and Spirit: The Feminine Christ Figure

Why is it important that these feasts are cooked and served by women, that those who arrange the feasts are women, and that the Christ figure or spiritual server is represented as a woman, in each case? Would it be different if all these were men? Yes, it would be different, for the main players in most cultures' food dramas are not men. Many traditions, both religious and secular, put females front and center in the role of feast preparer and server. Even in the symbolism of the eucharist, the (male) priest's role is often envisioned as feminine in medieval literature. What these films have done for us is to portray, cinematically, the *imago Dei* as feminine *and* universal. The three film directors are all men, but they have worked closely with female screenwriters and actresses. Gabriel Axel has faithfully brought Danish author Isak Dinesen's story to the screen. Alfonso Arau's ex-wife is the author and screenwriter of *Like Water for Chocolate*, Laura Esquivel; and Lasse Hallström's wife is the actress Lena Olin, who plays Joséphine in *Chocolat*.

All the main characters in *Like Water for Chocolate* are women; in some sense, all the men are ciphers or stereotypes: the father who has a heart attack when he is told that his wife has given birth to another daughter, the soldier in

Pancho Villa's army who is drawn in lust to Gertrudis (Claudette Maillé) by the smell of rose petals, the good American doctor John (Mario Martinez), and even the lovesick Pedro. The women are the actors—the producers and preparers of feasts, the artists of needlework and handwritten invitations, the bearers and nurturers of children; a woman (Mamá Elena) is even the boss of the ranch.

Tita, who "grew up in the kitchen," becomes a Christ figure early in the story, when her tears are so powerful that they make the wedding cake batter into a powerful emitic, causing vomiting and diarrhea in all the guests. Only a woman—Tita or Nacha—could have this spiritual power. When Pedro brings Tita roses to celebrate the completion of her first year as chief cook at the ranch (after Nacha's death), Tita's Christlike state is made physically manifest: she exhibits bloody stigmata (the wounds of Christ on the cross) on her breast from the roses. When she serves quail in rose petal sauce, everyone becomes suffused with passion; the narrator says that "Tita's blood had dissolved into the sauce." It is as if her body has become the quail and sauce that they eat, surely an image of the eucharist. Pedro and Tita find "a new way of communicating" as their love theme plays softly in the background.

At the end, when Rosaura's daughter Esperanza is getting married, Tita has prepared chiles with walnut sauce and pomegranates. The dish again suffuses everyone with passion, and Tita, answering a guest's query, explains that it "must be cooked with much love," underscoring the way her person is incorporated into the foods she prepares. There is a quick cutting back to Gertrudis's steamy passionate shower after eating quail with rose petal sauce, to remind us of Tita's magical powers. As Tita prepares the bed for the final (and first) love scene with Pedro, twenty-two years later, the love theme plays again. Now the elements in the Eucharist are the matches that ignite the first fire of love, and Tita is united forever with Pedro. As the daughter of Esperanza (the name means "hope" in Spanish) and the narrator of the story says, "She'll continue to live as long as someone cooks her recipes."

In *Chocolat,* Vianne functions as the Christ figure, for she heals people and brings them together across generational and class lines: Guillaume (Baptiste Marceau) and the widow (Leslie Caron); Armande and her grandson Luc (Aurelien Parent Koenig), and, ultimately her daughter Caroline (Carrie-Anne Moss); Joséphine, who shifts class and undertakes a new life as café owner; the gypsy Roux, Anouk, and Vianne herself; even the Mayor, the Comte de Reynaud, and Caroline. Vianne's method is to offer chocolate to everyone—the magical chile-flavored hot chocolate, or some "favorite" variety she can so miraculously discern from the Mayan calendar circle. She never disagrees with the mayor, the priest, with the ladies of the village, or with Armande; she just smiles a beatific smile and offers. The young priest, more interested in Elvis Presley music than in eternal damnation, finally changes his sermon (previously dictated by the Comte's instructions and focusing on original sin and retribution) to a meditation on tolerance: "We can't measure goodness by what we deny, but by what we embrace, who we include." It is Vianne who has brought about this new view of self and community.

Vianne uses 2000-year-old recipes as she offers a birthday feast for Armande and prepares a Chocolate Festival for Easter afternoon. A most interesting kind of shot is repeated throughout the film: frames, those around windows, doors, church pews and aisles—surround the actors as if in paintings. This is most evident at the end, when Vianne offers a healing glass to the chocolate-sodden mayor, just as Christ offered his hand to heal Jairus's daughter, the blind man, and the leper. Twice the two are framed by the window, these set pieces in frames suggesting a diorama or painting. The footage of Armande's feast, prepared by Vianne, uses the same cinematic techniques as in *Babette's Feast*—so similar, in fact, that it is clear that Hallström is quoting Axel: as the guests drink the wine and sample the seafood and then the turkey with mole, they smile, their faces lit with warm candlelight, their expressions almost angelic in the perfection of the taste sensations, friendship, and love.

Babette's role as a Christ figure, serving a "Last Supper" or eucharist, is underscored by costume, dialogue, lighting, and music. Not only does she wear a crucifix (while Protestant Philippa wears an "empty" cross), but her black dress sports a white collar, very much like a clerical collar. Even before she arranges the feast, we see her in a Christlike role of miraculous serving. When she arrives and the sisters tell her they cannot afford to employ her, she says, "If you don't let me serve you, I will simply die," the word *serve* foreshadowing what is to come. The night Babette arrived, the sisters were reading the newspaper, turned to a photograph of a woman bending over a steaming pot—again a foreshadowing. Once Babette is installed, her help in the kitchen and her wise shopping, in cooking and serving the poor and aged, miraculously enable the sisters to "have more money than ever." As with Jesus' miraculous feeding of the five thousand, they now have a surfeit of resources to help the poor. Other parishioners thank God for Babette. Before the feast, however, Martine's Protestant anti-Catholicism takes over: she is worried that Babette's dinner will be some kind of popish witch's sabbath and dreams of the giant tortoise burning and Babette spilling wine (or blood). The contrast between Protestant Denmark and Catholic France is underscored by the fact that when Maestro Achille Papin arrives, the pastor and his family immediately converse with him in French. Likewise, when Babette appears in 1871 and presents the letter from Papin, the sisters can read it and speak with her in French. Knowing French was a sign of class and of education in the nineteenth century, especially for women. The fact that the French people are "Papists" (Catholic) is a problem to the Protestant community, but both Papin and Babette are accepted, at least at first.

Dour, cold, dark unfeeling puritanical Protestant Denmark is contrasted throughout *Babette's Feast* with the warm, sensual, light world of Catholic France, even though none of the film takes place there. The first images in the film are those of the coastal plain and the drying cod. In fact, in the viewer's memory, the film recedes into black and white, because even in color, there is an abundance of grays and blacks: black houses, dark gray robes, dark interiors. The image of the small group of aging parishioners gathered around the table for their weekly prayer meeting, singing "Jerusalem," sets the stage for the importance of both music and camera angle in this film. The hymn, the commensal breaking of bread, and the communal table gathering are repeated in the final scenes.

At Babette's feast, there are twelve around the table, as at the Last Supper; the camera angle of the table repeats the prayer-meeting scene from the beginning of the film. As the food and the different spirits—from amontillado sherry through 1860 Veuve Cliquot champagne, 1845 Clos Vougeot bordeaux, and finally cognac—take hold, the lighting lingers in close-ups on the faces of the elderly guests, now coming to understand and forgive each other. Although they had taken an ascetic pledge not to pay attention to the food or drink, they soon begin to enjoy and understand. The candlelight is warm, soft and endearing; camera shots suggest Scandinavian genre painting. Ethereal music plays in the background, all of it suggesting a kind of beatific vision of the paradise they seek. The dinner, says the general, is a love affair, with no difference between the bodily appetite and the spiritual appetite. He reveals that the entrée, cailles en sarcophage, is just like he had once had in Paris at the Café Anglais, but somehow does not understand that Babette must be the very same chef. He teaches the other guests how to deal with the dishes—drinking the turtle soup, spooning up the sauce from the quail. The general's second speech, begun as he taps his glass (symbolic of the priest ringing the bell at the moment of transubstantiation), shows his understanding of the gift of grace (in the English translation in the film, he uses the word "mercy"—"Mercy is infinite; mercy imposes no conditions"). Finally, in the last scene, after all the guests have left, Philippa, also an artist, embraces Babette as an equal for the first time and reiterates what Achille Papin has said about Philippa's voice and the role of the artist. Now, Babette, the great artist, "will delight the angels."

In resurrecting the genre of the women's film of the 1950s, the three directors change and universalize it. In these films, it is women who have created and served, women who have assumed the burden of Christlike suffering, women who have given to all. For Babette's feast, Vianne's chocolaterie, and Tita's dishes of fiery and fertilizing passion are not for women only, but are truly gifts of grace for everyone, including the viewers.

Notes

1. *Chocolat*, directed by Lasse Hallström. Miramax Films, 2000; Joanne Harris wrote the novel in 1999. *Like Water for Chocolate*, directed by Alfonso Arau. Miramax Films/Arau Films International, 1993; the novel by Laura Esquivel was published in Mexico in 1989, in the U.S. in 1992. *Babette's Feast*, directed by Gabriel Axel. Panorama Film International/Nordisk Film A/S, 1987; Isak Dinesen's (Karen Blixen's) short story "Babette's Feast" was first published in 1958 in the volume *Anecdotes of Desire*.
2. Nelson Foster and Linda S. Cordell, eds., *Chilies to Chocolate: Food the Americas Gave the World* (Tucson: University of Arizona Press, 1996); Sidney Mintz, *Tasting Food, Tasting*

Freedom: Excursions into Eating, Culture, and the Past (Boston: Beacon Press, 1996); Carole Counihan and Penny Van Esterik, eds., *Food and Culture* (New York: Routledge, 1997). See also Sian Griffiths and Jennifer Wallace, eds., *Consuming Passions: Food in the Age of Anxiety* (Manchester: Manchester University Press, 1998); Warren Belasco, *Appetite for Change: How the Counterculture Took on the Food Industry* (New York: Pantheon, 1990); and Sophie D. Coe, *America's First Cuisines* (Austin: University of Texas Press, 1994). There are now beginning to be more studies that take gender into account, such as *The Anthropology of Food and Body; Gender, Meaning, and Power*, ed. Carole Counihan (New York: Routledge, 1999) and several books by Sherrie Inness, among them *Kitchen Culture in America: Popular Representations of Food, Gender, and Race* (Philadelphia: University of Pennsylvania Press, 2001).

3. Sue Thornham, ed., *Feminist Film Theory: A Reader* (New York: New York University Press, 1999); E. Ann Kaplan. ed., *Feminism and Film* (New York: Oxford University Press, 2000).

4. See, for example, Kristin Hohenadel, "Mounting a Feast That Can Satisfy Other Hungers," *New York Times*, 10 September 2000.

5. Johannes Tauler, quoted in Ninian Smart, "Johannes Tauler," in *Encyclopedia of Philosophy*, vol. 8, ed. Paul Edwards (New York: Macmillan, 1967), 82.

6. John A. Mourant, "Luis de Molina," in *Encyclopedia of Philosophy*, vol. 7, ed. Paul Edwards (New York: Macmillan, 1967), 338.

7. Julian of Norwich, *Revelations of Divine Love*, trans. Elizabeth Spearing (New York: Penguin, 1998), 140.

8. Julian of Norwich, quoted in Denise Nowakowski Baker, *Julian of Norwich's "Showings": From Vision to Book* (Princeton, N.J.: Princeton University Press, 1994), 132.

9. B. A. Gerrish, "Martin Luther," in *Encyclopedia of Philosophy*, vol. 5, ed. Paul Edwards (New York: Macmillan, 1967), 111. See also B. A. Gerrish, *Grace and Reason: A Study in the Theology of Luther* (Oxford: Clarendon Press, 1962).

10. Caroline Walker Bynum, *Holy Feast and Holy Fast: The Religious Significance of Food to Medieval Women* (Berkeley and Los Angeles: University of California Press, 1987), 298. Hereafter, page numbers will be cited parenthetically in the text.

11. M. F. K. Fisher, foreword to *The Gastronomical Me*, in *The Art of Eating* (New York: Simon and Schuster, 1971), 353.

12. Mary Elizabeth Podles, "Babette's Feast: Feasting with Lutherans," *Antioch Review*, 50, no. 3 (1992): 551–67.

13. See Homi K. Bhabha, *The Location of Culture* (London: Routledge, 1994), 112–15. Diane Long Hoeveler, "Like Words for Pain/Like Water for Chocolate: Mouths, Wombs, and the Mexican Woman's Novel," in *Women of Color: Defining the Issues, Hearing the Voices*, ed. Diane Long Hoeveler and Janet Boles (Westport, Conn.: Greenwood Press, 2001), 123.

14. See Elizabeth H. Boone, "The 'Coatlicues' at the Templo Mayor," *Ancient Mesoamerica* 10, no. 2 (1999): 189–206; and Gloria Anzaldúa, *Borderlands: La Frontera*, 2nd ed. (San Francisco: Aunt Lute Books, 1999).

15. Caroline Walker Bynum, "Women Mystics and Eucharistic Devotion in the Thirteenth Century," in *Fragmentation and Redemption: Essays on Gender and the Human Body in Medieval Religion* (New York: Zone Books, 1992), 110, 115, and passim.

10

Food, Sex, and Power at the Dining Room Table in Zhang Yimou's *Raise the Red Lantern*

ELLEN J. FRIED

The 1992 film *Raise the Red Lantern* (*Da hong deng long gao goa gu*), based on the novel *Wives and Concubines* by Su Tong and directed by Zhang Yimou, chronicles a year in the lives of the four wives of Master Chen, a wealthy merchant. Lauded by critic Roger Ebert as a "Chinese film of voluptuous physical beauty and angry passions,"[1] its story line exposes the increasing jealousy and competition among the women in the Chen household that ultimately leads to tragedy and death. Literally translated as *The Great Red Lanterns Are Raised Aloft*, the title describes the humiliating daily ritual of hoisting and lighting large red lanterns at the house of the wife who is to be favored with the master's company that evening. The news is delivered as the wives and their servants stand around a central courtyard, tensely awaiting placement of the initial lantern. The bellowing announcement of the master's choice resonates throughout the household.

The wife singled out by the lantern lighting is also granted other privileges in this early-twentieth-century household, among them her selection of favorite dishes to be served at the family's next communal meal. In a world where women have little currency, the wives quickly learn to manipulate food traditions to flaunt their favorable position with the master. The dazzling array of food prepared for every meal and the family rituals surrounding its consumption provide a glimpse into a life in which, according to E. N. Anderson, a noted historian of Chinese food and customs, "table manners took on a vital importance quite unknown in many cultures."[2] In short, ritual and food are inseparable.

The Chinese have long been passionate about food. Recipes were recorded on bamboo, wood, and silk as long ago as the Chou dynasty (425–122 B.C.E.).[3] Culinary rules set down in the *Li Chi* (or *Book of Rites and Ancient Ceremonies*) and the *Analects of Confucious* are full of directions that minutely detail how, what, when, where, and with whom, a proper meal may be taken.[4] The lofty pedestal upon which food is placed is evidenced, too, by the traditional sayings "To the people, food is Heaven" and "Heaven loves the man who eats well." People commonly greet each other with the phrase "Have you eaten already?" or, more specifically, "Have you eaten rice yet?"[5] This preoccupation with food and eating has led one leading author of Chinese history, Lin Yu-Tang, to make the timeless observation, "If there is anything we are serious about, it is neither religion nor learning, but food. We openly acclaim eating as one of the few joys of this human life."[6] Yet another oft-quoted Chinese historian-anthropologist, K. C. Chang, has opined, "To say that the consumption of food is a vital part of the chemical process of life is to state the obvious, but sometimes we fail to realize that food is more than just vital. The only other activity that we engage in that is of comparable importance to our lives and to the life of our species is sex."[7]

The Chinese are connoisseurs of both. East Asian studies scholar Frederick Mote has explored ancient Chinese works of literature, dating back to the sixteenth century, in which food and sex are the core activities: "The . . . experience of food leads to the experience of sex, leading again to food, and then back to sex."[8] Sociologist Jack Goody, writing on cuisine and class, pointed out that the Ch'ing dynasty (1644–1911) was characterized as a time when "'the vocabularies of food and lust' overlapped and blended into a language of sensuality."[9] Indeed, the Chinese have a long history of keen interest in foods and rituals believed to stimulate sexual appetite and maintain sexual health.[10]

In addition to being pleasurable, it has long been believed that food consumed in the correct combination of yin and yang elements is absolutely essential to one's health and well-being. A meal goes well beyond mere sustenance: "at each meal a Chinese adds to his virtue, strengthening resistance to the ills of body and mind, curing ailments, or possibly, rendering himself capable of better work."[11] Food historian Reay Tannahill compares Chinese and Indian food cultures: both encompassed the belief that "food and drink were intimately bound up not only with the health of the body, but also with that of the mind and soul." As Tannahill eloquently summarizes the Chinese food experience, "To eat and drink correctly [is] as much an instrument of virtue as an expression of it."[12]

Those who control the selection and availability of this powerful life force can wield it for good or evil purposes. Thus, an injured child can be soothed with a sweet and a lover can be wooed with a favorite food. Conversely, an angry spouse or rival can serve bad food (or worse, poison) or refuse to eat altogether. Indeed, in a society where table manners are critical to the maintenance of social order, requesting strange food, refusing to eat what others are eating, or acting in defiance of custom, can all be powerful weapons of manipulation.[13] The Chen wives learn to manipulate the rituals related to food as one of the few means they have of controlling their lives.

Historically, Chinese women, especially wives and concubines, had little power of any kind. They were severely oppressed and "inferior economically and legally to their sisters in almost all known civilized societies."[14] Women who were not needed to work in the fields were expected to stay at home. A foreign missionary in nineteenth-century China observed that woman "never go anywhere to speak of, and live . . . the existence of a frog in a well."[15] This confined space could get crowded. The purchase of brides and concubines, a custom that dated back hundreds of years, permitted the master of the house to bring secondary wives and concubines into the communal home after his principal marriage; their number was limited only by the master's desires and financial means.[16] *Raise the Red Lantern* focuses on just such an arrangement and the human drama it spawns with each communal dinner that reflects the business of the bedchamber, centuries of culinary etiquette, and the vengeance of competing concubines.

This essay argues that communal adherence to food etiquette and the rituals of dinner reflect societal behavior critical for all aspects of household and societal harmony; if dinner is disrupted, so is the flow of daily life. Conversely, an imbalance of power or discontent among family members can lead to the unraveling of family customs, including the deliberate sabotage of food rituals.[17] Thus, when the fourth wife of Master Chen attempts to elevate her status in the household by manipulating the rules of communal dining, the delicate balance of family power is disrupted and centuries of ancestral customs are threatened with extinction. Her punishment for challenging the established hierarchy is harsh and swift; once the threat to family harmony is removed, the rhythm of life—and, by extension, the ritual of communal dining—may resume.

Film critics and sociologists alike have interpreted the brutal subjugation of the Chen wives as a metaphor for the oppression suffered by all Chinese under both prerevolutionary and subsequent communist rule. One film reviewer described the machinations that rend the family fabric dutifully woven by generations of Chen patriarchs and their mistress as "a parable for the corruption of modern society in China."[18] Treatment of food custom and ritual in *Raise the Red Lantern* may be viewed literally as artful power play within the family, as well as a symbolic, theatrical device that reflects the dissolution of the family, and by extension, of an oppressed society. There is much to learn about all these social and political systems by observing the connections among food, sex, and power at the Chen family dining room table.

The Fourth Mistress

When *Red Lantern* begins, the image on the screen is the face of the leading character, Songlian, played by actress Gong Li. Her stunning beauty is evident, though she is clearly pained and stares straight ahead with little expression and mournful eyes. "Mother, stop. You've been talking for three days," she intones flatly. "You always speak of money. I'll get married . . . to a rich man." Her stepmother warns Songlian that she will be forever relegated to the role of a concubine. "Let me be a concubine," Songlian replies, "Isn't that a woman's fate?"

For millions of women in China, the answer was yes. Prenuptial talk was always of money; its transfer marked the entry of wives, concubines, and maids into a household.[19] Arranged marriages often resulted in unhappy unions.[20] The traditional Chinese family was organized around men and male authority. When the typical teenager first entered the new household, she was at her weakest and most miserable; she lacked status in the family and was quickly subordinated to her husband. Women were essentially outsiders, described by historian Kay Ann Johnson as doomed "temporary members or future deserters of their natal families and stranger-intruders in their new husbands' families."[21] It is little wonder that Songlian's spirit is defeated by the prospect of marriage.

As she sets out for the Chen household plainly dressed in a white shirt, dark skirt, and leggings, her hair in pigtails tied with ribbon, Songlian looks every inch the plaintive schoolgirl. She had attended university for sixth months, allowed briefly to taste freedom in the emerging China of the 1920s. When the death of her father decimates the family's finances, she finds herself falling through the looking glass of ancient, timeless custom, betrothed as fourth wife to a wealthy merchant. By walking alone on the dusty road that leads to her new existence, Songlian desperately tries to maintain her independence, ignoring the bridal sedan sent to fetch her. She carries a sole suitcase.

Addressed by the household servants as the fourth mistress, Songlian is chided for arriving in so pedestrian a fashion. She is quickly attended to by servants, bathed, coifed, and dressed in sumptuous silks. The red lanterns are lit; it is family custom for a new bride to enjoy nine consecutive nights of the master's attention. She is also introduced to another old family custom—a precoital foot massage administered by a servant. The massage is intended to keep a woman and her feet healthy so that she is better able to serve her man. The distinctive rhythmic sound of the massage echoes throughout the compound as a humiliating reminder to those who have not been chosen for the evening. The master settles himself into a chair in the fourth house, visually inspects his most recent acquisition and, obviously satisfied with the novelty of his new wife, remarks to a seemingly emotionless Songlian that "educated girls are different." He refuses Songlian's request to douse the lights, and without further fanfare, the marriage is consummated. The third mistress, however, disrupts the evening by feigning illness and sending a servant to fetch the master. Chen complains, but nevertheless leaves the marital bed; a loud announcement precedes the transfer of lanterns to the third house.

The next morning, Songlian is instructed to meet her "sisters" (the other wives) before breakfast.[22] The first mistress is appalled by Songlian's youth and inclusion in the household; to her, the master's multiple marriages subject them all to a life of sin. Second mistress, however, outwardly welcomes her "fourth sister." Songlian is prevented from meeting the third sister since the master is still asleep in her house.

Songlian is shown rooms where the daily family meal and important meetings are held. Enormous portraits of Chen family ancestors cast a watchful eye over the square, lacquered dining table surrounded by carved stools. The looming presence of the ancestors is customary; as culinary historian and cookbook author Eileen Yin-Fei Lo explains, "In Chinese households, the gods eat with us at our table, and food is what we offer as gifts, as sacrifices to them. We hang their images in our kitchens and dining rooms to remind us of their continual presence."[23] Songlian is brought before the ancestral altar, yet sullenly refuses to kowtow to their images. This is just the first of many occasions upon which she is admonished to obey family customs.

Chinese Foodways

Typically, everyday meals in China were communal occasions, a gathering of husband, wife, and other family members.[24] *Commensality* is the term used by sociologists for the activity of eating together; commensal partners are people who share a meal. Although commensal eating can be dangerous, with its risks of intentional or accidental foodborne illness and exposure to communicable diseases, the sharing of food has long been recognized as an important means of expressing social affiliations and customs. Commensal relationships are not static, but change continually in relation to other life events. As Jeffery Sobal explains, "Commensal relationships are revealed by who is present or not invited, who is seated at the same table or elsewhere, who is seated adjacently or opposite, and who is seated on the right or left. Propinquity during meals provides a social map of roles, reference groups, status, and social networks." In other words, "you are who you eat with."[25]

Individual and group behavior at meals is defined by social custom. Margaret Visser, an authority on many subjects relating to the table, explains that the proscribed "rituals of dinner" have been set in place for myriad reasons: for example, good manners are essentially imposed as a safety measure "to protect us from other people's roughness and greed, and from the consequences of pandering to our own lower instincts."[26] In China, intricate instructions that detail every aspect of proper commensal behavior have been the rule for thousands of years.[27]

Elaborate banquets were the hallmark of many Chinese imperial rulers. Literally thousands of people on the palace staff were responsible for food-related matters during the Zhou dynasty (1122 to 770 B.C.E.).[28] Equally elaborate table and food rituals provided the choreography for every participant. These behaviors, as well as simpler instructions for gentlemen to follow while going about the business of their daily lives, were chronicled in the *Li Chi* (*Book of Rites and Ancient Ceremonies*) some 1,200 years after the Zhou period. The rules of dining etiquette instructed, "Do not roll the rice into a ball; do not bolt down the various dishes; do not swill down (the soup.) Don't make a noise in eating; do not crunch the bones with the teeth; do not put back fish you have been eating; do not throw the bones to the dogs; do not snatch (at what you want.) Do not (try to) gulp down soup with vegetable in it, nor add condiments to it; do not keep picking the teeth, nor swill down the sauces. If a guest adds condiments, the host will apologize for not having had the soup prepared better."[29] These admonitions would be perfectly applicable at the Chen family table.

Confucius, too, weighed in on matters of the table. He said, of the perfect gentleman, "Even if meat is plentiful, he does not let it overpower the food. It is only with wine that there is no set limit, but he does not drink to the point of confusion. He does not eat to excess."[30] Author and historian Eileen Yin-Fei Lo, who was born near Canton, emigrated to the United States in 1959. She fondly recalls her Ah Paw's (grandmother's), many discourses about food according to Confucius: "[He] desired rice to eat at its whitest and meat to be finely chopped, but when food was overcooked he would not eat. When fish or meat had become tainted, or had lost its color, or had an odor he thought distasteful, he would not eat. He insisted that the food he ate be in season, not preserved, and sauce for it had to enhance it, not change it. He drank wine, but not to excess. Nor did he overeat and he would have no meal that did not have some ginger."[31]

For millennia, diners have observed a sequence of events related to each meal, whether a banquet or small family dinner. For example, the *Book of Rites* prescribes intricate ritual behavior for the host and his guests to follow before any food is eaten; much posturing according to social rank comes first.[32] Visser points out that table manners in all cultures have long traditions that specify "rituals of starting." These rules delay the beginning of eating and are critical to the concept of politeness. It is, she explains, a way of overriding the impulse to just dig in, as well as a means of controlling hunger so that other obligations may be tended to, such as gratitude for the food and the awareness of others at the table.[33] It is against this background of rich cultural history relating to food and ritual that the maneuvering by the Chen wives at successive family meals is best understood.

The First Communal Meal

On her second day in the household, Songlian is called to her first family meal. The master sits next to his first mistress; the second mistress and Songlian are also seated at the table. A phalanx of servants lines the walls. Each diner has a bowl of rice and chopsticks; the table is laden with assorted dishes. The third mistress is nowhere in sight; the family doctor is purportedly writing a prescription for her previous evening's illness. When she does appear, her sauntering gait and wordless inspection of Songlian underscore the insouciance of her late arrival. The master surveys the scene and instructs his wives, "Songlian is new here. You sisters must get along with one another. Let's eat."

This admonition is bound to fall on deaf ears. Studies reveal that women who are denied access to legitimate roles of authority within family and society will manipulate "interpersonal relationships and emotional ties to gain influence over their lives and to partially overcome the imposed handicaps of male-dominated authority structures." New brides are often viewed as a threat to the existing family solidarity. Barred from overt power, they turn to "informal, indirect or concealed ways" to influence their relationship with men. Of course, the wives and concubines may seemingly live in harmony, while in reality, they are constantly quarreling and maneuvering for a favorable position in the household.[34]

Bound by custom, the first and second mistresses reach out to offer Songlian food. It is the only time we see the first wife smile. The third wife does not participate in the welcoming ritual. The master notices that Songlian is not eating; she offers simply that she does not like meat.[35] The other women look both puzzled and pained that the new family member is not pleased with the meal, since this reflects poorly on their hospitality. The master inquires about the day's selection of vegetarian dishes. A servant pulls an extensive menu from his pocket and recites: "Fragrant mushrooms, chrysanthemum moss hair, bird's nest, thrice-fried mushrooms, five color vegetables, vegetarian hot-pot and hearts of cactus." All turn expectant faces to Songlian, assuming that one of the dishes will entice her to eat. She does not react. Master breaks the silence to explain that according to family custom, the wife with the lighted lanterns also enjoys the privilege of ordering a favorite dish. "What would you like?" he asks Songlian. Her answer is spinach and bean curd; simple and unadorned. The master orders an additional item of his own: young bean sprouts.

Although the menu seems extravagant, the wide variety of foods at one meal is typical, especially for an upper-class household. Food is a way of displaying one's wealth and good breeding, and a socially sanctioned indulgent pleasure. Moreover, by offering many dishes of meat, fish, and vegetables, a host affords each diner the opportunity to select foods he enjoys, while simultaneously consuming a meal comprised of balanced elements.[36] In the Chen household, a bountiful table is also a symbol of power and affluence. Several servants are devoted to producing food for the family's pleasure. The day's selection not only observes centuries-old food traditions; it also keeps the kitchen and household staff apprised of the political and sexual machinations of the master and his wives. Aware of each wife's favorite dish, the staff can surmise in which house the master spent the night based on the dishes requested for the communal meal.

For the Chinese, the consumption of the proper amount and type of food is essential to maintaining one's balance and health; imbalance may promote illness and disease. The ideal amount to eat at every meal, as every Chinese parent recites, is only *ch'i fen pao*—what can be described as "70 percent full."[37] Typical family meals and elaborate banquets both follow the same basic structural rules. Meals are based on the complementary pairing of yin (the feminine, cooling, dark and yielding foods) and yang (the masculine, heating, bright and hard foods). Eating is considered yin, while drinking is considered yang.[38] A properly balanced meal should include dishes that feature the five basic tastes: sweetness, brininess (or saltiness), sourness, spiciness, and bitterness.[39] Cooking methods also figure into the equation; dishes prepared by varying techniques will be incorporated into each meal to achieve balance. Cooking techniques thought to have a yang influence on food are roasting and frying in deep fat or by stir-frying. Yin influenced techniques include steaming, poaching, and boiling. Achieving the perfect balance of yin and yang is further complicated by the belief that the basic yin or yang nature of a particular food may change depending upon the foods with which it is paired and the cooking method used.[40]

Each meal must also reflect a balance of *fan* and *ts'ai*. *Fan* is rice or cooked rice; the term embraces all cereal and starch dishes including porridge, steamed bread and noodles. *Ts'ai* originally meant vegetable; it now refers to the accompanying dishes, such as vegetables, meat, or fish. Suitable quantities of both must be consumed at each meal to achieve the proper balance. Another balancing factor to consider, for both culinary and medicinal purposes, is the consumption of heating and cooling foods. The notion of hot—or *jeh*—foods in this instance does not refer to temperature, but instead to the food's yang properties; they need to be paired with cooling or *liang* foods to maintain balance.[41] There is no unanimity as to which foods are hot and which are cold. However, Anderson's categorizations are generally accepted; hot foods are comprised of animals with fatty flesh, such as mutton and dog, oily nuts, such as peanuts, spices including chili peppers and ginger, and strong alcoholic drinks; cold foods are comprised of most fruits, bland, low-calorie vegetables, and plants that grow in water, since water is considered cold. Most grains, such as rice, are neutral. Vegetables are considered cooling as they are generally bland and crisp, and prepared by steaming and boiling. The heavy, protein-rich fare of feasts is often stir-fried, spiced and heavily flavored; such foods are considered "heating."[42]

The pairing of yin and yang is also achieved through contrasting the textures of crisp and soft, colors, flavors, fragrances and cooking methods. Flavorings and seasonings also reveal the yin and yang pairing principle in sweet and sour (sugar and vinegar), soy sauce and rice wine, ginger and scallion, and salt and pepper. Chinese food expert Barbara Tropp explains the principle's application with chili: while chili alone presents a strong yang taste, adding a pinch of sugar (yin) rounds out the flavor; what Tropp describes as a "fiery full flavor instead of just fire." She adds that a Chinese cook's ability to harmonize yin and yang in each dish is "inbred in the culture . . . a gentle intuition and a visual and sensory confirmation of what does and doesn't go together."[43]

With these principles in mind, we turn to the vegetarian dishes on the Chen family table at Songlian's first communal meal. Each is being offered to the new wife in accordance with the timeless principles of Chinese culinary traditions; a study in contrasting tastes, textures, colors and medicinal benefits. The fourth mistress's refusal to partake of these ancient delights is symbolic, symptomatic of her refusal to participate in family customs. It portends her doom.

Fragrant Mushrooms and Thrice-Fried Mushrooms

Mushrooms are, according to Eileen Yin-Fei Lo, a basic necessity. They are most often dried and must be soaked before cooking. The variety known as fragrant mushroom (or shiitake, outside of China) has a flat, thin cap and is "prized more for its taste and dusky aroma than for its texture. Straw mushrooms, with long caps, are served to guests as a mark of respect. Cloud ears, a dried black fungus that is a relative of the mushroom are also dried; when reconstituted in water, they "soften and glisten and resemble flower petals." It is easy to imagine a delectable dish comprised of three different mushrooms, stir-fried. Or, the recipe may call for three different methods of cooking the mushrooms; first soaking, then boiling and finishing by stir-frying together with other ingredients. Fragrant mushrooms might be steamed with sugar, soy sauce, scallions, ginger, oil, and stock and served as an appetizer or a full course.[44]

Chinese gastronomy experts Hsiang Ju Lin and Tsuifeng Lin offer the following observations and advice regarding Chinese mushrooms: "People tend to misuse mushrooms, slivering them finely to spread out their flavour, but to their detriment. They should be left whole or cut in half, juicy, fragrant and smooth. Do not add other things to them, for it takes away from the pure enjoyment of mushrooms. Do not talk when eating mushrooms, or you spoil the flavour. Chew a mushroom as little as possible, only press out its hidden juices between tongue and teeth." The Lins consider properly selected mushrooms to be "almost perfect in shape, texture and flavour"; indeed, they describe their flavor as "sublime."[45] Such sentiments could certainly account for the preparation by the Chen cooks of two mushroom dishes for one meal.

Chrysanthemum Moss Hair

Moss hair is a variety of seaweed that enjoys several descriptive names—hair vegetable, black moss, or hair seaweed; it resembles thin, coarse, black strands of human hair. Like other dried ingredients, it must be soaked before cooking.[46] As it does not have much flavor of its own, moss hair is used primarily for its appearance and texture. Accordingly, renowned chef Kennth Lo's recipe for Chinese seaweed soup combines hair vegetable seaweed together with bamboo shoots, lotus roots, dried mushrooms, tiger-lily buds, wood ears, red bean curd cheese, snow peas and transparent noodles.[47] Chrysanthemum flower petals are used mostly as a decorative garnish, or steeped for tea.

Five-Color Vegetables

An infinite variety of vegetables may be combined for variations in color, texture, taste, and to balance hot and cold elements. A marvelous example is Eileen Yin-Fei Lo's "Harmonious Vegetable Stir-Fry," composed of ginger, mung bean sprouts, garlic, carrots, and cucumber stir-fried in peanut and sesame oils. Ms. Lo describes her preparation as "a dish of harmony, neither too *yin* nor to *yang*. The mung bean sprouts and cucumbers are essentially cooling, carrots are warming, and though garlic, like most spices, is warm, it is often added to other foods for its aroma and taste and as a digestive aid that tends to lower blood pressure and cholesterol. Stir-frying . . . is considered warming, but peanut and sesame oils are neutral."[48] Lo opines that the dish is quite healthy because of its careful balance of elements. No doubt, the Chen household's five-color vegetable dish was created with these same principles in mind.

Bird's Nests

Bird's nests are an expensive and exotic ingredient that were—and remain—a treat for special occasions. In addition to its culinary appeal, it is also reputed to have myriad health properties, including the preservation of skin's youthful appearance. It would find a place on the Chen table both because of its opulence and its medicinal attributes. The nests themselves are not consumed; rather, what is so prized is the dried spittle of a breed of swifts found in Southeast Asia; the birds secrete a mucous substance that acts as glue and dries to a thin layer that lines the nest.[49] To harvest this delicacy, boys traditionally climbed long bamboo scaffolding to enter cliffside caves where the birds nested.

The nests are sold dried and must be soaked for hours, and picked clean of feathers and other debris before cooking. The result is both jellylike and crunchy. Since bird's nests have virtually no flavor of their own, their taste will reflect the ingredients with which they are prepared. Traditionally, bird's nests are enjoyed as a sweet dessert or in a rich, savory soup.[50]

Hearts of Cactus

It is difficult, if not impossible, to find cactus in western Chinese cookbooks. The dish served at the Chen household's table might have contained "dragon fruit," a member of the cactus family. The fruit "appears shining red and olive-shaped" and its white or red flesh is sweet. It is most often compared to a kiwi. According to a Chinese purveyor, its versatility as a fruit, flower, vegetable, and medicine accounts for its popularity in many Asian cuisines.[51]

Vegetarian Hot Pot

The hot pot on the Chen table has a large round base for broth, which is heated by burning charcoal; the fire is vented through a funnel or chimney. These cooking vessels are often called Mongolian hot pots, although a Mongolian hot-pot dish would contain lamb.[52] Diners choose morsels of food from a selection on the table and place them in the steaming broth to cook. The participation of the diners in the cooking process often makes this a popular dish for festive meals; it is a quintessential commensal meal experience.[53]

Spinach and Bean Curd

Bean curd, or tofu, is ubiquitous in Chinese cooking. It is highly nutritious, provides a significant amount of protein, and assumes the flavor of whatever food it accompanies. The custard-like curd is made from soybeans that are soaked, ground, and mixed with water before being slightly heated and formed into cakes. Bean curd comes in many forms—fresh, wet, dried, and preserved with wine, as cakes and skins—and can often be prepared to mimic other foods such as meat and chicken. Spinach and bean curd is a common simple stir-fried dish.[54] Indeed, the third mistress seems both amused by Songlian's simple taste in food and disdainful of her refusal to eat meat.[55] Songlian does not elaborate on her distaste for meat aside from her simple statement; her behavior, however, sets her apart from the others. In the pantheon of vegetables, spinach is considered cool and slippery.

Young Bean Sprouts

Bean sprouts are most often grown from the green mung bean, though soybeans are also sprouted. Sprouts must be fresh and crunchy; they have a subtle flavor and are very nutritious. "Fragile, they must be eaten very soon after they sprout or they well lose their fresh, lovely taste," notes Ken Hom.[56] Bean sprouts are enjoyed as a salad, simply tossed with rice vinegar, salt and sugar, or in a stir-fry with other vegetables. The master's penchant for young bean sprouts is consistent with his taste in young brides.

More Food Games

After a bountiful, communal meal, Songlian visits with second mistress. Flushed with her seeming good fortune, the new wife giddily asks her "sister" if foot massages are a nightly occurrence. She is instructed that "if you can manage a foot massage every night, you'll soon be running this household." Songlian takes this advice literally; it will eventually lead to her descent into madness.

On the second marital evening, third mistress again attempts to lure the master out of Songlian's bed by feigning sickness; this time he refuses to leave. Undeterred in her quest to regain the master's attention, third mistress awakens the household at dawn with her operatic singing on the rooftop. Songlian ventures outside to investigate and returns to find the master fondling her maid; Songlian is visibly shaken. Master Chen goes on the defensive at first and chides Songlian for leaving their bed; he then scolds her for reacting child-ishly to his dalliance with her maid. Finally, master attempts to assuage Songlian's feelings by suggesting they go to her favorite dumpling house.[57] When Songlian rebuffs all attempts at appeasement, master punishes her by moving the lanterns to the third house.

The master cannot join his wives at the next day's communal meal. Left alone, the mistresses begin to bicker. The third mistress, who benefited from the master's displeasure with Songlian has selected the menu. Songlian remarks on the absence of spinach and bean curd; third mistress replies that there are too many vegetable dishes and orders another meat dish, pork steamed in lotus leaves.[58] Songlian storms away from the table, breaking both the rules of etiquette and family meal customs. The third mistress's sham attempt to maintain a balance of *ts'ai* dishes fools no one; the kitchen servants gossip about the abundance of meat dishes, well aware that the master has just taken a young bride who does not eat meat.

Acts of retribution begin to escalate at dizzying speed as the women vie for the master's attention. Songlian, aware that giving birth to a male heir is criti-cal to her status, is warned to be wary of the second mistress, who poisoned the third mistress's food when they were both pregnant. The second mistress wheedles Songlian into giving her a haircut that would make her appear more youthful and attractive to the master; Songlian manages to cut the second mis-tress's ear in the process. The second mistress uses the injury to her advantage to convince the master that she needs his comforting presence for many eve-nings. Meanwhile, Songlian mistreats her illiterate maid at every opportunity; she later discovers that the maid has a pin-studded effigy with Songlian's name written on it. Songlian wrings out of the illiterate maid the crushing news that it was the second mistress who, though outwardly friendly to Songlian, painted the calligraphy on the doll. The maid harbors a festering hatred for Songlian because Songlian's arrival as the fourth mistress has destroyed the maid's fantasy of being elevated to that status. Songlian also discovers that the third mistress is engaged in an illicit affair with the family doctor. Goaded on by the intense competition and a sense of emptiness, Songlian creates a plan to ensure that her own lanterns will be lit every night.

The first step toward achieving her goal occurs when Songlian unexpect-edly refuses to join the communal meal, even though spinach and bean curd—and the other mistresses—await her and the master. Chen balks at first and points out that staying in the fourth house to eat "is not right"; it is dis-turbing to him to disrupt the family food ritual. Nevertheless, to appease his new bride, he acquiesces. The mistresses, already seated in the dining room, are speechless when a servant informs them that the master and the fourth mistress will not be joining them. The third mistress quickly recovers, how-ever, and "wants to make it clear" that she, too, demands that her own meals be served in her house when her lanterns are lit. The three wives dine alone at the last communal meal depicted in the film.

Songlian, who has deceitfully announced that she is pregnant, uses this artifice to insist on taking all meals in her house. A jubilant master often joins her. While Songlian reclines in bed, the maid spoon-feeds her lotus-seed soup, intended to ensure fertility and longevity.[59] The other mistresses dine without the master. A Mongolian hot pot sits in the middle of the table; the mistresses carefully select tidbits of food to cook in the communal vessel. Steam rises from the broth to frame the third mistress's face as she verbally torments the second mistress about Songlian bearing a son; the second mistress has produced only a "useless girl." The first mistress listens to the other two women trade barbs and impatiently admonishes them: "All this food can't shut you two up! This family will perish some day in your hands."

The consumption of food is no longer a pleasure; rather, it is employed as another tool in the relentless struggle for recognition and influence. Songlian has broken the cultural and moral code that guides food consumption and social interaction in the Chen household. She had calculated that by having the master with her every evening, her fabricated pregnancy would soon become real. However, the subterfuge is soon uncovered by her maid, who, while casually spitting into her Mistress's laundry, discovers menstrual blood on a pair of white pants. Songlian is severely punished for deceiving the master; outraged, he orders that her lanterns be extinguished and covered with black cloth. To further her shame, Songlian is also blamed for causing the subsequent death of the maid.

Thoroughly disgraced, Songlian is forced to eat alone in her house. Once the desired end of much scheming, eating alone has become an instrument of ostracism and punishment. Seated at a small table, Songlian orders a servant to fetch some wine along with her food; she is celebrating her twentieth birthday. This desperate act is pitiful by any cultural standard; it is particularly painful in a culture that marks all rites of passage with food-laden celebrations and feasts. Songlian ignores the teachings of Confucius and drinks to excess. In her stupor, feeling abandoned and alone, she wallows in self-pity and tells of the third mistress's relationship with the family doctor. The second mistress pounces on this information and sends servants to hunt down the lovers; they are discovered in town, in a hotel, in bed. This transgression leads to the third mistress's death by hanging, by order of the master, at the hands of the family servants.

The last glimpse of Songlian reveals a woman who has lost her sanity; she wanders aimlessly through the house, unaware of the loudly announced arrival of the fifth mistress. Songlian is again dressed in the clothing of a university student, and she appears oblivious to the rhythmic tapping sound of the new wife's foot massage. Sentenced to live inside her own personal purgatory, it seems that Songlian will not be joining the communal family meal to welcome her new sister.

Film reviews and criticism

Western film reviewers were generally lavish in their praise for *Raise the Red Lantern*.[60] The film was nominated for many awards, including the 1992 Academy Award for best foreign language film. It captured quite a few prizes, including the best foreign film award at both the 1992 New York Film Critics Circle Awards and the 1993 British Academy Awards.[61] No work of art, of course, is entirely without its detractors. Among those few that found fault was a respected Chinese journalist who argued that Zhang created a film so "rife with historical and cultural inaccuracies" that it must have been created solely for "the casual pleasures of foreigners."[62] Others leveled criticisms at what they perceived to be Zhang's efforts to tailor his films to appeal to a Western sense of Eastern exoticism.[63] These critics accused Zhang of creating rituals centered on sexual practices that never existed, with the sole purpose of making a profitable film that would be attractive to Western audiences.

Although most of the reviews and essays mention the favored wife's menu selection, it is depicted as just one of many means of manipulation practiced by Master Chen and his wives. It is remarkable, however, that critics and scholars alike have otherwise ignored the central role of food and dining rituals, so important in Chinese culture. Donald Sutton acknowledges that Zhang has created specific rituals solely for dramatic effect, such as the central act of raising a red lantern to highlight the master's sexual intent for the evening. However, he points out that rituals of every conceivable type permeate Chinese culture and that the sense of *li*, or proper ritual, is "inseparable from social mores" and at the heart of Confucian tradition. Sutton argues that Zhang had to depict precommunist society on the screen in a way that would appeal both to Eastern and Western audiences and also appease rigid communist contemporary censors. Instead of criticizing the director's use of fanciful rituals steeped in visual and aural cues, Sutton praises the "invention of the red lantern ritual" as an effective means of recounting history. The ritual of the lantern is purposefully charged with sexual tension, is an object of intense competition, and represents a unifying image that governs the family's life. While the specific ritual may not be historically accurate, the behavior of the family around it is certainly consistent with social history.[64]

The activities and sentiments of the Chen family are mirrored in the descriptions of Chinese society detailed by Cheng Ch-eng-K'un in a 1946 issue of *Social Forces*. Cheng paints the "characteristic traits" of the Chinese with a very broad brush yet still provides an accurate overview of family behavior. He first hails the noble virtue of patience; this, he instructs, was developed as a result of living with large, multigenerational families that included concubines. Each member of the family had duties assigned by tradition; this gave the illusion of domestic harmony, "but no one who had lived in the institution could escape consciousness of the diversities of emotional conflicts which formed the cross-currents underneath and which were greatly complicated by all the elaborate codes of decorum handed down from antiquity." This code of conduct included the ability to "take an insult with all possible placidity" from a higher member of the family hierarchy and the repression of desires and impulses that were not acceptable in society, especially between the sexes. Chinese girls were essentially kept indoors after the age of twelve. Children were taught that their "life companion" was predestined; to choose a spouse on one's own was but useless rebellion against fate. A Chinese wife was expected to "strive to maintain her equanimity" when a concubine was brought into the home, though her faithfulness was expected even beyond her husband's death. Custom encouraged severe punishment for women who violated the rules. A sense of fatalism, particularly in matrimonial affairs, resulted in an attitude that it was both useless and against the process of nature to attempt to improve or change the conditions of one's life.[65]

The rituals of *Red Lantern* can be interpreted either as historical metaphors for the tyranny of a centuries-old male-dominated society or a thinly veiled criticism of a contemporary dictatorship; in other words, they are timeless. So, too, are the food rituals and food games of Master Chen and his wives. Chinese meals remain communal; each diner gets a bowl of rice and a pair of chopsticks. A variety of food is placed on the table all at once and diners choose what appeals to them. Chinese table manners have changed little from the ancient *Book of Rites*.[66] The unraveling of food customs, and the rituals of commensality, can portend the dissolution of the family or of a society. When the third mistress slams down her chopsticks and storms out of the dining room, perhaps patience is no longer available in the abundance described by Cheng: storming away from the table certainly demonstrates both a short temper and a lack of manners. It also delivers a powerful message, one that is understood in virtually all cultures.

As anthropologist Sidney Mintz explains, "For us humans, then, eating is never a 'purely biological' activity. . . . The foods eaten have histories associated with the pasts of those who eat them; the techniques employed to find, process, prepare, serve, and consume the foods are all culturally variable, with histories of their own. Nor is the food ever simply eaten; its consumption is always conditioned by meaning. These meanings are symbolic, and communicated symbolically; they also have histories. These are some of the ways we humans make so much more complicated this supposedly simple 'animal' activity."[67] The rituals surrounding the consumption of food in *Raise the Red Lantern*, while specific to Chinese culture, impart timeless cultural lessons for students of food and human nature.

Notes

1. Roger Ebert, "Raise the Red Lantern" (review), *Chicago Sun-Times*, 27 March 1992. *Raise the Red Lantern: Three Novellas* was written by Su Tong, trans. Michael S. Duke (New York: William Morrow, 1993).
2. E. N. Anderson. *The Food of China* (New Haven, Conn.: Yale University Press, 1988), 201.
3. Jacqueline M. Newman, "Chinese Meals," in *Dimensions of the Meal: The Science, Culture, Business and Art of Eating*, ed. Herbert L. Meiselman (Gaithersburg, Md.: Aspen, 2000), 163–77.

4. *Li Chi, Book of Rites and Ancient Ceremonies*, trans. James Legge (New Hyde Park, N.Y.: University Books, 1967), 163–75; *The Original Analects; Sayings of Confucius and His Successors*, trans. E. Bruce Brooks and A. Taeko Brooks (New York: Columbia University Press, 1998), 62.

5. Emily Hahn, *The Cooking of China* (New York: Time-Life, 1968), 7; Frederick Simoons, *Food in China; A Cultural and Historical Inquiry* (Boca Raton, Fla.: CRC Press, 1991), 15,14.

6. Lin Yu-Tang, *My Country and My People* (New York: John Day, 1954), 336–7. Lin notes that the Chinese, "gifted with teeth and driven by famine," have discovered that "roasted beetles and fried bee's chrysalis are great delicacies," but despite centuries of Mongol and European pressures to do so, "steadfastly refuse to discover or eat cheese."

7. K. C. Chang, "Introduction", *Food in Chinese Culture*, ed. K. C. Chang (New Haven, Conn.: Yale University Press, 1977), 3.

8. Frederick W. Mote, "Yuan and Ming", in Chang, ed., *Chinese Culture*, 248. The connection between the consumption of food and the consumption of one's partner during sex, both figuratively and literally, is itself an entire field of study. For example, the sexual aspect of cannibalism is the subject of Maggie Kilgour, *From Communion to Cannibalism: An Anatomy of Metaphors of Incorporation* (Princeton, N.J.: Princeton University Press, 1990); see also Joan Smith, *Hungry for You: From Cannibalism to Seduction—A Book of Food* (London: Vintage,1997). From a film perspective, the eating scene in *Tom Jones* (dir. Tony Richardson, 1963) is an unparalleled study in sexual foreplay.

9. Jack Goody, *Cooking, Cuisine and Class: A Study in Comparative Sociology* (Cambridge: Cambridge University Press, 1982), 114.

10. Simoons, *Food in China*, 25.

11. Hahn, *Cooking of China*, 7.

12. Reay Tannahill, *Food in History*, rev. and updated ed. (New York: Three Rivers Press, 1988), 127.

13. Susan Allport, *The Primal Feast: Food, Sex, Foraging, and Love* (New York: Harmony, 2000), 213–15. The author describes Gertrude Stein's cook's rebuke of Henri Matisse—she made him scrambled eggs instead of an omelet—as "a subtle gastronomic scolding that was understood by all." Similarly, angry Mexican wives may burn their husbands' tortillas, and a modern American wife may secretly serve dog food to a husband who rejects her attempts to change his daily fare to more refined cuisine. See Jeffrey M. Pilcher, "Industrial Tortillas and Folkloric Pepsi: The Nutritional Consequences of Hybrid Cuisines in Mexico," in *Food Nations*, ed. Warren Belasco and Philip Scranton (New York: Routledge, 2002), and Pat Conroy, *Prince of Tides* (New York: Bantam, 1987).

14. Olga Lang, *Chinese Family and Society* (Republic of China: Southern Materials Center, 1946), 54. (Lang's *Chinese Family and Society* was also published by Yale and Oxford University Presses in the same year.)

15. Kay Ann Johnson, *Women, the Family and Peasant Revolution in China* (Chicago: University of Chicago Press, 1983), 14.

16. The practice of keeping a concubine or mistress is so deeply ingrained in Chinese culture that contemporary lawmakers continue to grapple with its adverse impact on society. See "China Cracks Down on Bigamy, Concubines," CNN.com News, 29 April 2001. Online at http://www.cnn.com/2001/WORLD/asiapcf/east/04/29/china.marriage/; accessed 19 November 2002.

17. This essay does not attempt to provide an in-depth study of Chinese food customs; it focuses only upon those aspects of food and ritual depicted in the film that are crucial to the manipulative behavior of the wives. Thus, I have chosen not to explore the ritual importance of serving tea to a guest, ubiquitous in the film, nor have I provided a more detailed discussion of rice. The myriad sources cited in these notes may be consulted for excellent discourses on these two topics.

18. James Berardinelli, "Raise the Red Lantern" (review). Available online at www. Moviereviews.colossus.net/movies/r/raise.html; accessed May 23, 2002.

19. Rubie S. Watson, "Wives, Concubines, and Maids," in *Marriage and Inequality in Chinese Society*, ed. Rubie S. Watson and Patricia B. Ebrey (Berkeley and Los Angeles: University of California Press, 1991), 239. This study draws a clear distinction between wives and concubines: a wife enters a marriage accompanied by great ceremony, carried from her parents' home in a red sedan; concubines enter the new household quietly and are prohibited from riding in the bridal sedan. For life histories based on interviews with women who were concubines, see Maria Jaschok, *Concubines and Bondservants: The Social History of a Chinese Custom* (London: Zed, 1988).

20. Lang, *Chinese Family and Society*, 201, cites execution records from the Chinese Ministry of Justice for the period May through September 1925; almost half the total number involved the killing of spouses.
21. Johnson, *Women, the Family and Peasant Revolution in China*, 8–10.
22. Breakfast is not a communal meal in the Chen household. Chinese breakfasts are essentially simple fare: in the south, rice *congee* (a type of porridge), noodle soup, or dim sum is eaten; in the north, breakfast may typically consist of a deep-fried pastry, served with warm soy milk. Small dishes of peanuts, pickled vegetables, and other tidbits often accompany other breakfast foods throughout China. See Newman, "Chinese Meals," 168. Breakfast foods are rarely, if ever, mentioned in Chinese cookbooks.
23. Eileen Yin-Fei Lo, *The Chinese Kitchen* (New York: William Morrow,1999), 1.
24. Goody, *Cooking, Cuisine and Class*, 110.
25. Jeffery Sobal, "Dimensions of the Meal," in Meiselman, ed., *Dimensions*, 123.
26. Margaret Visser, *The Rituals of Dinner* (New York: Grove Press, 1991), 69.
27. Chang, "Introduction," 38.
28. Startling numbers are cited by historians. Chang, "Introduction," 11, offers the following statistics for the palace kitchens in the second century B.C.E.: Food and wine handlers numbered 2,271 persons, including 70 meat specialists; 128 chefs for family meals and another 128 guests; 335 grain, vegetable, and fruit chefs; 162 master dietitians; 342 fish specialists; 24 turtle and shellfish specialists; 28 meats dryers; 110 wine officers; 340 wine servers; 94 icemen; and 62 pickle and sauce chefs. Tannahill, *Food in History*, 140, notes that imperial banquets in the thirteenth century offered hundreds of dishes. Then, as now, the Chinese meal was comprised of a variety of dishes to ensure that each guest would find a few appealing and be able to construct a balanced dinner to suit his own taste.
29. *Li Chi*, 79.
30. *Sayings of Confucius*, 33.
31. Lo, *Chinese Kitchen*, 4–5.
32. Chang, Introduction, 38.
33. Visser, *Rituals of Dinner*, 145.
34. Johnson, *Women, the Family and Peasant Revolution in China*, 10; 17–18; Lang, *Chinese Family and Society*, 222.
35. Goody, *Cooking, Cuisine and Class*, 106–7. The influence of Buddhism required many meatless days in the calendar; however, meat was not consumed often because it simply wasn't available. According to Goody, "What there was, including dog, was eaten and even human flesh was not altogether taboo."
36. Tannahill, *Food in History*, 140.
37. Chang, "Introduction," 10.
38. Newman, "Chinese Meals," 173.
39. Ying-Shih Yu, "Han China," in Chang, ed., *Food in Chinese Culture*, 68.
40. Grace Young, *The Wisdom of the Chinese Kitchen* (New York: Simon and Schuster, 1999), 192.
41. Ibid., 166.
42. Anderson, *Food of China*, 203.
43. Barbara Tropp, *The Modern Art of Chinese Cooking* (New York: William Morrow, 1982),12.
44. Ibid., 21, 40, 539; Hahn, *Cooking of China*, 74; Lo, *Chinese Kitchen*, 27.
45. Hsiang Ju Lin and Tsuifeng Lin, *Chinese Gastronomy* (Vermont: Charles E. Tuttle, 1969), 142.
46. Lo, *Chinese Kitchen*, 24.
47. Kenneth Lo, *The Encyclopedia of Chinese Cooking* (New York: A and W, 1982), 73.
48. Ibid., 350.
49. Ibid., 75.
50. Bird's nests, along with the also exotic and expensive shark's fins, are often placed on the menu to impress and delight family and guest alike because of their expense. Both are extremely time-consuming and tedious to prepare. They do, however, figure prominently in Chinese gastronomy and are lovingly described in the authoritative Lin and Lin, *Chinese Gastronomy*, as "the gastronome's pets, the cook's burden, the host's pride and the guest's joy" (82).
51. China High Quality Farm Produce Network, online at www.vegnet.com.cn/gzncp/encpjj.htm Dragon Fruit; accessed November 15, 2002.

52. Lo, *Encyclopedia of Chinese Cooking*, 11. The Mongol invaders ruled for approximately one hundred years (*c.*1280–*c.*1368.) They were known for preparing enormous cauldrons of boiled mutton; this somehow became known as the Mongolian hot pot. However, the culinary practice of grilling thin slices of lamb is actually not Mongolian at all, but instead "the creation of twentieth-century Chinese Muslims."

53. Lo, *Encyclopedia of Chinese Cooking*, 74, describes several variations of hot pot; "First Rank Hot Pot" contains *beche de mer* (sea slug that is bought dried and must be soaked, cleaned, and boiled before use), cabbage, cauliflower, ham, dried mushrooms, chicken breast, duck, and hard-boiled eggs; "Chrysanthemum Fish Hot Pot" is comprised primarily of fish, but also includes chicken, port wine, kidney, chicken liver, roast peanuts, and plenty of vegetables. The petals of one large chrysanthemum bloom are used as garnish. Emily Hahn's recipe for Chrysanthemum Fire Pot is similiar; this version includes shellfish; see Hahn, *Cooking of China*, 26.

54. Ken Hom, *The Taste of China* (New York: Simon and Schuster, 1990), 24.

55. Simoons, *Food in China*, 35–36. Vegetarianism was primarily practiced according to religious, primarily Buddhist, beliefs; vows not to eat meat were often of limited duration and undertaken to achieve a particular goal.

56. Hom, *The Taste of China*, 24, 71.

57. Visits to a dumpling house for an afternoon snack of dim sum and tea was a popular Cantonese activity. See Lo, *Chinese Kitchen*, 363, for her memories of cherished childhood visits to a dumpling house. See also Young, *The Wisdom of the Chinese Kitchen*, 141–42, for a description of a traditional teahouse. Dim sum, which includes many varieties of dumplings (and which literally means "a dot on the heart") can be loosely translated as "heart's delight" or "to touch the heart." See Hom, *Taste of China*, 154.

58. Large dried, lotus leaves are used as wrappings for steamed foods. They are considered preferable to bamboo leaves, also used to wrap foods, because the lotus leaves add a slightly sweet taste. See Lo, *Encyclopedia of Chinese Cooking*, 26.

59. Simoons, *Food in China*, 115. The name for lotus seed is similar to the words for "many sons."

60. Berardinelli, "Raise the Red Lantern"; Janet Maslin, "Soulfully Speaking the Universal Language of the Oppressed," *New York Times*, 29 September 1995; online at www.spe.sony.com/classics/shanghai/nims/NewYork.html.; David Chute, "Golden Hours: On Location in China with Zhang Yimou," *Film Comment* 27, no. 2 (1991); online at www.filmlinc.com/fcm/archinv/yimou.htm.

61. Internet Movie Database, "Awards for *Da hang deng long gao gao gua* (1991)"; online at http://us.imdb.com/Tawards?0101640.

62. Qing Dai, "Raised Eyebrow for *Raise the Red Lantern*," trans. Jeanne Tai. *Public Culture*, no. 5 (1993): 333–37.

63. Mark Freeman. "Eastern Culture, Western Gaze: The Cinema of Zhang Yimou"; online at http://home.vicnet.net.au/~freeman/theory/zhangymou.htm.

64. Donald S. Sutton, "Ritual, History, and the Films of Zhang Yimou," *East-West Film Journal* 8, no. 2 (1994): 31–46.

65. Cheng Ch'eng-K'un, "Characteristic Traits of the Chinese People," *Social Forces* 25, no. 2 (1946):146–55.

66. For a contemporary description of Chinese table matters, see, Jacqueline Newman, "Chinese Table Manners," *Flavor and Fortune* 9, no. 2 (2002): 27–28.

67. Sidney Mintz, *Tasting Food, Tasting Freedom* (Boston: Beacon Press, 1996).

11

Anorexia Envisioned: Mike Leigh's *Life is Sweet*, Chul-Soo Park's *301/302*, and Todd Haynes's *Superstar*

GRETCHEN PAPAZIAN

Anorexia has become somewhat passé—at least according to my eighteen-, nineteen-, and twenty-year-old students at a women's college in the southeastern United States.[1] Unlike the college girls of the 1980s and early 1990s who held up the thin, emaciated body as an ideal, the women of the new millennium gaze at the anorexic body not with longing but with idle curiosity, indifference, and even disdain.[2] For them anorexia seems to be more of a historical phenomenon than a current one, or so they have said. The students in my recent course on food and culture seemed uninterested in the topic of anorexia. They read a variety of theoretical and literary representations/explanations of the disorder, but they didn't engage with the material or the subject. They were bored with it; their in-class comments and demeanor suggested that they'd heard it all before.[3] Then we watched Todd Haynes's *Superstar: The Karen Carpenter Story* (1987). The film galvanized them.

The visual text engaged their interest—their concern, their self-righteousness. Why? Most obviously, one might say it's because we live in a visual age. We go to films, watch television, and surf the Internet. Photographs, television, and film dominate print as modes of communication. We are "taught," through experience, how to "read" visual media. We understand character, elements of plot, techniques of narrative development, and even modes of argument from our experiences with visual forms. It should be unsurprising, then, if students perk up when confronted with visual texts in a course that traffics primarily in print ones. Nonetheless, I believe my students' response to

Superstar hints at something more. The visual representation of anorexia disarmed them; it reached past their boredom. It shook them up by making the disorder concrete and real in a way that went far beyond health class and girl power discussions of the topic. It also, I believe, undermined the defensive shield of repression that (young) women erect in the face of anorexia. They don't want to think about it because they don't want to think (or talk) about the ways they themselves (anorexic or not) use food in quirky (if not outright disorderly ways) as a means to define who they are. *Superstar* forced them to look—literally—at anorexia. And even more than this, their response suggests that the story of the anorexic is itself best—most effective—when told visually.

In discussing Mike Leigh's *Life is Sweet* (1991), Chul-Soo Park's *301/302* (1997), and Haynes's *Superstar*, this essay explores the relationship between anorexia and visuality, between stories of disorderly eating and visual representation, between structures of culture and structures of film. I want to be clear, however, that the essay is not about anorexia as a medical condition—nor could it or should it be. Instead, it is about filmatic representation, about how an idea of anorexia is represented. The essay contemplates how the disorder is visually constructed and displayed, and how the films meet the challenge of presenting the anorexic body and mindset. In doing so, it looks at the films' various accusations and conclusions about the disease (what causes it, sustains it, etc.). It takes up questions about representation, pondering the relationship of who (male directors) is representing whom (women and their bodies). It engages in a discussion about the nature of spectatorship, considering how we as viewers are taught to see and understand anorexia (through whose eyes? from what subject position?). All told, the essay argues that the anorexic's story is best told visually because, as a disease, as a disorder, anorexia is not only enmeshed in image—self-image, in particular—but it also manifests itself most compellingly (and most alarmingly) visually.

Although eating disorders (and accounts of them) have been around since the nineteenth century, they really only entered our cultural consciousness in a big way in the early 1980s. And for the most part this recounting took a literary form, beginning with Aimee Liu's 1979 autobiographical *Solitaire* and Steven Levencron's 1981 novel (and later made-for-TV movie) *The Best Little Girl in the World*. Accounts—fictional and autobiographic—abound from there. Despite the proliferation of such texts—or perhaps because of it—most fictions and autobiographies of anorexia are largely formulaic.[4] They focus on a good, middle-class white girl, beginning with either a diet (prompted by a comment about the girl's weight) or in the middle of the illness (focusing on the precariousness of the anorexic body). They then provide, in spectacular detail, the development of the disorder, including strange eating habits and exercise regimens. They end as Joan Brumberg notes "at the critical point of therapeutic intervention," which is generally also the moment at which the anorexic inexplicably decides to eat.[5] Mary Petrie demonstrates that the narrative voices in these texts are also remarkably similar— focused and obsessive in the early narratives, more sarcastic in the most recent ones.[6] Thus, as both Joan Brumberg and Mary Petrie remark, the fiction and autobiography of anorexia ultimately fail to offer significant insight into or real understanding of the anorexic and her experience. This is puzzling, especially given the scholarship that ties anorexic practices to narrative forms.

Literary and cultural critics have described and theorized historical and contemporary affiliations between food and the word, eating and reading, fasting and writing, and anorexia and the written text. In looking at the Modernist text, for example, Mark Anderson and Maude Ellmann argue that there is a connection between a rejection of language and food refusal—a link between the spare text and the slight body. Anderson claims that Modernist texts (such as Franz Kafka's *The Hunger Artist* and Herman Melville's *Bartleby, the Scrivener*) insist "on the relationship between writing and eating," refusing the latter so as to metonymically reject the tasty, multi-ingredient plots, rich verbiage, and resulting thick volumes that characterized pre-Modernist (late nineteenth-century) modes of writing.[7] Ellmann, somewhat differently, suggests that "the image of the starving artist [in the Modernist text] seems to stand for the crisis of high art in bourgeois culture; that is, for the exclusion of the artist from the life of commerce and [a] proud refusal to be 'fed' by capital."[8] To write, she argues, is to hunger. Thus, the body is converted into words as words take the place of food; the body itself becomes a text, a self-fashioned artifact. The process produces a somewhat circular reversal: while the text becomes lean like the dieting body, the body comes to "speak" like a text.

The link between anorexia and the text is not limited to a certain period, though. Sue Vice, for example, argues that the "various forms of control (or loss of it) that characterize anorexia, bulimia, and compulsive eating . . . inform the act of writing" more broadly.[9] Yet, if eating disorders can be a model for contemporary fiction, something clearly goes wrong with this process in fictions and autobiographies that are explicitly about eating disorders. These texts are not "lean," but usually rich with details (luscious descriptions of cakes not eaten; meals divided and subdivided on a plate; lettuce cut into pieces; the piles of food—colors, textures—eaten during a binge; vivid images of the plumbing bursting after a weekend of binging and purging). The body becomes an exhibit—not a text—offering little insight into the anorexic's interior world.

The disjuncture here may lie in the fact that the kind of text typically described as "anorexic" is a highly gendered text. Indeed, critic Leslie Heywood, in her formulation of what she calls "the anorexic aesthetic" of contemporary texts, suggests that gender plays a central role in the development of the lean-text/body-as-text formulation that dominates our time.[10] The "anorexic aesthetic," she argues, is part of a male-identified experience of life, and, in many ways, this aesthetic operates at the expense of women. This may be similar to, although not identical to, the ways in which media culture aestheticizes, objectifies, and sexualizes women's bodies in order to sell products.

In any case, the fiction or autobiography of anorexia is clearly female identi-fied—about a woman and her experience, if not always written by a woman. What may be "wrong," then, with the union of the anorexia story and the "anorexic text" is not the "story" but the form. Ironically, the anorexic text cannot tell the story of the anorexic experience.

Perhaps this is because anorexia is, in part, a disorder of *vision*. It is linked to misperceptions about body image. According to the *Diagnostic and Statisti-cal Manual of Mental Disorders* (*DSM*), anorexia is characterized by, among other things, a "disturbance in the way in which one's body weight or shape is experienced, undue influence of body weight or shape on self-evaluation, or denial of the seriousness of low body weight."[11] In other words, it is character-ized by seeing oneself as fat when one is radically underweight. It may also be a disorder tied to visual media—specifically, visual representations of women's bodies. Scholars looking to cultural causes of the disorder make this quite clear.[12] On the one hand, anorexia has been causally linked to images of the ideal female body as an extremely thin body. Here, the girl, in her anorexic behavior, becomes the *uber*-ideal woman; she becomes caught-up in her quest for the ideal (media-defined) look of femininity. On the other hand, anorexia may be a way of disavowing Western culture's objectification and sexualization of the female body.[13] Indeed, one of the physical symptoms of anorexia is, notably, "amenorrhea, i.e., the absence of at least three consecutive menstrual cycles" (*DSM*). To put it another way, the girl, in her anorexic behavior, may be rejecting the sexuality that her culture seems to force—through images—on her.[14] Regardless of how one understands anorexia's causal con-nection to the visual, though, it exactingly makes literal Marshall McLuhan's old claim, "The medium is the message." The anorexic appears to internalize the mass media and consumer culture's messages about women's bodies and externalize them on her own body, while she spectacularly uses her own medium—her body—to convey her *own* message. The spectacle of anorexia seems thus almost uniquely appropriate to representation via a medium of visual spectacle: film.

Trying to represent the anorexic story visually creates technical problems, though, for how does one produce the shrinking body on screen? This essay will touch on how three films grapple with this difficulty, but to some degree the question is beside the point, for the real thing film offers the story of anor-exia is a way to represent what the written text has not been able to—namely, the internal workings of the anorexic experience. Film, as a medium, is well suited to such a purpose in that, arguably, the cinematic experience mimics the workings of the human psyche itself.

Jean-Louis Baudry, for example, drawing on the work of Sigmund Freud, compares the filmgoing experience to that of the dream; he notes that "taking into account the darkness of the movie theater, the relative passivity of the situation, the forced immobility of the cine-subject, and the effects which result from the projection of images, moving images, the cinematographic apparatus brings about the state of artificial regression. It artificially leads back to an anterior phase of [the viewer's] development—a phase which is barely hidden, as a dream. . . Following this line of reasoning, one may then be able to understand the reasons for the intensity of the subject's attachment to the images and the process of identification created by the cinema."[15] By way of comparison, Christian Metz, drawing on theories of psychoanalyst Jacques Lacan, urges that the cinematic experience is less like dream than it is like the moment of psychic formation when we realize that we are individuals.[16] In this, Metz posits, the cinema offers viewers pleasure because it returns them to a preconscious moment (preseparation), while it also offers the pleasure of identification with perception itself. To put it another way: watching a film reenacts the (scary and pleasurable) moment when we recognize ourselves as individuals.

As we shall see, these arguments become more complicated when we begin to ask questions about how a specific cinematic experience genders the process of perception (and we must ask about gender given that anorexia has been codified primarily as a women's illness). However, for the moment it seems clear that, in its manners of mimicking psychic experience, film is perhaps the perfect medium through which to experience the process of psychic disorder, and thus the most effective medium to represent such a disorder. In fact, these theories mark film as perhaps the perfect medium through which to represent the anorexic experience specifically—a disorder of thinking, feeling, and *seeing*. Film—in its apparatus and experience, which are so unlike literary ones—can tell not just the story of the anorexic experience, but it can intimate and imitate the inner workings of the disease itself.

Of course, among the difficulties of representing anorexia is the nebulous nature of the disease itself. For, as a disease, anorexia is a bit of a puzzle. It has been described variously as a sense of self-fragmentation, as a black hole, as a desire for control, as a rejection of femininity, as an embrace of the feminine ideal. While the symptoms have been codified in the *DSM*, there is little consensus as to what causes it. Some suggest genetics or other biomedical causes.[17] Others find explanation in psychological models—specifically, issues of sexuality or identity formation in relation to parental models (usually the mother).[18] Still others argue that anorexia is a product of the messages contemporary consumer culture sends young women about ideals of beauty.[19] In their representations of the disease, *Life is Sweet, 301/302*, and *Superstar* each offers its own sense of what eating disorders are "about": What causes them? What sustains them? How do they work? How can we understand them? More than simply speculating about the workings of the disorder, though, each film offers an experience of anorexia by employing the unique representational technologies offered by the medium.

Of the three films this essay will discuss, Mike Leigh's *Life is Sweet* takes least advantage of the film apparatus to convey the anorexic experience. Instead, the film relies on plot—not conventional plot structure, though.

In fact, the film has very little coherence; it is more of a sequence of events than a story. In this, it mimics the experience of anorexia itself, which is often experienced as a kind of self-fragmentation.

The film centers on a family: "Mum" (Wendy, played by Alison Steadman) laughs gratingly at un-funny things, works at a fancy children's clothes store, and teaches children's dance; Dad (Andy, played by Jim Broadbent) is the kitchen manager and a chef at a restaurant. He's also a dreamer; early in the film he buys a junked mobile snack cart, with hopes of fixing it up and having his own business. The daughters, twins in their early twenties, living at home, are Natalie (Claire Skinner), a plumber, who spends her free time looking through travel magazines and planning a trip to America, and Nicola (Jane Horrocks), an unemployed college dropout and self-proclaimed feminist with an eating disorder, who spends her days taking showers and having kinky sex with her boyfriend (David Thewlis), and her nights bingeing on candy and vomiting into a plastic bag. The film also portrays the opening of Regret Rien, the French-esque restaurant of quirky family friend Aubrey (Timothy Spall), whose menu features tasty dishes involving brains, lamb tongue, and liver; prune quiche and pork cyst are a few of the specific menu items. The restaurant's décor—a stuffed cat head, fish encased in Lucite—doesn't make the dining experience seem appealing.

While it is difficult to pinpoint what the film is "about" (some argue it's a farcical look at the sitcom genre; others suggest it's a response to the social politics of Margaret Thatcher), it clearly gains thematic unity through food. And, I would like to suggest that, in doing so, it represents the anorexic experience. Like anorexia, the film links food to power and control. For example, Andy hates his job, and his purchase of the snack cart represents his wish to structure his life; he "could be [his] own man with a cart like that." Nicola calls him a capitalist and Tory for his efforts. Aubrey's restaurant is all about doing what he wants, doing it "right." And, when he finds himself with no customers, he smashes the place to bits, ripping tablecloths off tables set with china, throwing chairs across the room. Likewise, Nicola's eating/not eating throughout the film clearly emphasizes the food/power connection. She smokes cigarettes while her family has a snack, despite Mum's requests that she not. She refuses to eat dinner at the table with her family, preferring instead to take her plate into the next room, from where she tosses off snide comments in response to the family's dinner conversation. Nicola's relationship with her boyfriend also involves food and control. She wants him to lick chocolate off her during sex; he finds it "boring." Jump cut: he's doing the chocolate thing, complaining it's making him feel ill. Later in the film, though, he refuses to have sex at all, preferring to talk. "I don't want *it*," he tells Nicola, "I want you. Talk to me. About anything. Anything. What you think, what you know, what you care about." She doesn't want to talk. He leaves.

Although anorexic Nicola's "story" does not occupy the central role in the film, the film really comes together around her. In an interview with Leigh (about another of his films, *Secrets and Lies*), Susan Katz remarks that watching a Mike Leigh film is disorienting: "[One] start[s] out watching the movie thinking 'Who are these characters, and what am I doing watching such weird people on the screen?' And then about halfway through, something clicks in, and [you're] right there—in their living room, at their dining room table, at the birthday party. . . caring mightily about these people."[20] In *Life is Sweet* Nicola is the one who makes us care and we care, in part, because of her eating disorder, because the film enacts the disorder (or a version/vision of it) and the therapeutic process of coming to terms with such a disorder. This is what makes the film's vision of anorexia so effective.

In the beginning of the film, viewers don't know Nicola has an eating disorder. Leigh simply throws us into the midst of the family dynamic. Although all the characters are, as Katz puts it, "weird," Nicola is not just weird; her character is unpleasant, disquieting, and even hateable. She is hard to look at head on. Actually, she's kind of hard to see (clearly, Leigh's way of representing the anorexic body); her stringy, tangled hair hangs over her face, she wears oversized T-shirts that hang almost to her knees, and she has a range of strange body ticks and twitches. On top of that, she's sarcastic and rude, sneering and shouting "Bollocks!" and "Capitalist!" at everyone, refusing to answer the doorbell when she's standing right next to it, and neglecting to tell her family members they have guests when she does let such people in the house. Her mother and sister Natalie joke about how to get rid of her. "If we got a dog, a Rottweiler, maybe it could eat Nicola," Mum cracks at one point.

Forty minutes into the film Leigh presents Nicola having a late-night binge. Headphones on, crouching on the floor of her bedroom, hands and body shaking and quaking, Nicola yanks off bites of candy bar with her teeth and crams fists full of potato chips into her mouth. And then she vomits. And vomits. And sticks an object (pencil? toothbrush?) down her throat and vomits more. It's sickening to watch; but Leigh isn't yet interested in making Nicola into a sympathetic character. We can't connect with Nicola; the film doesn't allow us to identify with her.

For example, intercut with Nicola's binge and purge, we see Natalie in the room next door, in the dark listening to her sister vomit. Her face is blank. The film's built-in "response" to Nicola's disorder is so strangely nothing—not horrified, surprised, upset, or pained—that it is enlightening. For, in the film's failure to invite the viewer to sympathize with the anorexic, it creates an image of the anorexic that is startling: the anorexic is not, as represented in the majority of literary texts, the young, vulnerable waif-girl worthy of our pity (and envy). In fact, she is an intractable horror. She is the "difficult," "stubborn and willful," "annoying," and "terrifying" anorexic patient described by therapists.[21] Here, the film makes its impact. Beyond presenting a less romantic picture of the anorexic, the film offers us the experience of anorexia itself. Through our own efforts and then failures to identify with Nicola, we experience the numbness—the black hole—that sustains anorexia.

Toward the end, though, the film does offer the "therapeutic break-through." In a cathartic scene, Mum confronts Nicola—not about the eating disorder (it turns out that the family already knows about this; they had in fact hospitalized her at one point)—but about her lack of will, about the nothing-ness that both sustains and depletes her. Mother and daughter argue. "You've given up. You're not happy. You've no joy in your soul," Mum says as she con-fronts Nicola. Nicola insists that she is happy, just misunderstood. Mum persists in her claims, trying to make Nicola see that she's given up on every-thing—friends, her ambitions, and even eating. "You almost died," Mum yells at Nicola, who didn't realize how sick she'd been. Mum tries to make her daughter see that life is hard for everyone. Nicola simply feels she is being blamed for her mother's failure to make something of herself (Mum wanted to go to college and be a professional, but she got pregnant with the twins). "If you hate me so much," Nicola spits at her mother, "why don't you throw me out?" "We don't hate you! We love you," Mum replies, softly, gently, adding as she turns away, "stupid girl." Nicola sobs. Her pain is tangible, raw.

In all of this, Leigh proposes that the anorexic experience is like (and may in fact be) the condition of contemporary life. Experience is fragmented; life is empty. In Leigh's film, anorexia is, as scholar Susan Bordo phrases it, "the extreme expression of . . . a remarkable overdetermined symptom of some of the multifaceted and heterogeneous distresses of our age"; anorexia is simply a "crystallization of culture."[22] Leigh doesn't dwell on causes; it's never quite clear how Nicola came to be anorexic. Instead, Leigh highlights what it is like to be anorexic. And, in doing so, he reveals, that in some way, we are all "anorexic."

But for Leigh that doesn't mean life has to be joyless. It can be sweet (albeit bittersweet). He uses the anorexic experience as a foil. He suggests that the anorexic dwells in the misery that we all face, becomes consumed by her own grossness—when in fact we all are "gross." In the film's final scene, for exam-ple, Nicola, confronted by Natalie about her late-night purges, derides herself: "I am disgusting! Disgusting!" Natalie confesses that she too is disgusting: she puts her hands down toilets all day. The difference between the anorexic and the rest of us, for the film, is emphasis, where we choose to let our thoughts dwell—on ourselves (cleaning toilets, unsatisfying careers, lost prospects) or on our dreams (travels, snack carts, dancing around a room with a troupe of children singing the words "happy happy happy").

While *Life is Sweet* concludes on a healing note, Chul-Soo Park's *301/302* is nothing but disturbing. In part, this is because of content—sexual abuse of a child, the cooking and eating of a pet dog, murder, and cannibalism. But it is also because of the film's visuality—that is, the way the film looks. In its efforts to represent the anorexic experience, it relies on not only plot but also visual fragmentation and distortion.

The film concerns two modern (read: Westernized) women who live across the hall from one another in an upscale apartment complex in Seoul.

The woman who lives in apartment 301 (Eun-Jin Bang), a divorcee, is pathologically obsessed with cooking, eating, and feeding others. Through a series of flashbacks detailing her pre-301 life, the film links her food obsession to childhood loneliness and isolation, as well as to her husband's inability to value her efforts to please him, her efforts to be what she is supposed to be—namely, a wife (cook, lover, housekeeper, etc.). The occupant of apartment 302 (Sin-Hye Hwang), a writer of clinical-sounding sexual advice, is anorexic. The film's plot focuses on 301's efforts to make 302 eat, culminating in 301's realization that 302 cannot eat, and 302's request that 301 cook *her* (302). The film explores both women's lives, and how they came to be such dysfunctional people. In many ways it sets them in opposition to each other: one woman is about excess (sexual, alimentary); the other is about denial (sexual, alimentary). And, in the end, *301/302* implies, as one woman ingests the other, that social norms inhibit the possibility of a self-assured, independent woman. Only by breaking those norms, by breaking taboos, can a woman come into her own. Fascinatingly, the film reveals this dilemma of contemporary Western womanhood through its representation of the anorexic experience.

Although *301/302* is about the two women and spends approximately equal amounts of time on each, its framing device emphasizes the anorexic as especially important. The film's conceit involves a detective (Chu-Ryun Kim) trying to uncover what has happened to 302 (the anorexic), who has seemingly disappeared. In this, the film places "what happened to 302?" at its center, not only suggesting a concern with where she is but also foregrounding the puzzle of anorexia itself: what happened to make her anorexic? Why can't she—or won't she—eat? The concern is further emphasized through the film's story, for *301/302* is not really about the detective's investigation; it is about 301's obsession with 302. Here again, then, anorexia stands at the film's center.

Through the character of 302, Park suggests that anorexia is not—as Leigh implied—willful, but instead a response to trauma. As we learn over the course of the film, 302's disease is not that she won't eat, but that she *can't* eat; she can't keep anything down. As a child, she was repeatedly raped by her stepfather—not insignificantly, a butcher. In the flashback sequence, the mother seems passively indifferent, willingly blind, more interested in money than her daughter. Scholar Joan Kee goes so far as to suggest that the mother knowingly sacrifices her daughter to this man as a way of protecting herself from destitution.[23] Added to the trauma of rape and the pain produced by her mother's failure to protect her, 302 believes herself to be responsible for a neighbor child's death. This younger child, seeing the young 302 hiding from the stepfather, thinks it's a game. Wanting to play, the child sneaks into the butcher shop's walk-in freezer, where no one finds her until much later. These experiences have made 302 feel dirty. "It's not that I'm on a diet," she explains to 301 after recounting the events, "I'm just so full of dirty things. . . . How can I stuff myself with food or men? . . . I wish I could disintegrate." Her disease, in other words, stems from *dis-ease*, a fractured sense of self. Not eating is merely the symptom, the outward manifestation of the inner condition.

The film does not merely describe the anorexic experience as fragmentation, however; like *Life is Sweet*, it enacts this state, giving the viewer an experience of anorexia. The narrative is fragmented and disorienting. For one thing, the flashbacks have flashbacks within them, thus re-creating the embeddedness of the anorexic experience (in the film's representation, the symptom—not eating—masks feelings that hide an actual trauma). At times it is even difficult to keep track of which time frame the film is in. The film jumps from a dinner conversation between 301 and 302 to a dinner with 301 and her husband to a moment of shopping. Is the shopping for a meal for the husband or a meal for 302? Is it for a future meal or one of the meals currently going on in the narrative? At another point, 301 asks the detective if he would like some juice. When she turns around to serve it, the narative is in the past, and 302 takes the juice. When 302 accepts a refill, however, the narative returns to the present, and the juice goes to the detective.

Bodies, too, are fragmented. Park frequently uses a shot/reverse-shot super-close-up to show someone watching someone else eating. We see a mouth, lipsticked, chewing rhythmically, mechanically. We see a mouth messy, slurpy, tongue flicking in and out. We see eyes—eyes behind glasses, young 302's eyes. The camera pulls out; dialogue begins. Her mother distractedly jumps up from the table to count some money; she thinks she's made a mistake in the butcher shop receipts. Her stepfather leans over to 302. "Eat, eat," he says, "food is everything," grabbing a wad of beefy something-or-other and stuffing it into 302's resistant mouth. Her face contracts, eyes squinch. Jump cut, next scene: young 302 in bed, eyes squinched shut, clearly not sleeping. Stepfather sneaks into the room. She tries to squirm away, hide. He grabs her, pulls up her nightgown, and stuffs himself into her. In the juxtaposition of these scenes, it becomes quite clear why 302 cannot "stuff herself" with food or men.[24]

Park doesn't just fragment the body to get at the anorexic experience; he also distorts it. Part of this is done through exposition: "Disgusting. Such a pig!" (302 thinks of 301); "You look like a model" (301 says to 302). Remarkably, both actresses have slim, though not scrawny bodies. So effective is the film's representation of anorexia, however, that by the end we hardly notice that 302's naked body is not that of someone who exists on vitamins and water. In addition to the confusion about thinness, the film achieves body distortion through costume and makeup: 301 wears a fat suit and green-tinted makeup in some of the scenes. (As her husband increasingly rejects her and her love, she turns to food for comfort. By the time of the divorce, she has gained quite a bit of weight, which she quickly loses once she's on her own again). And 302, in one of 301's fantasies, also wears a fat suit. More typically, though, she wears draped, oversized black T-shirts and skirts. Bodies are also distorted as we see them reflected—in mirrors and other glossy surfaces;

refracted—through bottles in a shop; and blown up—a larger-than-life-size photograph of 301 hangs next to her front door. In all of this, *301/302* deftly conveys the subjective nature of perceptions of body size, at one and the same time representing the anorexic experience of body and commenting on body-size ideals themselves.

One might argue, in fact, that *301/302* uses anorexia as a means of think-ing about larger questions of perception itself—specifically visual perception. The gaze. Within the film, there is a lot of looking. People watch each other; 301 and 302 "check each other out" as they pass on the sidewalk in front of their building:

> 301 (thinking to herself): It's her. . . the walking mannequin.
> 302 (of 301): Disgusting.
> 301: All nutrition drained.
> 302: Her breasts could feed a hundred men. . . .
> 301: I've got to supplement her with animal fat.

In the flashback to her married life, 301 watches from a window as her hus-band kisses another woman (in response, the next morning she serves him his pet dog for breakfast). Skulking around corners and hunching her shoulders, 302 watches her stepfather. She is careful to avoid his gaze. Even the film's detective is a figure devoted to the gaze, whose role is to watch, to spy, to uncover that which is hidden.

Park uses the camera to highlight the film's interest in perception. Using a fish-eye lens, the plot begins with 301 looking through her apartment-door peephole at the detective. Later in the film (but earlier in time), Park shows us 302, trying to avoid 301, looking through her peephole before leaving her apartment. Throughout the film, Park gives us strangely high and strangely low camera angles, leaving the viewer feeling disoriented. The focus shifts quickly from deep to shallow (rack shots), confusing our eyes. And, there are even several scenes shot from above—straight down—placing us, the viewers, in an oddly omnipotent position. In short, Park very carefully and purpose-fully manipulates and plays with the viewer's usual way of seeing and perceiving, creating a sense of confusion not dissimilar to that experienced by the anorexic—or at least the experience of the anorexic in which Park wants us to believe.

The film *301/302* wants to see anorexia as a woman's experience, though, not as a condition of modern existence (as Leigh represented it in *Life is Sweet*). On the one hand, the film seems sympathetic to the experiences of women. In a culture—Western culture broadly defined—that neither nurtures girls (302) nor values the roles it sets up for its women (301), women can only ever experience the world anorexically—as a contradictory, confusing place.[25] Women can only ever be dysfunctional, parts of people. When 301 eats 302, when 302 asks 301 to eat her, the film suggests one woman alone cannot be whole. Highlighting this, even after her death 302 remains in 301's life—contained in her body, haunting her in her dreams, and frozen in her freezer (her severed head, anyway). In an odd way, the act of cannibalism even normalizes 301—the woman who rebelled against the patriarchy, the woman who fed her husband his dog. By ingesting her anorexic neighbor, 301 does what women are supposed to do according to Western (or Westernized) cultural definitions of womanhood: by literally consuming thinness, 301 buys into Western cultural ideals of femininity. The act of eating an anorexic woman goes far beyond mere dieting or even anorexia itself to this end. Of course, because Park draws on the perverse to make his point, he implies a critique of the (Western or Westernized) cultural forms that set thinness (and more, extremely, the anorexic) as the default—the ideal—state of womanhood. Beyond this, *301/302* indicates that, in many ways, the real tragedy in this state of affairs is that women can't even help each other.

Yet, while the film seems sympathetic to women's experience (as it defines it), one has to wonder at its version of feminism—a feminism that disallows sisterhood. Of note also is the fact that the film codes the anorexic experience as other, as not familiar. The film's literally anorexic character, for example, cannot see properly; 302 wears glasses. Likewise, the fish-eye lens shots, in one of the few instances in which viewers see through the two women's eyes, posit that both 301 and 302 perceive the world in distorted ways.[26] And, while *301/ 302* may ask its viewer to try to understand women's experience, in many ways the film itself reinscribes women as objects, reproducing the very process it condemns as responsible for women's anorexic experience of life. For example, in using the male detective to investigate what happened to 302, woman becomes object—subjected to the male gaze. The detective stands in for the film viewer, in other words, and as such it is not insignificant that the "viewer" is male. The story is being told, if not always to the male detective, at least because of him. The story emerges in response to his—both the character's and the gendered viewer's—curiosity.

Still, *301/302* also resists this interpretation, for ultimately 301 tells the detective nothing and asks him to leave; only she and the film viewer, those who have seen anorexic-ly, those who have consumed the anorexic (literally or visually), know what happened to 302.

Like Park's film, Todd Haynes's "biopic," *Superstar: The Karen Carpenter Story*, is extremely disturbing. Despite being the shortest (at just forty-three minutes) and the oldest of the films under discussion, it is the most intriguing. On the one hand, this is because the film is not commercially available. Threatened with lawsuits from Richard Carpenter, A&M Records, and Mattel, Haynes pulled the film from theaters and agreed not to screen or commercially distribute it (however, there are almost always bootleg copies available for sale on the Internet). On the other hand, *Superstar* stands out among films that look at eating disorders because of its form: it is highly experimental and extremely didactic. While its story follows the literary formula of the anorexia story (normal, white middle-class girl [a bit of a perfectionist], with controlling or demanding parents, gets told she's fat, starts to diet and gets addicted to the sense of power and control it gives her), its representation of the anorexic experience is visually daring; one feels almost assaulted by it. Through manipulation of film conventions, the image itself, and sound, Haynes and his collaborator Cynthia Schneider offer a raw, grim, anorexic envisioning of anorexia.

Superstar chronicles the rise of the 1970s soft-rock phenomenon the Carpenters, and lead singer Karen's fall into anorexia, as well as her eventual death from the disease. And it does so in part using not actors but Barbie dolls. The device, although familiar, is apt as it connects Carpenter's disease to contemporary ideals of the female body.[27] Through the Barbie body, which both reflects and promotes such ideals, the film visually accuses those ideals of contributing to disorders like anorexia. More than this, though, the plastic doll body—in its immutability, in its inability to change size, its inability to enact the physical process of anorexia—forces viewers to "see," to experience, the psychological process of the disorder.[28]

Haynes constructs this experience mainly through a very careful manipulation of image and sound. First, *Superstar* deftly mixes mediums and genres. It uses text, as well as images, to convey its message. It is part informational video, part docudrama. There are long sequences of exposition, of analysis of anorexia—excerpts from the *DSM*; passages from Susie Orbach's *Hunger Strike* and other books; and impromptu-seeming, fake-sounding "interviews" with people on the street ("What is anorexia nervosa?" one woman chimes, while others ask "Do anorexics ever get hungry?" and "Do they really think they look attractive like that?"). The film uses these materials to define its sense of anorexia explicitly: It is "a condition of self-starvation that primarily effects women in their teens and late-adolescence"; it is an "obsession" evolving out of a "complex internal apparatus of resistance and control"; it is "an addiction and abuse of self-control, a fascism over the body in which the sufferer plays the part of both the dictator and the emaciated victim who she often resembles." It is caused by the family dynamic, controlling mothers, and a culture that emphasizes an image and self-construction based on looks. Intercut with these health class–like materials, experts offer comments on Karen's music; we get bits of 1970s media footage (television shows, newscasts, newspaper headlines); and dolls enact scenes depicting Karen Carpenter's life. In the splicing together of these fragments, Haynes offers us not only a sense of the period's culture, but also an experience of the fragmentation that so often accompanies the anorexic experience.

The film opens with the discovery of Karen's body. Shot in black and white, using people (not dolls for this scene), the camera follows Karen's mom as she moves through the house looking for Karen; the camera shakes and sounds are undifferentiated (footsteps and door noises are too loud; mom's voice is flat, shifting from sunny to shrill as she becomes anxious, but not changing in volume). The soundtrack scrapes and echoes. It all stops for a moment as we see Karen's emaciated body in the closet. Mom screams. Here, while the soundtrack locates us in the horror genre, the conventions of the home movie (sound and camera work) tie anorexia to the family; the Karen Carpenter story is the private, horrifying tragedy of one family.

However, the film itself is to be no normal home movie. After mom's screams, the screen goes blank and then cuts to a shot of a white house. A male voice inquires, slowly, methodically, scientifically: "What happened? Why, at the age of thirty-two, was this smooth-voiced girl from Downey, California, who led a raucous nation smoothly into the seventies, found dead in her parents' home?" This film, Haynes reveals, is to be a case study. Like *301/302*, it sets anorexia at its center, aiming to discover how and why a girl becomes anorexic. And in setting anorexia at its center, it aims to uncover what the existence of the anorexic reveals about Western culture more broadly and American culture most specifically. The credits roll, along with a tracking shot of suburban houses, to the Carpenter's slow, dreamy song "Superstar": "Long ago / and so far away / I fell in love with you. . . ."

Throughout, *Superstar* uses the Carpenters' songs as commentary. The opening use of "Superstar" establishes the scene as a kind of fairytale world while it also frames the viewer's place in the cinematic experience: we are to (and do) fall in love with Karen Carpenter over the course of the film. The narrative itself begins with Karen alone in her room, half-humming, half-singing the chipper "I'll Never Fall in Love Again": "What do you get when you fall in love? . . ." In the next room, her mother, hearing Karen, decides that Karen should be the singer for son/brother Richard's band. "I'll Never Fall in Love Again" becomes nondiagetic, speeding up, as if things are out of control, and screeches to a halt with the sound of a record player needle scraping across a record as the scene shifts from the family home to the offices of a record executive (presumably Herb Albert, who first signed the Carpenters with A&M Records). The executive constructs an image for the Carpenters ("just a couple of kids next door. . . young. . . fresh"), urging them "put yourselves in my hands." While Richard eagerly embraces the idea, Karen seems less certain. The film cuts between increasingly closer shots of Karen's plastic face, the record executive, a looming shadowy hand, and images of emaciated bodies falling into a pit. In the context of this visual narrative, the soundtrack song "I'll Never Fall in Love Again" anticipates exactly what "you get when you fall in love," what happens to Karen when she becomes famous, when she becomes "loved." "Falling" into fame—a fame based on a particular image defined by the media—sets up Karen for, as the song goes, "only pain and sorrow." More than this, though, in the jump cuts Haynes conveys the panic that the film suggests undergirds the anorexic experience. The images are so fast they are hard to see, and the effect evokes anxiety, thus constructing—as well as representing—the experience of anorexia.

Haynes's anorexic representation of the disorder crystallizes further as he reverses the relationship between sound and narrative. Using the almost sickly sweet Carpenter sound against the narrative, the music now provides counterpoint. For example, peppy, uplifting "Top of the World" ("Such a feeling's coming over me. . . ") plays to a montage of shots chronicling Karen's descent into anorexia: A scale (the numbers keep dropping), boxes of Ex-Lax, a map of a tour schedule, TV clips, some home video. Here, the images resist the soundtrack, positing perhaps that anorexia itself resists the media and popular images of women, such as those reinforced by the lyrics of "Top of the World" —namely, that woman's reason for being, her ultimate fulfillment is the heterosexual romance. The film's sense of anorexia as resistance comes into focus even more as, at the end of "Top of the World," Karen and Richard are invited to the White House to sing for President Richard Nixon. There Karen sings the simple, childlike "Sing" ("Sing / Sing a song / Sing out loud . . . "). In affiliating the Carpenters ("young America at its best," Nixon called them) with Nixon himself and his pre-Watergate popularity, Haynes intimates discord between the lying simplicity of surface idealizations and the actual complexity of reality. Karen's anorexia develops in response to trying to live in the lies. She resists the false images, but because she cannot accept her resistance it backfires; it becomes anorexia. In other words, according to *Superstar*, Karen's anorexia is a means of rebelling against the life she wants but can't fully bring herself to live. She can't embrace the normative, nor can she bear rejecting it. As the image resists the soundtrack, it portrays what some theories see as the irony of anorexia itself: it resists proscribed ideals of femininity as it strives toward them. Anorexia is all about a crisis of identity.

The juxtaposition of cheery sound and gentle, sappy lyrics with disease and eventually death constructs the crisis of the anorexic experience itself and it does so anorexically. What you hear clashes with what you see; who you are clashes with who everyone else says you are or should be. Embodying this, the image itself in *Superstar* becomes increasingly anorexic—fragmented, contradictory, confused. And, toward the end, the images become increasingly startling, terrible, shocking, ghastly. Despite the fact that we never see the anorexic body, the anorexic experience Haynes depicts is horrifying. Late in the film, as Karen nears her death, the soundtrack becomes echoey, warbled, a mishmash of lyrics and musical phrases ("Long ago"; "only pain and sorrow"; "such a feeling"). The jump cuts increase in frequency; Haynes adds images of war and spanking to the sequence that represents Karen's state of mind and simulates the anorexic experience for the viewer.

No moment is more upsetting, perhaps, than when Haynes "forces" the viewer into the anorexic's subject position. Real hands (not those of a doll) open a drawer containing a row of small brown bottles; two are set on the counter; and their lids are unscrewed. The camera pans down and then up quickly, as "we" toss back the bottles of ipecac syrup. A shot of a toilet bowl; a gush of vomit splashing toward it. Small brown bottles thrown in a garbage can. Again, spanking; an emaciated body falling; a body being dragged along a road; the image of Karen's body in the closet that concluded the opening sequence. Darkness. And, finally, Haynes returns us to the tracking shot of the suburban houses that ran with the opening credits. Finally, we know "what happened." *Superstar* is, in fact, no fairy tale. The princess destroys herself.

According to the film, she does so because she has no choice; she can't imagine any other way. *Superstar* does not condemn the anorexic for her failure to commit to one thing (the normative) or another (rebellion). Instead, Haynes constructs a poignant and sympathetic rendering of the anorexic. When Karen goes to Steven Levencron's clinic in New York, for example, the film chronicles her therapy with the slow, lyrical "For All We Know" ("Love, look at the two of us / Strangers in many ways / . . . but love may grow / for all we know"). Over the course of the song, away from her family and career, Karen fully gives into the disease, reaching her lowest weight (according to the film's image of a bathroom scale). It is very sad; in committing herself to something—to her disease, to herself—she nearly dies. She does, in fact, die several scenes later, but here the film demands that we sympathize with the anorexic and the impossible position in which her culture has placed her. In making her a princess ("Long ago / and oh so far away / I fell in love with you . . .), it disallows her to love herself ("Love, look at the two of us / Strangers . . ."). Karen's "love" does not "grow"; it kills her.

Like *301/302*, *Superstar* is about perception. It is about the ways a star is constructed and how the star herself can neither live up to the image nor consciously rebel against it. Haynes clarifies this as he includes images of other female stars—most notably Judy Garland, singing "Over the Rainbow." *Superstar* is, as K. Burdette argues, "a film about the real-life 'not-ordinariness' of icons of normativity and the repressiveness of social institutions (the family, the mass media, the recording industry) which insist upon conformity with no regard for the individual's well-being."[29] Or, as one of the film's narrators puts it, "The story of Karen Carpenter's life and death . . . [provides us] with an extremely graphic picture of the internal experience of contemporary femininity." In its anorexic representation of anorexia, the film suggests that (young, white, middle-class/upwardly mobile) womanhood is always already fraught with self-doubt and anxiety. Anorexia represents a failure to come to terms with these things. It is driven by a sense of not ever being good enough, by always having to be something different—better, more perfect—than one is. The film is about self-perception, about identity, about the ways in which women see themselves and their place in the world as they struggle to find an identity. Accurate or not, it gives viewers a sense of this experience as it visually assaults them and even more, as it requires them to identify with a plastic doll.

Life is Sweet, *301/302*, and *Superstar* all quite successfully represent an experience of anorexia. They differ in their sense of what the disease is about and how it works. While Leigh suggests it is a symptom of despair, Park marks it as

a kind of *uber*-femininity, and Haynes suggests it is a rebellion against constructs of femininity. Taken together, these differences make it hard to come to
a totalizing sense of what anorexia *is* and is *about*. However, that was not the
goal of this essay. Instead, I hoped to suggest that film is a particularly effective
medium through which to represent an idea of—to construct an experience
of—anorexia. Unlike literary efforts at portraying the disease, these films don't
merely offer a chronology of the disease. Instead, they offer the viewer an
anorexic event, using elements unique to film to convey a fragmented, disorienting, anxiety-filled, anorexic cinematic experience.

Still, despite their success in constructing an experience of anorexia, which
primarily affects women, we must question their representation of women. It
is notable that men direct all three films. In his film, Leigh skirts the problem
by universalizing anorexia—claiming that it represents the modern experience. And Park invokes a kind of pseudo-feminism as his defense. Only
Haynes, who is openly gay and acknowledges his interest in the constructed-
ness of identities, has been forthright about the potential problems of a man
representing women and their experiences. His solution was to involve a
woman (cowriter/coproducer Cynthia Schneider) in his project: "Neither of us
has been anorexic," he tells an interviewer, "but I think that although men can
understand eating disorders and that kind of thing, *all* women know what
anorexia is about."[30] While there's no reason why a man can't represent a
woman's experience, we must ask: Do these films actually construct a woman's
experience or is it a man's experience of a woman's disease? In other words, do
Life is Sweet, *301/302*, and *Superstar* "other" and objectify their female subjects
and their female disorder? Do they, while critiquing the objectification of
women, actually reobjectify them?

Laura Mulvey's work on spectatorship suggests some answers.[31] Mulvey,
drawing on the same Freudian and Lacanian ideas as Baudry and Metz,
suggests that classic Hollywood cinema generates pleasure (why we like going
to the movies) by means of constructing female characters (and, by association, women generally) as erotic objects for both male characters and the
viewer who is "taught" by the film to identify with those male characters. If
this is how women come to be objectified in the cinema, then none of our
films objectify women. For, none are classic Hollywood movies and none use
typical filmatic structuring of the narrative. Before coming to this conclusion
too quickly, though, we need to think about Mulvey's idea of cinematic pleasure, which she argues develops from watching women. Both *301/302* and
Superstar place women at the center of their (and the viewer's) vision. *301/
302*'s detective, for example, might even stand in for the viewer; his curiosity
structures ours. *Superstar*'s male narrator ("What happened?. . . Let's see. Let's
go back . . .") could be said to serve a similar purpose, and interestingly
enough he, like we viewers, never *appears* in the film (than again, *Superstar*
also has a female narrator and the same things could be said of her). Still,

narrative perspective aside, neither film ultimately gives pleasure; instead, both offer the opposite: horror.

This, too, fits with Mulvey's ideas, for she argues that female characters are not only the source of cinema's pleasure but are also the source of its "unpleasure" in that they represent the threat of (metaphoric) castration—that is, the undoing of male power. In some ways, *301/302* and *Superstar* do "undo" male power and privilege: *301/302* in its refusal to give knowledge to the detective, and *Superstar* in Karen's death. Yet, while both films offer the "typical" construction of pleasure and unpleasure outlined by Mulvey, in the end neither actually establishes the male as the character with whom the viewer should ultimately identify. The detective in *301/302* is intrusive; we don't trust him. And, *Superstar*'s narrator switches so often between a male and a female voice that, in the end, the viewer's gendered position becomes mixed—queer, one might argue.

Leigh's film, likewise, remains vague in terms of whom the viewer is to identify with. The multiple narratives that don't cohere and the mostly unsympathetic characters shut out the viewer. Moreover, *Life is Sweet* explicitly tries to undo the cultural and filmatic conventions that construct women as objects. For example, Nicola and her boyfriend's kinky sex is more distressing or even funny than it is erotic. And, in fact, as we noted earlier, Leigh's "sensitive young man" wants Nicola to be more than a "shag bag." He doesn't want "it"; he wants *her*—to talk to her, to get to know her.

In some ways, while the question of the gendering of the spectator is important, a more important question raised by these films is: Can film itself as a medium ever do anything but turn people into objects, into stars? And, this is in many ways the problem of anorexia itself. When a person becomes an object in the world, unable to be who she thinks she should be, what does she do? This is the crux of the anorexic experience, according to all three films. Nicola shuts down when faced with college, when faced with having to prove she is smart; 302 can't eat because she's been filled with so many "dirty things"; and Karen Carpenter, according to Haynes, couldn't live with her image. In the end, then, these films' anorexic envisioning of anorexia gain effectiveness because they raise the very questions about the relationship between gender and culture that anorexia itself does. To put it another way: film, in its visuality and in its ability to mimic the workings of the human mind, can re-create the experience of contemporary womanhood.

And this may ultimately explain why the women students I spoke of in this essay's opening found *Superstar* so compelling. After viewing it, they wanted to know more about anorexia and disorderly eating generally—mostly, "Why?" but also, in some cases, "How?" "Why do people become anorexic?" "Is behavior X or Y anorexic?" "How can people live like that?" "How can people not see how they really look?" "Do people really die?" The film grabbed their attention not simply because it offered them a more visceral experience of the disorder, not simply because it presented the story of anorexia in a way that reconceived what they thought they knew and understood about the disorder. Rather, I think *Superstar* showed them that anorexic thinking, that the anorexic experience, is not that different from "normal" women's thinking—about food, about themselves and who they are and where they fit in the world. This troubled them; it confused them; it cut sharply through their indifference.

Notes

1. I would like to thank the students in my spring 2002 freshman seminar, Food for Thought, at Agnes Scott College for the inspiration for this essay and for allowing me to use their responses.
2. Susan Bordo, "Anorexia Nervosa: Psychopathology as the Crystallization of Culture," in *Unbearable Weight: Feminism, Western Culture, and the Body* (Berkeley: University of California Press, 1993), 139–64. Bordo's description of her students, as well as the facts, figures, and statistics she quotes, offer evidence of the 1980s–90s college women's mind-set.
3. Mary Petrie, "The Anorexic's Story," Ph.D. diss., University of Minnesota, 2000, 1. Petrie remarks on the extent to which anorexia has become what she calls, "a folk term." She tells of attending a youth gathering to discuss anorexia and finds herself surprised by "the amount of information these young people had about the disease," while she also wonders "if the group had any other psychiatric diagnoses at their fingertips."
4. Notably, fictional and autobiographical accounts of other eating disorders (bulimia, overeating), while still formulaic, follow a different formula, (tending to highlight recovery through Twelve Step programs or a religious community).
5. Joan Jacobs Brumberg, *Fasting Girls: The History of Anorexia Nervosa* (New York: Plume/Penguin, 1989), 17.
6. Petrie, "Anorexic's Story," 197.
7. Mark Anderson, "Anorexia and Modernism, or How I Learned to Diet in All Directions," *Discourse* 11, no. 2 (1988–89): 34.
8. Maud Ellmann, *The Hunger Artists: Starving, Writing, and Imprisonment* (Cambridge, Mass.: Harvard University Press, 1993), 70.
9. Sue Vice, "The Well-Rounded Anorexic Text," in *American Bodies: Cultural Histories of the Physique*, ed. Tim Armstrong (New York: New York University Press, 1996), 196.
10. Leslie Heywood, *Dedication to Hunger: The Anorexic Aesthetic in Modern Culture* (Berkeley and Los Angeles: University of California Press, 1996).
11. *Diagnostic and Statistical Manual of Mental Health*, 4th ed. (Washington, D.C.: American Psychiatric Association, 1994).
12. Bordo, *Unbearable Weight*; Kim Chernin, *The Obsession* (New York: Harper Collins, 1994); Jean Kilbourne, "Still Killing us Softly: Advertising and the Obsession with Thinness," in *Feminist Perspectives on Eating Disorders*, ed. Patricia Fallon, Melanie Katzman, and Susan Wooley (New York: Guilford Press, 1994), 395–418; Marcia Millman, *Such a Pretty Face: Being Fat in America* (New York: W. W. Norton, 1980); Susie Orbach, *Hunger Strike: The Anorectic's Struggle as a Metaphor for Our Age* (New York: Avon, 1986); and Marlene Boskind-White and William White, *Bulimarexia: The Binge-Purge Cycle* (New York: W. W. Norton, 1983).
13. Carolyn Costin, *The Eating Disorder Sourcebook: A Comprehensive Guide to the Causes, Treatments, and Prevention of Eating Disorders*, 2nd ed. (Los Angeles: Lowell House, 1999), and B. Dolan, "Cross Cultural Aspects of Anorexia Nervosa and Bulimia: A Review," *International Journal of Eating Disorders* 10, no. 1 (1991): 67–78. Although eating disorders are not exclusive to Western cultures, Costin and Dolan contend that Westernized women are at greater risk for them. Further, studies suggest that the degree of Westernization increases the risk.
14. Early psychoanalytic explanations of anorexia held that the disorder expressed a fear of sexual maturity and, specifically, a fear of getting or seeming pregnant. This theory has mostly been discredited as the trend in psychoanalytic explanations has shifted toward more general explanations (such as resistance to female identity of which sexuality is only one part). The idea does, however, persist in some pop-psyche literature and more broadly in that vague entity know as "popular thinking."

15. Jean-Louis Baudry, "The Apparatus: Metapsychological Approaches to the Impression of Reality in Cinema," in Film Theory and Criticism, 5th ed., ed. Leo Braudy and Marshall Cohen (New York: Oxford University Press, 1999), 773.

16. Christian Metz, "Identification, Mirror," in Braudy and Cohen, eds., Film Theory and Criticism. Metz draws on Lacan's idea of the "mirror stage" in which the child sees itself in the mirror and recognizes itself as both a subject and an object: THAT (over there) is ME (right here).

17. See Brumberg, Fasting Girls, 25–27, for an overview of some of these.

18. Hilde Bruch, The Golden Cage: The Enigma of Anorexia Nervosa (New York: Vintage, 1979). Bruch, a dedicated Freudian and one of the first psychoanalysts to focus her attention on anorexia, centered her theories on issues of sexuality. She believed that the anorexic feared becoming a sexual person and refused food as a way of refusing to become an adult—a sexual being. The anorexic, thus, uses her body as a mean of achieving control over her identity. Other theorists—notably Salvador Minuchin and Kim Chernin—find cause in the family dynamic. Here, food becomes a means of rebelling against an oppressive family dynamic (see Salvador Minuchin, Bernice L. Rosman, and Lester Baker, Psychosomatic Families: Anorexia Nervosa in Context [Cambridge, Mass.: Harvard University Press, 1978]) or a way of expressing anxiety over rejecting and/or surpassing the mother (Kim Chernin, The Hungry Self: Women, Eating, and Identity [New York: Harper Collins, 1985]).

19. Naomi Wolf, "Hunger," in Fallon, Katzman, and Wooley, eds., Feminist Perspectives on Eating Disorders; Orbach, Hunger Strike; and Bordo, Unbearable Weight.

20. Susan Bullington Katz, Conversations with Screenwriters (Portsmith, N.H.: Heinemann, 2000), 34.

21. Orbach, Hunger Strike, 6–7.

22. Bordo, "Anorexia Nervosa: Psychopathology as the Crystallization of Culture," 141.

23. Joan Kee, "Claiming Sites of Independence: Articulating Hysteria in Pak Ch'ol-su's 301/302" Positions 9, no. 2 (2001): 449–66.

24. Susan Wooley, "Sexual Abuse and Eating Disorders: The Concealed Debate," in Fallon, Katzman, and Wooley, eds., Feminist Perspectives on Eating Disorders, 171–211; and Mark Schwartz and Lee Cohen, Sexual Abuse and Eating Disorders (New York: Brunner/Mazel, 1996). Increasingly, researchers are finding connections between childhood sexual abuse and eating disorders. Some suggest a correlation in as much as 70 percent of cases.

25. Aside from the actual food cooked, 301/302 offers a remarkably Western representation of Korean life. Both 301 and 302 are marked as "modern" women, and this modernness is explicitly characterized as Western/American ways of being. (See note 13, above.) Still, I do not want to be inattentive or insensitive to cultural differences. Therefore, I must clarify that I am approaching the film (or all three films) from a "viewerly" perspective (adapting Roland Barthes "readerly" versus "writerly" notion of a text). That is, I acknowledge that what I see in the films is tainted by my own subject position as a viewer (woman, American, etc.).

26. Here, the similarity of the shots works to collapse the women into one person, one woman, as the actual cannibalism does at the end of the film. Again, in this fusion, the film suggests that the experience of womanhood in general is anorexic—fragmented, bewildering, distorted.

27. For Haynes's comments, see Mary Dickie, "Superstar: The Karen Carpenter Story" Graffiti, December 1998; available online at http://ca.geocities.com/need2bluv/carpenters/superstar.htm; accessed April 2002.

28. Over the course of the film, Haynes does mutilate the Karen doll in an effort to represent the ravages of the disease, but notably it is the doll's face, not the body, that he disfigures. As he describes the process to one interviewer: "all the faces are very full, with round cheeks. So I tried carving them down, but it made these huge sort of gashes in her face. So we ended up using pancake makeup to fill in the gashes, and it created a very kind of otherworldly effect"; Haynes, quoted in Dickie, "Superstar."

29. K. Burdette, "Queer Readings/Queer Cinema: An Examination of the Early Work of Todd Haynes," Velvet Light Trap, no. 41 (1998): 72.

30. Dickie, "Superstar."

31. Laura Mulvey, "Visual Pleasure and Narrative Cinema," in Braudy and Cohen, eds., Film Theory and Criticism, 833–44.

12

Production, Reproduction, Food, and Women in Herbert Biberman's *Salt of the Earth* and Lourdes Portillo and Nina Serrano's *After the Earthquake*

CAROLE M. COUNIHAN

Introduction

In this article I examine food symbolism in two films with Latina protagonists and explore how filming food can promote "oppositional consciousness," a way of thinking that challenges dominant ideologies.[1] The films are Herbert Biberman's *Salt of the Earth* (1954) and Lourdes Portillo and Nina Serrano's *Después del Terremoto* (*After the Earthquake*, 1979).[2] Food in these two feminist films becomes a vehicle for examining a topic fundamental to women's liberation—whether their work has social value.[3] Because food is so often women's work and language, food symbols can emphasize the importance of women and challenge the centrality of men. Because women are sometimes forced to serve and cook for others, or because their work is devalued, food can be a channel of oppression. Yet through cooking, feeding, eating, refusing food, or manipulating food's meaning, women can sometimes chart their own way around barriers.[4] In *Salt* and *Earthquake*, diverse food symbols play small but decisive roles in enacting key issues in women's lives and in demonstrating different paths toward gender equality.

Quite often and across cultures, an important component of women's work and an essential part of reproductive labor is provisioning food for children, husbands, and the larger community.[5] Whether this work is valued, shared, public, or private is a major determinant of women's status. A key feminist issue has been how under capitalism women can balance their privatized and devalued domestic chores with socially valued work, all too often an elusive goal. In the 1950s, there were strong propaganda and advertising campaigns to induce women to return to the home and give up their jobs to the decommissioned soldiers, as Connie Field's *Rosie the Riveter* (1980)[6] so effectively depicts. In the 1950s *Salt* was a pioneering film that addressed women's social value and agency, and it linked gender inequality to race and class stratification. Hostility to this message in the US was made clear by the near total extinguishing of the film for twenty years.[7] A quarter century after *Salt*, filmmakers Portillo and Serrano addressed the links between women's status and their work inside and outside the home in *After the Earthquake*, a film that followed a feminist vision by addressing the political through the personal.

I focus on food in these two films as an important indicator of women's social management of the crucial sectors of production and reproduction. Under capitalism, reproduction and production are split—reproduction into the domestic, private sphere of the family, and production into the public sphere of paid work to produce surplus.[8] Production is associated with men and is socially valued, while reproduction is viewed as women's "natural" duty, is privatized, and lacks monetary and social value. As Friedrich Engels originally pointed out in *The Origin of the Family, Private Property and the State*, and as feminists have elaborated upon, the splitting of production and reproduction led to the "world historical defeat of the female sex."[9] Interpreting Engels, Eleanor Leacock argued that a key factor in women's inequality was the "transformation of their socially necessary labor into a private service."[10] In the pioneering feminist anthropological volume *Women, Culture and Society*,[11] the reproduction/production dichotomy was a key issue. In Lydia Sargent's subsequent *Women and Revolution*, several articles focused directly on the importance of the production/reproduction divide in understanding how marriage and mothering reproduce patriarchy.[12]

Alison Jaggar and William McBride have complicated the feminist debate by suggesting that the very distinction between production and reproduction is a product of patriarchal ideology that links reproduction with female biology and isolates it from politics and history, whereas production is male, part of history, and subject to change. They have argued forcefully that this is a spurious distinction and that activities of nurturing and procreation are "forms of human labor" the same as all other forms of production.[13] In some ways this claim is supported by Louise Lamphere's recent summary of the anthropological literature and her conclusion that across cultures there are multiple ways of defining production and reproduction, of allocating them by gender, and of blurring their distinctions.[14]

Food is a useful lens with which to examine the gendering of production and reproduction because it is a central part of reproductive labor and can stand for all reproductive labor symbolically, but it also belongs to the public sphere of production and is central to the economy and politics of every culture. Furthermore, food is a flexible and multifaceted symbol that plays an important role in culture, art, and literature and can represent social issues in visual form in film.[15] *Salt* and *Earthquake* are two powerful feminist films that deserve attention. While there is of course more to these two films than their food-centered activities, these can suggest meaningful dimensions of women's work and their dignity.

Salt of the Earth

In defiance of active suppression by Hollywood, the International Alliance of Theatrical and Stage Employees (IATSE), and representatives of the U.S. government, *Salt of the Earth* (1954) was made with independent funds and financial support from the International Union of Mine, Mill, and Smelter Workers. Three men blacklisted by Hollywood were instrumental in its making: director Herbert Biberman (one of the "Hollywood 10"), producer Paul Jarrico, and Academy Award–winning writer Michael Wilson, who also co-wrote *A Place in the Sun*, *Bridge over the River Kwai*, and *Lawrence of Arabia*.[16] Shown in only a few theaters for a few months at the time of its making, *Salt* was suppressed until the 1970s when it was rediscovered and "hailed as a landmark in the authentic depiction of both Chicano and women's lives."[17] Since then it has gained an enthusiastic revival in universities and art cinemas.[18]

Filmed in a neorealist style in black and white with a stationary camera, *Salt of the Earth* tells the fictionalized story of a real labor strike by Mexican-American miners in southwestern New Mexico. Blacklisted by Hollywood studios, actors, and technicians, Biberman filmed *Salt* on location using local people in almost all roles. Only five actors were professionals, including the magnificent Mexican actress Rosaura Revueltas, who played the female protagonist, Esperanza Quintero, and who was also the film's narrator. Revueltas said that *Salt* "was the film I wanted to do my whole life,"[19] and she enacted with artistry and deep emotional range Esperanza's transformation from a timid, compliant housewife to a spirited and militant public actor.

Enflamed by low wages, unsafe conditions, and racial discrimination, Esperanza's husband Ramón (played by the real-life union leader Juan Chacón) leads the miners into a strike against the company. The men refuse the women's assistance until a Taft-Hartley injunction prohibits the men from picketing. Then the women take over the picket lines, defy the white power structure, and confront gender roles in the household. The film depicts the personal and social struggles that occur as the women become important actors in the strike and seek to validate their work and selves through sisterhood, while demonstrating what director Biberman called the "indivisibility of equality."[20]

Food Symbolism in Salt of the Earth

This paper focuses on food symbols and activities first in *Salt* and then in *Earthquake* to examine the unfolding of gender around production and reproduction.

In *Salt of the Earth*, a cake Esperanza bakes for her own birthday (or "name day") celebration plays a symbolic role in several early episodes that are intercut with scenes of Ramón working in the mine, a technique that emphasizes the female/male, private/public, reproduction/production divide. In one medium shot of Esperanza and her son Luís (Frank Talavera), facing each other in profile, Luís spies the cake and asks, "How come the cake?"

Esperanza replies, "Never mind the cake." Then the film cuts to a showdown at the mine between male workers and management. Then it cuts back to the kitchen to a close-up shot of the back of Esperanza's daughter Estella's (Mary Lou Castillo) head on a level with the cake on the table. The cake is obviously homemade, with a slightly lopsided shape and lumpy white frosting. Estella turns toward the camera and says, "Mama—?"

"Not a word about the cake, hear?" Esperanza replies. The cake reappears again after Esperanza and Ramón have an argument about their radio. He denounces the radio for the burden of monthly payments, but Esperanza defends it as her only pleasure and tells Ramón that she listens to it when he goes to the beer parlor. Ramón angrily announces he's going out and goes into the kitchen to wash, where in a medium shot the camera shows Esperanza to the left, Ramón in the center washing, and the cake on the counter to the right. Ramón fails to notice the cake, and Esperanza swiftly crosses the camera to pick it up and hide it on a shelf. Her repeated concealment of the cake may stand for her own self-silencing.

Finally, however, when Ramón complains that there is no hot water to wash with, Esperanza talks back. She reminds him that she chops wood five times a day to keep the water hot while the "the Anglo miners have hot water. In pipes. And bathrooms. Inside." She complains that the union men never prioritize these domestic issues and concludes, "What the wives want, that comes later, always later." The cake episodes visually reinforce this same message by showing that Esperanza's birthday was the last thing on Ramón's mind.[21]

The next scene shows Ramón and his friends in the beer parlor, drinking beer around a table. Luís comes in and sits at a booth in the background, waiting until he is noticed. Ramón walks back to him and when Luís reminds him that it's "Mama's saints day," Ramón invites the brothers over to sing "Las Mañanitas" to his wife later that night. In New Mexico, "Las Mañanitas" is "a song of lyric character sung usually as a serenade in the early morning hours" often for a Mexican American nameday or birthday celebration.[22] This song "belongs to a type of commemorative *canción* sung throughout the Rio Grande del Norte. . . . *Mañanitas*, or dawn songs . . . are beautifully expressive and convey the depth of regard *la gente* feel for their family and friends on birthdays and saints' days."[23] *Salt's* treatment of the community gathering to sing "Las Mañanitas" for Esperanza is culturally authentic. First the camera does a wide-angle shot from behind all the miners and their wives outside singing, then a shot of the people gathered inside Esperanza's house facing the camera, passing out beer and dancing. Later the camera shows Esperanza in profile in close-up outside, filling the frame, daydreaming and remembering her party in voice-over. Then we see a flashback medium shot of Esperanza surrounded by all her friends with the cake in the foreground, right in the center of the frame, as she blows out the candles to the cheers of all present.

Intercutting the cake scenes with the men's activities in the mine and bar emphasizes the separation between the men's and women's worlds that is a key issue in their relationships. What women want is "always later" because their needs are privatized and isolated in the home, lacking the public space and value that give them legitimacy. In the cake scenes, Esperanza trivializes and subordinates her own needs; she makes her own cake but is ashamed to give it to herself. The cake signifies the contested nature of Ramón and Esperanza's relationship that is critical to the film's plot and also points toward a central message of the film—the importance of community solidarity—when it becomes the central focus of collective support and of reconciliation between husband and wife.

As the film unfolds, food becomes a subtle yet steady index of the transformation of Esperanza into a social actor. At first, Esperanza enters the public world and continues to fulfill her domestic duties—a filmic rendition of one stage of feminist emergence.[24] In fact, initially forbidden to picket by Ramón, Esperanza uses her cooking—in particular her coffee-making skills—to overcome his objections. The camera shows several women in close-up serving coffee, then an extreme close-up shot of a coffee cup, and then a medium shot of Ramón walking away from the coffee shack with a disgusted look on his face, with the camera closing in on his face as he lifts the cup to his lips and grimaces while Esperanza recounts, in voice-over, "But Ramón is a man who loves good coffee. And he swore that the other ladies made it taste like zinc sludge." Then the camera runs through the same sequence of shots with Ramón in a different shirt and ends with a close-up shot of him drinking coffee and smiling broadly as Esperanza peaks out of the coffee-shack door behind him in the upper left hand corner of the frame. The camera then cuts to a medium shot of Esperanza, smiling in the doorway of the coffee shack, an apron covering her slightly pregnant stomach and her daughter at her side while she says, in voice-over, "So one day I made the coffee." From then on, Esperanza goes out to the picket line every day, participating in public actions while still fulfilling her reproductive duties.

But as the strike drags on, men are forced to take over some of the domestic chores. In one outdoor scene, the camera shows a medium shot of Ramón in the foreground on the left and his neighbor Antonio behind him in the center, hanging out the wash, while they complain about no hot water. Ramón says, "It should have been a union demand from the beginning," underscoring the need for men to take part in women's work to begin the process of reciprocal identification and empathy essential to solidarity. But in another scene, Ramón's displeasure with having to do the "women's work" while Esperanza pickets reaches the boiling point. In a medium shot of the interior of the house, the camera shows from left to right their son Luís, Ramón, Estella, and then Esperanza leaning over the baby's crib giving him a bottle. Ramón says, "Listen, if you think I'm going to play nursemaid from now on, you're crazy. . . I've had these kids all day!"

Esperanza turns up from the crib to face him in a close shot of their two heads and torsos in profile, and she replies resolutely, "I've had them since the day they were born!" When Ramón insists that he will not watch them, she responds firmly, still facing him, "Okay, then tomorrow, I'll take the kids with me—to the picket line," and turns away from him and walks out of the room. She is an increasingly forceful filmic presence, but though she projects her private chores into the public domain, she nevertheless still bears them. The film depicts the limits, however, on her ability to combine public and private roles, which emerge when the sheriff jails many of the picketing women in an effort to break their resistance.

We see a medium shot showing all the women behind bars crammed into a jail cell on the left of the frame and the two exasperated sheriff's deputies outside the cell on the right. The camera provides a close-up shot of Esperanza in jail in a Madonna-and-child pose with her baby in her lap and her young daughter on the right. The baby screams and turns away from the bottle Esperanza offers him while her friend Teresa enters the scene on the left. Esperanza laments, "He can't drink this milk; it makes him sick. He needs formula. I was a fool, I shouldn't have kept him with me." In this critical moment, Esperanza shows the difficulties of women's entrance into the public world while still responsible for reproduction, and she blames herself for failing to nurture her baby.

But Teresa, the women's picket captain, refuses to let her retreat into individualism, defeatism, and guilt. Teresa promotes a collective, active solution and says, "Don't you worry; we'll get some action." Then the camera cuts to a medium shot of Teresa and the women behind bars demanding formula from the sheriff and chanting, "We want the formula, we want the formula."

Annoyed beyond tolerance by the women's collective shouting, the sheriff gets Ramón, opens the cell, and calls for the baby. In a dramatic medium shot, Esperanza moves forward through the ranks of the women in the jail cell with the baby in her arms; all is quiet except for the baby's screams. There is a shot-reverse-shot sequence as the camera moves in close-up from Esperanza to Ramón to Esperanza, and then a medium shot while she hands the baby to Ramón, with the crowded jail cell full of women in the background. The camera focuses closely on Esperanza's face as the jail door swings shut and she turns from watching her family leave to facing the sheriff, whereupon a look of resolve crosses her face, and she chants forcefully, joined by all the other women, "*Queremos comida, queremos camas, queremos baños* (We want food, we want beds, we want bathrooms)." This scene marks the transition of food from a private issue to a public, collective demand. Furthermore, as Esperanza gives Ramón responsibility for child-care, she becomes a militant protestor.

Yet as Esperanza enters the public world, Ramón must increasingly inhabit the home. In the next scene, the camera frames a medium shot of Ramón and Luís in the kitchen washing and drying the dishes, and then alternates shot and reverse shot as Ramón tells Luís he has to help in the kitchen and Luís complains that his mother never made him do dishes. Ramón says, "You should have helped her without being asked." He underlines yet another critical issue for women—that having to *ask* for help reinforces that the work is "naturally" theirs.[25]

Esperanza bursts in, happy and glowing, from her four days in jail. Ramón again says he hopes she's not going back on the line, and he makes clear that he is resentful of having to do "her" duties at home, again underlining the tension between male and female, production and reproduction. But Esperanza will not give up her public militancy, and when she has a meeting of the women's picket team at her home, Ramon angrily leaves for the bar. When he returns, they have their major confrontation of the film in a long scene in the kitchen. In a long close-up scene Ramon is located in the lower left of the screen and Esperanza in the upper right as she speaks: "Have you learned nothing from this strike? Why are you afraid to have me at your side? Do you still think you can have dignity only if I have none? . . . The Anglo bosses look down on you, and you hate them for it. 'Stay in your place, you dirty Mexican'—that's what they tell you. But why must you say to me, 'Stay in your place?' Do you feel better having someone lower than you? . . . Whose neck shall I stand on, to make me feel superior? And what will I get out of it? I don't want anything lower than I am. I'm low enough already. I want to rise. And push everything up with me as I go."[26]

At the end of this speech, the camera does a long, shot/reverse-shot sequence from her to him, her to him, her to him, setting up a clear gender opposition in the editing rhythm. Enraged by her defiance, Ramón loads his gun, stalks out of the house, and goes hunting with several other miners, abandoning their strike posts and rejecting unity with the women. This is precisely the moment the company picks to issue an eviction notice to the Quinteros, and the camera intercuts the sheriff and his deputies taking all their furniture out of the house with shots of news of the eviction spreading throughout the community. People walk, run, hitch rides, and drive to the Quintero home, forming an increasingly agitated crowd, while Ramón in the woods realizes Esperanza was right and abruptly heads for home. There the women defy the sheriff and his deputies and start returning items to the house faster than the sheriffs can remove them. Hundreds of community members gather at the home watching, including workers from several other mines in the area. Ramón sees how the people, all working together, are able to foil the sheriff's efforts to evict them from their home. The camera intercuts a close-up shot of Ramón with a wide-angle shot of the crowd while he says, "Thank you, sisters and brothers. And Esperanza, thank you for your dignity. You were right. Together we can push everything up with us as we go." With the camera alternating between a close-up of Esperanza and a wide-angle shot of the departing people, she says, in voice-over, "Then I knew we had won something they could never take away—something I could leave to our children—and they, the salt of the earth, would inherit it."

Salt of the Earth uses food to further its project of challenging Hollywood's colonization of the public's mind. The film draws attention to how the subordination of Chicanos and women stems from the historical and economic exigencies of capitalism. It defines class, race-ethnic, and gender unity as critical to resistance. It demonstrates how gender equality depends on addressing the fundamental dichotomies between male and female, production and reproduction, valued work and taken-for-granted work. However, this dichotomy is reversed but not dismantled; the strike is won for the moment, but race/ethnic, class, and gender hierarchies persist.[27] *Salt* is important in defining the production/reproduction dichotomy as a key issue and showing the tensions involved in challenging it—an important stage in the struggle for gender equality.

After the Earthquake

The beautiful experimental feminist film *After the Earthquake* describes a more individual and complex path through the production/reproduction dichotomy. It was co-written and co-directed by Lourdes Portillo and Nina Serrano, whose other directing credit is with Saul Landau and Raoul Ruiz for *¿Qué hacer?* (1970).[28] Portillo is an independent filmmaker who was born in Mexico in the mid-1940s and came to the United States in adolescence. She became involved in filmmaking in the early 1970s as a member of the Marxist collective Cine Manifest and has since directed a dozen films known for addressing important issues with groundbreaking documentary and experimental film techniques.[29]

After the Earthquake was Portillo's first major film. She and Serrano addressed significant political issues through the personal story of the protagonist Irene, a Nicaraguan immigrant who came to the United States after the devastating Nicaraguan earthquake of 1972. This twenty-four-minute film, shot in black and white on a low budget, is set in the Mission District of San Francisco in 1976 at a time when the Mission was teeming with Salvadorans, Cubans, Guatemalans, and Nicaraguans, over 50,000 of whom had left their country, fleeing the earthquake and the repressive dictatorship of Anastasio Somoza.[30] The main characters are Irene (Vilma Coronado); her friend Luisa Amanda (Leticia Cortez); her aunts (the *tías*, played by Themilda Leiva and Maria Reyes); and her betrothed, Julio (Angelo Guzman), who has just arrived in the United States after being released from prison in Nicaragua, where he was tortured for his anti-Somoza political actions. The film moves from Irene's workplace to her home to the birthday party of a community elder, where all the characters come together and Irene reunites with Julio after three years of separation. Dialogue and subtitles alternate between Spanish and English, and Irene's fluid switching of languages is an important indicator of her ability to cross cultural boundaries as well as those between home, work, and politics.[31]

In *After the Earthquake,* Irene splinters the production/reproduction dichotomy in several ways. She does not have the role of wife and mother in the domestic sphere of home—not yet, at least, for whether she will marry Julio or not is a central question of the film; instead she works at a full-time job outside the home for wages. Yet her work brings her inside another home, as a domestic servant, "twelve hours a day, six days a week," as Luisa Amanda reminds her. Irene's outside-inside presence disrupts the binary opposition of production and reproduction and shows their permeability and linkage.

The film begins in Irene's room in the home where she works as a maid. After an initial opening shot of her dresser and radio, blaring a Spanish station in the background, the film shows Irene from behind in a medium shot, taking money hidden inside a book, and then she faces the camera and puts the money into her wallet. We soon learn that she is taking her money to buy a television set, symbol of "U.S. cultural imperialism" and commodity consumption.[32] The film, in its association of Irene with the television set, and with two different radios as well, reaffirms the connection between media consumption and women that *Salt* also establishes in the dispute over the radio. Whereas in *Salt* Ramón and Esperanza lose their radio as they lose the struggle for economic justice, in *Earthquake* Irene demonstrates her success in the economically stratified United States by going into debt to purchase the television set.

Food Symbolism in After the Earthquake

The film uses food in diverse ways to penetrate the boundaries between production and reproduction. While getting ready to go to the birthday party of a community matron, Luisa Amanda comments to Irene, "Yes, there is enough food and clothes here, but something is missing." Next we see one of Irene's tias praying to the statue of St. Anthony for a husband for Irene. Then the camera frames the other tia sitting at a table in a simple kitchen making tamales. She is on the left side, looking toward the door on the right side of the frame. The tia calls Irene in and asks her to buy her a Diet Pepsi. Irene leans into the room, holding the door frame, acquiesces, and then quickly exits the kitchen, representing in space her broader role as the mediator between the Nicaraguan world of homemade foods represented by the tias and the U.S. capitalist world of processed foods represented by the Diet Pepsi. A few scenes later, the camera shows Luisa Amanda and Irene exiting her room, approaching the camera down a hallway with a statue of St. Anthony and a picture of the Virgin of Guadalupe to the right. Luisa Amanda tells Irene that there is more to life than work and consumption and says, "Go to school, Irene." Then she hollers jokingly to the tias in Spanish, "Liberate the women from the kitchen! Let the men make tamales!"

The feminist vision of reversing gender roles espoused by Luisa Amanda is not well received by the tias who complain to each other while sitting at the kitchen table making tamales, "She thinks that wearing pants is independence. I don't like Irene running around with her, she thinks she knows it all. I wish Irene would marry Julio so we wouldn't have another spinster." Then the camera does an extremely close shot of one tia making a tamale, and then the beautiful, tidy tamale itself filling the frame, tied up to look like a gift, a gift presented for male consumption later on at the birthday party. Then the camera does a medium shot of the tias in a different kitchen, dressed up for the party, standing behind the kitchen table serving a tamale for a male guest who is flirtatiously teasing the tias and telling them he's going to eat as many as he can of their delicious tamales. The scene enacts an old-fashioned gender discourse centered on a male/female, production/reproduction, consumer/consumed dichotomy that is part of Irene's Nicaraguan-American world but which she does not adopt.

Irene's transcendence of this dichotomy is demonstrated through her relationship to the birthday cake. This cake is clearly store bought rather than homemade, for it has fancy bakery-made swirls all around the edges and "Felicidades Doña Mercedes" elegantly scripted across it. We first see it in close-up, and then see Irene bringing it to the table. Later, we see all the guests standing around the table in the dining room singing "Las Mañanitas" in a scene reminiscent of the one in *Salt*. Irene serves the punch while they all sing. She plays an intermediary role between production and reproduction by not inhabiting the quintessential domestic space of the kitchen but the more public space of the dining room. In not making the cake, she contrasts with her tias and with Esperanza in *Salt*, who produce homemade culinary specialties in their kitchens.

Portillo and Serrano dissolve the production/reproduction dichotomy in a different way by linking the political and domestic dimensions of food. In one scene, Luisa Amanda and Irene are in her room with their backs to the camera looking at photographs on Irene's dresser, with Luisa Amanda reflected back in the mirror above the dresser between their torsos, looking at the camera, doubling her image, perhaps implying her doubled social identity, her biculturalism. Luisa Amanda asks Irene why she keeps her photos of the Nicaraguan earthquake. The camera then shows Irene in profile facing left on the right half of the shot surrounded by the background of the diaphanous white curtain framing her lovely profile and black hair. Irene replies that the photos remind her of why she left home: "There was misery everywhere. There was hunger and thirst. My house was only rubble." While Irene continues to speak, the camera pans to Luisa Amanda looking out the window, then the camera looks out the window onto the street below where Luisa Amanda's brother is buying a joint while Irene continues, "The president stole all the supplies sent from other countries, then sold them to us at high prices—so what's new?" The stealing of food from the poor in Nicaragua is thus linked to the poor buying drugs in the United States, both important political issues linked to inequality.

Later in the film, at the birthday party, an old man comes up to Julio and says, "So they arrested you for trying to get the food after the earthquake? What a noble cause." Julio then shows his slides of Nicaragua and points out the poverty, hunger, and malnutrition caused by the Somoza regime, placing. Julio's connection to food clearly in the public sphere. That Irene mentioned these same issues earlier in the film creates a link between her and him, and shows her ability to span the public and private domains.

In the last long scene of the film, the camera shows a street in the Mission District and circles around Irene and Julio as they are walking down the street and sitting down on a bench. Julio tells her that everything has changed since they became betrothed three years ago, and Irene concurs, affirming that women are independent now, and she has bought a television set to prove her independence. While saying this, she rises and starts walking toward the camera in full shot and Julio follows, slightly behind her. The camera backs away from them as they walk forward. Aghast, Julio asks her how much the television set cost. When she tells him $300, he is horrified, saying, "You could feed two families with that in Nicaragua." She retorts angrily, "Calm down—here you don't have to support even one." He responds, "So we're not getting married?" And she responds, "*Por supuesto que no*" (which is usually translated as "of course not," but which the subtitles render here as "I guess not," thus playing with ambiguity through language).

But then Irene suggests that they should go somewhere, have "a cup of coffee," and talk about things. The coffee here recalls the coffee in *Salt*, but instead of proficiently making the coffee to get what she wants from her man as Esperanza did, Irene evades the subordinating dimensions of reproductive labor in the home by suggesting they go to a public place for coffee. She and Julio are walking along the street toward the receding camera the whole time they are talking until finally they walk past the camera and off down the street, where the camera follows their receding backs in a full shot with the street heading off behind them. Then the film ends with the words upon the screen, *Y empezó así*—"And so it began."

The openness of this ending parallels the openness of the entire film, which introduces multiple femininities and gender strategies. Production and reproduction, instead of being closed, mutually exclusive domains as they are in *Salt of the Earth*, flow constantly into each other. Thus Irene works outside the home inside another home; Irene understands both the work of food in the kitchen with the tias and the politics of food in the public sphere; Irene knows both the old gender ways and the new; and she will seek her own path over "a cup of coffee," in the public space of a café, not in the private space of home. Irene's ability to mediate between usually dichotomized domains opens multiple strategies of "oppositional consciousness"—what Chela Sandoval calls "differential consciousness," a concept applied by Rosa Linda Fregoso to *Earthquake*.[33] In the film, we see diverse women—who work, who stay home, who go to school, who seek more than "enough food and clothes," who seek husbands or do not, and who seek independence and self-realization in many ways. Thus the film dissolves the production/reproduction dichotomy and challenges oppressions lodged in traditional gender dichotomies.

Conclusion

Salt of the Earth and *After the Earthquake* advance "the project of Chicano cinema" to document "oppositional forms of knowledge about Chicanos" and the feminist goal of critically interrogating "gendered subjectivities."[34] These two films represent different historical moments in and cinematic approaches to women's social value and agency, which I have examined through the meanings embedded in food symbols. I have attempted to show how filmmakers can use food symbols that are highly resonant with viewers to complicate and challenge taken-for-granted assumptions about gender. Women's assumption of cooking duties or not, inside the home or out, for pay or not, becomes an important index of their social position. Although *Salt* and *Earthquake* are not "food films" per se, they demonstrate that powerful messages can be communicated through birthday cakes, coffee cups, tidy tamales, and infant formula. Showing these films to students and communities can open up visions of women's diversity, struggles for autonomy, and ability to juggle diverse roles simultaneously—lessons still of relevance a half century after *Salt* was produced, a quarter century after *Earthquake*.

Notes

1. Rosa Linda Fregoso, *The Bronze Screen: Chicana and Chicano Film Culture* (Minneapolis: University of Minnesota Press, 1993). See also Jason C. Johansen, "Notes on Chicano Cinema (1979)," in *Chicanos and Film: Representation and Resistance*, ed. Chon A. Noriega (Minneapolis: University of Minnesota Press, 1992), 303–7, on how a goal of Chicano cinema is "the decolonization of minds."
2. Herbert Biberman, *Salt of the Earth* (Independent Productions and International Union of Mine, Mill and Smelter Workers, 1954); Lourdes Portillo and Nina Serrano, *Después del Terremoto/After the Earthquake* (Xochitl Films, 1979).
3. See Henrietta Moore, *Feminism and Anthropology* (Minneapolis: University of Minnesota Press, 1988), 53, who writes, "it is the relationship between women's reproductive and productive labor which is the crucial determinant of their position in society."
4. Carole Counihan, *The Anthropology of Food and Body: Gender, Meaning and Power* (New York: Routledge, 1999).
5. Carole Counihan, *Around the Tuscan Table: Food, Family and Gender in Twentieth Century Florence* (New York: Routledge, 2004); Marjorie DeVault, *Feeding the Family: The Social Organization of Caring as Gendered Work* (Chicago: University of Chicago Press, 1991).
6. Connie Field, *The Life and Times of Rosie the Riveter* (Sundance, 1980).
7. Although blacklisted in the United States, *Salt* received enthusiastic welcome and critical acclaim around the globe. See Herbert Biberman, *Salt of the Earth* (Boston: Beacon Press, 1965); James L. Lorene, *The Suppression of: How Hollywood, Big Labor* Salt of the Earth, *and Politicians Blacklisted a Movie in Cold War America* (Albuquerque: University of New

Mexico Press, 1999); and Deborah Silverton Rosenfelt, Salt of the Earth: *Commentary* (New York: Feminist Press, 1978).

8. See Carolyn Merchant, *Ecological Revolutions: Nature, Gender and Science in New England* (Chapel Hill: University of North Carolina Press, 1989), 17–19.

9. Frederick Engels, *The Origin of the Family, Private Property and the State*. (New York: International, 1972), 120. See also Moore, *Feminism and Anthropology*; Karen Brodkin Sacks, "Engels Revisited: Women, the Organization of Production, and Private Property" in *Women, Culture and Society*, ed. Michelle Zimbalist Rosaldo and Louise Lamphere (Stanford, Calif.: Stanford University Press, 1974).

10. Eleanor Burke Leacock, Introduction, to *The Origin of the Family, Private Property and the State*, by Frederick Engels (New York: International, 1972), 41.

11. Michelle Zimbalist Rosaldo and Louise Lamphere, eds., *Women, Culture and Society* (Stanford, Calif.: Stanford University Press, 1974).

12. Lydia Sargent, ed., *Women and Revolution: The Unhappy Marriage between Marxism and Feminism* (Boston: South End Press, 1981); Sandra Harding, "What is the Real Material Basis of Patriarchy and Capital?" in *Women and Revolution*, ed. Lydia Sargent (Boston: South End Press, 1981); Christine Riddiough, "Socialism, Feminism, and Gay/Lesbian Liberation," in *Women and Revolution*, ed. Lydia Sargent (Boston: South End Press, 1981).

13. Alison M. Jaggar and William L. McBride, "'Reproduction' as Male Ideology," *Women's Studies International Forum* 8, no. 3 (1985): 185–96.

14. Louise Lamphere, "The Domestic Sphere of Women and the Public World of Men: the Strengths and Limitations of an Anthropological Dichotomy," in *Gender in Cross-Cultural Perspective*, ed. Caroline B. Brettell and Carolyn F. Sargent (Upper Saddle River, N.J.: Prentice Hall, 2000), 100–109.

15. See Cynthia Baron, "Food and Gender in *Bagdad Café*." *Food and Foodways* 11, no. 1 (2003): 49–74; Maggie Dunn, "Licking the Pots in Sorrow's Kitchen: Food as Metaphor in Fiction and Film." *Journal of the Association for the Interdisciplinary Study of the Arts* 5, no. 1 (1999): 33–41; Evelyn Hinz, ed.. *Diet and Discourse: Eating, Drinking and Literature*. Special issue of *Mosaic* (Winnipeg: University of Manitoba, 1991); Ruth D. Johnson, "The Staging of the Bourgeois Imaginary in *The Cook, the Thief, His Wife, and Her Lover* (1990)," *Cinema Journal* 41, no. 2 (2002): 19–40; Mary Anne Schofield, ed., *Cooking by the Book: Food in Literature and Culture* (Bowling Green, OH: Popular University Press, 1989).

16. *A Place in the Sun* (dir. George Stevens, 1951); *Bridge over the River Kwai* (dir. David Lean, 1957); and *Lawrence of Arabia* (dir. David Lean, 1962).

17. Linda Williams, "Type and Stereotype: Chicano Images in Film," in *Latin Looks: Images of Latinas and Latinos in the U.S. Media*, ed. Clara E. Rodriguez (Boulder, Colo.: Westview Press, 1998), 217.

18. On *Salt*, see Biberman, *Salt of the Earth*; George Lipsitz, "Herbert Biberman and the Art of Subjectivity," *Telos*, no. 32 (1977): 174–82; Lipsitz, "Herbert Biberman and the Art of Subjectivity;" Lorene, *Suppression of Salt of the Earth*; Esteve Riambau and Casimiro Torreiro. "This Film Is Going to Make History: An Interview with Rosaura Revueltas," *Cineaste* 19, nos. 2–3 (1992): 50–51; Rosenfelt, *Salt of the Earth*; Williams, "Type and Stereotype;" and Michael Wilson, *Salt of the Earth* (screenplay; New York: Feminist Press, 1978).

19. Riambau and Torreiro, "This Film Is Going to Make History," 50.

20. Biberman, quoted in Rosenfelt, *Salt of the Earth*, 94.

21. Further on, the film indicates the exchange of roles between men and women when after Esperanza gets out of jail, Ramón says, "We have to talk," and she says, "yes, but later," and Ramón in medium shot says, with a puzzled look on his face, "Later?"

22. John O. West, *Mexican-American Folklore* (Little Rock: August House, 1988), 118.

23. Jack Loeffler with Katherine Loeffler and Enrique R. Lamadrid, *La Música de los Viejitos: Hispano Folk Music of the Rio Grande del Norte* (Albuquerque: University of New Mexico Press, 1999), 113. See Gary Riebe-Estrella, "Critic's Corner: Latino Religiosity or Latino Catholicism?" *Theology Today* 54, no. 4 (1998): 512–15, who describes Mexicans singing "Las Mañanitas" on the feast of the Virgin of Guadalupe outside the church early in the morning and then gathering in the church courtyard "to eat *pan dulce* and drink *champurado*" (514).

24. Chela Sandoval, "U.S. Third World Feminism: The Theory and Method of Oppositional Consciousness in the Postmodern World," *Genders* 10, no. 1 (1991): 1–24.

25. DeVault, *Feeding the Family*.

26. Wilson, *Salt of the Earth*, 79–80.

27. See Barbara Kingsolver, *Holding the Line: Women in the Great Arizona Mine Strike of 1983* (Ithaca, N.Y.: Cornell University Press, 1989), which finds in her study of an eerily similar

1983 copper mine strike in Arizona that after women surged into leadership in the strike, many couples had difficulty accommodating their changed roles after the strike.
28. Saul Landau, Raoul Ruiz and Nina Serrano, *¿Que Hacer?* (Lobo Films, 1970).
29. Rosa Linda Fregoso, ed., *Lourdes Portillo: The Devil Never Sleeps and Other Films* (Austin: University of Texas Press, 2001). Portillo's most recent film, *Señorita Extraviada/Missing Young Woman* (2001) is a film of haunting beauty about the terrible murders of over two hundred young women in Juarez, Mexico. Portillo draws out the frightening social complicity that fails to stop the murders of young, poor, powerless women. In *Las Madres: The Mothers of the Plaza de Mayo* (1986), Portillo and codirector Susana Muñoz traveled to Argentina and recorded the poignant stories of some of the mothers of thousands of "disappeared" children. The film documents the subjective perspectives of several mothers to show how they came to protest in the Plaza de Mayo, draw attention to the horrors, and help topple the repressive Argentine government. In *The Devil Never Sleeps* (1999), Portillo returned to her birthplace of Chihuahua, Mexico to explore the gunshot killing of her favorite uncle in an intriguing "melodocumystery" that artfully questions the nature of truth. Fregoso, *Lourdes Portillo*. See Lourdes Portillo's website at http://www.lourdesportillo.com/ for further information on her films. *Las Madres: The Mothers of the Plaza de Mayo* (dir. Lourdes Portillo and Susanna Blaustein Muñoz, 1985); *Il Diablo Nunca Duerme/The Devil Never Sleeps* (dir. Lourdes Portillo, 1999); and *Señorita Extraviada/Missing Young Woman* (dir. Lourdes Portillo, 2001).
30. Fregoso, *Lourdes Portillo*, 207.
31. Fregoso, *The Bronze Screen*, chapter 5.
32. Fregoso, *The Bronze Screen*, 103.
33. Sandoval, "U.S. Third World Feminism"; Fregoso, *The Bronze Screen*, chapter 5.
34. Fregoso, *The Bronze Screen*, xiv.

13
Images of Consumption in Jutta Brückner's *Years of Hunger*

YOGINI JOGLEKAR

In *Years of Hunger* (*Hungerjahre in einem reichen Land*, 1979), director Jutta Brückner uses a first-person voice-over narrative to portray four years in the life of an emotionally starved adolescent, Ursula Scheuner, growing up in the midst of West Germany's 1950s "Economic Miracle."[1] The film depicts Ursula's gradual breakdown as a result of her inability to cope with the widening gap between her external surroundings—her family, school, and West German society—and her internal feelings of isolation, insecurity, and pain. Ursula takes recourse to food as a means of escaping from her disjointed existence. In addition to her voracious appetite for food, the teenage protagonist experiences an intense hunger for various kinds of inaccessible knowledge, including knowledge of sexuality and her female body, along with political knowledge about Germany's troubled past and its conservative and (sexually and politically) repressive present. As Gertrud Koch has rightly noted, the film combines the "outer history of an epoch with the inner (hi)story of an individual."[2] In fact, it is the theme of consumption that seams together political and personal history in Brückner's film. For Ursula as well as for the young West German state, economic progress becomes synonymous with an insatiable desire for food and commodities. Brückner thus creates a unique culinary narrative, juxtaposing a capitalist society thriving on its consumption of material comforts with Ursula's struggle to come to terms with the abundance of her surroundings as well as with the gaping void in her relationships to her body, her identity, and food itself.

The economist Alan Warde has distinguished three motives behind consumption and consumer behavior: (1) exchange, or the price of commodities; (2) use, or the satisfaction of needs and wants; and (3) identity, or consumption for the sake of belonging to social groups or for narcissistic purposes.[3] Warde contends that the fulfillment or denial of consumerist fantasies depends to a large extent on the perceived value and the corresponding price of a product and also on the consumer's perception of need compared to her desire for a new object. Interestingly, Warde determines that consumption for identity formation is an especially prominent feature in postwar economies. Consumption motivated by the desire to belong to a social group or to assert an eclectic individual taste often ignores the first two factors behind consumption—namely, price and need. In postwar West Germany's economy of plenty, an increasing belief that prosperity could be maintained only by ever-increasing consumption led to massive buying and accumulation of commodities regardless of their exchange value. However, Warde's third category, consumption for identity formation, is the most significant factor in the postwar West German context and for Brückner's film. The 1950s setting of *Years of Hunger* lends its images of consumption a special resonance, embodying an ideology of consumption as an antidote to wartime deprivation. The West German fascination with abundance—or the growing hunger for consumer goods during the Economic Miracle—is, therefore, a direct reaction to the penury and suffering of the war and the immediate postwar years. Indeed, the growing needs and wants of postwar consumers were in sharp contrast to the past, where saving and thrift were among the prize virtues. The excessive investment in economic prowess and indulgence, combined with a disinterest in political themes in the 1950s, becomes a deadly formula for a self-absorbed, but also group-dictated pattern of consumption under which Brückner's protagonist ultimately suffers.[4] As Sandra Frieden explains, "At the beginning [the character Ursula—played by Sylvic Ulrich] is bewildered because she is no longer permitted to like what she is. Gradually this leads to a more general bewilderment, expressed by her constant eating. She tries to consume everything, despite the title, until she is forced into silence and finally suicide. The problem . . . is the relationship between the individual and society, a central issue of the women's movement [and] of a whole period, of the fifties."[5]

Much of the film's reception has concentrated on its disturbing imagery and on its strong connection to the women's movement and to Ursula's grappling with her identity and sexuality, which Brückner herself foregrounded in her interviews about the film.[6] Barbara Kosta reads the film above all as an attempt by a woman director to represent female sexuality, especially in dialogue with feminist film criticism's connections among cinematic practices, voyeurism, and the "male gaze."[7] The cultural conditions of the 1950s produced not just confusion about female sexuality and social roles, but also—as my essay will demonstrate—the kind of food disorders we see in Ursula, namely her overeating and bulimia, which function in collusion with precisely these external conditions. The film's conscious instigation of several tensions— between body and mind, obedience and rebellion, plenty and want—all indicate the protagonist's gnawing spiritual hunger that hides behind the façade of overindulgence in food and consumption. Brückner's refusal to offer a straightforward "solution" to these paradoxes makes the film brutally, sometimes unpalatably honest, but also gives it a richly polyvalent texture, chiefly by exposing various personal and political levels on which the film's depiction of consumption operates.

Brückner's reliance on Ursula's overeating and bulimia to illuminate a self-destructive postwar consumer culture is consistent with Hilde Bruch and Susan Bordo's analyses of eating disorders among women as a manifestation of the ills of postwar society. Bruch's psychiatric view of adolescent eating disorders in conjunction with the postwar popularization of adolescent weight control creates a complex understanding of the significance of food behavior.[8] Bruch convincingly argues that an individual's misuse of eating functions to camouflage problems of living that to her appear insoluble. Brückner's commentary on this particular issue concurs with such a psychological approach: "[The film depicts] what happens to girls who become alienated from their own bodies . . . because they don't know how they are supposed to be in the eyes of others and therefore in their own eyes. For who would have been capable of passing a judgment that would put other judgments in question at . . . fourteen!"[9] Throughout the film, Ursula suffers under powerful cultural pressures toward the standardized female body disseminated, for instance, through the beauty contests she avidly watches. The bingeing and purging pattern she follows indicates her strong desire to fit her body into the socially acceptable mandates of weight and appearance, without any reflection on women's empowerment or social roles.

In her study of anorexia nervosa, subtitled "Psychopathology as the Crystallization of Culture," Susan Bordo asserts that eating disorders reflect and draw attention to some of the central ills of the society in which they appear. Bordo isolates three interrelated axes along which women's disturbed relationship to food is structured: (1) the dualist axis, or the heritage of disdain for the body; (2) the control axis, or fear of loss of control over the future; and (3) the gender axis, or the disquieting relationship between body ideals and gender.[10] First, Bordo takes up Michel Foucault's notion that the body is constantly under pressure from the cultural practices which inscribe themselves on it. The tenacious Western legacy of body-mind dualism, then, defines the body as alien, other than self, a material prison, the enemy. The way to win against the body is to control it through denial of food or through overeating to overcome and transcend it. Speaking of aspects of fashion, Bordo then reveals how the social manipulation of the female body becomes a central strategy in maintaining power relations between the sexes. Bordo traces the mythology/ideology of the devouring, insatiable female, back to texts such as *Malleus Malleficarum* (*The Witch Hammer*)[11] as well as social discourses linking excessive eating to excessive sexuality. In *Years of Hunger,* Ursula's grappling with her body and sexuality foregrounds this dualistic theme. The inability to effectively negotiate those forces that pull her in opposite directions—mind and body, desire and repulsion, obedience and rebellion, wealth and scarcity— expresses itself in Ursula's distorted relationship to food throughout the film.

Ursula's increasing dependence on food, central to the film, raises the question whether *Years of Hunger* should be classified as a "food film" such as *Eat, Drink, Man, Woman* (dir. Ang Lee, 1994), *Fried Green Tomatoes* (dir. Jon Avnet 1991), or *Like Water for Chocolate* (dir. Alfonso Arau, 1991).[12] In such food films, eating becomes a product and mirror of the organization of society on both the broadest and most intimate levels, a prism that absorbs and reflects a host of cultural phenomena. An examination of foodways—behaviors and beliefs surrounding the production, distribution, and consumption of food— reveals much about power relations and conceptions of sex and gender in these films. In Brückner's film, food intake becomes a means to fill the void in Ursula's life and to unlock the deepest secrets of the self. However, unlike the food films that feature extreme close-ups of food or devote large amounts of the narrative to the rituals of buying, preparing, and consuming food, Brückner's sparse film technique chooses to foreground hunger, relegating individual food items to long shots or situating them off-space (that is, outside the action normally captured on screen by the camera) while focusing on close-ups of Ursula's face in the act of consumption.

Rather than food itself, hunger and the need for consumption are the driving forces of Brückner's film. In addition, *Years of Hunger* also presents a total breakdown of the relationship between food and self. Ursula's eating disorders—her overeating and bulimia—can be read as self-directed violence, which culminates in her consumption of a "cake" made of medicine pills, toward the end of the film. Food, though separate from the body, becomes the body and crosses the boundaries between outside and inside when it is ingested and ejected. Yet, in a subversion of this idea, food also becomes a deadly means to negate the boundaries between outside and inside by generating death, the ultimate leveler of the animate and inanimate. Indeed, as Gay Poole observes in her study of food on film, "food's protean qualities of transience, physicality, and mutability and the digestive process itself are analogous to the process of transformation involved in dying and decay."[13] Instead of providing solace and nourishment, food embodies self-destruction in Brückner's film. Finally, the director's decision to make the theme of food consumption part of a complex set of discourses about 1950s West German society makes *Years of Hunger* a scathing commentary on the problematic politics and economics of a past decade. After devouring everything else, the consumer must resort to eating herself. In the West German political context, the obsession with consumption cannot gloss over knowledge of the Nazi past. Awareness of Germany's painful national history, then, becomes an antidote to overconsumption and must also lead to devastating self-criticism.

The painful process of food consumption equated with self-destruction, as it is enacted in the final sequence of Brückner's film, is echoed by the contradiction contained in the film's German title, *Hungerjahre in einem reichen Land* (literally, "Years of Hunger in a Rich Country"). The title appears twice in the opening sequence, highlighting two sides of the story's take on eating and consumption. The title appears for the first time after the historical context has been set up with the intertitle "1953," followed by scenes from Ursula's parents talking about their new apartment, from which earlier tenants, an unmarried couple, have been evicted. Ursula's curious question regarding the previous renters' "left-handed marriage" is followed by admonishment from her mother (Britta Pohland) that she does not need to know everything. As Kosta observes about the film, "[Ursula's] exclusion from certain spheres of knowledge, for which her mother is primarily responsible, leads to an increasing tension between the inner—her needs and desires to become a "normal girl"—and the outer—an oppressive bourgeois asceticism that her mother personifies."[14] The first appearance of the film's title after this scene of exclusion clearly points to the fact that the hunger central to this movie is multifaceted.

Hunger for food and eating as a theme appear relatively late in the film, which begins by focusing on the more abstract notion of a hunger for knowledge. An extreme close-up of rows of canned food is followed by the mother's voice on the soundtrack saying, "You never know when hard times will strike." We then hear Ursula's commentary on the soundtrack directing her to "be curious about myself." A close-up of a car being cleaned and waxed cuts to a long shot of the Scheuner family in the car, superimposed with the second appearance of the title in its entirety, as *Years of Hunger—In a Rich Country*. The appearance of the title directly after this montage brings together multiple meanings of consumption. Hunger becomes the place in the film where "the invisible soul can make itself visible,"[15] and where aspects of the visible world, including food, but also body image, gender roles, and social codes can inscribe themselves on the invisible soul, ultimately subjugating and destroying both aspects of this dualistic relationship, the shell of the body and the core of the soul.

In addition to the close-ups of food cans and some shots of cooking and eating, a ritual that recurs in the film to signify Ursula's confused relationship to her external surroundings is the eating of cakes on various occasions. Close-up shots of cake being eaten freely during an outdoor picnic while Ursula interacts and jostles with a male cousin give way to an increasingly differentiated use of food as a veiled metaphor for sexuality and interpersonal relations. For instance, the mother's coy description of Ursula's first menstrual period to the father, "She has a tummy-ache because she ate too much cake," sets forth the connection between food and sex she makes when describing her own first date with Ursula's father: "He got me candy, . . . and we must have eaten at least a pound of it between the two of us." The parallel between eating and courtship expresses the mother's confusion of the two kinds of pleasures and, more poignant, her inability to talk with Ursula about sexual topics. Later in the film, the mother helplessly exclaims: "We should talk about this sometime . . . but then you read so much." Left on her own, Ursula is drawn to books to satisfy her thirst for knowledge, but books are clearly inadequate for much of the knowledge she seeks about the self and the world.

Shots of Ursula eating cake invariably recur when she is confronted with new knowledge that she cannot fathom: after witnessing her parents' coitus, after finding out about her father's secret affairs with other women, and after her parents interrupt her date at a fast food restaurant and prohibit her from seeing men. The cake's multiple appearances suggest its status as a "comfort food" for Ursula, associated with feelings of familiarity, childhood, and a sense of social belonging. In other words, the recurring cakes recreate a perfect world in which she can continue to be a "good girl" in spite of her transgressions and find a level of security despite new and disturbing knowledge.

Hilde Bruch remarks that women and girls with eating disorders are typically known for being "good girls," for being overly compliant: "They have a difficult time asserting themselves, going against societal or familial programs: being fat then becomes a panacea. . . . They practise their rituals—of gorging, scrutinizing their bodies in the mirror—alone."[16] Ursula's disturbed relationship with food, characterized by extreme binges, complicates her grappling with her self-image. There are recurring close-ups in the mirror of Ursula's body in various states of dress and undress—such as examining her legs critically while she holds herself in a seductive pose on a chair. The diffusion of her reflected image—for instance, fragmented reflections of her face (or mind) in one mirror and body in another—shows the gradual dissolution of her self-understanding. In addition, scenes of Ursula's fragmentation are juxtaposed with footage from the Miss World competition, with extreme close-ups of beautiful bare bodies presented as models of identification: "'Woman' here is produced as a spectacle, as an object to be looked at. She advertises herself as a product whose purpose is to arouse the viewers' desire," notes Kosta.[17] At the same time, the parading of bodies indicates another kind of hunger for female role models, apart from her mother, with whom she can identify. Ultimately, however, Ursula's belief that "others are better than I am" is a result not so much of her own body image as of the excessively stringent authority exercised by her mother.

The ingestion of food, as Carole Counihan points out, is "a metaphor and vehicle for the ingestion of parental—particularly maternal—culture."[18] However, in the film, Ursula's mother is shown to be unskilled at creating a positive maternal culture. Mrs. Scheuner's decision to work goes against dominant ideas about female domesticity and maternal behavior under Chancellor Konrad Adenauer's administration, when women were propagandized back into the full-time job of wife and mother. The complete lack of scenes showing family meals also relates to a more mechanized eating pattern, suggested by the rows of canned and readymade food in Mrs. Scheuner's kitchen, which are contrasted with the self-made food of her mother-in-law. At the same time, the extreme close-ups of food cans are accompanied by the mother's fear of a relapse into wartime deprivation: "Let's hope there is no war; otherwise it's all been for nothing." Mrs. Scheuner's decision to work seems primarily motivated by her consumerist fantasies, for example, her desire for a larger apartment. At the same time, her anxiety about leaving Ursula alone in the apartment results in Ursula's entrapment in a regimen of forced domesticity, captured in the recurring image of Ursula standing behind a window, "caged" in her parents' apartment and value systems. Ursula compensates for both the lack of maternal reality and the reality of maternal oppression through her eating in a distorted attempt at self-mothering. The bingeing motif, then, indicates her attempts to fill the isolation and inner deficit by eating. For example, the school dance that Ursula is not allowed to attend is shown in a montage of still photographs intercut with images of her sitting on her bed ingesting heaps of food.

Instead of functioning as "comfort food," however, eating becomes a debilitating idée fixe that allows Ursula no distance on her situation, no freedom of thought, no chance of making any progress in leading the kind of active, creative life that her body and soul crave. The regime of isolation and enforced domesticity culminates instead in two suicide attempts and a nervous breakdown. Ursula's voracious consumption of food becomes her chief means of self-destruction. During her binges, she becomes increasingly lethargic and indifferent to the outside world, and is later shown doubled over with a stomach ache. Even as she flees from her body through compulsive eating, Ursula also writes poetry, which would seem to indicate a creative potential and urge to express herself. Much of her poetic imagery draws on cooking or food metaphors and is focused on her body. In the face of her incapacity to deal with self-imposed ideals such as those of body image (for instance, the ideal of beauty queens) and of being a star student, Ursula's nonconformist combination of food and poetry becomes a creative act that offers some solace but also underlines her complete withdrawal from the outside world.

By plundering the refrigerator at night and by eating differently from family members, Ursula defies communally endorsed patterns of consumption. Postwar consumption, as depicted in *Years of Hunger,* becomes equivalent to a consensus on what comprises a decent and good life. Ursula's parents desire mass-produced commodities—such as vacuum cleaners and cars—that are little differentiated from others by fashion. Their identity forming consumption results not from an expressive choosing of items particular to their own taste, but in conforming to social pressures and belonging to a group of consumers. Interestingly, patterns of consumption in *Years of Hunger* also become a site of generational strife and difference. Alan Warde observes that a "crucial effect of affluence in postwar capitalism has . . . been to justify the ideology and allow the practice of individualism and to link the acquisition and use of consumer goods to values which emphasize the importance of the search for personal identity."[19] Warde's account of the difference between a younger and older generation's postwar consumption emphasizes the gradual erosion of social embeddedness or group constraints in buying, and emphasizes individualization and self-direction for younger consumers. The adolescent consumer's distinct and eclectic taste in food becomes a sign of how she situates herself with relation to others generationally and socially.

The frequent voice-overs of Ursula or her mother reading through an inventory of possessions emphasize the generational difference between their consumer desires. For instance, Ursula's list includes exotic objects such as a fan with a peacock embossed on it, while her mother's list highlights objects that will add to their comfort or status as a middle-class family: "a bigger apartment with a study and dining area, Chippendale cabinets, a vacuum cleaner." Her mother's frustration at Ursula's constant demands for more material possessions reflects the distance between them: "She wants and wants and doesn't realize how much we are sacrificing for her . . . or that other children's parents are rich business-owners." The complete miscommunication between generations becomes most evident after Ursula's mother discovers heaps of pills to aid digestion in her daughter's room. Mrs. Scheuner's remark, "If you would eat with us at proper times, you wouldn't have to raid the refrigerator at night," reveals both her inability to understand Ursula's bulimic behavior and her failure to offer her viable means to overcome her disorder. Given this kind of response from her mother, it is easy to understand Ursula's refusal to interact with her parents. In the following sequence, Ursula holds the telephone receiver far from her ear when her mother calls from work to check on her. When her mother's voice pours through, suggesting that she stay away from bed and do homework, Ursula responds intermittently with "yes" and then promptly goes back to bed. Ursula also reacts to her mother's unproductive one-way telephone communication with a militant ingestion of food.

In addition to foregrounding her struggle with the physical, sexual, and social image she strives to attain, Ursula's gradually specialized and self-endangering consumption of food amounts to a politicizing of consumption in the course of the film, reflecting her increasing distance from her parents' generation and from society's messages regarding consumption or from its "transmission of cultural capital."[20] Her ingestion of food in the two suicide sequences toward the end of the film can thus be read both as consumption and anticonsumption. In both, she gorges herself, thus consuming in rabid excess not unlike her parents and the surrounding culture. But her individual rebellion emerges in her unique attempt to conquer materialism through self-destruction.

The first suicide sequence starts with a medium shot of Ursula trying to buy sugar. She can muster up the words describing the commodity only with great difficulty— "that white, sweet thing"—as she pretends to be a foreigner: "I felt superfluous and made no attempt to convince myself otherwise." The conflicting feelings of being "as transparent as parchment paper" and "heavy as a stone" echo her nightmare of being pulled in two different directions by the globe under her feet and the sky above her, a conflict also reflected in the poem she writes about burning like a candle at both ends. Her first suicide attempt, when she cuts herself in the classroom, is prevented by a custodian's arrival. This is followed by a medium shot of Ursula consuming the sugar she has purchased, chewing down huge quantities in one go, while the soundtrack plays her voice saying "devouring . . . burning, coldness in fire, eating up." The combination of the ingredients on-screen and the fire from the voice-over creates a unique recipe for self-destruction that reaches its highpoint in the final sequence. The soundtrack ends with the central question of the film, "How can one live inside and outside at the same time?" followed by explosions. The date 1789 (referring to the year of the French Revolution) written on the chalkboard when Ursula attempts to kill herself suggests that while self-destruction could be one answer to the question, another possible solution could be revolution— and an active confrontation of history.

Throughout the film, Ursula's gradual rebellion against traditional patriarchal structures and the protective core of institutions like the family or school system is depicted as a painful process of coming to terms with selfhood as well as with troubling external, political conditions. The film makes explicit the connection between the food motif and the historical context of the Cold War and a divided Germany when Ursula's teacher makes a list of food items that could be sent to East Germany: "oil, meat, sugar, powdered eggs, and above all, bananas and oranges." Cinematic versions of moments of significant change and historical shifts captured through foodways can also be found in other films, such as Peter Greenaway's *The Cook, the Thief, His Wife, and Her Lover* (1989). Feeding characters on screen becomes synonymous with feeding the audience with history. In Brückner's case, the film's difficult confrontation with Germany's troubled past and its revisiting of the Third Reich is echoed in the disagreeable quality of its images of food and eating. Brückner uses scenes of Ursula's confusion-filled teenage years as the basis for treating the thorny matter of growing up during the 1950s in West Germany, grappling with those elements of the Nazi past that form a continuum with the present.

A good example of this technique occurs in the sequence in which Ursula's high school teacher fondly reminisces about her childhood in Nazi Germany. Ursula's critical questioning of the past in these scenes and her probing into the political conditions in West Germany are constantly balanced with footage from key political events between 1953 and 1956, such as the uprising in Berlin's Soviet sector in 1953, Chancellor Adenauer's reinstatement of compulsory military service, and the prohibition of Germany's Communist Party in 1956. These documentary inserts powerfully highlight World War II's continuing influence on all fronts. Further, the confrontation with history, particularly with the Nazi past, becomes a means of confronting personal history and the parents' past. Ursula's realization that her father exploits his underground seditious activity of distributing flyers against the Nazis to court his female acquaintances problematizes the private and public nature of the lies she confronts while growing up in the 1950s.

Years of Hunger uses the theme of eating to focus on the painful realizations made by a young girl who confronts her body and the world, and simultaneously rebels against both. The protagonist's hunger for self-understanding and self-discovery as she confronts disturbing and repressive mechanisms at work in the society and in the politics of her country, culminates in Ursula's second suicide attempt in the final sequence. In this sequence, Brückner once again subverts traditional expectations of food as the source of comfort, nourishment, and health, and transforms it into a source of anxiety, illness, and destruction. The sequence begins with Ursula's voice-over saying, "I'm baking a cake of almond, poppy seeds, orange peels, butter, sugar, eggs—but without flour. No flour." The voice-over is accompanied by a long shot of Ursula sitting at a table covered with different kinds of food and drink, and continues with a close-up of her face as she removes several boxes of medications from the medicine cabinet in the bathroom in her parents' apartment. The next few frames consist of extreme close-ups of Ursula in the act of bingeing on handfuls of pills, the "flour" for her cake, chewing them slowly and washing them down with sips from a water bottle. The soundtrack remains silent except for the sound of her swallowing, and minimal camera movement tracks her controlled gestures of moving her hand to different bottles of pills, and then eating the pills.

Brückner's visual choices are deliberately unsavory, making her images more difficult to digest than the alluring close-ups of food in most food films. The hunger of the film's title penetrates the visual images of food to produce a stark, deprived quality; at the same time, the film's abundance of imagery and its reliance on visual montage to compress multivalent messages in a single frame or sequence suggest its own hunger for images as a means to confront the void of repressed truths. Using discontinuous editing to shift rapidly among autobiographical, fictional, and documentary modes, *Years of Hunger* frequently creates a discord between image and sound, between form and content, and thereby hearkens back to the inherent contradiction contained in its title, the contrast between hunger or scarcity and satisfaction or wealth. Its intentional paucity reflects the emotional hunger in a decade of plenty, a hunger that eats at the self, as is evident in the film's final image of a burning photograph of the thirty-year-old Ursula. While the older first-person narrator's voice-over in the frame narrative assures viewers that she has survived the 1950s and her "years of hunger" unscathed, the final fiery image seems to explode in violent self-consumption. Ursula's burning photograph appears to indicate autobiographical filmmaking's consumption of self as film image.

And yet, echoing the flashback, the film ends in a freeze frame with the photograph half-burned and thereby saved from destruction.

The self-reflexive play on eating oneself away to death powerfully connects the self-destruction of the frame narrative to Ursula's suicide attempts through eating during the Economic Miracle. The sense of survival and security in emerging from both self-mutilating acts can only partially mitigate the nagging hunger that has beleaguered the bulimic first-person narrator and 1950s West Germany, and above all, the hunger felt by a first postwar generation for a truthful confrontation with the past. Ultimately, both narrative levels of Brückner's film explore the kind of hunger that cannot be satisfied by food. Instead of culminating in pleasurable satiation like most food films, *Years of Hunger* whets viewers' appetites for more understanding of its social context and political message, voicing a desperate protest against external conditions. Melancholy and death coexist with Ursula's consumerist excess. The normally pleasurable food that she turns into poison becomes an allegory for the waste and greed of the Economic Miracle and for the deadly consumerist impulses unleashed at that time.

Notes

1. The 1950s were the first decade of West Germany's Economic Miracle (*Wirtschaftswunder*). Economic support from the West—for example, through the Marshall Plan—led to the rapid recovery and growth of the West German economy to such an extent that unemployment sank to below 1 percent by 1961. An increase in wages, coupled with generous state subsidies, led to a higher standard of living. Rabid consumerism, brand consciousness, and luxurious lifestyles became the order of the day.
2. Gertrud Koch, "*Hungerjahre-in einem reichen Land.*" *FAZ*, 23 October 1980.
3. Alan Warde, *Consumption, Food and Taste: Culinary Antinomies and Commodity Culture* (London: Sage, 1997), 197.
4. Kristin Ross, in *Fast Cars, Clean Bodies: Decolonization and The Reordering of French Culture* (Cambridge: MIT Press, 1996), identifies two types of consumers that rose in prominence in the 1950s—namely, the housewife and the teenager—and the mother-daughter relationship in *Years of Hunger* spans both these "consumer types."
5. Sandra Frieden, ed., *Gender and German Cinema* (Oxford: Berg, 1993), 256.
6. See, for instance, *Abend*, 23 February 1980 or *Frankfurter Rundschau*, 26 August 1980.
7. Barbara Kosta, "Representing Female Sexuality: On Jutta Brückner's Film *Years of Hunger*," in *Gender and German Cinema*, ed. Sandra Frieden (Oxford: Berg, 1993), 24.
8. Hilde Bruch, *Eating Disorders* (New York: Basic, 1973), 5.
9. *Abend*, 23 February 1980.
10. Susan Bordo, "Anorexia Nervosa: Psychopathology as the Crystallization of Culture," in *The Anthropology of Food and Body: Gender, Meaning, and Power*, ed. Carol Counihan (New York: Routledge, 1999), 241.
11. *The Malleus Maleficarum*, first published in 1486, served as a guidebook for inquisitors during the Inquisition, and was designed to aid them in the identification, prosecution, and dispatching of witches. Many women—midwives, old women, and others who did not fit in within the contemporary view of pious Christianity—were suspected, tried, and burned at the stake.
12. Gay Poole, in *Reel Meals, Set Meals* (Sydney: Currency, 1999), 13, traces the food motif in literature and art over the centuries, and points out that film directors were quick to grasp and exploit the implications of food, starting with the Auguste and Jean Luois Lumière'a *Baby's Lunch* (1897) and Charlie Chaplin's films.
13. Ibid., 156. Poole also contends that Claude Lévi-Strauss's views on the human habit of eating and baring our teeth (principally to tear flesh) only in trusted company are prompted by the recognition that the consumption of an everyday meal may have a destructive element.

14. Kosta, "Representing Female Sexuality," 245.
15. Brückner, cited in Kosta, "Representing Female Sexuality," 249.
16. Bruch, *Eating Disorders*, 212.
17. Kosta, "Representing Female Sexuality," 247.
18. Carole M. Counihan, *The Anthropology of Food and Body: Gender, Meaning, and Power* (New York: Routledge, 1999), 58.
19. Warde, *Consumption*, 7.
20. Ibid., 189.

3
Making Movies, Making Meals

14

Appetite for Destruction: Gangster Food and Genre Convention in Quentin Tarantino's *Pulp Fiction*

REBECCA L. EPSTEIN

Over the past few years, "food films" have been making moviegoers salivate. Stanlet Tucci and Campbell Scott's *Big Night* (1996), George Tillman, Jr.'s *Soul Food* (1997) and Lasse Hallström's *Chocolat* (2000) are just three examples of recent, popular feature films in which the production, presentation, and consumption of food fills the screen and tempts the audience. In 1997, *New York Times* food critic Molly O'Neill observed that food in Hollywood films was increasingly becoming "both plot and motive."[1] Indeed, the food-related activity in these productions is not only aesthetic; it also serves as a locus for social relations and cultural values, organizing narrative lines and soliciting audience response.

But how might we interrogate the use of food in "*non*–food films?" How does food factor into the structure, themes, and characters typical of traditional Hollywood genre films, such as the western, musical, or screwball comedy? Does food imagery serve symbolic, thematic, or narrative ends in films where culinary and gastronomic activity are seemingly subordinate to established generic codes and conventions? How, for instance, might we discuss the food in *Pulp Fiction*, writer/director Quentin Tarantino's 1994 neo-noir gangster film, critically prized for its witty banter, graphic violence, and generic self-reflexivity?

Pulp Fiction was a popular and critical success immediately upon its release; the film's postmodern complexity, narrative stealth, excessive violence, and comedic irony led to seemingly endless discussions of its formal content, cultural context, and audience appeal. Yet for all the critical recognition attending this film, little of it has focused on *Pulp Fiction's* substantial display and diegetic use of food. According to my count, eighty-three of the ninety-three scenes in the published screenplay bear some reference to food. In these scenes, food lends depth to characters, advances the narrative, and, ultimately intensifies the brutal displays of violence.[2] Indeed, by foregrounding scenes involving the discussion, presentation, or consumption of food, Tarantino creates a culinary discourse integral to *Pulp Fiction's* diegetic intent and generic success. In other words, the film's food enriches our reception of the film and its generic codes. How this value escaped most critics' eyes may be tied to what folklorist Michael Owen Jones has stated: "The subject of food customs and symbolism is one of the most overlooked and least understood topics in research." This, though "eating is unique. No other activity in which human beings engage involves so many senses and sensations."[3] While the amount of food-related scholarship in the humanities has increased significantly over the last decade, it remains minimal within the discipline of film studies. This essay, therefore, employs food as a means of textual analysis. Additionally, food's presence in *Pulp Fiction* is in many ways similar to its use throughout the gangster genre. As such, it is a generic convention and merits discussion in generic terms. Indeed, a food-based approach to *Pulp Fiction* expands the possibilities of film genre study as a whole.

Pulp Fiction—"three stories about one story"—takes place in modern day Los Angeles and as Tarantino describes, "hangs out" with a small variety of gangsters over a thirty-six-hour period.[4] The characters, most of whom are male, are modern incarnations of those from the genre of literature to which the film's title refers; urban outlaws who are tough, droll, and engaged in tests of their virility. Integral to this updating of pulp narratives is an attention to the kitsch of late twentieth-century American popular culture; there are references to a broad spectrum of television shows, B movies, and pop music (primarily 1950s surf and 1970s disco and soul).[5] Completing the environment are references to brand-name junk foods and definitively American restaurants, including fast food chains, diners, and theme museum/entertainment eateries.

The film opens, in fact, at a coffee shop meant to resemble "a normal Denny's."[6] It is late morning, and a couple of liquor store robbers who call each other Honey Bunny and Pumpkin sit in a booth discussing their next heist. They face each other, presumably having finished their breakfast despite only one used plate on the table between them. As they talk, Honey Bunny (Amanda Plummer) pours an indiscriminate amount of cream and sugar into her coffee and Pumpkin (Tim Roth) chain-smokes cigarettes. After considering a range of possibilities, Pumpkin suggests they hold up a restaurant, perhaps even the one they're sitting in. When Honey Bunny asks him to explain, Pumpkin spouts a torrent of racial epithets before arguing that the establishment is undoubtedly insured, and the (low wage) "wetback" employees are unlikely to resist or show protective loyalty. Pumpkin then considers the likely similar passivity of the patrons, adding, "Customers are sitting there with food in their mouths, they don't know what's going on. One minute they're having a Denver omelet, next minute somebody's sticking a gun in their face." Now worked up, Pumpkin calls for more coffee, insulting the waitress in the process by shouting "Garçon!" ("Garçon means boy," she retorts, refilling his cup.) Suddenly Pumpkin and Honey Bunny decide to act, sealing the deal by kissing over the empty plate, which represents the food they consumed to nourish their bodies, their plan, their partnership, and their love. The two turn into the room with guns drawn. "Alright everybody, this is a robbery!" Pumpkin shouts. Honey Bunny follows, screaming "Any one of you fucking pricks move and I'll execute every one of you motherfuckers!" According to the script and as played by the actors, Pumpkin is "in-control and professional" while Honey Bunny appears a "psychopathic, hair-triggered loose cannon."[7]

This first scene conveys all the manners in which food is presented throughout the film: culturally (American fare such as a Denver omelet), spatially (a diner), temporally (a late morning breakfast) and sexually (Honey Bunny's hysteria after excessive use of cream and sugar is coded feminine, whereas Pumpkin, who doesn't eat and displays outward aggression, is coded masculine). Food also impacts language (the pet names "Honey Bunny" and "Pumpkin"), and sets up power relations between those eating and those preparing and serving food. Nonnutritive stimulants are also "consumed" (in this case, cigarettes). Finally, mealtime is presented as social, fostering communication, which leads to action. Indeed, as the couple kisses over the table, we witness a transition from a comfortable, harmonious moment "over food" to a charged, violent one.

In a rare reference to his copious use of food and food sites in the film, Tarantino claims he shot the film mostly in restaurants, "as they are ideal for long conversations."[8] Although he wrote this scene based on his own habit of hanging out with friends at diners, his remark indicates an understanding of the social mechanism of food consumption. Dining with others typically facilitates communication, problem solving, and social comfort. Honey Bunny and Pumpkin, for instance, socially and emotionally bond over their breakfast of coffee, cigarettes and strategic planning. Similarly, later on in the film, only after sharing a meal with his boss's wife does lead protagonist and hit man Vince (John Travolta) finally agree to enter a twist contest with her, of course, *Pulp Fiction* also reveals how the table can be rife with conflict. Pumpkin is the first to air the film's preoccupation with the threat of social difference. In addition to calling the busboys "wetbacks" and condescending to the waitress, he rants that "too many foreigners own liquor stores. Vietnamese, Koreans that can't speak fuckin' English . . . and if it's not the Gooks, it's the Jews." Xenophobia also occurs in the "you are what you eat" scenarios of the film, in which differing food preferences illustrate cultural tensions among characters. Sympathetic characters indulge in meat-laden American fast food and diner cuisine, while the (few) unsympathetic characters eat "lighter" continental fare or in the case of the pawnshop owners, metaphorically eat insects ("Spider just caught a coupla flies"). Meat is so sacred that even the renaming of commercial American hamburgers strikes these characters as peculiar, as evidenced by the film's famous "Le Big Mac" dialogue. Stranger still are what Vince calls the "little differences" of foreign foodways: his partner, Jules (Samuel L. Jackson), for example, is disgusted when he learns the Dutch commonly eat French fries with mayonnaise.[9]

Breakfast selections most frequently convey the film's culinary bias toward American cuisine, especially diner fare. Vince indulges in a "Grand-Slam" style breakfast of pancakes, eggs, bacon and coffee, while his boss, the oppressive Marcellus Wallace (Ving Rhames), prefers the "continental" fare of croissant, juice, and tea while dining al fresco. (Notably, Marsellus's socially deviant body is also impressively larger than that of anyone on his staff, so that his physicality, like his food choices, expresses his formidable power rank. But when Marsellus teams with Vince as Vince's new partner, we see Marsellus carrying a box of doughnuts. In his less powerful capacity, Marsellus has "changed sides," now choosing breakfast fare that is fried, sweet, and widely beloved in America rather than food that is baked, savory and European. Marsellus's changed diet further points to the gangster film's subtext of (failed) class mobility. When Marsellus gives up his role as a manager to be a worker, the doughnuts signal his social decline and foreshadow his total humiliation, and thus our sympathy, when, in the next scene, two hillbillies sodomize him.

Breakfast also provides the metaphors for Jules's retreat from gangsterism, which is traceable based on his food choices over the course of the film. Jules eats and talks about hamburgers in his first two scenes in the film, but at his last appearance he eats a bran muffin. He also rebukes Vince's heavy, hungryman breakfast. Indeed, Jules's approach to food is intellectual while Vince's is sensual: Jules theorizes about pork ("[Pigs] are filthy animals. Pigs sleep and root in shit. I don't wanna eat nothing that ain't got enough sense to disregard its own feces") while Vince simply delights in food's flavors ("Sausage tastes good, pork chops taste good"). After this exchange, Jules announces his decision to "go straight" and leave the corrupt underworld in which he dwells. With Jules, food choices represent levels of moral consciousness, his "light" bran muffin exemplary of his phasing out of the heavy meals associated with gangster life. The interaction first suggests a generic convention of gangster films in which the sidekick of a criminal duo gives up a life of crime and returns to social order.[10] Here, however, the convention is reinscribed through Jules's talk of kung fu films (which also employ complementary gangster duos) and his changing food preferences.

Pulp Fiction also codes masculinity through food selection. Highly androcentric, the film extols stereotypical notions of American manliness through the consumption of beef. When we first meet Jules and Vince they are driving to a "hit" and speaking about fast food hamburgers overseas, from McDonald's Le Big Mac to the Burger King Whopper. In the next scene, Jules boasts of his masculine prowess and intimidates a group of young men by slowly savoring one of their Big Kahuna burgers. Jules, whose food choices become increasingly devoid of meat products as the narrative progresses, lovingly bites into a Big Kahuna burger as if fueling his essential, masculine being. "MMMM, that is one tasty burger!" he exclaims. "My girlfriend's a vegetarian so I don't get to eat them very often, but I do love the taste of a good burger." Along the same lines, highly carnivorous Vince later craves and orders a steak "bloody as hell." Consumed often and primarily by hit men, meat in *Pulp Fiction* is revealed as the most manly of food choices.

Beef also helps to define the boy-man subtext typical of the gangster genre. As Thomas Schatz noted in his groundbreaking study of the "classic" gangster films from the early 1930s, the gangster (a "willful individualist") typically must confront, and is often undone by, "his own inability to escape the influence of mother, home and culture."[11] While *Pulp Fiction* reveals the extent to which mother figures have largely disappeared from the gangster genre, food factors into the film's images of boyishness, which serves as a foil to the (male) gangster's arrogance and criminality. The young men to whom Jules confesses his love of burgers, for instance, are eating cheeseburgers at 7:30 A.M. in a messy apartment, only one of them dining at a table. The image suggests orphaned boys who do not know how to take care of themselves—after all, even in America it seems gastronomically inappropriate to eat hamburgers for breakfast. Accordingly, Jules and Vince take on parental roles, allegorically scolding and then punishing the boys' errant behavior by blowing them away. Some critics have also noted how the renegade boxer, Butch Coolidge (Bruce Willis), embodies a tension between boyish needs and manly displays, a depiction to which food contributes. As the authors of *Tarantino, A to Zed* noted, "For what else is Butch but a big baby? His wide eyes and shaven head mark him thus physically; he shares an exclusive childish language with his baby-doll cute paramour, Fabienne . . . Hell, he even eats Pop Tarts."[12] The unsophisticated diet and dining habits illustrated by Butch's Pop Tart penchant and the boys' hamburger breakfast also show up with Lance (Eric Stoltz), Vince's drug supplier. Lance, always in pajamas, eats Cap'n Crunch sugared cereal for dinner while watching television in bed. Dana Polan sees such childlike food choices as indicative of a "regressiveness centered on orality" within the film, as characters experience an infantile comfort from the food they discuss and ingest.[13] And ultimately, these physically vulnerable men find womblike protection in their gastronomy. (Even Vince's excitement over his pork sausage, with its focus on instant gratification, verges on the juvenile.)

Food in *Pulp Fiction* also codes femininity and femaleness. The women's voracious appetites align them with their sisters in noir: as sexually insatiable and (therefore) dangerous. For instance, Fabienne (Maria de Medeiros), Butch's petite girlfriend, lounges in bed in underwear while speaking of her desire for a huge breakfast of blueberry pancakes with maple syrup, eggs over easy, five sausages, a tall glass of juice, and black coffee. (Although she is

French, Fabienne is apparently an American culinary convert.) For dessert, she wants a slice of blueberry pie. "Pie for breakfast?" Butch teases. "Anytime of the day is a good time for pie," she counters, with "pie" serving as a pun on female genitalia. "Blueberry pie to go with the pancakes," she continues, "and on top, a thin slice of melted cheese." Neither timid nor ashamed of her hunger, Fabienne personifies the film's ultimate critique of American physical and material mass consumption. Men may crave meat, but *Pulp Fiction* defines excessive appetite as feminine, a sign of weakness and lack of self control.

Notably, this food-based mode of articulating highly charged female sexuality is highly condemnatory, and each female character within the film endangers the man with whom she comes in contact. Fabienne, for instance, jeopardizes Butch's plan when she forgets to pack his gold watch, and her oversight requires him to return to their old apartment and face Marsellus's men. The model of a foodie femme fatale is most clear, however, in Mia (Uma Thurman), Marsellus's notoriously seductive wife, who breaks Vince's resistance to her over the course of a meal. During what Vince refuses to refer to as "a date," the two go to Jack Rabbit Slim's, a themed restaurant that "both mocks and celebrates the garishness of commercialized 1950s Hollywood nostalgia."[14] Like Fabienne, Mia shows her dangerous sexuality by ordering heavy: a "Durwood Kirby" burger and a "Martin and Lewis Five Dollar Shake" (vanilla flavored, as opposed to a chocolate "Amos and Andy"). In another of the film's many attacks on modern consumer excess, Vince scoffs at the cost of the Sheko, what is "only" milk and ice cream. His resistance is low, however, in the comforting, domesticated space of the restaurant (recall Pumpkin's theory of unsuspecting Denver omelet eaters) and in the company of a sexually seductive woman. When the shake arrives and Mia sucks on the white, creamy phallus, Vince can't help but be sucked in by Mia's charm. Significantly, all of the film's uses of and references to dairy products and eggs, foods commonly associated with females and fertility, connote vulnerability and lack of control—from Pumpkin's unsuspecting omelet eaters to Honey Bunny turning hysterical after drinking coffee with lots of cream.[15] Because of Mia's manipulative skills with a milkshake, Vince, too, crumbles, and Mia holds the shake's cherry in her mouth to symbolize his stolen strength and submission to the feminine.

Strikingly, in *Pulp Fiction*, nonnutritive stimulants and depressants such as alcohol, cigarettes, caffeine, cocaine, and heroin are depicted as comestibles. Recall, for example, that Pumpkin was smoking heavily in the opening scene as if dependent upon cigarettes to think clearly. The correlation of drugs to food is also apparent when Vince stops by Lance's house to purchase some heroin. There, Lance displays a buffet of white powders from which to choose. In extreme close-up we watch the preparation and "cooking" of the drug with a spoon, scale, and hot skillet. Shots then alternate between a stoned (or "full") Vince and the hypodermic needle, the utensil with which he consumes his selection and satisfies his "hunger." In the next scene, while waiting for

Mia, Vince fixes himself a scotch while Mia snorts cocaine in another room. In this way, each has an appetizer of drugs before their restaurant dinner together. Heavy drug use is never portrayed attractively, however, as its presentation is consistently tied to blood, vomit, and mental sluggishness. Drugs are the health-destructive "junk food" (or junkie food) in *Pulp Fiction's* fast-food-based gastronomic hierarchy.

Butch, also a smoker, orders a pack of "Red Apple" cigarettes at a bar, and with this sly commentary on the unhealthfulness of cigarettes reveals another way food appears in the film: in metaphors, puns, and other verbal play.[16] Honey Bunny and Pumpkin's names of endearment are echoed by Fabienne and Butch, in what Polan describes as the "sugary way they talk to each other." Butch calls Fabienne "Sugar Pop," "Lemon Pie," and "Jelly Bean" to convey his love and affection.[17] Noirish amoral heavy Marsellus, on the other hand, uses food analogies to express his ferocity. He lectures Butch that boxers do not "age like fine wine" but instead "turn to vinegar," and later tells his men to be "hiding in a bowl of rice" if the betraying Butch ends up in East Asia. Jules speaks similarly to Pumpkin when he foils the diner robbery ("Normally your ass would be dead as fried chicken"), and both Jules and Lance refer to America's renowned soft drink war to illustrate their spiritual and commercial beliefs. Jules talks of God having "changed my Coke to Pepsi," and Lance says he'll "take the Pepsi Challenge with that stuff from Amsterdam any day" to prove the superiority of the heroin he deals.

As shown, food in *Pulp Fiction* operates thematically, enhancing recurring narrative and generic tropes. However, food also significantly informs the film's structure. For instance, in addition to signifying masculine (im)maturity, the characters' undisciplined eating habits mirror the film's temporal flow. The inversion of culturally determined breakfast and dinner foods (burgers in the morning, cereal at night) is coterminous with the deliberate nonlinear chronology of the film; characters eating foods at the "wrong" time confuses the audience and assures surprise when the narrative puzzle is resolved. When Mr. Winston "The Wolf" Wolfe (Havvey Keitel) appears at Jimmie's (Quentin Tarantino's) house at 8:30 A.M. wearing a tuxedo, having been called away from an unusually early cocktail party, this too is consistent with the film's "movie moments" in which realism is subverted for generic recognition (that is, Mr. Wolf as the familiar, suave problem solver).[18] Significantly, such collapsing of cinematic time always depends on food.

The film contains its temporal sprawl with symmetrical opening and closing scenes at the diner and tight shots of the actors, a mode of visual framing that allows the audience to feel present in the scene, as if sitting at the table with them.[19] The parallelism of the first and last scenes suggests the film has come full circle, even if we're not yet clear on how all the pieces fit together. On closer inspection, however, we see that coffee drinking operates as the film's spine: In act 1, Honey Bunny and Pumpkin have coffee to jack themselves up for the robbery; in act 2, Fabienne talks about coffee and Marsellus carries it (with the doughnuts); and in act 3, Jimmie serves coffee at his house (where, distinguishing their class differences, Jules calls Jimmie's brew "gourmet shit"). The film then closes at the diner when Jules realizes his coffee has grown cold. Because each of these scenes take place the same morning, coffee, the one food in the film designated to only one time of day, helps to cohere the narrative fractures, delineating the temporal links of the film's three stories.[20]

The most striking employment of food within the film's structure is that food scenes consistently precede, or turn into, violent ones. Polan, one of the few academics to address the use of food in *Pulp Fiction*, has described the consumption and discussion of food in the film as a "snack break," "a way to slow down the forward movement of the narrative, for people to find leisurely respite before going out again into the cruel harsh world."[21] I would argue, however, that the structural juxtaposition of food scenes immediately followed by, or merged with, displays of violence, is emotionally effective and narratively progressive. Thus, when the fearsome Wolfe barks at Vince—"Pretty please, with sugar on top, clean the fucking car!"—he not only conveys his anger and superiority, he also speaks to the essence of the film's vitality: the constant volley between displays of nourishing food and destructive violence. The boys' Big Kahuna burgers lead to their massacre, a milkshake at Jack Rabbit Slim's ends with Mia's brutal resuscitation from a drug overdose, and breakfast turns a diner into a site of armed robbery. In addition, the popping up of toaster pastries prompts Butch to pop caps into Vince, and after Butch lurches into a doughnut-toting Marsellus the two find themselves violently sexually assaulted.

In the end, because the food in *Pulp Fiction* is iconic and its use comedic, the food-based scenarios intensify our experience of the film's impassive aggression. Tarantino has stated that he structured his first film, *Reservoir Dogs* (1992), to get laughs despite its gory violence. "I like the idea that the audience is laughing and that BOOM, the next moment there is blood on the walls. Then there are more laughs."[22] In both *Reservoir Dogs* and *Pulp Fiction*, however, he elicits laughs through the "ultrarealism" of popular culture, which in these films often involves food—from commercial products to sites in which food is served. "Real life is *absurd*, like the conversation you hear at Denny's in the next booth. My characters define themselves and talk to others through pop culture, because they all understand it."[23] Not only do the characters "understand it," but so does the audience, laughing at generic tough guys enmeshed in the ridiculousness of commercialized American foods.[24] In other words, food presentation, consumption, language and depictions of drugs as food all work as soporifics; they lull us, the audience, into a relaxed state in which we feel safe, secure, and well fed—that is, until the next gun goes off. Ultimately, *Pulp Fiction*'s culinary discourse not only informs characters and relationships, it also manipulates the audience so the violence consistently takes us by surprise. *We* are Pumpkin's (always unsuspecting) Denver omelet eaters.

Tarantino has alluded to this effect of the film, stating that he likes "pulling the rug out from under" his audience, defying their expectations with surprising twists and turns.[25] But his comments have primarily focused on the narrative and intellectual surprise, rather than the film's phenomenological effects. Polan, on the other hand, likens the experience of the film to that of a theme-park ride, "a roller-coaster experience made up of lulls and high sensations," and does suggest, albeit briefly, the role of food to that end. Polan also draws parallels between *Pulp Fiction's* experiential drama and postmodern discourse, which subsumes textual purpose to sensation. Noting Frederic Jameson's theory on the "waning of affect," Polan writes, "It might well be that post-modernity also has to do with an intensification of sensory experience—a rendering of viscerality so intense that it substitutes for all concern with deep meaning."[26] This may also explain in part why critiques of *Pulp Fiction* have more often spoken of the film's violence, the shocks to the system, than the comforting, familiar food moments that "strap in" the viewer before the ride's next drop. Or, as described by Tarantino, how the audience will go "from the frying pan into the fire."[27]

While Polan's discussion of postmodernity is apt given the film's release toward the end of the twentieth century and contemporary critical debates in the academy surrounding it, what I see as *Pulp Fiction's* structure of contrasts directly relates to the role of contradiction in genre films. The gangster genre and genre study as a whole have been greatly informed by scholars who have focused on inherent contradictory play within generic texts. Rick Altman, in particular, has forwarded this idea through his early studies of the Hollywood musical.[28] Additionally, scholars of the gangster film have discussed the structuralist binaries in play throughout most gangster works. These include high class/low class, boys/men, domestic/antidomestic, masculine/feminine, urban/pastoral, and individual/group.

Food has often played a role in the expression of these generic tensions, regularly enhancing if not in fact determining the thematic, visual, and structural conventions of the Hollywood gangster genre. When Tom Powers pushed a grapefruit into his girlfriend's face in *The Public Enemy* (dir. William Wellman, 1931), he brutally dismissed the domesticity she represented. From that same era, the ascent of Rico Bandello (Edward G. Robinson) to mob boss in *Little Caesar* (dir. Mervyn LeRoy, 1930) delivers him to formal banquets far removed from the modest dining experiences he'd known during his humble beginnings. Many years later, *Bonnie and Clyde* (dir. Arthur Penn, 1967) not only used meals to demonstrate each incarnation of the ever-changing, ever-running Barrow gang "family" (the car becomes their most constant dining room), but also exploited the narrative contrast of food and violence that *Pulp Fiction* enjoys. (Parley Ann Boswell has suggested that because food scenes in *Bonnie and Clyde* are always followed by destructive violent ones, food allegorically "betrays" the outlaws. I tend to see this consistency less as a betrayal than an indication of Bonnie's quest for acceptance and domestic normalcy.[29]) As echoed in *Pulp Fiction*, pie is an ongoing sexual motif in *Bonnie and Clyde*: Wanting to have her photo taken with a captive Sheriff Hamer (Denver Pyle), Bonnie (Faye Dunaway) moves demurely toward him and delivers her immortal line, "Everybody's gonna see Captain Frank Hamer of the Texas Rangers with the Barrow Gang . . . and all of us just as friendly as pie." (In this film, however peach, not blueberry, is the edible pie of choice, made especially significant when Clyde [Warren Beatty] calls Bonnie "a peach" who is sexually "as good as she looks").[30]

Both *Bonnie and Clyde* and *Pulp Fiction* depict a landscape of Americana that is inextricably linked to American fast food—especially hamburgers. In the early 1990s, "gangsta" films located in urban ghettos, such as Allen and Albert Hughes's *Menace II Society* (1993), also involve fast food hamburgers, but do so to highlight the corrupted space of the dining room (now outside at barbeques and fast food stands that render diners vulnerable to drive-by shootings) and the nonnutritive environment in which these gangsters dwell (there are few fresh, noncommercial foods available to them). Thus, a brief look at "cycles" of the gangster genre, begins to reveal how food commonly informs these works.

Tarantino and his critics have been very outspoken about the director's predilection for derivative images and generic cliches. Tarantino himself referred to *Pulp Fiction* as the film in which he sought to calm his obsession with movie gangsters.[31] Accordingly, the film is packed with allusions to popular gangster and noir films, including the brightly lit briefcase in *Kiss Me Deadly* (dir. Robert Aldrich, 1955) and the elliptical narrative style of *The Killing* (dir. Stanley Kubrick, 1956). Certainly, gangster films have been self-reflexive throughout the genre's history. Writers and directors have often quoted previous works to acknowledge cinematic virtuosity and, consequently, canonize the genre. Such referential and reverential moments are also winks at the audience, references begging for recognition. In this way, *Pulp Fiction*'s familiar characters become familial ones: We have a history with them. The what, where, and why of food in *Pulp Fiction* is often subtly but certainly linked to previous gangster and their films and literature. For instance, in James M. Cain's books, which became seminal mid-century Hollywood noir/crime films, including *The Postman Always Rings Twice* (dir. Tay Garnett, 1946) and *Mildred Pierce* (dir. Michael Curtiz, 1945), we find the author manifesting simultaneous attraction and repulsion to mass produced (fast) foods. Robert Dingley claims that in Cain's works, food is in fact a "determinant of action."[32] Tarantino has also confessed that one of his favorite shootouts on film takes place in a restaurant (*Year of the Dragon*, dir. Michael Cimino, 1985).[33] Most predominantly, *Pulp Fiction*'s food scenes provide representations of normalcy and social stability, what cinematic gangsters are necessarily unable to attain.[34]

As I have demonstrated, food is abundant and significant in *Pulp Fiction*, so it's a wonder that anyone would ask, "*What* food in *Pulp Fiction*?" Perhaps one explanation lies in the many peculiar paradoxes of mass American dining practices. Just as beef has the characteristic of having a high status and being universally accessible at the same time, food in America is at once everywhere and out of sight. With the exception of those in need, the majority of the population's food supply is so completely taken for granted that it seems an infinitely available and therefore unremarkable part of everyday life.[35] In addition, the majority of Americans are increasingly unappreciative of the sensory aspects of eating. We place emphasis on food's convenience and cost (and sometimes on calorie counts and nutrients) more often than indulging in the numerous positive sensual and social experiences eating can engender—including those that would assist us in noticing food in "*non*–food films." In contrast, Western Europeans, more actively integrate their gastronomy into their cultural practices. This difference is referenced in *Pulp Fiction* through Fabienne, the French woman who is the only character to eagerly anticipate a meal. Riddled with generic contradictions and paradoxes, *Pulp Fiction* also presents American food and foodways in a manner so consistent with cultural practices that they seemingly disappear.[36]

The absence of discourse about the food in *Pulp Fiction* confirms how much we take for granted the ways that food-centered activities structure, inform, and nourish our lives. Indeed, the distance between our biological need for food and our awareness of its social and cultural weight is exemplified by the plethora of reviews and articles that employ food-based analogies to describe the film, but fail to mention the film's culinary references, if not foundation. Film critic Manohla Dargis mentions "tenderized bodies" and Tarantino's "prodigious appetite for the good the bad and the idiotic," and joins the *Chicago Tribune* film critic Michael Wilmington in calling the women's roles "juicy."[37] Wilmington also calls the film a "bloody stew," and Pat Dowell speaks of the film's "salt and pepper casting."[38] Finally, Foster Hirsch describes the film as "junk food for cineastes," yet even he passed over the value of the film's junk-food foodways in his interpretation of the text. How can we discuss masculinity without discussing the food on which male characters feed? How can we talk about the film's cultural economy of excess without talking about the primary consumptive practice of eating? As illustrated in this essay (and throughout this volume), the study of food can be meaningfully applied to the study of film, from individual texts to generic traditions.

As to *Pulp Fiction*'s audiences' seeming lack of awareness about the movie's multivalent uses of food, we cannot scold the critics without noting that Tarantino himself seldom speaks of the signifying complexity of the film's edibles. The writer/director/actor has stated how much he wanted the film to feel like aspects of his own life, to have the audience "hanging out" at diners as he does. "There are restaurant scenes in all of my scenarios," he stated in a 1994 interview, "and I think every viewer can identify with this kind of scene. I often go to restaurants and just like to sit there and talk with friends. My characters talk a lot and you open up in this kind of conversation."[39] The Le Big

Mac dialogue was also autobiographical, inspired by his own experience living in Amsterdam.[40] Nevertheless, in terms of the film's preponderance of food images, Tarantino has been relatively silent. In yet another nondeliberate self-reflexive act, he has called the film's characters "the oldest chestnuts" and has stated that he left "a trail of bread crumbs" so the audience could decipher the film's more subtle details. In the same interview, Tarantino also spoke of latching onto novelist Stephen King's insight in *Danse Macabre* "about how you have to drink a lot of milk before you can appreciate cream and you have to drink a lot of milk that's gone bad before you can appreciate milk."[41] Writers as food-minded as Tarantino and his critics owe it to themselves and all cultural consumers to "drink the milk" that churned *Pulp Fiction* into "cream." Everything about the film—and film genre study in general—will then become richer.

Notes

1. An early version of this article was presented (as "Tasting the Essence: Food and Meaning in *Pulp Fiction*") at a conference for the Association for the Study of Food in Society, 6 June 1998. Molly O'Neill, "Eye Candy," *New York Times Magazine*, 16 November 1997, p. 149.
2. Quentin Tarantino, *Pulp Fiction: A Quentin Tarantino Screenplay* (New York: Hyperion, 1994).
3. Michael Owen Jones, "Afterword: Discovering the Symbolism of Food Customs and Events" in *We Gather: Food and Festival in American Life*, ed. Theodore C. and Lin T. Humphrey (Ann Arbor: University of Michigan Press, 1998), 235, 244.
4. Gavin Smith, "When You Know You're in Good Hands," *Film Comment* 30, no. 4 (1994): 32; Quentin Tarantino, "Quentin Tarantino on *Pulp Fiction*," *Sight and Sound* 4, no. 5 (1994): 10.
5. Stanley Crouch, "Pulp Friction," *Los Angeles Times*, 16 October 1994.
6. Tarantino, *Pulp Fiction*, 1.
7. Ibid., 7.
8. Manohla Dargis, "Quentin Tarantino on *Pulp Fiction*," *Sight and Sound* 4, no. 11 (1994): 16.
9. Peter Farb and George Armelagos, *Consuming Passions: The Anthropology of Eating* (New York: Washington Square Press, 1983). Farb and Armelagos suggest that French fries and mayonnaise are not typically served in America because of a learned aversion to "doubling up" on greasy foods. Meat and cheese combinations are acceptable but side dishes demand balance as they in turn balance a meal. The Dutch, however, customarily combine heavy and oily foods (222).
10. Thomas Schatz, *Hollywood Genres: Formulas, Filmmaking and the Studio System* (Austin: University of Texas Press, 1981), 93. Schatz notes that "sidekicks" in the classic gangster film would typically "reject the gangster-hero for the more traditional values of marriage, home, and family. Rejection by his junior partner leads directly to the hero's death in these films, indicating that his gangster-family cannot displace society's traditional family structure." Indeed, Jules ultimately obeys his vegetarian girlfriend and Vince dies shortly thereafter.
11. Ibid., 93.
12. Dana Polan, *BFI Modern Classics: Pulp Fiction* (London: British Film Institute, 2000), 49.
13. Polan sees this as reverence for "comfort food," the bland, often "mushy cuisine (such as mashed potatoes) that brings one nostalgically back to the succor of childhood." He also notes the correlation between the infantilism expressed through food choices and the film's "obsession with scabrous anality." See Polan, *Pulp Fiction*, 49.
14. Greg Johnson, "The Diner Niche," *Los Angeles Times*, 4 February 1996.
15. Another feminine-coded food is the egg which, despite the preponderance of breakfast foods in the film, is only mentioned twice: Once by Fabienne ("eggs over easy"—another sexual reference) and once by Pumpkin ("Denver omelet"). Both references imply weakness and submission.

16. Paul A. Woods calls this an attempt to avoid further product placement in the film, which had been endorsed already with the Coke, Pepsi, McDonald's and Burger King references. Nonetheless, calling cigarettes a name implying healthfulness is also (appropriately) absurd. See Woods, *The Wild World of Quentin Tarantino* (New York: Thunder's Mouth Press, 1996), 110.

17. Polan, *Pulp Fiction*, 49.

18. As Tarantino has stated, "'The humor comes to me from this realistic situation [a mess to be resolved] and then in waltzes this complete movie creation, the Wolf—[played by] Harvey Keitel. The movie star walks in, sprinkles some movie dust, and solves the problems'"; quoted in Woods, *Wild World of Quentin Tarantino*, 122.

19. Tarantino has stated that the subject of this scene is not Jack Rabbit Slim, rather "what happens between the these two characters. That's why during their conversation there are no shots of the set." Quentin Tarantino, "Interview with Quentin Tarantino (1994)" by Michael Ciment and Hubert Niogret, in *Quentin Tarantino Interviews*, ed. Gerald Peary (Jackson: University Press of Mississippi, 1998), 86. And yet, the director's penchant for tight shots and confined spaces doesn't deny the significance of the setting. In the case of restaurant scenes, the close camera work places the viewer seemingly "at the table" with the characters.

20. I believe the diner setting is crucial to this film. Woods calls the diner "part of the LA Milieu Tarantino identifies with," coffee shops being his version of a Parisian café where, Tarantino has said, "'[Instead] of discussing existentialism, my friends and I were talking about New World Pictures and whether we were going to be with a woman'"; Tarantino, quoted in Woods, *Wild World of Quentin Tarantino*, 104. Tarantino even refers to the opening diner scene in *Reservoir Dogs* as having "'that *cinema verite* give and take'"; Gavin Smith, "When You Know You're in Good Hands (1994)" in Peary, ed., *Quentin Tarantino Interviews*, 101). However, in Tarantino's hands, this middle-class dining room reads both hip and unassuming, suiting the film's clashing of tough-guy coolness and ironic absurdity. In addition, the diner is the location where we see Vince and Jules "decompose" before our eyes—their dress has turned casual as they've been wasted by their profession, and by a script bent on exposing their humanity (see Ciment and Niogret interview, 97).

21. Polan, *Pulp Fiction*, 51.

22. Quentin Tarantino, "Interview with Quentin Tarantino (1992)" by Peter Brunette, in Peary, ed., *Quentin Tarantino Interviews*, 31.

23. Ibid.

24. Woods, *Wild World of Quentin Tarantino*, 123.

25. To this end, Tarantino has drawn inspiration from the trickery in the pulp crime and science fiction works by author Frederic Brown; see Woods, *Wild World of Quentin Tarantino*, 103.

26. Polan, *Pulp Fiction*, 77.

27. Woods, *Wild World of Quentin Tarantino*, 119.

28. See Rick Altman, "The American Film Musical: Paradigmatic Structure and Mediatory Function" in *Genre: The Musical*, ed. Rick Altman (London: Routledge and Kegan Paul, 1981), 197–207.

29. Parley Ann Boswell, "Hungry in the Land of Plenty: Food in Hollywood Films," in *Beyond the Stars III: The Material World in Popular Film and Culture* (Bowling Green, Ohio: Bowling Green State University Popular Press, 1983), 16. My opinion complements numerous arguments that have shown how *Bonnie and Clyde* was told through Bonnie's point of view. Note also that Bonnie is most happy just prior to her death, when she drives with Clyde (the car is their true home), sharing with him a succulent pear (she has by now forsaken fast foods for natural ones, having come to understand and accept her "natural" self). It is also worth noting that the similarities between *Bonnie and Clyde* and *Pulp Fiction* extend to the use of humor (much of it with food) amid a sea of carnage. Upon release, both films incurred extensive criticism for this duality.

30. This occurs when Clyde's brother, Buck (Gene Hackman), nudges Clyde to tell him about what it's like to have sex with Bonnie. "Is she as good as she looks?" Butch asks, excitedly. "She's better," Clyde answers, with a nervous grin. The audience sees through Clyde's facade, however, knowing that, because of Clyde's impotence, the couple has yet to consummate their love.

31. Smith, "Good Hands," 114.

32. Dingley based his argument on Caine's own identity as a gourmand, and his fear of the "dehumanization" of people in a machine age. See Robert Dingley, "Eating America: The Consuming Passion of James M. Cain," *Journal of Popular Culture* 33, no. 3 (1999): 63–78.

33. Joshua Mooney, "Interview with Quentin Tarantino (1994)" in Peary, ed., *Quentin Tarantino Interviews*, 72.

34. Schatz, *Hollywood Genres*, 29, assesses the "shared social function" of all genres to "tame" threats—actual or imagined—that "threaten the stability of our everyday lives." As evidence here, the food in *Pulp Fiction* provides narrative and structural moments of stability.

35. For a consideration of food as defined within "everyday life," see Michel de Certeau, Luce Giard, and Pierre Mayol, *The Practice of Everyday Life*, vol. 2, *Living and Cooking*, trans. Timothy J. Tomasik (Minneapolis: University of Minnesota Press, 1998).

36. Moreover, as elaborated by Elspeth Probyn, eating and drinking is the one act everyone, no matter age or background, performs. Referring to the writings of George Simmel, Probyn also remarks upon the "brute physicality of eating," which we can only passively experience. "As the morsel is going into my mouth, pricking up my tongue and taste buds, and sliding down on its route to digestion and then finally defecation, you cannot be anything more than a witness." See Probyn, *Carnal Appetites: FoodSexIdentities* (London: Routledge, 2000), 62. This comment supports my reading of the film as correlating eating with victimization.

37. Dargis, "Quentin Tarantino on *Pulp Fiction*," 8.

38. Michael Wilmington, "Bad to the Funny Bone," *Chicago Tribune*, 14 October 1994; Pat Dowell, "Two Shots at Quentin Tarantino," *Cineaste* 21, no. 3 (1995): 4.

39. Ciment and Niogret interview in Peary, ed., *Quentin Tarantino Interviews*, 86.

40. Brunette interview in Peary, ed., *Quentin Tarantino Interviews*, 32. In this 1992 interview Tarantino divulged, "I'd never been to other countries before this year, but I've now been to other countries, and I love going to McDonalds. The difference? In Paris McDonalds, they serve beer. And they don't call it Quarter Pounder because they have the metric system there: Le Royale with cheese! They don't know what a fucking Quarter Pounder is!"

41. Tarantino, "Quentin Tarantino on *Pulp Fiction*," 10.

15

"Leave the Gun; Take the Cannoli": Food and Family in the Modern American Mafia Film

MARLISA SANTOS

When the Little Caesars of the 1920s and 1930s in American film became transformed into the Michael Corleones of the 1970s, the filmic treatment of the Mafia began to involve home and family as much as guns and gambling. This shift signified a more complete treatment of the Mafia and its role in Italian American immigrant culture, including depiction of a wider range of forces that informed the world of Italian-American organized crime. It is perhaps these details of home and family that make the *Godfather* movies and other Mafia films that came later so fascinating to the American movie world; these films began to reveal subtexts about immigration and assimilation—issues that transcend the organized crime underworld.

Food is one of the most obvious elements to appear in this later depiction of the Italian-American cultural world, through meals themselves and their preparation. The addition of such scenes provides a clear sign in modern American Mafia films of the cultural foundation that informs the seeming dichotomy of life in such "families." Food highlights the power structure of the "family" as a military hierarchy, but also highlights the family as the foundation of home and tradition. The depiction of food in these films is the glue that binds together the often contradictory elements of the American Mafia way of life—the seeming incongruities of family, tradition, and religion joined with murder, bloodshed, and brutality. Food becomes the emblem of what it means to be civilized, the reinforcement of whatever cultural rules or aspirations Italian-American Mafia families live by.

When director Francis Ford Coppola began shooting *The Godfather*, he tried to think of some way to assemble the very diverse members of his cast in order to build some cohesion before rehearsals started. To begin creating the mood of the Corleone household and to inspire the actors to undertake character development, he brought together the entire cast for a real family dinner, the evening becoming "not only an opportunity to explore the characters, but to actually *assume* characters in a natural setting."[1] Nothing would seem more natural than a family dinner for building the character bonds that would be necessary for this film; the actors had to begin to realize the complicated burden of being in this family. But some explanation of the term *family* is necessary to understand the cultural implications that involve food in American Mafia films.

Hierarchies in Mafia organizations were traditionally structured as both armies and family trees, with blood relations existing among many of the branches of an organization, and those not linked by biology expected to accept ties of loyalty that made them as tightly integrated into the group as actual blood relatives. The rise of Mafia organizations in America added the additional complexities of immigration woes and assimilation difficulties. The ordering of "families" as an insular structure against the confusing—albeit opportunity-rich—American lifestyle ultimately merged tradition with new freedoms, yielding new complexities and tensions. The newer cinematic depictions of the Mafia, beginning with *The Godfather*, open themselves up to more comprehensively display the full lives of Italian American immigrant crime families. As Manohla Dargis points out, "the immigrant story that winds through the first two *Godfather* films is very much about the dissolution of class boundaries, as well as, importantly, the fear of the dissolution of those boundaries."[2] Food becomes a binding force that holds the cultural past of the "family" together in all senses of the word, reinforcing that there is some strangely moral order to the brutality and violence that preserves their way of life. Food also becomes a metaphor for the consuming nature of this lifestyle, with its rapacious devouring of territory and money; both little fish and big fish in this food chain are spit out when they threaten to poison the body of the family. Once you are eaten by the family, you are absorbed into its structure—the only way out is death.

Several key scenes in Coppola's *The Godfather* (1972) and *The Godfather, Part II* (1974) revolve around food and reveal food to be integral to the duality of violence and familial bonds.[3] Coppola's parallel opening scenes of the wedding of Connie Corleone (Talia Shire) in *The Godfather* and the First Communion celebration for Anthony Corleone (James Gounaris) in *The Godfather, Part II* both include meals and are deliberately similar, signifying the rise to power and then the demise of the Corleone family. However, they are also significant in showing the cultural metamorphosis that the family undergoes and the inherent duality and contradictions of life in *la famiglia*. According to George De Stefano, one of these seeming contradictions is that "the head of a brutal crime syndicate can be a loving father who wants better for his son than the family business; the college-educated and assimilated son can become a more ruthless don than his Old World father."[4] What the differences in the meals that open the two films reflect is the cultural differences that the family, in its most complete sense, is experiencing.

Connie's wedding is extremely traditional, not only in its music and dancing, but especially in its food and drink. At this point, the viewer sees Michael (Al Pacino) as somewhat of an outsider in his family, dressed in his Marine uniform and escorting a woman who is clearly neither Italian nor Italian American, but rather, white-bread Protestant American. However, it is over food that Michael tells Kay (Diane Keaton) what appear to be the first questionable stories she has heard about the darker side of his family and the "business" of his father and brothers. He tells her about the nature of Luca Brasi's bloody relationship to his father and his adopted brother Tom's role as *consiglieri*. Immediately following these stories, he asks, "You like your lasagna?" Even though he makes a point of saying, "That's my family, Kay; it's not me," he may as well be asking her, "How do you like this world?" The lasagna—with its rich layers of meat, cheese, pasta, and sauce—functions here symbolically to represent the fruits of the family's work and the delights of life in America, but of course, the price of this delicious lasagna has been blood and crime. Michael will come to see that the cultural trappings of his family are inextricably interlayered with its "business," and he will be unable to straddle the line forever.

The sharp contrast in the nature of food representation between the opening of the first and the second films speaks volumes about the metamorphosis that Michael has imposed on the family since he became Don. In *The Godfather, Part II*, the nature of Anthony's first communion party is decidedly un-Italian, having no visible signs of Italian culture—no Italian music, food, or dancing. Not only does the "honored" guest, Senator Geary (G.D. Spradlin), botch the pronunciation of the name Corleone, he also displays outright disrespect and bigotry to Don Michael (Pacino (as stated earlier)), who seems to partially blend in with Geary's pseudo-legitimate world, yet is still an outsider and therefore does not fit in anywhere. This line between tradition and assimilation is of course highlighted clearly in *The Godfather, Part II*'s overall structure, as it cuts back and forth between Michael and the present and Vito and the past.

The cultural divide within the family is also sharply displayed in the opening scene by the character of Frank Pentangeli (Michael V. Gazzo), who represents the "old" life of New York and the old way of the family. He arrives at the communion party and is clearly a fish out of water in the setting of Michael's new vision of the family. "What's with the food around here?" he asks Fredo (John Cazale). "A kid comes up to me in a white jacket, gives me a Ritz cracker and chopped liver, he says 'Canapes.' I said, 'Can-o-peas, my ass, that's a Ritz cracker and chopped liver.' . . . Bring out the peppers and sausage!" Michael later calls Pentangeli an "old man," but though he may seem to be a throwback to an earlier time, Pentangeli is able to see through the facade that Michael has created as he has tried to legitimize his family. The white jacket, Ritz cracker, and chopped liver are part of a different culture, that of establishment upper-class privilege. A similar incongruity is displayed when Pentangeli tries to get the band, "not one Italian" among them, to play a tarantella, only to succeed in getting them to play "Pop Goes the Weasel." Traditional music that would have been a symbolic expression of Italian culture at any other family ritual function like this, becomes instead a children's song that ridicules and taunts Pentangeli, as if that song were a symbolic messenger, a trickster who has transformed the family culture into one that Pentangeli no longer recognizes.

The split between the style Michael is trying to fashion and his family's traditions is most apparent, however, after the dinner—at which not one sensory image relates to Italian food—when Pentangeli complains that Michael will not allow him to run his family the old way and is forcing him to "lie down" to the Rosato brothers. Michael tells him, "Your family's still called Corleone. And you'll run it like a Corleone." Pentangeli fires back, "My family doesn't eat here, doesn't eat in Las Vegas . . . and doesn't eat in Miami . . . with Hyman Roth!" This exchange holds weighty significance, as Michael tries to equate the quality of being a Corleone with obeying his own will, rather than the kind of traditional bonds and actions that made the Corleone family strong to begin with, the traditional bonds that matter in Pentangeli's view. Pentangeli feels less like a Corleone now, especially if being part of this modern family means "eating" away from his own table, his own traditions and heritage and figuratively "swallowing" the injustice of the Rosato brothers' actions because Michael has business dealings with Hyman Roth. Pentangeli wants Michael to answer the question of who, exactly, the family is and what it means. Family, to Pentangeli, means who you eat with, who sits at your table, something that goes beyond the physical act of putting food in one's mouth. "Eating" means sharing culture, sharing values, and here seems to blend into the idea of blood loyalty and also loyalty that goes beyond blood.

It is this expanded notion of "eating" and experiences with food that permeates the "Vito" segments of The Godfather, Part II. The richness of the sensory culinary detail in these segments clearly shows the cultural foundation on which Vito's "family" will eventually be built. From his job in a grocery store and his meat-and-cheese lunches with his friend and future consiglieri Genco Abbandando (Frank Sivero) to the nightly meal of soup and bread that he shares with his wife, Carmella (Francesca De Sapio), food is the catalyst for human bonding and affection. Forced to leave Sicily as a child because of a Mafia vendetta against any remaining son of his dead father, Vito has made a life for himself in New York's Little Italy, only to see that life begin to slip away when he is forced out of his job to make room for the nephew of the "Black Hand," Fanucci (Gaston Moschin), the extortionist who runs the neighbor-hood. Vito innocently asks Genco, "If he's Italian, why does he bother other

Italians?" This is a simple principle to Vito, who only begins a criminal life to earn a living, and continues it later, to prevent the parasitic Fanucci from continuing to terrorize the neighborhood. In a crucial scene, while Carmella fills plates with spaghetti in their tiny kitchen, Vito serves Clemenza (Bruno Kirby) and Tessio (John Aprea) as he explains to them why they should not give in and pay Fanucci the cut of money he is asking from them. This is the moment when Vito Corleone becomes Don Corleone, even more so than when he shoots Fanucci later. It is at this point, over mounds of food and wine, that he tells Clemenza and Tessio that he will "take care a everyting" for them, even though he does not divulge exactly how he will manage to do so. He only wants them to remember that he did them a favor. What he is going to do, he says, "is my business." And what becomes his "business" thereafter is real protection, loyalty, and mutual respect and consideration—a trading of favors that shows a set of cultural bonds.

Contrast the richness of these ideas tied to the sensory imagery of food to the austere parallel scenes of Michael in *The Godfather, Part II* wherein he barely eats. At one point he has a solitary meal on a train with a white tablecloth (reminiscent of the white jacket alluded to by Pentangeli), or sucks on an orange, the "fruit" of his dealings with the Florida-based Hyman Roth, but most of the time he is removed from food. This austerity begins symbolically when Michael commits the act that will essentially seal his fate in the family business, that of killing Solozzo and McCloskey, and tellingly, does not eat in Louis' restaurant. In scenes after he becomes Don, he will commonly eschew food, such as the tuna sandwich at Hyman Roth's house. In the scene in which he shows up unannounced at Pentangeli's house, Pentangeli is upset because if he had known Michael was coming, he "coulda prepared something" for him. Michael's surprise visit robs Pentangeli of the opportunity for such hospitality in order to express the Don's power—a power based not on cultural bonds, but on strength to turn away from them. Michael turns inward for his sustenance as he turns his back on what he views as the past corruptions of his father, but only succeeds in eating himself alive—and consuming what remains of the family as well. Tom Hagen asks him, "You wanna wipe everybody out?" and Michael responds, "[J]ust my enemies." However, when his enemy turns out to be his own dim-witted, misguided brother, Michael's desire to purge and purify the family ultimately dooms it. As we have seen, everything depends on the integrity of blood relationships in the family. This integrity is breached when Michael assumes control and Fredo feels passed over as the elder brother, a feeling that sets in motion Fredo's betrayal. Fratricide is traditionally a taboo crime, but so is allowing disloyalty to go unpunished in a Mafia family. Fredo's murder, similar to the multiple killings at the end of the first film, is yet another of Michael's efforts to force those elements out of the "family" body that threaten to poison it—in the words of Richard Combs, "a purging of the family in order to reconsecrate the family."[5] However, in the process, he actually removes one of its vital organs—a son to the former godfather and a brother to the present godfather. Though the family body can abide such apparent contradictions as family loyalty versus violence in the interest of self-preservation, this kind of action is as poisonous as allowing Fredo to remain to sabotage the family further. His murder of Fredo thus places Michael in a position of paralysis. Though wealthy and bridging the gap to legitimacy, the "family" that he has saved is culturally a starved skeleton of its former self.

It is somewhat fitting that the character of Pentangeli was one created only because the character of Peter Clemenza was not reprised fully in *The Godfather, Part II* (Richard Castellano wanted more money than the studio would pay). Clemenza's character in the first film is one of the best vantage points from which to view the cultural significance of food in the dynamic of family; his proxy, Pentangeli, plays out much of this dynamic—an unraveling of family continuity—in the second film. Clemenza loves food; in *Part II* we see his ravenous appetite and growing stomach as a young man. In the later years, portrayed first in *The Godfather*, he is short and round and, moreover, a good cook. After Vito is shot and the rest of the family is on more or less martial alert, Clemenza gives Michael a cooking lesson, saying, "Hey, come on over here, kid, learn something. You never know, you might have to cook for twenty guys someday." He then proceeds to show Michael how to make sauce, browning garlic in oil, sautéing tomatoes, adding meat, wine, and sugar (his "secret"). The display of cooking in this scene is crucial to the portrayal of the family structure, a mixture of blood and military loyalty. Soon after this, following the hit on Solozzo and McCloskey, Coppola shows a "going to the mattresses" montage, in which the men are in soldier mode, living together in small rooms and eating communally. In the words of Norman Silverstein, "with the head of the 'family' in the hospital and a gang war in progress, the body of the 'family' lives on eighteen mattresses and eats Clemenza's cooking . . . . As a romance of the Mafia [*The Godfather*] reinforces the myth of fealty in the masculine life it extols."[6] Clemenza's role is essentially that of an army cook and has the symbolic significance of sustaining the masculine allegorical family body. Ironically, the most overtly masculine member of the family, Sonny Corleone (James Caan), intervenes in Clemenza's cooking tutorial for Michael, saying, "Why don't you cut the crap? I got more important things for you to do." The "more important thing" is actually the assassination of Paulie Gatto (John Martino), which Clemenza has already accomplished in one of the film's earlier and most notable scenes.

The scenes of Paulie's traitorous neglect and ultimate punishment are imbued with food—fittingly, considering that the problems Paulie creates are too often the kind of business that is integral to robbing the family of sustenance. Because Paulie has called in sick, Vito is left under the protection of only the inept Fredo; this situation leads to Vito being gunned down while he is buying fruit. Later, while the brothers and capos are assembled to plan a strategy, Paulie is back, seemingly still ill. Sonny, feigning concern, offers him something to eat because he looks peaked: "There's some food in the ice-box—you hungry?" When Paulie leaves, Sonny tells Clemenza, "I want you to take care of that son of a bitch right away . . . I don't want to see him again." Here, the offer of food is almost like a bait of trust—because Sonny offers him food, appearing to care about his well-being, Paulie would not expect that he is suspected of disloyalty. But Clemenza indeed follows Sonny's orders, the hit ironically being framed by the ubiquitous Italian cannoli. Clemenza's wife, as they depart from his house, calls to him not to forget the cannolis. They drive around, ostensibly to look for possible sites if they have to "go to the mattresses," and after Paulie is shot, Clemenza instructs Rocco, in one of the film's most memorable lines: "Leave the gun; take the cannoli."

One reason why this particular line is memorable is its apparent black humor or incongruity: the fact that a man has just been shot to death is given equal weight with a wife's reminder to bring home dessert. But, as Thomas Ferrarro points out (picking up on Silverstein's allusions to medieval conventions), Mafia crime families run so well because of "their cult of family honor. The Corleones believe, with a kind of feudal fervor, in patriarchy, patronage, and protection. *The Godfather* is saturated with the imagery of . . . social events—weddings, christenings, funerals, meals, and so forth—that embody the culture of family honor. Always, the business of crime is interlaced with the responsibilities of family."[7] Therefore, what appears as humorous irony here, is in fact the key to the success of the family: the integration of culture into business, so that the "family" rules in the largest sense of the word. The innocent cannoli takes on a still darker meaning in *The Godfather, Part III* (1990) as an instrument of death, when Connie Corleone gives poisoned cannolis to Don Altobello (Eli Wallach) as a gift, assuring him that "the nuns who made these cannolis took a vow of silence."[8] The sweets are thus imbued with religious sanctity; things that should be emblems of trust are, however, instruments of betrayal. And Altobello's betrayal of the family is repaid in kind.

While food signifies the glue of tradition in the family in the *Godfather* films, food plays a somewhat different but no less significant role in another modern American Mafia film, Martin Scorcese's *Goodfellas* (1990).[9] If Henry Hill (Ray Liotta) is anything like Michael Corleone, it is because they both are struggling to define their own identities and their level of power in the postimmigrant world. Henry does not have the pure Italian bloodline that would allow him to ever become a "made" man, but he covets money and power and the apparent freedom that both of these bring. Food in *Goodfellas* signifies less about codes of tradition, honor, and loyalty and more about opulence, power, and what it means to be "civilized."

Henry introduces the viewer to what life was like for him in Paulie Cicero's family, as he paid his dues and "broke his cherry" on his first pinch. We make the rounds with him and see the world through his eyes at the Bamboo Lounge. Among the long tables full of food, Henry explains, "For us to live any other way was nuts. Uh, to us, those goody-good people who worked shitty jobs for bum paychecks and took the subway to work every day, and worried about their bills, were dead. I mean they were suckers. They had no balls. If we wanted something, we just took it." And the results of their success were never-ending supplies of food and drink, rolls of cash, cars, clothes. When the Bamboo Lounge starts to fail and is taken over by Paulie (Paul Sorvino), it is chewed up and spit out, set on fire when it has no more to give.

Food also manifests itself in a domestic location, in traditional ways that display the same kind of incongruity, the same mixture of violence with sustenance that is seen in the *Godfather* films. For instance, after Tommy (Joe Pesci) and Jimmy (Robert De Niro) beat Billy Batts (Frank Vincent) to a pulp, they and Henry are in quest of a shovel. They end up at Tommy's mother's house in the middle of the night, at which point she proceeds to make them a full meal. They sit down at the table as if it were the most normal thing in the world, while the half-dead man writhes in the trunk of the car outside. Tommy even takes a knife from the table, telling his mother that he needs it to "hack" off the paw of a deer that hit the car. The structure of this traditional meal includes impromptu cooking in the dead of night and uses the same utensils for eating as are used for killing. Not once does Tommy's mother ever question any of these circumstances, because there is nothing necessarily strange about them. She is Sicilian, and she accepts the elements of the life common to her family.

The elements of food and death become even more horrifyingly mixed when, six months later, Jimmy, Tommy, and Henry have to move Batts's body because it is in danger of being found. Tommy is desensitized to such an enterprise and mocks Henry as he vomits: "Hey Henry, hurry up—my mother's gonna make some fresh peppers and sausage for us. . . . Here's a leg—here's a wing. Hey, what do you like, the leg or the wing, Henry? Or do you still go for the old hearts and lungs?" Food and death thus serve the same function—vehicles of sustenance. Henry has had his fill of death here and regurgitates the violence, but ironically it is for violating the code of killing a "made" guy that Tommy gets killed in the end.

The dichotomy of food being portrayed in an unconventional venue even as it is valued for its symbolic "civilizing" power is evident in the prison scenes of *Goodfellas*, when Henry explains how wise guys did not really suffer in the joint. Henry says, "In prison, dinner was always a big thing. We had a pasta course, and then we had a meat or a fish. . . . Paulie did the prep work . . . he had a wonderful system for doing the garlic. He used to slice it so thin that it used to liquefy in the pan with just a little oil." Though it could not subvert the criminal justice system and avoid imprisonment, the "family" is able to exert its power in prison to eat and drink fairly well, as is evident from the bottles of liquor and the boxes of steaks and lobsters on ice coming in.

However, an even more striking juxtaposition of crime/violence and food comes in the climactic scenes that depict Henry's arrest by narcotics agents. A drugged-up, paranoid Henry is trying to juggle unloading stolen guns, moving a shipment of cocaine, and cooking dinner for his family, the last of which takes equal priority with the other tasks. He is planning an extensive menu: ziti with meat "gravy," roasted peppers, string beans with olive oil and garlic, as well as some veal cutlets "cut just right" to fry as an appetizer. He has to balance getting dinner started—braising the "beef, pork butt, and veal shanks for the tomato sauce"—and doing a multitude of errands. Most people probably would have taken shortcuts on the dinner, if anything had to give, but Henry runs himself ragged trying to make the dinner turn out well even while he is working hard to stay away from the surveillance helicopter and unload his illicit packages. Henry even jokes that he's been either "watching sauce or watching helicopters all day"; watching both is equally important to him because both making the traditional dinner and moving the drugs and guns are integrally related. Cooking this dinner functions as a symbolic effort to maintain a traditional core, bridging the gap between dealing guns (old) and dealing drugs (new).

Like Don Vito Corleone, Paulie Cicero is averse to drugs, seeing them as "dirty business," and he admonishes Henry to stay away from them and all the danger they entail. Paulie adheres to a fairly traditional mindset, as is also evident when he counsels Henry to make peace with Karen (Lorraine Bracco) after she finds out about his affair, saying that "there's no other way. You're not gonna get a divorce. We're not *animali.*" Henry stubbornly tries to straddle the line between the traditional wise-guy philosophies that he learned from Paulie as a kid and the newer, more brutal tactics of Jimmy and Tommy. His struggling to cook the very traditional dinner for his family on the night of his arrest illustrates this conflict, and ultimately, his failure to walk that line. His final punishment is fitting: relocated to the witness protection program, living in a cookie-cutter house, he is alive, but trapped in suburban, whitewashed hell. He comments, "There's no action . . . . I can't even get decent food. Right after I got here, I ordered some spaghetti with marinara sauce, and I got egg noodles and ketchup." Henry breaks the third wall and gives viewers a smirk that communicates all that needs to be said about his new life.

It is evident that food in modern American Mafia films is a most useful signifier of changing, complicated lifestyles. Food is used as a symbol of old world traditions, binding Mafia "families" together and also implying the inherent contradictions that push and pull on family bonds. It is always the second or third generation of immigrants that find assimilation most difficult; for them the tensions between the old, traditional ways and modern ways are most desperate, ripping their families apart.

In a scene from another modern film with a Mafia theme, Mike Newell's *Donnie Brasco* (1997), the cooking of Lefty Ruggiero (Al Pacino) illustrates not a connection to tradition but a willful departure from it.[10] Lefty wants to separate himself from what he perceives as low-class Italian immigrant roots. When Donnie (Johnny Depp) comes over on Christmas Day, Lefty tells him, "You think I cook like them goombas in Brooklyn? All they know is 'manicotti, manicotti'; a hundred years, they're gonna be, 'manicotti.' You never had coq au vin, eh?" He cooks a French rather than an Italian dish, serving something that he thinks is higher class than manicotti. This scene illustrates how, in so many ways, Lefty wants to rise above his station in life, even while knowing that such a desire is futile. Lefty indicates that his cooking is sacred, calling it "communion," but when a kitchen fire starts, he steps back to let his wife put it out. His ineptness here and his sad striving to be better than a third gun in his Mafia family are one and the same.

This scene from *Donnie Brasco* is closely linked with those we have already considered in the *Godfather* films and in *Goodfellas* in that food represents the reinforcement of whatever cultural rules—or aspirations—characters live by. For the new Italian immigrants of the early twentieth century, food was a link to the past and tradition as they began to assimilate; it signified bonds of trust and loyalty. As depicted in contemporary films, the children of these immigrants display ambivalence in their relationship to food, for it troubles their sense of identity. They struggle between the old and new ways of life, and usually fail to find success and peace, their lives holding all of the violence but none of the culture of their ancestors.

Notes

1. Harlan Lebo, *The Godfather Legacy* (New York: Simon and Schuster, 1997), 88.
2. Manohla Dargis, "Dark Side of the Dream," *Sight and Sound*, vol. 6, no. 6 (1996): 16–19.
3. *The Godfather*, directed by Francis Ford Coppola, produced by Albert Ruddy (Hollywood: Paramount Pictures, 1972), DVD; *The Godfather, Part II*, directed and produced by Francis Ford Coppola (Hollywood: Paramount Pictures & The Coppola Company, 1974), DVD.
4. George De Stefano, "Family Lies," *Ariel* 23, no. 4 (1997): 22–25.
5. Richard Combs, "Coppola's Family Plot," *Film Comment* 38, no. 2 (2002): 38–44.
6. Norman Silverstein, "*The Godfather*—A Year Later: An Examination of the Movie's Internal Structure," *Italian Americana* 19, no. 1 (1974): 105–17.
7. Thomas J. Ferraro, "Blood in the Marketplace: The Business of Family in the *Godfather* Narratives," in *The Invention of Ethnicity*, ed. Werner Sollors (New York: Oxford University Press, 1989), 176–208.
8. *The Godfather, Part III*, directed and produced by Francis Ford Coppola (Hollywood: Paramount Pictures & Zoetrope Studios, 1990), DVD.
9. *Goodfellas*, directed by Martin Scorsese, produced by Irwin Winkler (Hollywood: Warner Brothers, 1990), DVD.
10. *Donnie Brasco*, directed by Mike Newell, produced by Louis Digiaimo, Mark Johnson, Barry Levinson, Gail Mutrux (Hollywood: TriStar Pictures, 1997), DVD.

16

All-Consuming Passions: Peter Greenaway's *The Cook, the Thief, His Wife and Her Lover*

RAYMOND ARMSTRONG

> Bad men live that they may eat and drink, whereas good men eat and drink that they may live.
>
> — Socrates, *Plutarch's Morals—How a Young Man Ought to Hear Poems*

In his 1989 film *The Cook, the Thief, His Wife and Her Lover*, Peter Greenaway presents us with what is perhaps the most comprehensive and outrageous compendium of food-related ideas and images ever to be seen in a major motion picture. Set almost entirely in the environs of a spectacularly grand though rather surreal French restaurant, this extraordinary cinematic feast even begins with the admonishment, "Come on now, open your mouth . . . learn to appreciate your food!"[1] Notwithstanding the many dainty dishes on the bill of fare, the audience is then offered a scene of coprophagia as a starter, and later treated to an act of cannibalism for dessert. In the intervening two hours, Greenaway, as our host, serves up a veritable smorgasbord of arresting connections between the world of food and other key areas of human experience, such as power, money, learning, sex, death, and even the cinema itself. The result is an extremely rich and challenging film that manages to be simultaneously visceral and cerebral, and is never less than pictorially sublime.

A fascination with food has always been one of the hallmarks of Greenaway's cinema. We can see this pattern emerging even in his debut dramatic

219

feature, *The Draughtsman's Contract* (1982), which opens with a close-up of Mr. Noyes eating a plum and ends with a similar shot of the statue-impersonator biting into a pineapple and then spitting it out. Moreover, the whole of that film is replete with allusions to many different types of fruit; from damsons and raspberries to pears and pomegranates. Staying with images of fruit, we might also note how the decomposition of a single apple is featured prominently in *A Zed and Two Noughts* (1985), how there are apples lying literally all over the place in *Drowning by Numbers* (1988), and how the occasional piece of orange is all that Stourley Kracklite can manage to keep down in *The Belly of an Architect* (1987). Indeed, unaware that he is suffering from stomach cancer, the corpulent Kracklite (whose most famous building—"a monument to carnivores"—had been inspired by his penchant for "frankfurters, hotdogs, hamburgers, salamis, [and] baloney") even accuses his wife of trying to kill him with some supposedly poisoned figs. In all of these contexts, the matter of eating is clearly an abiding preoccupation for both the director and his characters. With *The Cook, the Thief, His Wife and Her Lover*, however, Greenaway raises the stakes dramatically, for here we have a film in which the "central point of departure is food coupled to the idea that everything is eatable. Absolutely everything!"[2]

By far the most accessible of Greenaway's films, *The Cook, the Thief, His Wife and Her Lover* has a surprisingly simple and straightforward plot. Richard Borst (the cook, played by Richard Bohringer), a cordon bleu well known for his adventurous and ambrosial cuisine, is the proprietor of a stylishly upmarket restaurant called Le Hollandais. However, the business has recently been commandeered by Albert Spica (the thief, played by Michael Gambon), a fiendishly depraved gangster with grandiose affectations, who chooses to dine there every evening with his retinue of ruffians. Mr. Spica, as the cook tartly refers to him throughout, is also dutifully accompanied on these occasions by the pensive but chic figure of Georgina (his wife, played by Helen Mirren), whom he is wont to bait in public and batter at home. One evening Georgina happens to catch the eye of another regular at the restaurant, an unassuming bookworm named Michael (her lover, played by Alan Howard). Irresistibly drawn to each other, these unlikely sweethearts subsequently embark on a series of rapturously torrid encounters under the auspices of the ubiquitous cook. After five nights of unbridled intimacy in various parts of the restaurant, their secret affair is discovered and brought to the attention of Spica, the thief. At this point, events take a very dark and sinister turn, as the film betrays its debt to the macabre machinations of Jacobean revenge tragedy.[3]

The director himself has said that *The Cook, the Thief, His Wife and Her Lover* is very much part of a time-honored tradition of films that deal with the subject of food. The classic example of this genre, according to Greenaway, is Marco Ferreri's black comedy *La Grande Bouffe* (1973), which focuses on a group of highly successful middle-aged men (a chef, a television personality, a

pilot, and a judge) who conspire to wallow themselves to death in an omni-
vorous orgy of grossness and luxury.[4] It is particularly interesting that
Greenaway should have singled out this film for special mention, not least
because there are a number of striking connections between it and *The Cook,
the Thief, His Wife and Her Lover*. First, the opening sequence of Greenaway's
film—wherein a motley pack of dogs is pictured sniffing and slavering over
some large pieces of meat in an area outside the restaurant—effectively replicates the closing frames of *La Grande Bouffe*. Moreover, in both these instances,
there is a certain amount of stylistic distortion: not only have the dogs themselves been rendered in a slightly abstract fashion (via the dusky tones of slow
motion and the deliberate blurring of a long shot, respectively), but their
barking has also been subtly modulated to segue into the theme tune. Second,
in an apparent homage to *La Grande Bouffe*, where the five main characters
famously have the same first names as the actors who play them, Greenaway
had originally intended that each of the characters in his titular quartet should
likewise be identified by the first name of the actor for whom that part had
been written.[5] After the tortuous business of casting, however, the only role
that adhered to this nomenclature was that of Richard, the cook, played by
the French actor Richard Bohringer: nonetheless, this remnant is itself suffi-
cient to adumbrate the overall correlation.[6] Third, the scene in which Ferreri's
gastronomes view a series of antique erotic slides as they binge on oysters and
champagne effectively prefigures the triangular preoccupation with haute
cuisine, voyeurism and projected images that exercises the character of
Richard in *The Cook, the Thief, His Wife and Her Lover*.

One of the most beguiling aspects of Greenaway's film is the way in which
he contrives to merge his celluloid evocation of a fabulously plush restaurant
with the actual circumstance of being in the cinema.[7] During the opening
titles, the viewer is effectively ushered into the milieu of Le Hollandais, with
the subjective camera being escorted by two liveried attendants who pull back
a pair of blue velvet curtains, revealing the rear entrance to the restaurant. It is
at this very moment that the thief and his entourage drive into the parking lot,
and the drama proper begins to unfold. For the duration of the film, it would
seem that the viewer has not only been reserved a table in this impressive
establishment, but has also been granted access to all of its areas. As we follow
Albert's band of brigands on their progress through the cavernous kitchen and
into the crimson splendor of the dining hall, our attention is immediately
drawn to the back wall, which is dominated by a huge reproduction of Franz
Hals's famous painting "Banquet of the Officers of the St George Civic Guard"
(1616). It soon becomes apparent that what we have here is in fact another
company of virtual diners, sharing the same experience and mirroring the
perspective of the cinema audience. Indeed, despite being dressed identically
to the men in Spica's outfit, these painted warriors are actually Dutch doubles
of ourselves. Like the patrons in front of the projection screen, the various
figures on the seventeenth-century canvas gaze in fascination at what is

happening at the thief's table, which seems to be located midway between them and us. With the action taking place over a nine-day period, Greenaway is further able to exploit this dining motif as a framing device. At the start of each episode, he quite literally presents the viewer with a menu, focusing on the house specialties for that particular day of the week. The one exception to this pattern is the film's final sequence, Albert's last supper, where, instead of the usual list of dishes, we have a simple caption announcing that "The Restaurant is closed for a Private Function" (89). Significantly, as this soirée reaches its deadly dénouement, the camera, despite having been privy to all that has transpired, finds itself being maneuvered into reverse and steadily begins to pull away from the assembled cast of staff and clientele, whereupon the proscenium-style red curtains abruptly close and the credits start to roll. The viewer has thus been discreetly ejected from the theatrical world of the restaurant and returns once again to the reality of sitting in the movie theater.

Interestingly, this connection between the culinary and the cinematic realms is also insinuated by the pivotal figure of the cook, who explicitly identifies himself with the viewer, when he compares his own habitual scopophilia to the activity of watching a film. Yet paradoxically, Greenaway has indicated on several occasions that the cook actually represents the filmmaker himself—a professional voyeur whose business permits him to watch other people eat and make love. As he explained to Andreas Kilb: "Obviously, I am the cook. The cook is the director. He arranges the menu, the seating order of the guests; he gives refuge to the lovers; he prepares the repast of the lover's body. The cook is a perfectionist and a rationalist, a portrait of myself." In a subsequent interview with Marcia Pally, he stated that: "with each film I invite people to my table and I make the meal. I take the cultural systems I admire and try to set them out in one place. I demand, as we all do, some sense of coherence, of order in [the] world. And we are always defeated. This is the human condition."[8]

Just as the cook has "a reputation for a wide range of experimental dishes" (85), so is Greenaway widely renowned for his unconventional and innovative style of filmmaking. It could be said, moreover, that every one of Greenaway's films is made according to a recipe. For each of his concoctions, the director assembles all of the requisite ingredients and then skillfully blends them together according to a clearly defined procedure. While the format of the recipe is constantly being revised to reflect the concerns of each individual film, a systematic modus operandi is always apparent. The rationale for this resides in Greenaway's highly idiosyncratic use of onscreen devices—including lists, grids, shapes, texts and other alphanumerical signs—to emphasize the schematic development of his narratives. In *The Draughtsman's Contract*, for example, we have the twelve sketches that Mr. Neville is commissioned to draw of the Herberts' house; then we have the letters of the alphabet in *A Zed and Two Noughts*, the symmetrical patterns in *The Belly of an Architect*, the figures from 1 to 100 in *Drowning by Numbers*, the daily variations in the menu of Le Hollandais in *The Cook, the Thief, His Wife and Her Lover*, the eponymous articles in *Prospero's Books* (1991), the procession of placards in *The Baby of Macon* (1993), and so on.

If Greenaway is to be seen as a kind of cinematic master chef, then the studio is undoubtedly his dream kitchen, for it is here that he can keep a controlling eye on every aspect of his creations. How fitting therefore that *The Cook, the Thief, His Wife and Her Lover* was the first of his *chefs-d'oeuvre* to be produced entirely within a studio. The synthetic environment of the studio was perfectly suited to the director's purpose, since he was primarily interested in cultivating a heightened sense of artifice and theatricality—something that he would develop even further in his subsequent films, notably *Prospero's Books* and *The Baby of Macon*. To this end, he is admirably assisted here by the magnificent cinematography of Sacha Vierny, the imaginative production design of Jan Roelfs and Ben Van Os, the capricious costumes of Jean-Paul Gaultier, and the fantastically baroque music of Michael Nyman.

In terms of visual language, the most intriguing aspect of *The Cook, the Thief, His Wife and Her Lover* is the way that Greenaway uses color-coding, not simply to evoke atmosphere and emotion but—more importantly—to highlight the artificiality of the action. The filmscape is topographically divided into six different areas, each of which is quite distinctive in color: the parking lot is arctic blue, the kitchen is jungle green, the dining hall is blood red, the toilet is heavenly white, the book depository is golden brown, and the hospital is egg-yolk yellow. What makes this chromatic dispensation all the more fanciful is that whenever Georgina, Albert, or his minions move among these zones, their costumes automatically change color to match that of the décor. Significantly, though, the clothes of all the other characters remain colorfast. Notwithstanding our paramount preoccupation with food, it would seem here that Greenaway is concerned almost as much with the palette as he is with the palate.

Accepting the notion that the cook represents the film director himself inevitably prompts us to speculate about the possible significance of the other three main characters. If we extend this metaphorical framework, then the thief could be said to embody the more commercial elements of the film industry (Hollywood executives, financiers, distributors, entertainment journalists, etc) who are naturally hostile to the "highbrow elitism" of Greenaway's approach. Like an overbearing producer, the thief patronizingly praises the cook's skills, but is constantly reminding him who's boss, by interfering with the creative process, trying to impose his own dubious taste on things, and threatening to shut the whole operation down if he doesn't get his way. In this context, the wife may be viewed as the malnourished filmgoer, quietly yearning for a more vital and sophisticated diet, but endlessly frustrated by the stranglehold of the "dominant cinema."[9] For his part, the lover may be seen as the very personification of that enlightened and stimulating type of film culture. The fact that he is killed off by the thief symbolizes the apparent triumph of the dominant cinema over the cinema of ideas. As it turned out, though, Greenaway, rather like the wife at the end of the film, was destined to have the last laugh: just as the exquisite taste of the lover causes the thief to retch, so the remarkable box-office success of *The Cook, the Thief, His Wife and Her Lover* must have stuck in the throats of many in the mainstream movie business.[10] Having used his cinematic magic to confound his detractors with this film about food, it was curiously appropriate that the director's next project should have been *Prospero's Books*—an adaptation of William Shakespeare's *The Tempest*— if only for the scene in which the indignant sorcerer conjures up a vision of a sumptuous banquet to tantalize those who conspired against him.

As well as raising Greenaway's profile with a larger international audience, *The Cook, the Thief, His Wife and Her Lover* also marked his only foray into the arena of domestic politics. There is, however, a certain irony in the fact that this film, which proved so much more lucrative than any of his others, should be the one in which he affirms that the love of money is the root of all evil. Conceived as "a passionate and angry dissertation" on the cultural situation in Britain after a decade under the monetarist policies of Margaret Thatcher, *The Cook, the Thief, His Wife and Her Lover* represents a blistering indictment of this "rich, vulgarian, Philistine, anti-intellectual" climate that only seemed to encourage the rapacious villainy of individuals like Albert Spica. In essence, as Greenaway himself explained, "this is a movie about consumer society, it's about greed—a society's, a man's."[11]

In "a society where consumerism has run riot," it is perhaps inevitable that the business of eating should be concerned more with what is fashionable than with what is functional. The emphasis here is very much on haute cuisine—a "false art," according to Greenaway, that serves only pretension and ostenta-. tion in a futile "effort to de-food food."[12] One of the most vital of human requirements thus has to be packaged and prettified before it reaches the table. Food is no longer viewed primarily in terms of its nutritional value or gusta-tory appeal, but rather as a modish accessory or a status symbol: "Eating tells you a great deal about people—like all those young middle class people, the yuppies, who go out to eat all the time at places where it's more important that the tomatoes match the wallpaper than it is the food tastes good or is nourish-ing. They don't go out to eat so much as to show off their clothes or the way they can handle a knife, fork and wine glass. Food is a very good way to cri-tique the people who eat it."[13]

Observing how the art of great cooking often involves a combination of the most unlikely ingredients, the thief claims that he himself is also something of an artist, because of the ingenious way he combines his business (money) and his pleasure (eating). It is through the restaurant business that he acquires his cash—whether by creaming off the profits of Le Hollandais or by extorting protection payments from rival caterers (whom he threatens with food poi-soning)—and he takes full advantage of this circumstance by gourmandizing himself and his cohorts every evening. The connection between money and food is vividly illustrated on Friday night, when the proceeds from Albert's racketeering activities are laid in front of him on the restaurant table, effectively displacing that evening's meal. Borrowing a line from Oscar Wilde, Greenaway has described the cynically avaricious thief as "A man who knows the price of everything and the value of nothing" (93).[14] When it comes to good food, though, Albert is always ready to put his mouth where his money is. Not content to be just a connoisseur, he sees himself as more of a crusader. His mission is to teach other people how to dine properly and thus fully appreciate their food. Every evening he holds court in the restaurant and pontificates to his gauche commensals, rebuking them for their ignorant eating habits, mispronouncing French phrases, and relating dubious anecdotes about food. At one stage, he even boasts that he intends to compose a guidebook on how to eat exotic delicacies, such as "asparagus—oysters—artichokes—lobster—crab—snails—no we'll forget snails. I'll write it all down and Georgina can type it out—'Notes for Gourmets'—French for a good eater—." Who knows? Such a publication might even provide him with an additional source of revenue. For all his gastronomic pretensions, the bottom line for Albert is always money. When push comes to shove, he makes little distinction between "stuffing the mouth and feeding the sewers," because, as he himself later says, "It all comes out as shit in the end" (21, 23, 80). The fact that the thief appears to have a special fondness for seafood is possibly symptomatic of his Mussolini-like megalomania. After a rather savage demonstration of the correct way to eat a crayfish, he expounds his theory that great military leaders throughout history have always favored seafood. Equally interesting is his hesitation about whether to admit snails, which perhaps alludes to the issue of his repressed homosexuality, since it seems to echo the famous "snails and oysters" sequence from Stanley Kubrick's *Spartacus* (1960), where a bathing Roman senator (Laurence Olivier) tries unsuccessfully to seduce his bondsman (Tony Curtis).

As Alan Woods has pointed out, all of the thief's "tortures" are concerned with eating.[15] Yet, on each of these occasions, Albert himself would have us believe that he is merely seeking to educate a recalcitrant palate. He routinely advises the people on the receiving end that they are being taught a lesson in prandial etiquette, and that it is in their own interest to "learn some manners" (13). The one thing that he reproves all of his victims for is not paying enough attention to their food. His remedy for this is simple but radical. He personally selects something that is guaranteed to enliven their taste buds, and then relentlessly forces it into their mouths. In the course of the film, the thief is responsible for four such episodes of malign nutrition.[16]

The first of these vicious victuals is administered to Roy (Wille Ross), the owner of a small pie shop, who has failed to pay some protection money to Albert. The thief gets his hoodlums to denude the defaulter in the car-park of Le Hollandais, and then proceeds to shove dog excrement into his mouth, before urinating over him as he lies helpless on the ground. A weary Georgina protests, but Albert declares that he must ensure that the animals are fed and watered. The purpose of this scene is clearly to establish the thief's utter contempt for his fellow human beings. Coprophagia is an activity that is commonly associated with the canine community; as if to emphasize the obscenity of Roy's degradation, the spectacle of him having to eat dog shit is preceded by images of dogs themselves eating meat. This nauseating exhibition of cruelty is highly reminiscent of Pier Paolo Pasolini's *Salo, or The 120 Days of Sodom* (1975), where the sadistic masters of the revels had likewise sought to deny their victims' humanity by compelling them to participate in a fecal feast. However, for all its emetic excesses, even Pasolini's notorious opus didn't dare show us such an outrage in the opening minutes, as Greenaway does here.

The second frenzied feeding involves a customer in the restaurant whose table needs to be moved out of the way when the thief calls for an exotic cabaret to entertain one of his crooked associates. In a less than diplomatic bid to expedite matters, Albert "*shovels*" several spoonfuls of mushroom soup into the mouth of this unfortunate diner, and then empties the whole soup tureen over the man's head(56).

The third person to be treated to one of Albert's special slap-up meals is Pup (Paul Russell), the singing kitchen boy, who is intercepted on his way back from delivering food to the lovers' hideaway. Ruthlessly determined to get some information out of him, the thief rips the buttons off the boy's uniform and forces him to swallow them one at a time. When there are no buttons left, Albert decides that the boy will have to swallow his own belly button. He takes a knife and begins to excise the navel; however, not surprisingly, this operation proves too much for the lad, who faints and so narrowly avoids having to eat his own flesh.

The fourth and most heinous act of force-feeding is perpetrated on Michael, the wife's lover. A book curator by profession, the mild-mannered Michael is the very antithesis of the barbarous thief. In Le Hollandais, he is a regular but solitary diner, who sits unobtrusively at his table, completely absorbed in his reading matter. On Friday night, the swaggering Spica twice picks up a book from Michael's table and contemptuously tosses it away. In an ironic reference to the crafty art of embezzlement, the thief subsequently complains to Richard that the book "needs cooking" and advises him to "grill it with some mashed peas." The next evening Albert sits down beside Michael and reminds him, "This is a restaurant, not a library." It is a place for feeding the body, not the mind. What is more, as well as being an insult to the chef, "reading gives you indigestion—didn't you know that?" asks the thief somewhat prophetically. It would seem that Georgina, despite having fallen for Michael's charms, is also tainted to some extent by her husband's illiterate and consumerist outlook. Surveying the countless titles on the shelves of the book depository, she inquires of her lover, "What good are all these books to you? You can't eat them!" Unfortunately, though, this is precisely what Michael will have to do in order to satisfy the vindictive lust of the thief. Having managed to track down the "wife snatcher," Albert commands that he must be "stuffed with the tools of his trade"—a decree that is evidently as much about vandalism as it is about vengeance (39, 44, 70, 81, 78). The book depository is thus reduced to a state of total devastation, and one by one the pages of Michael's favorite book (*The French Revolution* by Pascal Astruc-Latalle) are stuffed into his mouth and rammed down his throat with the handle of a wooden spoon. Coincidentally, this is the very same book that Albert had earlier instructed Richard to cook: Michael has to eat it raw, but it will in due course be baked inside the lover for the thief himself to taste. The manner of Michael's death grotesquely parodies the diet of the book lovers in Ray Bradbury's novel *Fahrenheit 451*, who metaphorically consume and digest classic works of literature in order to preserve them from the incinerators of the philistine state. And indeed the fiery destruction of the written word is something that would feature prominently in two of Greenaway's subsequent films—*Prospero's Books* and *The Pillow Book* (1996).

Common to each of these assaults is Albert's peculiar fixation with the removal of the victim's clothing—especially the nether garments. Thus, Roy is left completely naked, Little Willie is threatened with being spanked on his bottom, Pup has his trousers pulled down, and Michael is stripped to his underpants. There can be no doubt that all this below-the-belt business has some perverse sexual significance. Each of these incidents is not just an affront to male dignity, but is in fact tantamount to an act of rape. The brutal and nonconsensual insertion of foreign elements—dog excrement, mushroom soup (Albert himself loathes mushrooms), buttons, paper—into the mouths of these men clearly represents a violation of their bodies, and perhaps even a kind of emasculation. Bearing in mind what Georgina says about Albert's bedroom antics—"He wasn't really interested in sex—not with me—not with women . . . " (83)—we are invited to conclude that the thief is actually a latent homosexual, and that he has been striving to sublimate this inappropriate predilection through these seemingly wanton acts of violence and humiliation. Neither concerned about nor capable of satisfying his wife sexually, it would also appear that he is virtually impotent. His callous use of phallic substitutes to penetrate Georgina's body would seem to be an attempt to compensate for his own inadequacy in that department.

It is in fact Albert himself who describes "how sex and eating are related" (23). Significantly, it is at this precise moment that Georgina exchanges a first furtive glance with her soon-to-be paramour, who is inserting a forkful of food into his mouth. Georgina herself is starved for affection and seems to have little interest in food. When the wife expresses her disgust at Albert's odious remarks about the starving in Ethiopia, Grace (Liz Smith)—the harridan who sits at the thief's table (and who is identified in the screenplay as Georgina's mother)—asks, "Now what do you know Georgina about the starving? You can have anything you want" (32). Anything that money can buy, that is, but neither love nor respect from the man who is her keeper. As far as Albert is concerned, Georgina is his "property" (29), and he believes he can do whatever he wants with her. While his wife is finding solace in an adulterous engagement in the ladies' toilet, Albert amuses himself by adulterating the food on her plate. Like a puerile prankster, he gleefully spills wine over her meal, and then douses it with vinegar and pepper. When she returns, Georgina stoically eats the food as if there is nothing wrong with it, and thereby denies Albert the satisfaction of watching her suffer.

Ironically, the only meal that actually seems to be enjoyed in the course of the film is served not in the restaurant, but in the book depository. It is there that the holed-up lovers tuck into a late-night supper that has been specially prepared for them by the cook. There is a suggestion that the lovers here are able to enjoy their food because they are very much in harmony with one another—both sexually and spiritually. In other words, there seems to be a connection between gastronomic satisfaction and consummate intimacy. This would certainly seem to be the case with Georgina, who elsewhere hardly touches her food or is inclined to eat in a rather apathetic and mechanical fashion. Moreover, when the lovers are torn asunder, it is significant that she should turn to the idea of food in a bid to restore their idyllic union. Traumatized by the discovery of Michael's lifeless body, Georgina beds down beside him and talks dreamily about the delicious breakfast that they will have together in the morning. This poignant fantasy of having breakfast with a resurrected loved one anticipates the scene in Greenaway's *Eight and a Half Women* (1999) where Storey Emmenthal (Matthew Delamere) attempts to repudiate the fact of his father's death by rushing to the kitchen and making him breakfast.

The tenderness of the wife's relationship with Michael is strikingly contrasted with her account of the torment she has suffered at the hands of the thief. As she lies beside her dead lover, Georgina falteringly begins to describe how she has been sexually abused by Albert. While she is speaking, her head is turned on its side (looking toward Michael and the camera), and we are presented with a rare close-up of her face. Center-right of the screen is the image of her mouth; however, the very fact that her lips are represented vertically rather than horizontally insinuates that the focus is actually elsewhere on her body. Having first given her a beating, and then subjected her to some unspeakable degradation in the toilet, Albert would always conclude his heartless conjugal rites by thrusting (or forcing Georgina to insert) one of a number of specially selected objects—including a wine bottle, a wooden spoon and a toothbrush—into her vagina. The fact that the majority of these objects have an oral significance serves to highlight the morbid link between Albert's crazed obsession with force-feeding and his baleful molestation of his wife. As a result of this persistent abuse, Georgina sustained serious internal damage and is now unable to have children. In this context, the process of being fed clearly has more to do with mortification rather than nutrition, punishment rather than pleasure, and ultimately (in the case of Georgina's three miscarriages and the choking of her lover) death rather than life.

The cook is tacitly involved at every stage of the romance between Georgina and Michael. He is a party to the significant glances that are exchanged surreptitiously across the crowded dining hall. And while circumstance compels the lovers to sit at separate tables, Richard symbolically endorses their secret intercourse by serving them both with the same complimentary dishes. Having observed the perils of their synchronized trips to the toilet, he subsequently leads them to the various recesses of his kitchen kingdom, where they can enjoy one another's company in relative safety—and where he can keep an eye on them. In the course of their couplings, the illicit lovers are shown to the pie pantry, the dairy pantry, the plucking room, the crockery and cutlery store, and, in the state of emergency that ensues when Albert learns about their affair, the refrigerator room. During one of these liaisons, Greenaway intercuts a scene of Michael and Georgina undressing and making love with images of food preparation. As the couple recklessly engage in intimacy under the nose of the prowling thief, we are presented with a series of close-ups of various vegetables—sequentially suggestive in both their color and shape, we see a pale green cabbage, a deep purple cabbage, a ripe red pepper, and finally a large cucumber—being expertly sliced by the cook, whose nimble fingers seem to flirt with the newly sharpened edge of the oncoming knife. The juxtaposition of these two actions is highly effective in conveying their mutual sense of delicacy and danger.

For all his curious proximity, the cook remains a semidetached and ambiguous figure throughout. As a pathological voyeur, he obviously derives a considerable amount of pleasure from watching the amorous activities of Georgina and Michael. Yet Richard's presence is crucial for the lovers, and not just because he offers them every practical assistance, but, perhaps more importantly, because his studious observations represent an objective confirmation of the reality of their lovemaking. Indeed he is later called upon to give a full account of all that he witnessed, and the graphic truth of his testimony offers the wife some consolation in the midst of her sorrow for her lover.

During this tête-à-tête with the grieving Georgina, the cook also reveals how the prices on his menu are fixed in relation to the idiosyncrasies and aspirations of his customers. While happy to cater to all tastes, Richard insists that people should be made to pay extra for their faddishness and vanity. Certain categories of diner, therefore, such as the vegetarian, the beautiful, the elderly and the athletic, are subject to special surcharges. Prices are also inflated for diet foods (+30 percent) and aphrodisiacs (+50 percent). However, the most expensive dishes on the menu are those that are black. Items such as grapes, olives, blackcurrants, black truffles, and caviar are all exorbitantly priced, because "People like to remind themselves of death—eating black food is like consuming death—like saying—ha, ha, Death!—I'm eating you. . . . " (85). The hubris of this conceit notwithstanding, a much more sobering connection between food and mortality is illustrated in the scene in which the cook helps the lovers to escape from the rampant thief by stowing them away in the back of a delivery truck. Unfortunately, the truck in question is full of rotting meat—rankly deliquescent, riddled with maggots, and swarming with flies. Huddling together, and almost overcome with the stench of putrefaction, the naked and shivering lovers struggle to keep their balance amid the swinging carcasses and the carrion slime. As well as being redolent of the time-lapse sequences of bestial decay that appear throughout Greenaway's enigmatic zoo story, *A Zed and Two Noughts*, this scene reminds us that even though these healthy human beings have just been sitting pretty at the very top of the food chain in a fancy French restaurant, ultimately they too are mere flesh, perishable bodies that will themselves one day be eaten by the lowest forms of life. And, in the case of the lover, that process will begin a lot sooner than expected—in the mouth of the despicable Albert Spica.

Much of the controversy surrounding the film has inevitably focused on its cannibalistic finale. In the modern world, we tend to associate cannibalism with the activities of the criminally insane (e.g., serial killers such as Ed Gein and Jeffrey Dahmer), or with stories about stranded survivors desperate to avoid starvation (like the members of the Uruguayan rugby team whose plane crashed in the Andes in 1972, and whose story was told in Frank Marshall's 1993 film *Alive*). From an anthropological perspective, however, research has shown that in those ancient and remote communities where cannibalism was practiced, it often had less to do with savagery or survival and more to do with ceremonial concerns. In terms of its ritual significance, the practice of eating human flesh appears to have had two quite distinct symbolic purposes: first, as a funerary act through which the mourner hoped to achieve a lasting sense of communion with the deceased loved one; and second, as a triumphal feast, through which the victor sought to assimilate the intrinsic strength—and so disarm the vengeful spirit—of his defeated foe. Oddly enough, both these aspects can be related to what happens in *The Cook, the Thief, His Wife and Her Lover*.

With regard to the consoling power of cannibalism, Georgina's request that Richard should cook Michael appears to be born of a desire to be close to her departed lover. We may recall that her last words to Michael (as she was rushing off to the hospital to visit the hapless Pup) were "Leave me something to eat"—a statement that retrospectively assumes a rather ominous significance. Convinced that her lover is bound to "taste good," she even goes so far as to speculate about which of his body parts would be the most pleasing to the palate (76, 85). From Richard's point of view, it seems that Georgina believes that if she consumes Michael's remains not only will his spirit come to life again in her body, but she and her lover will become one flesh, joined together in an eternal and indissoluble union. However, when Georgina reveals that it is in fact Albert who will be eating Michael, the cook—clearly taken aback at her audacious ingenuity—immediately offers his services free of charge, realizing that this is also the ideal way to avenge himself on the thief.

The conquering side of cannibalism is sardonically implied in the film's final sequence. Observing Albert's uncertainty about how to proceed when faced with the cooked cadaver of her lover, Georgina wryly recommends that he sample Michael's most succulent member: "Try the cock Albert. It's a delicacy. And you know where it's been" (92). Not only does the emboldened wife flaunt her infidelity here, but she also taunts the thief about both his latent homosexuality and his own penile inadequacy. Furthermore, she appears to suggest that, if Albert were to eat the vital part of his vanquished rival, he might even take on some of Michael's redoubtable virility.

Albert's cannibalistic tendencies had been suggested earlier, when he stuck a fork into the face of Patricia (Emer Gillespie), the mistress of one of his henchmen, after she revealed that he was being cuckolded by Michael. Seething with jealousy, the thief set off on a homicidal rampage, tearing through the restaurant in search of his wife and her lover. After causing pandemonium in the ladies' toilet, he stormed into the kitchen, where he went completely berserk, demolishing everything in his path. And then, looking "*like a demonic diner*"—his napkin still tucked into his shirt collar, as he brandished a large knife in one hand and a carving fork in the other—he repeatedly bellowed what he intended to do when he apprehended Michael: "I'll kill him and I'll eat him!" (66, 67). These words, as we have seen, later come back to haunt the thief.

The first instance of actual cannibalism in the film almost occurs when Albert attempts to feed Pup his own navel. This idea of cannibalism by proxy would seem to have a perverse appeal to Albert, since it is also insinuated during the horrendous episode in the book depository. Despite the fact that he had threatened to eat Michael himself, the thief, when it comes down to it, suggests that his young lieutenant should have a taste of the bookkeeper first: "Right Mitchel—this is where you're going to eat bollocks." Having earlier registered his disgust when tricked by Albert into eating an ersatz "prairie oyster," Mitchel finds the prospect of munching on real human testicles even less appetizing. Significantly, however, the thief suddenly becomes anxious that this might make the whole thing look too much "like a sex murder" and insists—albeit a little unconvincingly—that he was speaking metaphorically (77, 43, 78).

Characteristically undaunted by the problems involved in dealing with such a taboo subject as cannibalism, Greenaway was nevertheless keen to stress the ironic nature of his film. He pointed out that his approach was not unlike that of Jonathan Swift's A Modest Proposal, wherein the great eighteenth-century satirist had mordantly suggested that the problem of hunger in Ireland could be eliminated virtually overnight if its citizens would just eat the babies of the poor. In his introduction to the published screenplay, Greenaway describes cannibalism as "perhaps the furthest obscenity practiced by one human being on another; a savage proposition that, to mask the difficulties of comprehension, is normally treated with amused incredulity" (7). There were in fact a surprising number of movies released around this time that dealt quite explicitly with the issue of cannibalism. The most notable of these were *Eating Raoul* (Paul Bartel, 1982), *Eat the Rich* (Peter Richardson, 1987), *Society* (Brian Yuzna, 1989) and *Parents* (Bob Balaban, 1989). And, as if confirming the truth of Greenaway's dictum, all of them sought to temper the sensationalist horror of their subject with a large measure of surreal comedy. However, none of these films attracted nearly as much controversy as *The Cook, the Thief, His Wife and Her Lover.* There are perhaps two reasons why Greenaway's treatment of cannibalism proved harder to swallow for some people. The first has to do with the idea of perception; the second has to do with the question of ethics.

Amy Lawrence has noted that whereas in the majority of "cannibal texts . . . people do not know what they are eating . . . [in] Greenaway's film, they do."[17] However, the truly exceptional thing about *The Cook, the Thief, His Wife and Her Lover* is not so much that Albert *knows* what—or rather whom—he is eating, as the fact that he *sees* the person he is eating. Unlike most other cannibal films, no attempt is made to conceal the human source or semblance of the food being offered. On the contrary, the strategy of revenge requires that the lover's body be kept in one piece, since the cook must ensure that Albert is confronted with the atrocious reality of his own murderous appetite. Instead of being chopped up and put into an amorphous casserole or disguised as regular cuts of meat, the body remains very much intact and is indeed instantly recognizable as that of Michael. (Compare this with the wanton dismemberment of the fetishized bodies of both the "miracle child" in *The Baby of Macon* and the tattooed beau in *The Pillow Book.*) When Georgina removes the white cover from the table, we see her late-lamented lover laid out on a giant silver plate and surrounded by a generous selection of sautéed vegetables. His body, having been roasted to a crisp golden brown, is garnished with parsley and butter, and topped off with a few fancy orange slices. The camera lingers on this extraordinary dish, panning slowly from the feet up to the head, and savoring the contrast between its sumptuous presentation and its abominable content. Simultaneously mouthwatering and stomach churning, this sequence epitomizes the aesthetic of the entire film, which consistently manages to enthrall the viewer with its blend of visual splendor and aural sophistication, while unflinchingly portraying some of the least appetizing and most distasteful aspects of human experience.

What is so uniquely disturbing about *The Cook, the Thief, His Wife and Her Lover* is that the cannibalism itself takes on a moral dimension. The last supper of Albert Spica represents a communal spectacle of retribution. Nearly all of the people whom the thief has terrorized and abused in the course of the film are on hand to see him get his just deserts. Moreover, the viewer (having been sutured into the filmic context by Greenaway's highly subjective camerawork) is also implicated in what is taking place here. Despite the clandestine nature of the court, we are very much in sympathy with those bringing this action against the thief. We do not regard these stealthy plaintiffs as depraved, desperate, or insane; on the contrary, their behavior seems to be fairly measured and even appropriate in the circumstances. Characters and audience are thus joined together for a common purpose. Not only do we all want justice to be done, but we all want to see it being done—nothing less will satisfy us. The problem is, though, that here "justice" means forcing a man to commit an act of cannibalism. Greenaway unsettles the audience by challenging us to accept that such a thing can be morally defensible. There can be no denying that Albert Spica is (what the tabloid press would call) an evil monster, but deep down we still feel somewhat queasy about our complicity as we watch him get his comeuppance.

Elegantly attired in a reticulated gown with a ruff of sable plumes, Georgina dominates the proceedings. Having frequently used unflattering animal images to describe his wife, Albert now finds himself at the mercy of this magisterial version of a black widow spider. Ice cool in her delivery, she acquaints the quaking thief with what he has in front of him: "[I]t's Michael. My lover. You vowed you would kill him—and you did. And you vowed you would eat him. Now eat him" (92). Albert is thus condemned twice over by his own mouth. First, by what came out of it—the sentence that he passed on Michael, now to be terminated with extreme prejudice; and second, by what is about to go into it—the forbidden flesh that became of his words. On both of these counts, the cannibalistic meal is poetically justified, for it is meet that the murderer should have to chew over the fate of his victim. The thief, who has for so long been voraciously feeding off other people, is finally compelled to take in the consequences of his greed and inhumanity. With the tables having been turned, every one of Albert's trademark tactics now rebounds on his own person: he must learn a very hard lesson; his manly credentials are exposed to ridicule; and he is forced to consume a most unsavory substance, while being patronized with a Gallic culinary cliché—"*Bon appetit.* It's French" (92). Moreover, all of this happens on a Friday—the night he would normally expect to receive what is due to him. In a frantic bid to escape, the thief pulls out a small pistol, but this is immediately snatched away from him and passed among his victims. Eventually it comes to his missus, now also his nemesis, who pauses until he has put a forkful of the vile stuff into his mouth and begun to masticate. She then calmly shoots him in the forehead, denouncing him as a "Cannibal" (92). And so he dies, with a bullet from his own gun.

Greenaway sees cannibalism as the perfect metaphor for the end of consumerist society. A sign of the fundamental breakdown of civilized culture, cannibalism abolishes the hierarchical distinction between the person who is doing the eating and the thing that is being eaten. It therefore represents the ultimate negation of a common sense of humanity. Having started off *The Cook, the Thief, His Wife and Her Lover* by echoing the works of two Italian maestros, Pasolini and Ferreri, Greenaway bows out with a nod to another of his European cinematic heroes—Jean-Luc Godard, one of whose most cele-brated movies, *Weekend* (1968), likewise concludes with a scene of autophagy. The final message of both these films is that if the insatiable juggernaut of capitalist consumerism is allowed to go unchecked then the logical result will be wholesale cannibalism. As Greenaway says, "when you've finally devoured everything there is to be eaten, you end up eating one another."[18]

Notes

1. These are the actual words used in the film. However, the wording in the published screen-play is slightly different: "Okay, open your mouth. Come on! Take an interest in your food!" (Peter Greenaway, *The Cook, the Thief, His Wife and Her Lover* [Paris: Dis Voir, 1989]. 10). All subsequent quotations are taken from the published screenplay and will be cited paren-thetically in the text.

2. Hartmut Buchholz and Uwe Kuenzel, "Two Things that Count: Sex and Death," in *Peter Greenaway: Interviews*, ed. Marguerite Gras and Vernon W. Gras; Conversations with Film-makers series (Jackson: University Press of Mississippi, 2000), 59.

3. Greenaway has acknowledged that "the main template" for the film was John Ford's play, *Tis Pity She's a Whore* (1833). See Joel Siegel's "Greenaway by the Numbers," in Gras and Gras, eds., *Peter Greenaway*, 69.

4. Buchholz and Kuenzel, "Two Things," 59.

5. While the four male leads—Ugo (Tognazzi), Michel (Piccoli), Marcello (Mastroianni), and Philippe (Noiret)—were already established as household names in European cinema, Andréa (Ferréol), the quietly voluptuous schoolmistress who catalyzes the terminal excesses of her gluttonous hosts, was less well known at the time. She would go on to star in many noteworthy films, including Greenaway's *A Zed and Two Noughts*, where she plays the leg-less heroine Alba Bewick.

6. Of the other roles, the thief was to be played by Albert Finney (who flatly rejected the script), his wife was to be played by Georgina Hale (who was unavailable), and her lover was to be played by Michael Gambon. Had these original choices been fulfilled, the result would probably have been a very different film. In the event, Greenaway decided to keep the same names for the characters, but recast Gambon as Albert, alongside Helen Mirren as Georgina and Alan Howard as Michael—all of whom put their nominal antecedents in the shade and made the roles very much their own. See Siegel, "Greenaway by Numbers," 82.

7. There is, incidentally, a comparable sense of confusion between the restaurant and the movie theater at the start of Juzo Itami's *Tampopo* (1986), which, curiously enough, also focuses to some extent on the consuming passions of a vainglorious mobster and his diffi-dent female companion.

8. Andreas Kilb, "I Am the Cook: A Conversation with Peter Greenaway," in Gras and Gras, eds., *Peter Greenaway*, 62; Marcia Pally, "Cinema as the Total Art Form: An Interview with Peter Greenaway," in Gras and Gras, eds., *Peter Greenaway*, 108.

9. Siegel, "Greenaway by Numbers," 81.

10. Made for around $2.5 million, the film was a huge hit in Europe, and, despite the commer-cial handicap of an NC-17 rating, grossed almost $8 million in the United States alone.

11. Siegel, "Greenaway by Numbers," 81; Gavin Smith, "Food for Thought: An Interview with Peter Greenaway," in Gras and Gras, eds., *Peter Greenaway*, 93.

12. Pally, "Cinema as the Total Art Form," 119, 108, 107.

13. Ibid., 119.

14. Although unacknowledged here by Greenaway, this much-quoted line comes from the third act of Oscar Wilde's play *Lady Windermere's Fan*.

15. Alan Woods, *Being Naked Playing Dead: The Art of Peter Greenaway* (Manchester: Manches-ter University Press, 1996), 98.

16. Similarly nasty instances of force-feeding also occur in *A Zed and Two Noughts*, in which the zookeeper is coerced into consuming a rancid prawn, and *The Belly of an Architect*, in which the paranoid protagonist tries to make his pregnant wife eat one of the figs that he suspects she has poisoned.

17. Amy Lawrence, *The Films of Peter Greenaway* (Cambridge: Cambridge University Press, 1997), 184.

18. Siegel, "Greenaway by Numbers," 85.

17
Jean-Pierre Jeunet and Marc Caro's *Delicatessen*: An Ambiguous Memory, an Ambivalent Meal*

KYRI WATSON CLAFLIN

To eat or be eaten—that is the question

—August Strindberg, *The Father*

French journalist Pierre Hamp wryly observed in 1945 that in Paris, the world capital of gastronomy, "the culinary art, the fine sumptuousness of the table [was a] French invention, so tenacious that it continued even in time of real shortages."[1] Food is important in French culture on many levels, but for our purposes, following anthropologist Claude Lévi-Strauss, "food is good to think with." Reflections on the meaning of food in France during troubled times offer more than a morsel of cultural insight.

This essay explores the uses of food in the French film *Delicatessen* (1991).[2] A gustatory perspective gives us the firmest grasp on the diverse visual elements in the film and the mixture of humor and violence that directors Jean-Pierre Jeunet and Marc Caro throw at us. Food gives the film its context and meaning, and it does so by illustrating the questions the film is asking and by suggesting some possible answers. The first part of this essay will place the film in the context of the French memory of the era of the World War II German Occupation from 1940 to 1944, a phenomenon called the Vichy

*I am very grateful to Priscilla Parkhurst Ferguson for reading and commenting on an earlier version of this essay.

Syndrome. The film is an allegory of and recalls the Occupation era, both as illustration and trope. *Delicatessen* came out as France was grappling with the controversial history of the war years, and the film portrays ways in which the French had conducted life under German Occupation. Its plot and characters confront the national patterns of dealing with the ambiguity of the choices people made during those years under exceptionally trying circumstances.

The second part of the essay addresses the special significance of meat in French "culinary grammar," a phrase Claude Fischler uses to describe a culture's particular meanings for foods. Meat functions in *Delicatessen* as the centerpiece of the narrative, the drama, and the comedy. Meat eating has "gustatory semantics" of its own,[3] a symbolic structure that conveys meaning. The essay reveals why the message of this film can best be "read" in the butcher shop. In films, novels, art, and on the table, food can be a thing in itself, nourishment for the body. Artists, writers, and historians use food mimetically to represent the reality of eating at particular times and places. Yet food is also symbolic, its importance in this case being cognitive not physiological. Can anyone argue that in Western culture, a single red apple is not laden with meanings, sometimes sinister ones (from Eve to Snow White); sometimes domestic, comforting ones (Mom's apple pie)? As Roland Barthes argues, "Who can claim that in France, wine is only wine?"[4] Foods that figure largely in a nation's cuisine become institutions, so to speak, involving images, dreams, taboos, tastes, choices, and values. Food of all kinds, and especially meat, can represent a myriad of symbol systems and cultural traditions.

Many reviewers didn't know what to make of *Delicatessen* when it came out. Some called it a "cult film," "impenetrable," "a fantasy about cannibalism." One critic even wrote, "Only the French could come up with something this twisted."[5] The film tells the tale of a cannibalistic butcher and the near Armageddon his actions provoke for his daughter and all of the tenants in the apartment building he owns above his *boucherie-charcuterie*. What can we make of a butcher who murders a series of employees, and of customers who knowingly indulge in an appetite, indeed craving, for human flesh?

By proposing cannibalism as the solution to disastrous alimentary circumstances, the representation of what philosopher Carolyn Korsmeyer calls "terrible eating," *Delicatessen* brilliantly renders timeless themes in a contemporary form. Ambivalence and ambiguity are qualities Jeunet and Caro accentuate to make their statement. The ambiguity of choices, the ambivalence of self-control, the bonds that hold a society together, and the meaning of individual and collective actions: all of this is questioned, whether we read the film as an allegory of the occupation or as a cautionary tale about human appetites run amuck. Cannibalism symbolizes a civilization that has crashed, but the vision of the homicidal butcher getting his just desserts means that the way back is still covered with breadcrumbs. In the end, the film provides a hopeful pronouncement on a relatively grisly set of circumstances.

Delicatessen is set in an unspecified French city; the time is vaguely in the past. There are severe material shortages. Even the name of the newspaper is *Les Temps Difficiles* (*Difficult Times*). There is no prosperity in sight. The neighborhood looks bombed out: some buildings standing, some skeletal, some marked only by gaping holes in the landscape. There is a perpetual thick fog hanging in the air. The characters feature a villainous and hefty butcher all too aptly named Boucher ("butcher" in French),[6] played by Jean-Claude Dreyfus; his pretty, innocent and vegetarian daughter Julie (Marie-Laure Dougnac); the main protagonist, a former circus clown named Louison (played by Jeunet's favorite actor Dominique Pinon); Boucher's libidinous younger girlfriend, Mademoiselle Plusse (Karin Viard); and a team of vegetarian do-gooders, the Troglodistes, or "Troglos." The building tenants resemble a large dysfunctional family, each member feeding the strange needs, desires, and fears of the others. The arch rivalry in the film is between the underground Troglos and the surface-dwelling meat eaters. Each considers the other the enemy. But each character contributes a nuance to the meaning of the film and each appetite thickens the plot.

The charming Louison has to abandon his career as a circus clown when hungry marauders eat the other half of his act, a monkey named Livingstone, after a performance. Louison's search for a job brings him to Boucher, who needs a new building handyman. The last handyman tried to escape in a garbage can, but didn't quite get away. Each time the butcher hires a man, after the odd jobs are finished—voilà!—the man disappears and a supply of fresh meat appears, which Boucher sells at a pretty profit to the people who live in the apartment building he owns above his delicatessen. As the purveyor of this rare, sought-after commodity, Boucher becomes rich, or as rich as one can get in a society where paper money no longer has any value. He has thirty huge sacks of corn in his back room, a gold mine in a barter society where most people have had to become vegetarians due to a lack of meat.

When times are hard, how far will people go in order to get the food they need? The unsavory story that *Delicatessen* tells can be analyzed within historian Henry Rousso's theory of the Vichy Syndrome,[7] his name for the complex and ongoing negotiation in France with the events and the memories of the years of German Occupation. Jeunet and Caro use food in *Delicatessen* as one piece of the matrix of imagery that evokes wartime conditions of food and other material shortages. And they use it as well to conjure a *mentalité,* or frame of mind, that every choice was a matter of life and death. Food, and what hungry people would do to have it, serve as metaphors for the decisions a person was forced to make during the war. The choices that people made about food on a daily basis were full of ambiguities, just as the choices every French person had to make about how to conduct a life under Occupation were embedded in an atmosphere of ambiguity. The struggle over food portrayed in *Delicatessen* symbolizes the Franco-French conflict of the 1940s—the "civil war" that followed defeat in France as it did in so many countries conquered by the Nazis. Rousso correctly argues that the lack of consensus about the true nature of French actions during the Occupation is an ideological phenomenon that continues to resonate in French society. Ambiguities mark the era and characterize the French approach to the history of the Occupation to the present day. *Delicatessen* inventively portrays ambiguity and ambivalence as it revisits questions about French survival under Nazi domination.[8]

Ten years after the launching of *Delicatessen* and the publication of *The Vichy Syndrome*, in the spring of 2001, the legendary and beloved French singer and songwriter Charles Trenet died. As the nation grieved, his image appeared all over Paris. One poster in a metro station—depicting the young Trenet and the words to one of his most well known songs, *Douce France*—caught my eye on my regular morning ride. Then, one day not long after it had gone up, the poster was defaced with a large graffito in bold, black marker. In contrast to the sweet face of Trenet and the pretty lyrics of *Douce France*, the graffito at the bottom of the sign accused him starkly: "TU CHANTAIS ÇA SOUS L'OCCUPATION;" and written underneath, even larger, was "ENFOIRÉ!" ("YOU SANG THIS UNDER THE OCCUPATION . . . MOTHERFUCKER!")

Here was graphic evidence of Rousso's assertion that "obsession with the war is not yet a thing of the past."[9] Fifty-seven years after the Allies and the Free French Forces defeated the Germans in France, ending the Nazi Occupation and pulling down the wartime Vichy government, Trenet's choices during that pivotal era were the object of obscene accusations and resentment. Especially as subway graffito is not the likely pastime of someone old enough to have lived through the Occupation, it is clear that this experience still profoundly marks French society.

Food in *Delicatessen* addresses the struggle in the minds and hearts of the French that went on in the "dark years" (as they are called in France), a struggle still going on in 1991 when the film appeared. How did people make their choices and what did those choices mean? This is a thorny issue for a society to confront when it has lost a war. Historians Jean-Pierre Azéma and François Bédarida wrote in 1992 that the ambivalent character of behaviors during the Vichy period has been one of the factors most difficult for the French to understand.[10] They argue that the ambivalence of the reactions under the Vichy regime is the "best key to understanding the relative complexity of the attitudes of a large part of the population."[11] Treated comically, motivations are easier to understand. When the ogre is a cannibal, the people dependant on him who stupidly follow his philosophy of survival can be caricatured. But on a deeper level, when we read cannibal as collaborator, the characters resonate rather differently in a society torn apart by guilt and blame. This film, which portrays French society working through the ambiguity of behaviors during four of the most tragic years of French history, demonstrates how the Vichy Syndrome operates.

Naomi Greene, in her book *Landscapes of Loss*, which explores postwar French cinema, includes a discussion of *Delicatessen* but does not see its relevance as a film about the war. In Greene's analysis, the earliest films that represent the Vichy Syndrome, such as those by Alain Resnais (e.g., *Night and Fog*, 1955), evoke the period of the not-so-heroic past without representing it directly because of media censorship in the new Fifth French Republic under Charles de Gaulle. The films that followed in the Vichy Syndrome are those that are set in and re-create the Occupation, such as *Lacombe Lucien* (dir. Louis Malle, 1974) and *Le Dernier Metro* (The Last Metro, dir. François Truffaut, 1980). Greene argues that these were "retro" films, "marked by a new willingness to explore the somber realities of the Vichy era."[12] In categorizing *Delicatessen* as the genre known as the "Cinéma du Look," Greene and other film historians place it in a tradition of French filmmaking that tries to evoke memories of a "golden age" of French popular life in the early decades of twentieth century, and of a type of French cinema itself that has vanished. Cinéma du Look films are believed to be without intrinsic meaning. Such an argument is patently too confined. This essay shows the ways that *Delicatessen* obliquely, but not less powerfully, is a portrayal of the Occupation and a manifestation of the Vichy Syndrome.

Appetite for Survival

Jeunet and Caro imagined *Delicatessen* as a fairy tale.[13] The story takes place "once upon a time." The time and place are left to the viewer's imagination. The clothes, décor, and material shortages in *Delicatessen* strongly evoke the 1940s, and the presence of black and white television sets in most apartments and the television shows, of which we see bits, suggest the 1950s. In my reading, the juxtaposition of time frames that has confused some viewers recalls most powerfully the opening line of Marcel Aymé's 1943 short story "En Attendant": "Pendant la guerre de 1939–1972, il y avait à Montmartre, à la porte d'une épicerie de la rue Caulaincourt, une queue de quatorze personnes . . . . " ("During the war of 1939–1972, waiting at the door of a grocery on rue Caulaincourt in Montmartre, there was a line of fourteen people . . . .)

"During the war of 1939–1972": In other words, in 1943 the French felt that Occupation and war would last forever. And especially as food restrictions and shortages continued beyond the end of the war itself, they wondered if they would ever escape the day-to-day burdens of poverty and want and become again a prosperous country with abundant food supplies for everyone. Many, even most, city dwellers were hungry, not only the traditionally poor classes, and this was, after all, the land of François Rabelais, Jean Anthelme Brillat-Savarin, and Escoffier. Collective memory of this endurance contest has not faded over time. When one factors in the cultural power of the belief in the greatness of French cuisine as an integral piece in French nation building and national identity since the nineteenth century, one can understand that sudden deprivation of this cherished symbol of French civilization was not only a physical assault but also a psychological one. The Vichy regime's economic theories and professional organizations came under intense scrutiny and attack as food disappeared from the cities, except at black market restaurants and other places where people could see that with lots of money, one could indulge in almost every delicacy of fine French cuisine, and plenty of it. Good food was still a French birthright, but only for those with money or goods enough to deal on the gray or black markets. The social hierarchy, like the social structure portrayed in *Delicatessen*, was now based on access to food. In 1942, the dairyman's wife for the first time had the means to buy haute couture clothes, the grocer and his wife dined at Maxim's.[14] In the film, only a food trade can provide prestige and wealth, and other endeavors seem meaningless, even hopeless.

During the Occupation most French were obsessed with *la bouffe*, or eating, and it is the overarching obsession in *Delicatessen*—finding food becomes the master metaphor. At the same time, the film recalls the fairy tales and fables of the type Charles Perrault and Jean La Fontaine wrote, which the French still grow up reading. The main characters—the hideous ogre, the lovely daughter, a heroic fellow and a band of merry men who do good deeds—all act out a dramatic tension between the clever and the too clever. The approach the film takes to the question of how to triumph in an uncertain world is almost formulaic, although in no way Manichean. Historian Robert Darnton analyzed peasant tales of early modern Europe to discern characteristics that define a distinctly French cultural style and worldview. The recurrent theme in French tales is the hero who solves problems by cunning, craftiness, and intrigue. Darnton argues that this tradition functions to instill in the French the idea that these traits will work "as well as anything in a cruel and capricious world."[15] *Delicatessen* uses the literary devices common in traditional French popular literature to create the framework for its story.

Delicatessen is not the only work to have dealt with food and the Occupation. Its central character, Boucher, may be the archetypal "*boutiquier*" of the Occupation,[16] but there have been others like him. The greedy, detestable B.O.F.,[17] or dairy shop, owner was the subject of one of the most widely known novels about the Occupation, Jean Dutourd's 1952 *Au Bon Beurre*. It is still in print and was made into a popular 1970s television movie in France. The perfidious butcher is a legend of the Occupation. The most renowned French film about the black market, war profiteers, and the Occupation is *La Traversée de Paris* (*Crossing Paris*), a truly dark comedy by Claude Autant-Lara about another butcher, released in 1956. Two enterprising characters, played by Jean Gabin and Bourvil, lug four enormous suitcases stuffed with a freshly slaughtered pig across Paris after curfew, taking all night, all the while dripping a trail of blood and being followed by increasing numbers of dogs. This film is about traversing the Occupation, as well as the city, and it is a pessimistic vision of how the French negotiated the era.[18] It was the first film that appeared after the Occupation that treated the behavior of the French in a questioning and cynical way. *Delicatessen* picks up that tradition, with a lighter touch. The sign of the pig that hangs over the delicatessen in Jeunet and Caro's film is a fitting homage to the source of greed and betrayal that led to the downfall of the men in the earlier film, black market pork. In the short story on which the 1956 movie is based, the author coyly refers to "the victim" that is about to be killed for several pages, before the reader knows the victim is a pig. In *Delicatessen*, it is very amusing that it is the monkey Livingstone that is sacrificed. It is hardly a coincidence that the French referred to the wartime canned meat rations, which they thought were bad for their health and their palates, as *singe* (French for "monkey").

In *Delicatessen*, people must make different kinds of food choices. Most surface dwellers are carnivores, but have to assuage their hunger for meat by eating other people. Monsieur Potin (Howard Vernon) lives in the building's waterlogged basement and farms snails and frogs for his food.[19] He also catches the occasional insect in very inventive ways to supplement his diet. The hapless, vegetarian heroes of the film, the Troglodistes, live in the sewers. The Troglos, literally living underground, represent the Resistance, the metaphorical "underground" during the Occupation. Their comic treatment and bungled missions reflect very vividly the questioning of the Resistance myth that was created by Charles de Gaulle after the Liberation, and was dominant in Vichy historiography until the early 1970s.[20]

The "surfacers" represent both the French citizens who collaborated with the Germans and people who simply went about their lives and survived the times. The interplay of these groups in the film, and their choices about food, demonstrate the many choices that faced the French during the Occupation. These included out and out collaboration with the Germans for the benefit of the enemy or for personal profit or power; collaboration due to circumstance rather than ideology; sheer survival by *débrouillardise* (the triumph of *Le Système D*, which translates as survival by resorting to one's wits); or outright rejection of the New European Order and a commitment to resist and fight back from within the society. In Boucher's well-fed and voluptuous girlfriend, Mademoiselle Plusse, we even have another category represented. She goes along with Boucher for a while until she becomes disgusted with the destructive outcomes of his choices, at which point she switches sides and helps rescue Louison from Boucher's gleaming cleaver. This element of the population was called *attentiste*, or those who waited to see how things were going to turn out before choosing sides. These men and women, probably the majority of the French, generally began the Occupation supporting or tolerating the Vichy collaborationist regime, then gradually became disenchanted with its empty rhetoric of national restoration and the evidence that the Germans were pillaging France's resources with Vichy's cooperation.

Portraying the food shortages of the Occupation creates a situation in which you can ask the most basic questions about people: What are you willing to do to survive? What choices will you make given your individual philosophy of survival? Quite naturally one chooses life over starvation. Food is the first need, but that is where the certainty ends and the choices and the ambiguity begin. Sociologists, anthropologists, and historians argue that choices are fraught with cultural meanings. Food choices are believed to have especially significant cultural connotations.[21] The question is, can we "read" characters' choices, and can we then judge what kind of people they are? *Delicatessen* clearly addresses issues about choices in the most difficult of times, and about whether the French of today should judge the French of the 1940s. In the decade prior to the release of *Delicatessen*, France witnessed the trial of Nazi SS officer Klaus Barbie (who was called "the Butcher of Lyon"), and that of Paul Tourier, in which it became clear that some French had committed the ultimate collaborationist act of causing the deaths of innocent fellow Frenchmen, some of them children, and went undetected and unpunished, living in peace for many years. The debate over forgiveness was carried on in France in the wake of the trials with little consensus in public opinion. *Delicatessen* poses this question: How does one choose the ultimate food taboo, cannibalism, and does that choice merit forgiveness or condemnation?

When Julie asks Louison if he is angry and bitter about losing Livingstone to those ravenous thugs, he replies, "One must always forgive. No one is entirely evil. It's circumstance or they don't realize they've done wrong." Several scenes later, our antagonist, Boucher, is talking with his girlfriend, telling her he's going to "throw in his apron." He's losing his touch, with so many victims: "I feel sorry for them." Then he says nearly the same words that Louison had said to Julie: "No one's entirely evil. It's circumstance. Or you don't realize you've done wrong." Boucher sighs, "Some say you have to forgive." He wants his daughter's forgiveness for having become a monster of a butcher, not just a meat eater but also a real murderer, the butcher of *Place des Albumines* (literally translated, "Protein Square"). In her eyes, he is not fighting the enemy; he *is* the enemy, just as before and after the liberation the collaborator was branded an enemy of the French. What was initially an innocuous word meaning to act together came to mean only treason in French postwar vocabulary.

Thus we move from the use of food to illustrate a historical period and metaphor for the problems it experienced, to the use of food as a metaphor specifically for the Franco-French war, and the ideological, social, cultural, and mental fractures that followed June 1940. This period divided families, lovers, and neighbors over issues that had been creating dissonance at different levels of French society throughout the interwar years. When the Occupation came, it spared no one. It pitted diverse groups in society against one another in a more violent way than had been experienced in the interwar years. That rupture in the social fabric hurt France deeply as a nation and became an integral part of the memory of the experience of defeat and Occupation. In the film, the Troglos and the meat eaters are metonyms for the two broad rival categories of Resistance and Collaboration, but there are multiple and varied conflicts within the film that illustrate the many ways the Occupation influenced French society.

As mentioned earlier, there is the hatred and yearning for forgiveness between father (bloodthirsty butcher) and daughter (vegetarian lover of the next intended victim). The building's tenants, too, become an integral part of the divisive drama, not merely innocent bystanders. The man who is behind in his rent, Monsieur Tapioca (Ticky Holgado), offers up his mother to Boucher. He has, after all, a family to feed, and his wife complains constantly that she's hungry. Their share of the previous handyman lasted them a week, "not counting the bouillon." The next morning when this couple buys their cut of the old woman in Boucher's shop, Madame Tapioca (Anne-Marie Pisani) wipes away tears, saying, "I would have liked to say 'goodbye.'" Thus by questionable choices in difficult times, another family is brutally divided. In another apartment live the Kube brothers,[22] Roger (Jacques Mathon) and Robert (Rufus (actor uses one name only)), who make little boxes that make a "moo" sound. Pasting on the illustrated cow box covers, one brother notes that the glue smells like fish: "It brings back memories." The illusion of the cow's noise, when there are no more of the real thing, must evoke memories as well. When Robert ventures out into the stairwell after dark, something one should never do, he loses his leg to Boucher, who mistakes him for the old lady lured into the hall by her son and scheduled for slaughter that same night. The brothers' facade of togetherness breaks down, and bickering and jealousy surfaces when Roger brings Robert's leg into the apartment the next day, wrapped in brown butcher's paper. By now, Robert has lost his appetite.

There is no system in place to mitigate the conflicts and breakdowns that occur between citizens and families. The only evidence of the existence of a government in the movie is the presence of the mailman who is in and out of the building. We never otherwise see any authority figures in *Delicatessen*, not even police. This shows us that the state is divided from civil society, much as it was during the Vichy years, without much relevance to solving the problems of real people and real families divided by questions of collaboration, resistance, and survival. There was government in name, but the real authority was the *débrouillards*, men and women clever enough to get some control over a supply of food. The grocer with a real camembert under the counter, for instance, or a middleman bringing in food from the countryside, the farmer himself, and consumers—all were complicit in the "food at any price" philosophy. The mailman in the film (Chick Ortega) delivers a package to Julie, which is instantly recognizable as a *"colis familial,"* a legendary fact of everyday life during the Occupation. Friends or relatives in the country sent these packages of food, often some butter, a chicken, a rabbit, some vegetables, eggs or fruit, to people living in the cities to help them supplement their insufficient official rations.[23] When le Facteur ("mailman" in French) hands the package of "tidbits" to Julie, he fumbles with it on the stairs, and all the tenants instantly emerge from their apartments to grab for it. This illustrates well the idea that what one can get to eat in these hard times is an out and out free-for-all.

During the war, people who were the most resourceful were the ones that tended to triumph in the end, as in the fables of La Fontaine. Men and women were on their own to make decisions and act on them. In *Delicatessen*, the law of the land is *sauve qui peut*, or the attitude that it's every man for himself. Yet the fast-thinking Louison, helped by the love of Julie, a just-in-the-nick-of-time rescue by the Troglos, and the essential good-heartedness of Boucher's girlfriend are the elements of this society that counteract the each-man-for-himself ethos. Their efforts end the butcher's reign of power and rapaciousness. Here we recall the lawless purges of suspected collaborators in 1944 and 1945, a kind of vigilante justice that swept France in the wake of Liberation. In the end, the Troglos, and Julie and Louison, triumph over the dark vision of Boucher's man-eat-man philosophy, but there could have been another possibility, another ending. Again, ambiguity recurs as a key theme.

Delicatessen has fun with food both visually and linguistically, but that is not to say that this playfulness is without meaning. The Troglos' communication over portable radios is in code of course, but this is code written to sound like a recipe. When a mission begins, you hear the Troglos talking to each other: "Scout to Sauce-Master. . . ." Scout warns his comrades, "Watch your steaks, guys!" One of the Troglos is called Onion Sniper. The target of the rescue operation, Louison, is code-named Artichoke Heart. When Julie gets on the radio to direct and time the mission to snatch Louison from the apartment building, she says into her transmitter–cum–coffee grinder, "Recipe 8: Cordon Bleu to Sniper. Artichoke heart soufflé. Preparation: H minus thirty-five minutes. Throw in the onions. Simmer the snipers. Cover them for fifteen minutes. H minus twenty minutes, stir the sauce." Not only a funny send-up of so many movie scenes of French Resistance members coordinating their clandestine activities, this is one of many scenes that reflect a hungry society's obsession with food—especially filling and flavorful foods that are not available. When people are very hungry, they talk about food, they look at images of food, they even dream about food. Anthropologist Marvin Harris reminds us that in the Communist-led countries of Central and Eastern Europe, the shortage of meat after the Second World War led to the most visceral complaints and even violent public action. He notes that for decades the citizens subjected to strict state-directed economic planning judged political regimes by the "meat regime" the state was able to supply.[24]

Appetite for Flesh

The centrality of meat in the film thus compels us to look beyond the historical allusions and metaphorical uses of food I have discussed so far. It is significant that the action in *Delicatessen* is set in a butcher shop rather than a bakery or a grocery. In French culture, at peace or at war, meat itself has a symbolic significance, a history and a "social life" of its own. Sociologists, philosophers, and anthropologists have written on the special nature of meat and meat eating in a number of cultures. Meat functions on many levels in French food culture and supports a varied mythology.

Meat is a social marker, a product that signifies status. We can define a social hierarchy of meat eaters depending on the cuts, the frequency, and the amount of meat one is able to consume. In addition, the place where one buys and eats meat can indicate social status. The method of preparation one chooses is at least a signifier of social aspirations, if not of status itself. In Paris, even more than in the rest of France, ever since the eighteenth century political authorities have considered meat to be one of two foods that constitute the basic subsistence to which all citizens had a right. The other is, of course, bread. Even after the leaders of the French Revolution of 1789 abolished the regulation of food trades and practices, it was still legal for the state to fix the price of both bread and meat, and those two products alone, so that the French at every socioeconomic level could have some of each daily. French culinary culture considers meat simultaneously a necessity and a luxury.

Joan Jacobs Brumberg writes that the Victorians believed that eating the flesh of animals stimulated passion, which was clearly acceptable for men. However, "no food caused Victorian women and girls greater moral anxiety than meat." Victorian beliefs linked an excessive appetite for meat to (female) adolescent insanity and nymphomania. Frequently adolescent girls themselves expressed disgust for eating any form of meat.[25] Sociologist Claude Fischler argues that flesh "cannot be characterized only as a type of food, sought after or rejected; it is above all the food that carries the greatest ambivalence, encompassing at the same time desire and repulsion."[26]

Fischler adds that cuisine is not merely a set of ingredients and preparation techniques, it is comprised of representations, beliefs and practices shared by a group—this comprises a "culinary grammar" specific to a culture.[27] In the culinary grammar of traditional French cuisine there is an understood distance between the eater and the eaten.[28] Even with that distance, often the animals one typically eats in France still undergo a name change when they become food on the plate: *vache* becomes *boeuf; cochon* changes to *porc*.[29] The French do not classify some animals, like monkeys, as edible. Even during the Prussian siege of Paris in the winter of 1870–1871, when Parisians dined on the elephants from the zoo as well as on rats, dogs and cats, the monkeys in the Jardin d'Acclimatation were still taboo in a Darwinist interpretation of proximity between self and other. The monkeys were too close to human.

In *Delicatessen*, the dialectic of desire and repulsion remains a part of meat's strange magic. But necessity and luxury are no longer the issues. The line between man the eater and animal the eaten doesn't exist. The distinction between man and animal breaks down completely, and a whole segment of society eats not only monkey, but its neighbors as well! Scarcity has reduced the social hierarchy of meat consumption to the man who eats and the man who is eaten. The distance "civilized" humans maintain between self and other, and expectations of sociability are turned upside down in a Carni-valesque reordering of the world the characters inhabit. The line of culinary propriety and sociability completely disappears to reveal the utter degradation of man in a deadly eating contest. French culinary grammar is still communi-cating meaning about the culture, but what it says has changed dramatically. The new social hierarchy is a food chain where you must always "watch your steaks."

In part because of its connection to the invention of haute cuisine, French culture is considered one of the great civilizations in Western history. Margaret Visser writes, "Civilization itself cannot begin until a food supply is assured. And where food is concerned we can never let up; appetite keeps us at it."[30] In *Delicatessen*, that which makes civilization possible at the same time threatens to destroy it. Visser argues, "Cannibalism is to us massively taboo and forbid-den with far greater success than is incest." And because it has been so success-fully rendered horrific, an artist can count on it to create the effect of "an atrocity to make our skin crawl. . . . Cannibalism is a symbol of our culture in total confusion: a lack of morality, law and structure."[31]

Food, eating, and meals are associated with the formation of a community, sociability, sharing, and bonding. We have carefully separated the idea of can-nibalism from ordinary discourse. In Western culture the impossibility of the idea that humans might become food for each other has over the centuries propelled the West through a civilizing process—a reduction of violence, increasing civility in relations between people, and the development of table manners.[32] Visser writes, "Behind every rule of etiquette lurks the determina-tion of each person present to be a diner, not a dish."[33]

When cannibalism *is* part of our discourse, it becomes a commentary on societal breakdown. As philosopher Carolyn Korsmeyer puts it, representing the "dark side of eating," we discover "horrifying possibilities that are the counter-point to food as a civil and binding aspect of society."[34] Ogres in folk-tales, for instance, are distinguished by their desire for tasting human flesh. She points out these stories are "rife with terrible eating and hideous appe-tites." In *Delicatessen* the civilizing process is quite obviously teetering on extinction. Korsmeyer writes that cannibalism inspires "a particular revulsion because [it] violates a basic tenet both of what is edible and of what is accept-able conduct."[35] She notes that in art the depiction of food is often intended as an expression of passions that are "dangerous, terrible and abhorrent."[36] Certainly cannibalism in *Delicatessen* represents the unruly power of human appetites. Most of Jeunet and Caro's characters are under the influence of their passions: hunger, libido, love, power, or greed. Julie and Louison don't deny their appetites; they are in love, but they do retain their civilized nature. We literally see this distinction in their body types: both exemplify Byronesque thinness and, thus, spiritual purity. Boucher, every inch the perfect ogre, has an excessive appetite for flesh as food, as power, as sex and money; and he appears hideous to the viewer, enormous *clapet* (French slang for "mouth") and all. Gourmandise is revered in French culinary culture, and gourmandise involves a certain, although refined, degree of gluttony. But gluttony gets one uncomfortably close to animality, to the brink of civilized eating. Again we confront ambivalence in French culture: the ambiguity of appetite. How will you control it? Can you control it? Korsmeyer and Visser also remind us that most of what we eat was at one time alive, if not sentient, and must be treated with violence in order to be made edible—killed, chopped, cooked. It is a question of where one draws the line. Food is the first need, but eating is anything but natural.

Conclusion—Appetite for Meaning

In the film genre called Cinéma du Look there are "cinematic allusions and echoes" that serve as "constant reminders that we have entered a world of 'pure appearances.'"[37] In the Cinéma du Look there is pure seduction on the surface, "the triumph of appearances"—to disguise old, worn-out motifs drawn from classic French films of the 1930s. A great deal of critical comment has been generated by what is labeled the "falseness" of these films, their use of borrowed images. A harsh view of "incessant borrowings from and allusions to earlier works" associated with the Cinéma du Look has caused some to say that *Delicatessen* is all sizzle and no steak.[38] Naomi Greene writes about *Delicatessen* that "this black farce is nothing other than a somber rereading, a kind of evil twin, of the comic operettas René Clair brought to life in the early 1930s."[39] There is a superficial visual resemblance to images in Clair's 1930 film *Under the Roofs of Paris*, but the surface is where the similarities end.

Greene also writes that the films of the Cinéma du Look "display the bleak view of the present that reaches its grotesque apogee in Jeunet and Caro's sinister parable about contemporary cannibalism." Critic Susan Hayward chalks up the Cinéma du Look to "necrophiliac trends in French cinema."[40] Certainly an amusing connection in the case of *Delicatessen*, but again confined to the surface. Critics charge that currents of nostalgia are presented through a pastiche of glitzy special effects that mask a meaningless content based on no reality. The accusation is that Cinéma du Look has gotten away from the search for "truth" manifest in the great New Wave films of the 1960s.

Delicatessen is unquestionably visually vibrant, as are Jeunet and Caro's second film *City of Lost Children* (1995) and Jeunet's huge hit *Amélie* (2001). Jeunet recognizes that their visual style is animated and exaggerated, like a cartoon or commercial. He acknowledges the influence of some of the great French filmmakers, such as Marcel Carné, on his craft. But he also comments that he and Caro are not "*cinéastes*"; they are "*cuisiniers*."[41] They have done far more than slap together French cinematic traditions to tell a story without meaning that just entertains by looking good. This essay argues that they have indeed delivered a great feast to "think with."

A tale of a gruesome butcher who is the messiah of anthropophagy and about to cause the end of civilization could appear as simply a somber reading of Parisian populism, but my analysis of *Delicatessen* challenges this view by demonstrating the meaning and content of the film as seen through food. Viewed in this way, the film depicts a society searching to understand its values; it is a tale in which good, not evil, triumphs in the end. Food is at the center of the film. Placing the story within the Vichy Syndrome one sees the primary obsessions of the nation during the German Occupation—hunger, survival, choosing sides—while recasting questions about the painful dark years for a younger audience. Jeunet and Caro seize upon the themes of meat eating and cannibalism to show a whole spectrum of human appetites and conflicts. In the tradition of Rabelaisian vulgar and excessive food comedy, *Delicatessen* uses the truth that edible things have troubled civilized humans for centuries to illustrate the very human vicissitudes that civilization must overcome.

Notes

1. Pierre Hamp, *Et Avec Ça, Madame?* (Paris: Gallimard, 1947), 218.
2. For a very different interpretation of this film, see Stephen C. Infantino, "Delicatessen: Slices of Postmodern Life," *Arachne* 4, no. 1 (1997): 91–100.
3. The phrase is from Carolyn Korsmeyer, *Making Sense of Taste: Food and Philosophy* (Ithaca, N.Y.: Cornell Press, 1999), 184.
4. Roland Barthes, "Pour une psycho-sociologie de l'alimentation contemporaine," *Annales* 16 (1961): 977–986.
5. There may be in this statement a bit of truth of which the critic was unaware. In French popular imagery, the butcher was a favorite bogeyman that adults evoked to terrify young children into behaving.
6. Boucher does in fact have a name, Clapet, which is French slang for a big, talking mouth, as in "*Ferme ton clapet!*" ("Shut your big mouth!")
7. Henry Rousso, *The Vichy Syndrome: History and Memory in France since 1944*, trans. Arthur Goldhammer (Cambridge, Mass.: Harvard University Press, 1991).
8. On film, the Occupation, and memory, see also the insightful article by Lynn A. Higgins, "Two Women Filmmakers Remember the Dark Years," *Modern and Contemporary France* 7, no. 1 (1999): 59–69.
9. Rousso, *The Vichy Syndrome*, 305.
10. Jean-Pierre Azéma and François Bédarida, eds., *Vichy et les Francais* (Paris: Fayard, 1992),769.
11. Ibid.
12. Naomi Greene, *Landscapes of Loss: The National Past in Postwar French Cinema* (Princeton, N.J.: Princeton University Press, 1999), 9.
13. Jean-Pierre Jeunet, "Bicéphal ou presque," interview with Gilles Ciment, Philippe Rouyer, and Paul Louis Thirard, *Positif*, no. 364 (1991): 44. See also, "Rencontre avec Deux Tronches de l'Art," La *Revue du cinéma*, no. 471 (1991): 32.
14. See, for example, Henri Amouroux, "Le Crémier-Roi sous l'Occupation," *Historia*, no. 179 (1961): 464–71.
15. Robert Darnton, *The Great Cat Massacre and Other Episodes in French Cultural History* (New York: Basic, 1984), 61.
16. This translates literally, as "small shopkeeper." However, *boutiquier* is generally meant as a pejorative epithet.
17. The store that was commonly called a B.O.F. sold *beurre*, *oeufs*, and *fromages* (butter, eggs, and cheeses).
18. *Ecran Noir*, in its commentary on *La Traversée de Paris*, states that this was the first film after the war to take a nontraditional view of the period: "ici pas de résistants, pas de héros . . . le seul film à avoir bien traité cette face cachée de la France occupée est *Delicatessen*" ("Nothing here of resisters, of heroes . . . the only film to have really portrayed the hidden face of occupied France is *Delicatessen*"). Vincy Thomas, "Crime et Chatiment," available online at www.ecrannoir.fr/films/56/traversee.htm.

19. Félix Potin is the name of a well-known chain of specialty grocery stores in Paris, the kind of place that might well sell *escargots* and *cuisses de grenouilles* (snails and frog legs).

20. Portrayals of the Resistance after 1944 reflected Charles de Gaulle's vision of France as an entire nation of people who resisted the German occupiers, imposing a vision of a renewed France, and ignoring the evidence of those who were tried and condemned for treason after the war. This heroic image of a nation of resisters was shattered in the early 1970s—Rousso refers to this period as "the mirror broken"—with the near simultaneous appearance of historian Robert Paxton's landmark book about the Vichy regime, *Vichy France: Old Guard and New Order, 1940–1944* (New York: Columbia University Press, 1972) and Marcel Ophuls's documentary film *The Sorrow and the Pity* (*Le Chagrin et le Pitié,* 1971). This was bitter medicine that both shocked the French with the extent of widespread French complicity in collaborating with the Germans, and painfully exposed the core French belief about resistance during the Occupation as a myth.

21. See Barthes, "Pour une psycho-sociologie," 977–986. See also Carole Counihan and Penny Van Esterik, eds., *Food and Culture: A Reader* (New York: Routledge, 1997), especially the introduction, 1–7.

22. "Kube" evokes the brand name of a beef bouillon sold in France, KUB.

23. This concept was created by the first Vichy minister of food and promoted by the head of the government, Marshal Petain, who acknowledged that the inadequacy of the official rations could only be mitigated by some sort of activity on the "parallel market."

24. Marvin Harris, cited in Claude Fischler, *L'homnivore: Le gout, la cuisine et le corps* (Paris: Odile Jacob, 1990), 117.

25. Joan Jacobs Brumberg, "The Appetite as Voice," in Counihan and Van Esterik, eds., *Food and Culture,* 166–67.

26. Fischler, *L'homnivore,*123.

27. Ibid., 32.

28. Ibid., 125.

29. Ibid., 132.

30. Margaret Visser, *The Rituals of Dinner: The Origins, Evolution, Eccentricities, and Meaning of Table Manners* (New York: Penguin, 1991), 2.

31. Ibid., 6.

32. See Norbert Elias, The *Civilizing Process: The History of Manners,* trans. by Edmund Jephcott (New York: Urizen, 1978).

33. Visser, *Rituals,* 3.

34. Korsmeyer, *Making Sense,* 189.

35. Ibid., 191–92.

36. Ibid., 147.

37. Greene, *Landscapes,* 160, but see also generally chapter 6.

38. Ibid., 160.

39. Ibid., 182.

40. Susan Hayward, quoted in Greene, *Landscapes,* 161.

41. That is, they are not "filmmakers"; they are "cooks." Jean-Pierre Jeunet, "Rencontre Avec Deux Tronches de l'Art" (interview), *La Revue du cinéma,* no. 471 (1991): 31.

18

Futuristic Foodways: The Metaphorical Meaning of Food in Science Fiction Film

LAUREL FORSTER

Both food and science fiction have been of particular interest to cultural critics in the twentieth and early twenty-first centuries. In their different ways, they provide meaning and interpretation of the world at large, illuminating social, national, and even global structures, agencies, and order (or more often, disorder). In addition, critical inquiry into both subjects reflects changes and traditions in the quotidian habits that inform our lives. And both are useful cites to investigate the relationship between social function and individual existence, as it becomes, in a postmodern sense, more obscure and remote, more complex and more pressing. Food and science fiction provide a valuable means of understanding the link between the individual and controlling powers around her/him, often because of their ongoing concerns with the body and with technology. Food already links the external with the internal as far as the body is concerned, and has itself been subject to all manner of technological processes. Technological advancement (or deterioration) of machines, computers, and the body has long been seen as an index for social, cultural, and even political change, and science fiction has served as an insightful reflector (to say nothing of catalyst) of such change.

Food and foodways have been the subject of much recent academic study and debate.[1] From the structural analysis of a meal,[2] to detailed cultural studies,[3] to the foodways that determine the progress of the natural product in the field to the food on our tables at dinner, food has been critically discussed in a number of ways. Different races, communities, classes, and genders, at different times in our history have been shown to have differing relationships to foods. As Carole Counihan and Penny Van Esterik note, "Food is life, and life can be studied and understood through food."[4] Science fiction, understood by most at some level, yet notoriously difficult to define,[5] has always adopted different modes to express changing human anxieties and dreams at various times in our history. This adaptability and ability to reflect the personal, political, and the cultural has made science fiction an enduring genre in literature and film. Indeed, it has been argued that "Science Fiction film has simply proven to be one of our most flexible popular genres—and perhaps for that reason, one of our most culturally useful."[6]

Of course, there are many science fiction films that make little or no reference to food: people (or aliens) often exist over days, months, even years, make journeys through space and across galaxies, invade planets, conquer new worlds, and simply never eat. At other times, food is treated prosaically or as a mere prop to help the spectator engage with the story line; something to add a sense of completeness to the leap of imagination needed to believe in the cinematic illusion of a future world. Some science fiction movies use food and foodways in an unproblematized way, for example on the starship *Enterprise*, where food and eating occur in the recreational off-duty zones, merely as part of the futuristic mise en scène of the leisure scenes in Robert Wise's 1979 *Star Trek: The Motion Picture*. Food here is part of the extrapolated representation: it adds little to the larger narrative structure of the story. Other films make use of the idea of "consumption," without addressing food per se. *Dune* (dir. David Lynch, 1984) for instance, is structured around two major obsessions: the mind-enhancing spice "melange," which gives a superior mental capacity; and water retention for survival on the arid planet of Dune. The ownership, production, and consumption of these two highly prized commodities is the driving force behind the action and there are many points where, it could be argued, the film acts as an ecological metaphor about scarce natural resources and overconsumption by powerful nations: a clear indictment of Western power and values. However, food itself, with all its unique and pervasive cultural meanings, is not really explored.

More generally speaking, food appears in a surprising number of ways in a wide range of science fiction films. Many humorous science fiction films, for instance, which rely on kitsch or even the ridiculous for their entertainment value, use food and other domestic issues as a focus for their humor. Kitchen gadgets of the future; anthropomorphized, malfunctioning robots; and peculiar food are regular aspects of many popular science fiction movies.[7] Even science fiction films with an ultimately serious message often use humor about food as a way of drawing the audience into a new world, as a buffer zone in which one can suspend disbelief and engage with the underlying impetus of the tale.

My primary focus in this essay, however, is those films of the science fiction genre that use the subject of food, either generally or specifically, to help provide meaning in cinematic terms where food, foodways, and cooking carry a deeper, textual significance. Food appears as an important element in a surprising number of serious science fiction films. It is one of the essential elements of human life, and by interference with or disruption to established foodways, human life may be threatened. By interpreting a range of food scenes in some of these films, this essay will discuss the metaphorical meaning of food as part of the political and cultural comment made by science fiction regarding both futuristic messages and reflections on contemporary society.

There are many points of convergence between food and science fiction, making food such a helpful point of illustration for metaphor and exemplification of social concerns. For instance, both food and science fiction are concerned with the increasing impact of technology; in the case of food there is the globalization of mass-produced foods, the homogenization of cuisine such as the "MacDonaldization" factor,[8] as well as international cartels and subsidized farming and food production of, say, the European Economic Community. These mass, international means of producing and distributing foods have been a factor in global food concerns regarding surpluses in some nations and food shortages in others, with no politically satisfactory means of ensuring the obvious equality of food supply.[9] In a similar way, science fiction has long been concerned with the controlling, domineering power of the industrial complex, and the way the pursuit of company profit and corporate ideology have taken precedence over justice and moral codes of behavior for the individual. Science fiction has examined not just the physical impact of mass technology on our lives but its psychological impact too, often pointing to an invidious controlling force, invisible to normal consciousness, as in *The Matrix* (dirs. Larry and Andy Wachowski, 1999), where human lives have been refashioned to align with technological needs, not the other way around. In both the cases of mass industrialized food production and of a society dominated by computers and technology, we can see how the grand narratives of normalcy, natural morals, and human compassion have gone awry.

Another similarity between the study of food and science fiction is in their relevance to the body. The food we eat, or desire to consume, or indeed purposefully deny our bodies, signifies, at least in the wealthy Western world, much more than basic nutrients and energy calories. It is associated with social status, disposable income, and body image. The acts of cooking and eating are regarded by many as a means of controlling the impact of the exterior world on the interiority of the body, so that the relationship between food and the body is about control, both psychological and physical. Similarly, many if not most science fiction narratives rest on the impact of alien forces or technological advances on the fragile human body. The body in science fiction is a deliberately targeted zone, whether threatened from the interior or exterior. The central point is often that the body, being assumed, in the last resort, to be all that we truly own or control, is ultimately vulnerable to outside social, cultural, or technological forces. What is visible regarding foodstuffs may conceal deliberate or unavoidable toxins and impurities hidden within.

These two critical concerns—technology and the body—of such importance in discussions of food and science fiction, have also been central to the two most dominant modes of cultural thinking in the twentieth century, modernism and postmodernism.[10] Many science fiction films fall, broadly speaking, into alignment with one mode of thinking or the other. Therefore, the first part of my discussion will concentrate on issues of modernism and modernity that I have seen as either celebration or, conversely, anxiety concerning new technologies,[11] issues surrounding urbanization, a belief in human consciousness (albeit a fragmented one), and an investigation into the internal and external workings of the body. The cultural enquiries in such films are manifestly experimental, with the wider social messages of the narrative predicting utopia or dystopia. As will be seen, these are issues as relevant to food as they are to science fiction.

Soylent Green (dir. Richard Fleischer, 1973) is a science fiction film permeated by discussions of food at differing levels, which approaches the subject of impure or improper food from both corporate and bodily perspectives. The main story line is about the discovery and confirmation of the terrible fact that Soylent Green, the green foodstuff made by the Soylent corporation as a substitute synthetic food due to food shortages, is made out of processed human corpses. This deception of a hungry general public into a reworked cannibalism is depicted as symptomatic of a corrupt and divided society, where social and moral codes have disintegrated alongside the collapse of any urban infrastructure. Fresh natural food and drink, now so scarce, are the privilege of the rich or the dishonest. For the rich there are expensive, luxurious, modern apartments that include female partners known degradingly as "furniture," and food stores behind security fencing known as "food inventories." For the majority of the population there is overcrowding, scruffiness, malfunctioning technology, and processed food substitutes. Underlying the didactic warnings of the film are the vestiges of a modernist impulse toward empowerment of the individual and a belief in a degree of autonomy in the battle against degradation.

When Thorn (Charlton Heston), the hero investigator, retrieves some goods from the apartment of a wealthy murder victim, he brings them home to Sol (Edward G. Robinson), his elderly research assistant. The cache of rare goods includes soap, alcohol, vegetables, and beef. A meal is carefully prepared by Sol, who can remember such foods from a long time ago, and is overwhelmed with the reminder of the loss of proper food and its significance. The meal is eaten by Thorn and Sol with great reverence in a strikingly civilized fashion that provides great contrast to the clamor and chaos of daily life outside their home. The meal of salad, beef stew, and a fresh apple is appreciated without conversation, but with full attention on the food, causing the old man to declare afterward, "I haven't eaten like this in years." All three courses are accompanied by classical music. The ritual and structure of this meal is a hiatus of civilization in the film,[12] and offers a glimpse of how life was or could have been for the ordinary people of New York. The contrast between order and disorder, harmony and chaos, highlighted by the contrast between this ritualized meal and the daily queuing and squabbling over food in the city streets, remains a strong metaphor for the future social chaos predicted by the film generally, contrasted with the implied retrospective civilization of the current real world of the 1970s. Sol's sense of reminiscence, combined with his horror at the confirmation of the institutionalized cannibalism through the processed Soylent Green, leads him to opt for euthanasia; he trades his remaining years for half an hour of soothing music and picturesque archival film footage depicting natural landscapes, wild animals, and beautiful sunsets. Although idealized and sentimental, the contrast between the filmic memory of the world as it was, perhaps the world of Sol's childhood, and the general contemporary setting of the film is stark and disturbing. Thorn, on learning the truth about Soylent Green, investigates the processing factory for himself and tries to inform others on his return. Even when he has confirmed the dreadful truth, his hysterical appearance and the chaos around him conspires against him being taken seriously. Closure, then, is achieved through personal knowledge rather than "saving" society from itself. A modernist fear of the inexorability of urban deterioration and moral decline, brought about by the oppressive power of the corporation is made manifest.[13] *Soylent Green*, then, serves as a warning against the negative outcomes of the mass production of modernity, to a point where overconsumption has led to self-consumption.

The first of the Alien series, *Alien* (dir. Ridley Scott, 1979) also focuses on corrupt corporate power and the vulnerable human body, bringing together capitalism and the individual to predict an undesirable future society. Food in this film helps to cement the story line, reflecting the different stages of the narrative, as the corporate ideals impact upon the human characters. Set in opposition to the huge corporation is the central character of Ripley (Sigourney Weaver), a woman governed by her intuition, her strong sense of justice, and her maternal instincts. The combination of these three aspects of her personality enable her to stand apart from corporate ideals. After the film's long opening sequence of the spacecraft and the emergence of crew members from their hypersleep pods, a breakfast-type meal follows. The meal consists of cereals, dried fruit, coffee, corn bread, and so on. The crew are seated together around the table, and there is a sense of cohesion and harmony, even of a familial domestic scene. The table itself is littered with cereal bowls, storage jars, and melamine tableware. As in a family, there are jokes, asides, and whispers. The atmosphere is relaxed, and some start smoking. The picture is drawn for us of a team who live together. But in case the audience is too taken in by the illusion of domestic harmony, we are reminded that this is a workplace, as the conversation turns to snipes about inequalities in salaries and bonuses. Nonetheless, this meal has a number of codes and conventions that signify a sense of the traditional meal.[14]

The next meal, however, is in sharp contrast to this harmonious scene. The more disparate and disharmonious nature of the team has been caused by serious professional differences over safety procedures and undisclosed sinister alternative objectives of the company. This meal is taken standing up, with the crew not sharing food but eating separate portions of food out of individual cartons, like individual take-out meals. The unshared, even isolationist, aspect of this meal allows the crew to avoid contact with each other, some even standing with their back to others: the nature of the meal permits hostile body language. The differences of opinion arose over Kane (John Hurt), a crew member attacked by a face-hugging alien creature. Against safety regulations, and against Ripley's orders, he was brought into the craft, thus putting the rest of the crew at risk, but in fact this action complied with the company's hidden agenda of weapons research. The fragmented meal echoes and enhances the crew's disharmony.

However, Kane awakes from his coma and seemingly recovers from the attack. The alien carcass is contained, and the problem seems to have been solved. The crew welcome Kane back and he requests a meal before their long sleep on the journey home. Once more the crew sit around the table and share a meal together, this time a celebratory meal, similar in tone to the breakfast meal, but with some psychological and physiological traumatic distance having been traveled since that earlier shared meal. The conversation turns to home, sex, and food; friendly adult conversation has been resumed, hostilities are forgotten, harmony is restored. However, in *Alien*'s most famous scene, Kane lapses into a fit, collapses, and an offspring of the alien creature explodes out of his stomach. A harmonious meal with superficial equanimity was not enough to countermand the corruption of the corporate objectives or the horror of the alien creature. The human body has been corrupted, not by contaminated food, but by company-authorized impregnation by an alien creature. Corruption, immorality, and horror "consume" the frail human literally from the inside out. Even though the third meal takes place so quickly after the second, and so rather disrupts the narrative time of the film, it is no accident that the alien erupts from its male human host at a mealtime. As the alien bursts into its new life form, killing Kane in the process, a reversal of consumption takes place, blurring boundaries between the internal and external being. The food at the meal represented a return to the social and interpersonal order and harmony of the crew, reminding us of the strong moral order embodied in Ripley. The shocking appearance of a baby alien, directly from Kane's stomach onto the dinner table, represents the ultimate disruption of that order. The assumed purity of function of life-giving food is inexorably corrupted by the death and decay caused by the corporation. Modernist anxieties about weakened self-empowerment in the face of the uncontrollable power and drive of modernity's technological and consumer culture are made manifest. There is no longer any harmonious meal, the moral order is destroyed and revealed as naive: barbarism and self-interest take their place. The meals therefore follow a Todorovian narratological schema of an initial harmony, a disruption, and then a new equilibrium (much simplified). However the new equilibrium is an uneasy compromise among Ripley, the alien, and the corporate objectives. This film has many false endings and a final harmony is not truly reached until Ripley has eventually disposed of the alien and climbs into bed for her hypersleep once more. The meals consumed reflect the constant play between harmony and discord in the film.

The Stepford Wives (dir. Bryan Forbes, 1974) is in part a satire of patriarchal aspirations toward harmonious domestic living and manages to be simultaneously critical of both the present and a predicted future. It extrapolates toward a modernist dystopia of women's domestic role: all gleaming gadgets and no subjective consciousness. Central to this depiction is cooking and the kitchen. The actual woman's body is also in question, with its role and functions being subjected to extreme sexism and patriarchy. The first encounter with an automated Stepford wife occurs when, on the new family's arrival in Stepford, a neighbor, dressed in modest housewifely attire of long skirt, demure shirt, and clean frilly apron drifts dreamily across the lawn with a casserole. The eerie music, the stilted exchange, the extremely soft focus all indicate something unnatural about this woman. Echoing many strands of 1970s women's liberation, the difference between the mother of the new family, Joanna (Katherine Ross), her like-minded friend, Bobby (Paula Prentiss), and the rest of the wives is illustrated in many ways. The film challenges what it is to be an individual, with satirical comment on the enforced domesticity of women by patriarchal dominance. The men of Stepford, as part of their sinister "men's club," assume a godlike role in creating stereotypical imitations of real women, by a mind/body transference operation, transforming the women into sexual and domestic servants. One of the contrasts between Joanna and Bobby and all the "alien" women is their attitude to their kitchens. The two normal women keep normally scruffy kitchens, while the Stepford wives all have immaculate and gleaming homes and kitchens. When Bobby meets Joanna, they drink whiskey and smoke. This liberated behavior is contrasted with the selfless domestic toil apparent at a neighbor's party, where the quality and quantity of food is stunning. But the falseness of the situation becomes clear when one of the reprogrammed wives has had a car accident and is malfunctioning. Like an automated doll she keeps repeating the same phrase: "I'll just die if I don't get this recipe." The focus of the doll-like women has been turned away from a consciousness of an independent self to an all-consuming consciousness of the role within the family and home. The total control exerted over these women by their menfolk creates a feminist dystopia, echoing concerns expressed in other feminist media at the time.[15]

The Stepford wives are those women who have been sanitizd against the male-perceived threat of the unfettered female, and made to conform to a simplified gender-stereotyped existence. They are a filmic expression of a reaction against the idealized women's role, revealing the entrapment, restriction, and claustrophobia of a domestic "angel." This film exposes the dark underside of many early modernist concerns, such as the uncontrolled female consciousness, female control of "breeding" potential, the "function" of women in our society, and human and eugenic experimentation with an antidegenerative impetus. There are similarities here with the creation of the machine-woman, the false Maria in *Metropolis* (dir. Fritz Lang, 1926). As Andreas Huyssen has argued about this earlier android, "(T)he film does not provide an answer to the question of why the robot is a woman; it takes the machine-woman for granted and presents her as quasi-natural."[16] Huyssen's discussion extends to nature, technology, and male control.[17] The aggressive action of the men in *Stepford Wives* against their female partners echoes these concerns, and using issues surrounding the domestic, such as food and drink, makes a feminist statement. This is a film that, following Vivian Sobchack's summary of films of this moment of great social upheaval (1968–1977), certainly predicts a near future for women that is worse than the present.[18] The food and drink in this film are eternal tropes of women's work around the home, looking backward to traditional roles as much as forward to a new male-centered world. In fact, so closely intertwined in this film are issues of a feminist present, past, and future that the Stepford wives constitute, for feminists at least, a permanent threat of the nonfeminist other.

In *Alien Nation* (dir. Graham Baker, 1988), sameness through difference is explored as alien "otherness" becomes a metaphor for racism. The story combines humor with philosophy, where food and drink are part of the comedic aspect, but also provide scope for cultural philosophizing. In the opening sequence, we learn that in the New York district of the "Newcomers" (alien slaves whose space ship lost its way and landed on earth) there is as much crime as in any similar ghettoized, down-beaten district. The story is of two policemen—one human, one alien—who together investigate a brutal crime. One of the opening shots is of an alien drunk approaching the police car reeking not of alcohol, but of sour milk, as intoxicating to an alien as any alcoholic drink to a human. The humor is doubled: not only is he totally inebriated and trying to talk to the policeman, but is drunk on something repulsive and regarded by humans as food waste, something to be discarded. This acts as an ongoing filmic metaphor for the human attitude toward the aliens, also known derisively as "slags." The assumed superiority of the human race and inferiority of the alien race is a dichotomy that continues well into the film. The alien officer's name, San Francisco (Mandy Patinkin), is another point of derision, and Matt (James Caan), the human officer, renames San as George to save his own embarrassment. Differences in the eating habits of the two police officers provide Matt with another opportunity for condescension. When they call in at a fast-food stall, their food boxes get mixed up. George eats raw beaver meat, and Matt, faced with the wrong food, is repulsed and throws his meal away in disgust. Unable at this stage to accept difference as unthreatening, Matt belittles his alien partner, claiming he has fur on his teeth, implying an unattractive savagery and lack of sophistication. However, in the very next scene the audience sees Matt as the blundering unsophisticate, while the alien succeeds in obtaining some relevant information through subtlety and sensitivity.

The superior/inferior relationship continues to shift around, and there is a pivotal moment in the film when opinion is finally forced to change. One evening the two men get drunk together—one on liquor, one on soured milk—and Matt's conversation deteriorates to a puerile joke, which George fails to understand. George, however, gets philosophical in his drunkenness and opts for a much deeper observation about his human hosts: "You humans are very curious to us. You invite us to live among you in an atmosphere of equality that we have never known before. You give us ownership of our own lives for the first time and you ask no more of us than you do of yourselves. I hope you understand how special your world is, how unique a people you humans are. Which is why it is all the more painful and confusing to us that so few of you seem capable of living up to the ideals you set for yourselves."

The gratitude, simplicity, and clear truth of this statement provide a stark contrast to the cynicism of the regular American citizen. This filmic juxtaposition of the comic with the serious, acts as a narrative hiatus, providing space for the audience to reflect on much wider issues concerning U.S. freedom and citizenship. (Here we note that science fiction films often make manifest observations about society that otherwise might remain comfortably concealed by our version of daily reality.) So what starts as a drinking session, not without its comic elements, becomes a turning point in the film as the balance of the relationship between the two officers subtly changes. The mutual consumption of inebriating drink acts as a social/racial leveler here, where hierarchies are abandoned and an equal footing permits free speech. Analogies with racial oppression and class differentiation are not to be missed. This is an optimistic science fiction action movie in which comradeship and loyalty win over divisiveness, greed, and crime. Despite the physiological differences, emblematized by different food requirements, the similarities between alien and human, with the alien even as an idealized human, come to the fore.

Postmodern science fiction films, however, almost totally abandon an impetus toward an idealized vision of the human race, either latently or manifestly. Postmodernism may be understood as Jean-François Lyotard's "incredulity towards metanarratives,"[19] where an individual's sense of dislocation and disaffection results in an inability to resist the impact of technology, corporate power, or the "other," and also yields an impotent acceptance of a dysfunctioning society. Other significant aspects of postmodernism are questions of memory and history, and relatedly, the act of telling stories, the use of irony as a means of questioning truth, and the existence of a "hypertext."[20] Science fiction in relation to postmodernism has been relatively widely discussed;[21] the two areas have natural affinities in their joint regard for history and the future, and in operating on more than one level, offering the spectator both spectacle and metaphor. In the postmodern disruption of boundaries, the impact of technology upon the human body is of significant concern. The cyborg, the android, and the replicant all evidence the influence and integration of technology and the human, changing our definition of *human* and causing reflection upon the meaning of such a term.[22] Postmodernism, then, may be understood as individual disorientation and loss of control, a disintegration, corruption even, of personal and cultural norms and boundaries, a commodification of society, and a loss of coherent identity.

Blade Runner (dir. Ridley Scott, 1982) is frequently regarded as the archetypal postmodern film. It adopts the central theme of the interface of the human with the "other"—this time replicants, artificial humans designed for specific purposes. As a film it is a pastiche of retrospective styles of noir, detective, and action movies, and yet also is highly futuristic in appearance. As a story, the combination of old and new technology, the contrast of the futuristic and the decrepit, create an imaginative ambience of familiarity yet disaffection. In the apartment of Deckard (Harrison Ford), for instance, we recognize the codes of a home: sofa, piano, photographs, etc., but can only watch in amazement as he uses a machine to investigate a 2-D photograph from a 3-D perspective, and literally looks around the corner using a mirror in the picture. The familiar and down-at-heels images coexist with the futuristic and extrapolative. At one moment we see Deckard's old boss drinking vending-machine coffee out of a styrofoam cup in a scruffy office, and a few scenes later, Deckard is getting drunk on weird cocktails in a bar, telephoning Rachel (another replicant) via a videolink. There are no "meals" in *Blade Runner*; there are only half-eaten snacks and drinks, consumed on the run, on the way to something else. In this futuristic, multicultural version of Los Angeles, which is dark, dank, and degenerating, Deckard goes to a food stall, and failing to speak the language of the stall holder, points to the kinds of noodles he wants. The lack of interaction and ceremony are part of the postmodern anti-cultural stance. Deckard then stands in the street eating from his carton, only to be interrupted by a policeman sent to look for him in order to reemploy his particular skill as replicant assassin: a blade runner. The snatched food snack is discarded, compounding the sense of waste and decay, foreshadowing death and disillusionment.

While *Brazil* (dir. Terry Gilliam, 1985) also explores individual disillusionment within the chaos of postmodernism, this film creates a world of exaggeration and irony. With its sustained attack on technological and bureaucratic "improvements," the film mocks and criticizes an assumed teleology of modernity: improvement through technology. By revealing the chaos and dysfunction of an overengineered society in both the domestic sphere and the workplace, *Brazil* at once makes us laugh at technological overload, mock the naïveté of modernist ideals, and yet worry about the startling similarities to our own postmodern existence. Exercizing his interest in hybridity, Gilliam has produced a film that refuses simple generic classification: *Brazil* is science fiction and a whimsical love story; it is about technology but also about human determination and will; Sam Lowry (Jonathan Pryce) the hero, is both a fantasist and a pragmatist. When Sam is phoned at home from work because he has overslept, his tea–toast–boiled egg breakfast machine malfunctions resulting in soggy toast, so he skips breakfast and rushes to work. The absent breakfast for Sam is just part of the ever-present failure of domestic technology, and as the film continues, is just one of many aspects missing from his life.

Following a grotesque indictment of plastic surgery, where the patient, Sam's mother (Katherine Helmond), is fully conscious through the procedure, Gilliam juxtaposes a restaurant scene; both are deliberate consumer experiences. The restaurant, like the plastic surgery, operates largely as a statement of social status, and Sam's mother insists he accompany her to both. Sam's mother's ambitions for Sam operate in many directions: promotion at work, marrying the right young woman, and being seen in the right places. His lack of ambition and refusal to become embroiled in her ostentatious existence highlight the differences between her superficial existence and his pursuit of an inner life with real meaning. The restaurant and the food served offer a good example of this. Lunch, with overt irony, is ordered from a menu of pictures and numbers. Sam, who yet again seems to fail to understand the "system," struggles to communicate with the unhelpful waiter who must have a number, not a description. And, after all this fuss, when the food finally arrives it is a disappointing homogeneous dollop in one of a range of colors.[23] The point of the restaurant is clearly not the food, but the desire to see and be seen in a fashionable place. So strong is this determination among this particular social group that when a terrorist bomb explodes as a protest against social inequalities and half the restaurant is destroyed, a folding screen is provided to obscure the devastation, and the superficial and inane conversation continues. The restaurant, then, is the site of a literal class protest, but the political and social inertness of the moneyed class, echoed by the blandness of the food they eat, is impenetrable. Sam's disaffection from his social environment is made manifest at the restaurant in a number of ways, but, in a mode characteristic of postmodern identity, he has neither stability of character nor steadfast values. A central message of the film is postmodern valuelessness and confusion, and although people act with self-importance, nothing has lasting value in the day-to-day world of *Brazil*. Only pursuit of fantasy has meaning for Sam, the rest is disconnected experience. The food scenes in the film add to the postmodern sense of powerlessness and dysfunction; just as society has been corrupted by superficiality, so has food. Taste and texture have given way to technological overkill and pretence.

Ultimate technological control of the human race is the premise of *The Matrix*. There are three main occurrences of food in this film, each offering a different set of meanings to human existence in the matrix and the "real world," each reflecting philosophically on the postmodern human condition and subjective consciousness. A central question underlying *The Matrix* is whether it matters if we live in an artificial state, a kind of computer cyberspace. That is, how important is consciousness of reality to human fulfilment? Could we not all live perfectly satisfactory lives if we merely believed ourselves to be living normally? Vivian Sobchack argues, referring to Michel Foucault and Frederic Jameson, that in later postmodern science fiction films the alien in the film is understood as an alienated image of ourselves. Either the alien is different, just like us, or we are aliens too, there being no original version in the postmodern circulation of simulacra.[24] *The Matrix* explores this play between levels of consciousness in a postmodern world.

When Cypher (Joe Pantoliano), one of the revolutionary group, agrees to reveal the location of his comrades, he does so over a steak in a restaurant. This scene of Judas's betrayal focuses particularly on the high meat content of the meal, with extended close-up shots of the steak oozing its juices, giving up its flavor. Cypher consumes his steak, just as he is about to agree to be consumed by the system of the Matrix once more. He craves immediate gratification; "You know I know that this steak doesn't exist . . ."—and yet he desires it, just as he desires unconsciousness of the miserable "real" world as he agrees to enter the "normal" cyberworld once more. His betrayal of his colleagues and friends is worsened by his betrayal of himself: "I don't want to remember nothing. Nothing! You understand? And I want to be rich. Someone important. Like an actor. You can do that, right?" Unconscious, unquestioning acceptance of simulated luxury and celebrity then, are preferred to the "real" world, one full of hardship, basic living, and deprivations. The choice between two worlds—one false but comfortable, the other real but full of adversity—is made clear for the audience through the example of food. The unreal beef steak with its lurid redness and flowing juices, contrasts with the following food scene, which underscores the deprivations incurred by living outside the matrix. The film turns to the ship's mess or dining room of the Nebuchadnezzar where Neo (Keanu Reeves) and his newfound compatriots are having breakfast. The meal consists of a pale glop that, though it is made of "a single-celled protein combined with synthetic aminos, vitamins, and minerals; everything your body needs," could be, as another character suggests, "a bowl of snot." It might be nutritiously complete, but it provides no pleasure. Difficult issues of ecology, environmentalism, and health are brought to the fore by these two scenes. The pleasure experienced through food's taste and texture is seen as more meaningful than the nutritional quality any food may contain. Human judgment and consciousness are brought into question through these two examples of food.

There is also a further dimension of food that becomes significant in *The Matrix*. When Neo visits the Oracle (Gloria Foster) to find out whether he is "the one," and is asked to consider another level of consciousness, the Oracle, significantly, is baking cookies. This act of home baking, so imbued with meaning in a traditional American household with implications of homemaking and family values, takes place in a seemingly normal apartment. But it is within this apparent normalcy that Neo becomes aware of the abnormalities of the system of the matrix, and the role human consciousness must play in order to overcome the matrix's omnipotence. The contrast between the everydayness of the Oracle peering at her cookies in the oven, and the disconcerting things she says to Neo acts as a metaphor for his growing understanding of the nature of the matrix itself. What seems to be normal is not always to be believed in the matrix; it is within the supernatural events (conveyed through special effects in the film) that "truth" and a new reality may be discerned. Neo, as part of his development, needs to learn this before he can adjust his mind-set to believe a different truth about the matrix: he needs to have faith in the "uncanny." During Neo's conversation with the Oracle, she tells him he will have difficult choices to make, and, psychosomatically, his anxiety over what she says makes it difficult for him to breathe. Neo's heightened anxiety is caused by his growing appreciation of the difference between simulation and reality: a central dichotomy of postmodernism. Relief from his anxiety comes through a present of one of the cookies. The Oracle says, "I promise by the time you're done eating it, you'll feel right as rain." Neo recovers his sense of equilibrium when his thoughts are directed back to the food in his hand.

Despite the cookie being baked in the unreal world of the matrix, it represents intangible qualities, beyond the limits of simulation, such as sincerity, compassion and farsightedness. It acts metonymically to indicate the deeper aspects of life missing from the Matrix, just because of its already existing resonances of homemaking and nurturing. And yet in its delicious luxuriousness (even if false), it is an inverse reminder of the tasteless slop that is in fact, in terms of the film, the real food of the real world. In the postmodern world of *The Matrix*, the "real" world (outside the matrix) is a dystopia in contrast with the false but comfortable world of the computer simulation. Food becomes a metaphor for these complex postmodern issues, and a measure of the hardship of facing up to reality. The steak gives sensory pleasure, the cookies give familiarity and comfort, the nutritious slop demonstrates the sacrifice involved in denying false pleasures and following the path of conscious reality. In true postmodern style, food in *The Matrix* offers no easy answers, but instead a complex melange of history and future, memory, fantasy, and reality.

As a result of food's pervasiveness in our culture and in our consciousness, it can be used metaphorically to both draw on existing meanings and, perhaps simultaneously, suggest new understanding of futuristic new worlds. Food acts as a varied and malleable metaphor in science fiction film: it may shape the main story line, or support the general narrative structure; it may allude to dystopian lifestyles in general; or more specifically, it may metonymically stand for cultural difference and otherness or a shift in consciousness. Food in science fiction films provides a focus for memories, personal histories, and perhaps regrets. It also provides a focus for the end result of technological processes, perhaps taken to extremes. In this way, food creates a link, and a powerful filmic symbol between emotional histories, technology, and the body.

The power of food as a metaphor lies in the fact that food affects us both on an individual level and on a cultural level too, like film itself. Food, like film, gives us much pleasure in its personal meanings, its rituals, and its processes. In addition, food, again like film, gives us a means of intervening in and understanding our culture. These two aspects of interpretation mean that both food and film have become highly significant in structuring our lives. Thus, when food and this culturally critical film genre—science fiction—come together, they can make a memorable statement, as in the many science fiction films that demonstrate our weakening engagement with our culture. In postmodern science fiction films like *Brazil, Blade Runner,* and *The Matrix,* food metaphorically demonstrates our loss of meaningful connections with society, and our loss of stable identities. Ritual and habit are no longer guiding principles, and a sense of self can no longer be habitually achieved through the production, preparation, and eating of food. The pleasure has gone, and so have the connections between what we eat and what we are. All that is left is a sense of mourning through fantasy-memory moments of a beef stew or a home-baked cookie. Life cannot be measured or structured by the "dishonest" food in recent science fiction film: like so much else in the postmodern world, food is not to be trusted.

Notes

1. To name but a few: Carole Counihan and Penny van Esterik, eds., *Food and Culture: A Reader* (London: Routledge, 1997); Michel de Certeau, Luce Giard, and Pierre Mayol, *The Practice of Everyday Life,* vol. 2, *Living and Cooking,* trans. T. J. Tomasik (Minneapolis: University of Minnesota Press, 1998); Deane Curtin and Lisa Heldke, *Cooking Eating Thinking: Transformative Philosophies of Food* (Bloomington: Indiana University Press, 1992); and Alan Beardsworth and Teresa Keil, *Sociology on the Menu: An Invitation to the Study of Food and Society* (London: Routledge, 1997).
2. Claude Levi-Strauss, "*The Culinary Triangle*" in *Partisan Review* 33 (1996), 586–597; Mary Douglas, "Deciphering a Meal" in *implicit meanings: Essays in Anthropology* (London: Routledge, 1975); Mary Frances Kennedy Fisher, "The Anatomy of a Recipe" in *With Bold Knife and Fork* (London: Chatto and Windows, 1983).
3. Carole Counihan and Steven Kaplan, *Food And Gender: Identity and Power* (Amsterdam: Harwood, 1998); Stephen Mennell, Anne Murcott, and Anneke H. van Otterloo, *The Sociology of Food: Eating, Diet and Culture* (London: Sage, 1992).
4. Counihan and Esterik, introduction to *Food and Culture,* 1.
5. As a few examples see Adam Roberts, *Science Fiction* (London: Routledge, 2000), chap. 1; J. P. Tellotte, *Science Fiction Film* (Cambridge: Cambridge University Press, 2001), chaps. 1 and 2; Vivan Sobchack, *Screening Space: The American Science Fiction Film* (New York: Ungar, 1991), chap. 1.
6. Telotte, *Science Fiction Film,* 10.
7. See King and Krywinska *Science Fiction Cinema: From Outerspace to Cyberspace,* 88–89. (London: WallFlower, 2000) Geoff King and Tanya Krywinska.
8. See George Ritzer, *The McDonaldization of Society: An Investigation into the Changing Character of Contemporary Social Life* (London: Pine Forge Press, 1993).
9. Margaret. Mead, "The Changing Significance of Food," (1970) report in Counihan and van Esterik, eds. *Food and Culture,* 11–19.

10. Critics disagree over the relationship between film and modernism. For instance, Anne Friedberg, in *Window Shopping: Cinema and the Postmodern* (London: University of California Press, 1994), 162–63, has argued that "the very apparatus of the cinema makes the stylistic categories of modernism and postmodernism inappropriate," and claims that the relation between the apparatus of cinema as one aspect of modernity and cinematic modernism is ambiguous at best. Other critics see modernist films as those that revel in the apparatus, technology, and experimental techniques of early filmmaking, often alluding to or revealing the reality of the filmmaker's art and even presence, such as in *The Man With the Movie Camera* (Vertov, 1929) (dir. Dziga Vertor, 1929).

11. In discussing Fritz Lang's *Metropolis*, David Desser, in "Race, Space and Class: The Politics of Cityscapes in Science-Fiction Films," *Alien Zone II: The Spaces of Science-Fiction Cinema*, ed. Annette Kuhn (London: Verso, 1999), 81, has argued that this film "reveals strong fears of economic collapse and Communist revolution overlaid with anxieties about modernisation and urbanization and barely repressed fears of racialized Others. Alternately, it revels in the modern, with its magnificent vistas of towering cities and wondrous technology." In discussing an archetypal modernist film, Desser draws our attention to the inherent contradictions of the modernist aesthetic that I have extended, in this account, to films beyond the accepted modernist period of the first half of the twentieth century.

12. See Douglas, "Deciphering a Meal," for an extensive analysis of the structure of meals and associated codes.

13. For an extensive discussion of modernity and consumerism see Don Slater, *Consumer Culture and Modernity* (Cambridge: Polity Press, 1997).

14. See Jonathan Bignell, *Media Semiotics: An Introduction* (Manchester: Manchester University Press, 1997), 1–7, for a further discussion of semiotic meaning in cultural terms.

15. There was much discussion of housework and women's roles at this time; see for instance the feminist magazines *Spare Rib*, *Red Rag*, and *Shrew*. Ann Oakley's *The Sociology of Housework* (Oxford: Martin Robertson, 1974) was one of the early critical discussions of the issues surrounding domestic labor.

16. Andreas Huyssen, *After the Great Divide: Modernism, Mass Culture and Postmodernism* (Basingstoke, England: Macmillan, 1988), 70.

17. Ibid., 65–81.

18. Sobchack, *Screening Space*, 226.

19. Jean-François Lyotard, *The Postmodern Condition: A Report on Knowledge*, trans. Geoff Bennington and Brian Massumi (Minneapolis: University of Minnesota Press, 1984), xxiv.

20. Cristina Delgi-Esposti, ed., *Postmodernism in the Cinema* (Oxford: Berghahn, 1998), has paid particular attention to this postmodern hypertext and the attention of the spectator, which is demanded on a variety of levels, to a variety of communicative means. Notes Delgi-Esposti, "One of the most distinctive characteristics of a 'postmodern text' is the overt demand on the attention of the spectator whose active and indispensable participation is summoned and called upon in various levels of 'interpellation'" (introduction, 6–8).

21. See, for example, Telotte, *Science Fiction Film*, 54–58; Sobchack, *Screening Space*, 241–305.

22. Donna Haraway, "A Manifesto for Cyborgs: Science, Technology and Socialist Feminism in the 1980s," *Socialist Review*, no. 80 (1985): 65–107.

23. Janet Staiger, "Future Noir: Contemporary Representations of Visionary Cities in Kuhn," *Alien Zone II*, 115, makes a similar point here.

24. Sobchack, *Screening Space*, 292–305.

19

Supper, Slapstick, and Social Class: Dinner as Machine in the Silent Films of Buster Keaton

ERIC L. REINHOLTZ

> The two essential forms of the gag in Keaton—the trajectory-gag and the machine-gag—are two aspects of a same reality, a machine which produces man 'without a mother', or the man of the future.
>
> —Giles Deleuze[1], *Cinema 1: The Movement Image*

> Buster will fit into their schemes, if only to challenge them at their own game. . . . The machine functions well in any aspect of daily life that corrodes into a routine or mundane operation, and dinner is no exception.
>
> —Gabriella Oldham[2], *Keaton's Silent Shorts: Beyond the Laughter*

In the introduction to his recent book *Class, Language, and American Film Comedy* (2002), Christopher Beach asserts, "It was not until the sound era . . . that comedies moved beyond slapstick caricatures of middle-class and upper-class society and began to reflect more nuanced social distinctions."[3] With this pronouncement, Beach dismisses the work of Buster Keaton, Charlie Chaplin, Harold Lloyd, and Harry Langdon, as essentially "physical, slapstick, or clown comedy" incapable of examining questions of social class in anything more than "crude dichotomies."[4] While such a contention is undoubtedly excessive with regard to silent comedy in general, it is certainly unwarranted in the case of Keaton, whose films examined, more than any others, the problematic nature of "modern" society at the zenith of the industrial age in America. While much has already been written about Keaton's parodic treatment of modernity with regard to high technology (automobiles, ships, telephones, cameras, etc.), little attention has been paid to his equally subversive handling of the more mundane aspects of domestic life—most notably, foodways. In films ranging from early two-reelers like *The Scarecrow* (1920) and *The Electric House* (1921) to full-length features such as *The Navigator* (1924) and *College* (1927), the ritualized consumption of food serves as the springboard for a highly nuanced representation of inter- and intraclass relations that is as astute as it is humorous. Far beyond the crude social "caricatures" suggested by Beach, the viewer discovers such depictions of mealtimes to comprise a subtle commentary on the profound social transformation taking place in America: snapshots of changing values in a society whose members—from working-class minority groups to the Anglo-Saxon ruling class—were experiencing the necessities governing their transition from a traditional agrarian way of life to a modern urban existence. Interpreting this transformation of American foodways from a communal activity into the mechanical exercise in production and consumption through the lens of comedy—what Gabriella Oldham so aptly terms "dinner as machine"—Keaton shows himself to be one of cinema's most astute commentators on social class. Moreover, in his use of food production and consumption to illustrate this cultural metamorphosis, Gilles Deleuze's "man of the future" was undoubtedly the first American filmmaker to bring modernity into the dining room.

Before examining Keaton's filmic texts themselves, it is important to understand the distinction between Keaton's exploration of foodways and that of his contemporaries. For this purpose, it is useful to begin with examples from two of Charlie Chaplin's more memorable comedies: *The Gold Rush* (1925) and *Modern Times* (1932). Commenting on the "tight focus" used in shooting "the celebrated boiled-shoe dinner and bun-dance" in *The Gold Rush*, Walter Kerr observes that Chaplin "did not discard intimacy" even in his most "epic" film.[5] In noting that Chaplin's character "is never at a loss in any situation," André Bazin also references *The Gold Rush*: "It looks as if things are only willing to be of use to him in ways that are purely marginal to the uses of society. The most beautiful example of these strange uses is the famous dance of the rolls which contribute to a sudden outburst of highly unusual choreography."[6]

Central to the insights of both Kerr and Bazin is the recognition that the act of eating is an extension of Chaplin's heroic comedy. Food functions in the same way as other objects of desire, such as women and social status: the tramp must subvert social codes and undermine the mundane in order to obtain those things the world denies him. Indeed, while it was actually Roscoe "Fatty" Arbuckle who invented the dinner-roll dance in *The Rough House* (1918), the genius of Chaplin's appropriation of the routine lies in his transformation of a gag into a comic metaphor: in his dream, the lone prospector breaks the etiquette of formal dining by transforming the function of forks and rolls in order to win the attention of his female dining companions.

Modern Times, the much-admired critique of industrial capitalism, features a scene in which Chaplin's proletarian hero serves as the guinea pig for a feeding machine. Once again filmed in close-up, the scene has Chaplin being force fed by a malfunctioning invention that leaves most of the meal on his face and clothes. If the initial imagery invokes the theme of man versus machine, the latent message—one that pervades the second half of the film—is that of the triumph of the human spirit over alienating technology. Not only is the feeding device a failure, but later in the picture Chapin reverses the roles by having his character perform the same humiliating procedure on a supervisor who is caught in the cogs of one of the massive factory engines. Finally, as the slapstick of the industrial parody gives way to the love story between Chaplin and the "gamin" (a lionized stereotype of the street urchin played by Paulette Goddard), Chaplin inserts another fantasy sequence involving food. In the pastoral setting of a country cottage (complete with a cow passing by with milk for Chaplin's coffee), the couple enjoys the proverbial home-cooked steak dinner. This daydream will prefigure the film's final scene, with Chaplin and Goddard happily making their way down a country road, away from the troubles of "modern times." This resistance to and retreat from the conventions of modernity, whether in the vastness of the Yukon or the countryside outlying an urban metropolis, makes clear why Martin Rubin has characterized Chaplin's "universalized eccentric" as, "a semi-Victorian figure [who] is never quite at home in the Machine Age, [neither] its master nor its servant."[7] It is also a clear indication as to why Christopher Beach sees silent film class characterizations painted in such broad strokes. The representation of foodways in these two films reflects not only Chaplin's Manichean view of class relations, but also his nostalgia for an earlier, less technologically driven era.

In contrasting Buster Keaton's style with that of his comic rival, Rubin describes Keaton as "more aggressive and contemporary than Chaplin. . . . He is at home in the Machine Age."[8] In the late 1920s, a young Luis Buñuel put this distinction less kindly, complaining of "the latest Chaplin productions, with their mawkish romanticism." Referring specifically to one of the scenes discussed above, he remarked, "Remember the Christmas Eve scene in *The Gold Rush*. In that regard, Buster Keaton is far superior."[9] For all his harshness, Buñuel was no doubt one of the first commentators to identify two aspects of Keaton's films that made them distinct from those of Chaplin—two aspects central to understanding the function of foodways in pictures such as *The Electric House* or *The Navigator*. The first of these, as Rubin suggests, deals with technology. Eric Mottram observes that "Buster Keaton never actually triumphs over the machine he is caught up with" but rather "becomes a machine himself, hence the emotionless mask."[10] The second addresses the question of social class. Contrasting him with Chaplin's proletarian persona, and especially Harold Lloyd's parody of middle class upward mobility, Robert

Sklar notes, "Where Lloyd accepted middle-class order and made comedy from the foolish antics of the man on the make, Keaton's existence within the same social setting was predicated on a recognition not of his but *its* absurdities."[11] At the crux of these two points is the dynamic underlying the function of foodways in Keaton's films. The great bourgeois myth of progress, embodied in the implementation of technology, has distorted the most fundamental act of human communion into an exercise in technology for its own sake. Unlike Chaplin's working-class rebel in *Modern Times*, Keaton's middle-class antiheroes, would-be masters of the means of production, are thus transformed into cogs within the machines of their *own* making.

This departure from previous treatments of food and foodways in silent comedy can be seen in Keaton's earliest two-reelers. Although Keaton always emphasized his comedic debt to Fatty Arbuckle,[12] there is a sharp divergence from the pie-throwing antics of Arbuckle/Keaton shorts like *The Rough House* (1918) and *The Butcher Boy* (1917). In December 1920, less than a year after establishing his own studio on the former Chaplin Lone Star lot, Keaton first unveiled his vision of "dinner as machine" in *The Scarecrow* (1920). Decribing "the film's cleverest routine," Eleanor Keaton offered the following synopsis: "Buster and Joe Roberts play farmhands who share a one-room house that is filled with surprising time- and space-saving devices: the phonograph doubles as a stove; the bookcase also serves as an icebox. . . . Breakfast involves a series of strings dangling from the ceiling, which pull down condiments that the two men swing back and forth to each other over the breakfast table."[13]

This marks the first, and one of the most elaborate, utilizations of a Rube Goldberg device in a Keaton film. While critics like James Agee have long praised these "mechanistic gags," Robert Knopf astutely observes, "In Keaton's films the whole world frequently seems to operate as one gigantic Rube Goldberg device."[14] In *The Scarecrow,* made the very year that the nation's urban population first exceeded the number of its rural inhabitants, this mechanized world makes a particularly telling statement.[15] While its title, characters, and setting all invoke a rural way of life, the film's breakfast scene subverts these elements and hints at the profound cultural changes taking place in the United States in the first decades of the twentieth century. Although the foodstuffs consumed by Keaton and Roberts—biscuits, butter, pork, coffee, milk—are completely consistent with what had remained a typical farmer's diet since the late 1800s,[16] their context is not. In a dwelling whose quaint exterior belies an interior more closely resembling a New York apartment ("ALL THE ROOMS IN THIS HOUSE ARE IN ONE ROOM"), their array of gadgets alludes to the explosion of "time- and space-saving devices" that had been appearing in upper-and then middle-class urban households since the turn of the century: the egg beater (1901); the thermos bottle (1904); the electric toaster (1908); cellophane (1911); Pyrex glass (1915); the home refrigerator (1916), the electric mixer (1918), and the automatic pop-up toaster (1918).[17] Of course, the mass of pulleys, strings, and weights—as well as the two human beings—engaged in this mechanical "ballet"—are a mockery of the modern middle-class kitchen, governed not by the weltanschauung of progress through technology, but by "the maniacal illogic of farce."[18]

While Tom Gunning argues that scenes such as this one "often serve little narrative purpose,"[19] there are several clues that this and other scenes in *The Scarecrow* are intended as more than gratuitous comedy. First, an element of the breakfast ballet never mentioned by critics is the presence of a coin-operated gas meter in the supposedly simple country cottage. Second, as Keaton and Roberts exit the dwelling, a wide-angle shot of the two reveals a country skyline dominated by an immense palm tree—another reminder that this is only a farmland fantasy. (Keaton would repeat this gag in *The Black-smith* (1922), his parody of Henry Wadsworth Longfellow's paean to the forge. A title card bearing the verse "UNDER A SPREADING CHESTNUT TREE THE VILLAGE SMITHY STANDS" precedes a shot of Keaton leaning against a spindly California palm: in the modern age, there are neither bucolic landscapes nor rugged heroes to populate them). Finally, in another food-related gag, *The Scarecrow*'s audience is told that an angry daughter (Sybil Seeley) plans a culinary revenge on her father (Joe Keaton) for mocking her fantasy of becoming a famous dancer: "STUNG BY HER FATHER'S TREATMENT SHE PLANNED TO RUIN HIS RURAL STOMACH—SO SHE BAKED HIM A CREAM PIE." This otherwise inexplicable adjectival use of *rural* is perhaps the best evidence for reading *The Scarecrow* as an intentional commentary on America's changing demographics. Not only does the scene use food humorously to underscore the transformation of the farmer's way of life, but it is also a clear reference to a younger generation's rejection of a rural existence in favor of the more alluring city.

If one accepts Oldham's view that the film is structured around "mechanical transformations [that] turn into a personal transformation,"[20] then it might be observed that *Scarecrow*'s underlying base is the transformation of a rural culture into an urban one, with food as a principal ideologeme. Indeed, in light of Delueze's comment on the metamorphic effect of machines on Keaton's characters, the breakfast scene's final gag takes on a much deeper meaning. As Keaton and Roberts complete the cleanup after their mobile breakfast, they hang the folding dining table on the wall, revealing the sign: "WHAT IS HOME WITHOUT A MOTHER." At face value, this is an amusing commentary on the irony of the charcters' domestic situation. But as one considers the encroachment of the metropolis on the farmlands, of modernity on tradition, this apparently inoffensive tribute to motherhood underscores the extent to which machines have transformed rural society. Just as Seeley's character has no use for conventional patriarchy (and ultimately does elope with Keaton by means of another machine, a motorcycle), so Keaton literally spells out for his audience his own status as a "man without a mother."

Less than two years after *The Scarecrow*, Keaton revisited the modernization of American society in *The Electric House* (1922). Once again, the rituals of eating constitute a central element in his satire. The difference between the two films lies in their class targets: whereas *The Scarecrow* focuses on the transformation of agrarian America, *The Electric House* takes aim at the suburban upper middle class and its obsession with progress through technology. In describing the set for the film as "futuristic," Marion Meade identifies an important trait not readily appreciated in Keaton. Preceding Fritz Lang's *Metropolis* (1927) by five years, and *Modern Times* by seven, *The Electric House* presents a technological distopia of a more intimate nature.[21] While the other two films attack the abuses of capitalism on a grand scale, casting monolithic villains in the form of government or corporation, Keaton's infinitely more subtle critique strikes the bourgeoisie quite literally where it lives.

For Robert Benayoun, the subject of Keaton's film is "a house [that] disastrously turns against its owner."[22] Such a view is not wholly accurate. On the contrary, it is the owner (once again Keaton regular Joe Roberts) whose obsession with modernity (the title card states "A MODERN HOME WHERE ELECTRICITY IS TO BE INSTALLED") results in the disastrous transformation of his house. The unwitting agent of this metamorphosis is, of course, Keaton. After an error at the People's University graduation, hair stylist Keaton winds up with a classmate's electrical engineering degree and an offer to electrify the Roberts's elegant Tudor residence (the exteriors were shot in Los Angeles at Keaton and wife Natalie Talmadge's Westmoreland Place home). With a how-to book in hand, Keaton rewires the mansion while Roberts and his family are away on vacation. It is upon their return that the film begins to unfold its ideological message, once again with foodways as a central component. After viewing a staircase-turned-escalator, a self-draining and -refilling pool, a revolving bathtub, a Murphy bed that raises and lowers itself, and an automatic billiard room/library, the family and their "engineer" guest sit down for an automated dinner.

Among the many gadget gags mentioned above, the dinner scene is key, for it is here that Keaton's house of tomorrow begins to go awry. In contrast to the rural working-class table in *The Scarecrow*, the setting is now an elegant Edwardian dining room. Equally significant is the distinction between the former's mechanical and the latter's electrical configuration. Farcical in the farmhouse, "improved technology, in the form of better stoves [and] electric appliances" had become the norm in bourgeois households by the mid-1920s.[23] Finally, whereas Keaton and Roberts perform a flawless juggling act in *The Scarecrow*, the second film becomes a comedy of technological errors. Crosscutting from the dining room to the kitchen, Keaton reveals both ends of a food production line that carries the meal from the cook's hands to each individual diner by means of a miniature train complete with tracks, drawbridge, and crossing signal. The table itself features a rotating center for condiments and a complement of chairs that move in and out at the push of a button. Returning to the kitchen, an ad-like title card proclaiming "SOMETHING FOR THE HOUSEWIFE" reveals a cook stacking plates on a conveyor belt–driven automatic dishwasher. Just as disaster is about to strike, Roberts's character boasts, "THIS IS REALLY A WONDERFUL INVENTION!" Although Keaton's nemesis, the true engineer bent on revenge, soon arrives to sabotage the house, it is significant to note that the meal-related fiasco is prior to any malfeasance. After pulling the chairs out from beneath his hosts by an errant touch of the control, Keaton inadvertently derails the arriving soup course resulting in a lapful of broth for the lady of the house. Finally, in a scene that has been partially lost to chemical damage, a crosscut to the kitchen finds the cook shooing away several curious felines. The next shot has the train entering the dining room. As Keaton informs his host, "HERE IS YOUR DESSERT, SIR," the latter pulls away the cover to reveal a dish of kitten.[24]

Oldham has criticized the particularly stagey look of the meal scene, believing it to have been designed primarily to highlight "Buster's technical wizardry" at the cost of "intimacy," but she seems not to have considered the possibility that this was done by design.[25] Given that the implementation of high technology in food preparation and service had become a status symbol in the "modern home," the essence of Keaton's comedy lies precisely in the subversion of that bourgeois variation of the myth of progress. The "housewife" (whose greatest convenience is not any machine, but human labor in the form of a cook), is rewarded with a soup-stained dress. The modern-minded husband discovers that the latest technology is no match for a playful young cat. Most important, the would-be ruling class unwittingly finds itself on a culinary assembly line more suggestive of industrial factory workers than well-to-do suburbanites—an effect achieved principally through Keaton's masterful use of alternating montage. Crosscutting between the kitchen and the dining room blurs the distinction between production and consumption while at the same time both hastening and fragmenting the mealtime ritual. Harvey Levenstein comments that when the post–World War I middle class was confronted with both a "servant crisis" (due to a steady decline of cheap immigrant labor), "new household technology," and a range of "new leisure activities" outside the home (made increasing possible because of the automobile), the "traditional role of food-sharing in reinforcing family solidarity and establishing lines of authority also declined."[26] Just as Keaton had understood the transformation of rural America when choosing the dinner table as the focal point of his humorous commentary in *The Scarecrow*, so *The Electric House* suggests that he had no less of an awareness of the evolving position of the suburban bourgeoisie—and an even greater desire to focus on the dining room in his wicked assault on technology as a social status symbol.

When Keaton moved from shorts to feature films in 1923, he recognized the importance of developing his characters and story line rather than simply staging a series of gags—especially those of an "impossible" or unrealistic nature.[27] So while he would never again take his comic treatment of foodways to such an extreme as in *The Scarecrow* or *The Electric House*, mealtime would remain a popular subject in Keaton's films. From *The Three Ages* (1923), his first independent production, to *The Cameraman* (1928), his last before MGM deprived him of creative control over his films, at least one food-related gag appeared in every Keaton feature. Many times these are nothing more than slapstick. In several instances, as with *Go West* (1925) or *Battling Butler* (1926), the humor, while connected to social class, is based upon the kind of broad stereotypes described by Christopher Beach. There are, however, two important instances of "dinner as machine" that merit critical attention; these occur in Keaton's much-admired classic *The Navigator* (1924), and the less acclaimed but socially insightful *College* (1927). Both films underscore their creator's ability to utilize foodways as a vehicle for subtle social commentary. And, perhaps more important in considering Keaton's impact on the cinematic representation of food, both works can be seen as seminal models anticipating discreet use of the dinner motif as both comedy and social critique in the works of directors like Federico Fellini, Luis Buñuel, and Woody Allen. Such is the opinion of Keaton biographer Larry Edwards in his synopsis of *The Navigator*:

> In *The Navigator*, Buster plays a spoiled millionaire named Rollo Treadway. As the film opens, Rollo finds himself adrift at sea on the U.S.S. Buford, where he thinks he is alone and left to die on a sinking ship. Unknown to Rollo, he is not the only person on the ship; his estranged girlfriend is also on board and she, too, thinks she is alone. As the film continues, Rollo Treadway and his estranged girlfriend (portrayed by Katheryn McGuire) finally run across each other. The scenes of Rollo and his girl are truly classics of the comedy cinema. At one point, Rollo goes into the ship's kitchen (galley) and attempts to fix a meal for them. In the course of this culinary action, everything goes wrong. This scene has been copied in films ever since, including the famous kitchen scene in Woody Allen's classic, *Annie Hall*.[28]

The scene to which Edwards refers finds the ruling class couple attempting to prepare breakfast, hampered by both their own unfamiliarity with such menial tasks, and by the massive proportions of the industrial galley and its equipment. In this way Keaton brings the issue of social class back into the context of dinner as machine.

While it can be argued that the character of Rollo Treadway, the same type of spoiled rich boy played by Keaton in *The Saphead* (1920) and *Battling Butler*, is in itself a class stereotype, the genius of *The Navigator* lies in Keaton's choice of setting. Isolated from the world in which they hold a privileged status, the couple is revealed for the drones they are. "COLD AND HUNGRY," as McGuire's character grumbles, the two make their way to the massive galley, an interior space echoing the dimensions of the ship. Daniel's Moews's description of the scene underscores its social significance: "Rollo and the girl move into the ship's galley, a large room equipped to prepare food for hundreds, with outsized utensils and working spaces. Struggling with the giant apparatus, the two will become diminutive, like children playing house, spoiled children, in fact, so used to being waited upon that they are ignorant of how to do the easiest things for themselves."[29] These "easy things" constitute the preparation of breakfast: making coffee, setting the table, frying bacon, opening cans of hash and condensed milk, and boiling eggs. Their successive failures each underscore not only the couple's lack of practical knowledge, but even more so the paradox that the perpetuators of industrial capitalism are, in fact, unable to master the means of production they possess. McGuire fills the oversized coffee pot with only a few beans and brews it with seawater. She slices off strips of bacon only to tie them into dainty but uncookable bows. Keaton, after breaking the key attempting to open several cans of hash, turns on the stubborn containers with knifes and a meat cleaver, leaving himself covered with splattered meat. In the same vein, he drills open a can of milk but perforates both ends, leaving a white liquid trail to the table. Finally, having dropped four eggs into an enormous institutional cooking pot, he succeeds in breaking them one by one as he fishes them out with a slotted spoon. The two characters then confront their inedible meal with place settings of metal dishes and enormous chopping knives, roasting forks, and mixing spoons. Only the sighting of a potential rescue ship through the porthole saves them from both their cooking and the admission of their own incompetence.

The Navigator's status as one of Keaton's greatest pictures is evidenced by his sophisticated use of foodways as a motif. Whereas the dinner gag, for all its humor and ideological content, is limited essentially to one scene in the early shorts, in full-length features like this, it is skillfully transformed into an important narrative device within the film's broader structure. So it is that Keaton has his couple revisit their breakfast debacle "WEEKS LATER—STILL ADRIFT." This parallel scene begins with Keaton emerging from a bedroom that is revealed to be a cylindrical boiler compartment. When his shipmate appears at the "door" of her own cabin, the two make their way to a reconfigured galley. Utilizing a series of Rube Goldberg devices reminiscent of The Scarecrow, the couple has overcome its previous dilemma. Pulleys and strings light the stove and raise a cage of freshly boiled eggs from the huge pot. Tubes run from water bottles to fill the coffee pot, which is then whisked away to the stove. Condiments suspended over the table are lowered into place by the pull of a chord. Meanwhile, in the pantry, a bicycle-powered hacksaw opens a large can of hash as Keaton pedals leisurely, buffing his fingernails on the front wheel.

This latter scene is significant for the way in which it advances the narrative. Returning systematically to the exact same breakfst tasks, it utilizes the morning meal on a number or levels. First, and most obvious, is that Keaton and his companion have found a means of sustenance: survival is predicated on eating (and thus one scene can substitute for all the other potential problems to be overcome). Second, the domesticity implicit in breakfast, underscored by a level of teamwork so seamless that no communication is required, alludes to the couple's growing degree of intimacy. Finally, on an ideological level, the scene allows Keaton to represent a social transformation impossible in his two-reel shorts. While it would seem at first glance that this change, as Rubin suggests, deals with Keaton's ability to "master" the machine,[30] such a view is inconsistent with both Keaton's comic universe and the images in *The Navigator*. Emerging from the boiler rooms as they do, Keaton's and McGuire's characters have not taken control of the ship; they have become a part of it. Moews is clearly cognizant of this transformation when he describes the refitted galley as "a mechanized food factory."[31] If the suburban family of *The Electric House* is served by an assembly line, here the two patricians, with their silent, rehearsed movement, have become cogs within such a manufacturing system. The antithesis of Chaplin's proletarian rebel in *Modern Times*, Rollo Treadway is wholly integrated into the machine: not the unwilling guinea pig of a feeding contraption, but rather an extension of it. In noting that "*The Navigator* inevitably invites comparison with Chaplin's *Modern Times*," Rudi Blesh asserts, "In the assembly line's mechanized jungle it is Chaplin the human being who is hero. Keaton, on the contrary, shares his role with a hostile costar, The Machine." For Blesh, the result is a comedy whose undercurrent is "a deep and hopeless irony."[32] Part of this irony is visible in the conclusion to the second breakfast scene. Moews observes, "Though efficiently produced, the assembly line breakfast is never eaten."[33] Such is the futility of Keaton's own "modern times." Marx's capitalist-turned-proletarian, as his name suggests, Rollo Treadway becomes a stinging metaphor for the alienated individual trapped on the circular treadmill of the industrial age: peddling along in ignorant bliss, oblivious to the reality that he will never taste the fruits of his own labor.

It is easy to see why *The Navigator* enjoys such an elevated status among Keaton's cinematic works. In this epic of modernity, its hero is no more than a consequence of The Machine (even at the end of the film, the couple is about to be captured by cannibals when suddenly rescued by a machine—a submarine that appears in an instance of *deus ex machina*, as it were). The function of dinner, beyond representation of social class, takes on a metaphorical quality, a signifier of both the film's literal machine, the ship, and the function of machines in human lives in a broader sense.

College (1927) should not be seen in such a broad context. Following the financial failure of what is today considered Keaton's masterpiece, *The General* (1926), *College* represents producer Joe Schenck's desire to return to a more proven hit formula. It can hardly be considered mere coincidence that it came on the heels of Harold Lloyd's "huge success" and "most popular picture," *The Freshman*.[34] This said, *College* is not wholly lacking in merit. In particular, it offers two of the most fascinating food-related scenes in all of silent cinema. Reflecting the dramatic increase in public dining, the film utilizes a restaurant setting on two different occasions: the first, a comic, but socially pointed vision of the prohibition-era phenomena of the soda fountain; the second, a compelling statement on race and class in a 1920s college dining hall.

The plot of *College* is unquestionably formulaic. Keaton's character, Ronald, is the bookish son of a lower-middle-class or working-class family. He follows Mary (Ann Cornwall), the girl of his dreams, to sports-obsessed Clayton College, where he hopes to woo her by becoming a star athlete. Food figures into the film when Ronald is obliged to seek employment to help pay for the private education his single mother cannot afford. He is first hired by the local druggist to work behind the store's soda fountain. As he sees from another soda jerk's acrobatic exhibition of milk pouring, egg cracking, ice cream juggling, and glass sliding, the job requires not only quick and efficient production, but also a combination of artistry and athleticism. Keaton, of course, will turn the spectacle into a fiasco: milk is spilled; eggs are dropped; ice cream stubbornly refuses to fall from the scoop into a glass; and a customer ends up with a lap full of milkshake. While the humor is pure slapstick, it is also a clear return to the theme of dinner as machine. The soda fountain, itself all chrome, glass, and machinery, emerged as a true cultural phenomena in the wake of Prohibition. Levenstein comments that numerous saloons were converted into fountains in the 1920s with "soda jerks replacing a generation of deft bartenders." Moreover, he notes that drug stores that had "invaded the light lunch market, setting up their own soda fountains" were seeing food and beverage sales accounting for more than two-thirds of all income by 1929.[35] In short, these confectionaries—cutting across both class and gender boundaries—became at once feeding machines and social settings for a modern urban workforce.

While Ronald's ineptitude behind the counter foreshadows his incompetence on the playing field, the character can also be grasped essentially as a defective part in this feeding machine. Such an image in turn underscores the character's social status vis-à-vis his more economically privileged classmates. When Mary arrives unexpectedly in the company of Ronald's rival, "star athlete" Jeff Brown, the hero slips from behind the counter and onto a stool, pretending to be a patron rather than an employee. The soda fountain was an unprecedented public eating space in terms of both accessibility and affordability. Ronald, caught between his incompetence as producer and his economic disadvantage as consumer finds himself completely marginalized. Thus, the character moves quickly to his only possible conclusion: a defeated retreat from the drug store in search of another job.

Understanding the social implications of the soda fountain scene, it becomes easier to comprehend Keaton's now controversial donning of blackface for Ronald's second attempt at employment in the school's dining hall. Keaton, a veteran vaudevillian by his teens, was highly familiar with minstrel acts, even including one in his short *The Playhouse* (1921). While today's viewer finds this historically specific kind of racism disturbing at best, the dining hall scene in *College* is in many ways one of the most lucid commentaries on class and race in all of silent film. Ronald's decision to respond to the ad, "WANTED COLORED WAITER" reflects the social consequences of what might otherwise be seen as the democratization of public eating spaces in the 1920s. Keaton contrasts the synthetic spaces that are the kitchen and the dining room (already utilized in *The Electric House* with the ethnicities of their respective inhabitants: kitchen = African American = working class = inferiority; dining room = Caucasian = bourgeoisie = superiority. In disguising himself as a black man, Ronald is able to resolve the dilemma created by the public dining space. He does not disguise himself as an African American because there is no other work for him; rather, he does so because it allows him to perform menial labor such as serving dinner to economically advantaged white youths without exposing his own class status. Moreover, Keaton shows his awareness of the implicit racism accompanying this degrading work. When Ronald brings a bowl of soup to one white student, the latter refuses the dish, insisting, "BRING ME SOMETHING YOU CAN'T STICK YOUR THUMB IN." Ronald does return with more soup, now in a cup covered with an inverted soup bowl, honoring a request made with clearly prejudicial overtones. He also brings the condescending patron a second food item consistent with his wishes: a whole coconut. Thus, a gag that appears quite literally on the surface as racist, should be seen, at least in part, as a stinging retort to the kind of arrogance displayed by white diners toward black food service workers. Hidden behind grease paint, Ronald unexpectedly encounters—and responds to—a much more virulent form of discrimination that the class barrier that was his original concern. The makeup also achieves its desired purpose when Mary and Jeff arrive for dinner. Although he draws some scrutiny from the couple, his disguise works.

It appears that in changing ethnicity Ronald has solved the problem of his social status at Clayton. But at this point the scene takes an unexpected turn. Ronald, having passed through the symbolic kitchen doors that divide the white consumers and the black producers, is unaware that the steam from a pot is melting his blackface. The pleasant conversation of his coworkers, a cook and a waiter, turns quickly to shock and then anger over the deception. The scene cuts to a shot of Ronald with the cutlery brandishing cook and waiter in close pursuit. He flees back into the dining room, past the confused diners, and out of his second job. He is excluded from the white elite by his economic status, and rejected by those who comprise the most exploited of all human machines. The dining hall sequence, despite its moments of humor, is too painful to be funny. Racist on the surface, it is even more disturbing as it strips away, like Keaton's grease paint, the complex realities of institutional racism in the public eating spaces that characterized "modern society" in the 1920s.

From *Metropolis* to *Modern Times*, silent filmmakers consistently associated modernity with the machine. For Lang and Chaplin, the image was blatantly menacing. For Keaton, more "at home in the Machine Age," the machine was no less imposing, but his response was infinitely more subtle. Nowhere is this more evident than in Keaton's treatment of foodways. Beginning with mechanistic gags in *The Scarecrow* and *The Electric House*, and following with powerful statements on the nature of society in *The Navigator* and *College*, Keaton's films capture the essence of modernity in the most traditional of settings, the dining room. Much more so than his contemporaries, Keaton shows his audience that the issue is not "humans versus machines," but rather humans—both individually and collectively—*becoming* machines. It is no doubt for this reason that Delueze has commented, "There are . . . two very different 'socialist' visions, the one communist-humanist in Chaplin, the other anarchistic-machinic in Keaton."[36] And while we cannot know if Walter Benjamin thought of Keaton when he wrote "The Work of Art in the Age of Mechanical Reproduction," his words offer a perfect description of the comedian's "anarchistic-machinic" vision as *auteur*: "[B]y focusing on hidden details of familiar objects, by exploring commonplace milieus under the ingenious guidance of the camera, the film, on the one hand, extends our comprehension of the necessities that rule our lives; on the other hand, it manages to assure us of an immense and unexpected field of action."[37] Keaton's representation of the "commonplace milieu" that is a meal does indeed reveal to what extent the modern fascination with machines and technology ruled, and continues to rule every aspect of human lives. Leading his audience beyond a Chaplinesque nostalgia for a "simpler time," he forces viewers to confront the truth of the modern condition. Like the coconut in *College*, Keaton's representation of foodways promises to fulfill our appetite for comedy while its problematic consumption obliges us to rethink our assumptions about film, food, and society in "the age of mechanical representation."

Notes

1. Giles Deleuze, Cinema 1: *The Movement Image* (Minneapolis: University of Minnesota Press, 1986), 177.
2. Gabriella Oldham, *Keaton's Silent Shorts: Beyonds the Laughter* (Carbondale Southern Illinois University Press, 1996), 216.
3. Christopher Beach, *Class, Language, and American Film Comedy* (Cambridge: Cambridge University Press, 2002), 2.
4. Ibid., 3.
5. Walter Kerr, *The Silent Clowns* (New York: Alfred A. Knopf, 1975), 247.
6. André Bazin, "Charlie Chaplin," in *What is Cinema?* vol. 1 (Berkeley and Los Angeles: University of California Press, 1967), 146.
7. Martin Rubin, "The Crowd, the Collective, and the Chorus: Busby Berkeley and the New Deal," in *Movies and Mass Culture*, ed. John Belton (New Brunswick, N.J.: Rutgers University Press, 1996), 62.
8. Ibid., 62.
9. Luis Buñuel, *An Unspeakable Betrayal* (Berkeley and Los Angeles: University of California Press, 2000), 103.
10. Eric Mottram, "Blood on the Nash Ambassador: cars in American films," in *Cinema, Politics and Society in America*, ed. Philip Davies and Brian Neve (New York: St. Martin's Press, 1981), 222–23.
11. Robert Sklar, *Movie-Made America: A Cultural History of American Movies* (New York: Vintage, 1975), 117.

12. Buster Keaton with Charles Samuels, *My Wonderful World of Slapstick* (New York: Da Capo, 1982), 95.

13. Eleanor Keaton and Jeffrey Vance, *Buster Keaton Remembered* (New York: Abrams, 2001), 72.

14. James Agee, "Comedy's Greatest Era," *Agee on Film: Criticism and Comment on the Movies* (New York: Modern Library, 2000), 408; Robert Knopf, *The Theater and Cinema of Buster Keaton* (Princeton, N.J.: Princeton University Press, 1999), 70.

15. James Trager, *The Food Chronology* (New York: Holt, 1995), 431.

16. Elaine M. McIntosh, *American Food Habits in Historical Perspective* (Westport, Conn.: Praeger, 1995), 93–102.

17. Trager, *Chronology*, 369–421.

18. Oldham, *Keaton's Silent Shorts*, 45.

19. Tom Gunning, "Crazy Machines in the Garden of Forking Paths: Mischief Gags and the Origins of American Film Comedy," in *Classical Hollywood Comedy*, ed. Kristine Brunovska and Henry Jenkins (New York: Routledge, 1995), 101–2.

20. Oldham, *Keaton's Silent Shorts*, 46.

21. Marion Meade, *Buster Keaton: Cut to the Chase* (New York: Da Capo, 1997), 107.

22. Robert Benayoun, *The Look of Buster Keaton* (New York: St. Martin's Press, 1982), 103.

23. Harvey Levenstein, *Revolution at the Table: The Transformation of the American Diet* (New York: Oxford University Press, 1988), 163.

24. Rudi Blesh, *Keaton* (New York: Macmillan, 1966), 210.

25. Oldham, *Keaton's Silent Shorts*, 298.

26. Levenstein, *Revolution*, 162.

27. Keaton and Samuels, *Slapstick*, 174–76.

28. Larry Edwards, *Buster: A Legend in Laughter* (Bradenton, Fla.: McGuinn and McGuire, 1995), 66.

29. Daniel Moews, *Keaton: The Silent Features Close Up* (Berkeley and Los Angeles: University of California Press, 1977), 113.

30. Rubin, *Crowd*, 62.

31. Moews, *Keaton*, 120.

32. Blesh, *Keaton*, 251.

33. Moews, *Keaton*, 121.

34. Tom Dardis, *Harold Lloyd: The Man on the Clock* (New York: Penguin, 1983), 156.

35. Levenstein, *Revolution*, 187.

36. Gilles Deleuze, *Cinema 1: The Movement Image* (Minneapolis: University of Minnesota Press, 1986), 176.

37. Walter Benjamin, *Illuminations: Essays and Reflections* (New York: Schocken, 1988), 236.

20

Banquet and the Beast: The Civilizing Role of Food in 1930s Horror Films

BLAIR DAVIS

In the horror films of the 1930s, the relationship between food and identity is a common element in the various stages of acceptance and rejection from society that the monsters encounter. Food, and frequently food with strong Christian associations, commonly serves a civilizing role in the monsters' development, as it is with the engagement in human dining customs that these creatures learn about societal norms and traditions. The monsters seek to pass themselves off as normal—or human—through the mastery of such customs.

One obvious way of denoting someone (or something, in the monsters' case) as "other" is in the distinctions between what they eat in relation to our own, supposedly "normal" cuisine. When the food of others is different, it is often thought to be strange, even repugnant, or at the very least unappetizing. Monsters are an extreme form of "the other," feared because they might hurt us, with the given assumption that we will be eaten, as predators eat their prey. While some monsters in these horror films do in fact possess beastly appetites, many instead prefer the taste of regular, human food. This should come as a certain comfort to humanity, yet it frequently is not; the panicked villagers never stick around long enough to find out whether a monster wants to break their bones or to break bread with them instead. Furthermore, the Hollywood monsters often eat food with religious significance, such as bread and wine—sacraments used in performing the Eucharist in Christianity. This could be viewed as a worthy attempt to learn human traditions and the morality behind them, yet the more common view is that the monsters' appropriation of these religious symbols is to be deemed sacrilegious. Thus rejection is based on the unholy nature of these monsters, which will be examined in four films. In Tod Browning's *Dracula* (1931), vampires are described as unholy creatures that can actually be harmed by Christian symbols such as the crucifix. Also directed by Tod Browning, *Freaks* (1932) depicts actual human monstrosities in a tale of vengeful circus sideshow performers—thought by some to have been rejected by God ("What kind of God would do this?"). Both Erle C. Kenton's *Island of Lost Souls* (1932), an adaptation of the H. G Wells novel *The Island of Dr. Moreau,* and James Whale's *Bride of Frankenstein* (1935) feature scientifically created monsters.[1] Being man-made rather than divine creations, they are as such unholy. The role of food in each of these films will be analyzed in relation to questions of morality and civilization. In a variation on the old adage that "you are what you eat," Susan Allport writes, in *The Primal Feast,* "Our lives are a reflection of the foods that we eat."[2] Count Dracula does not consume food in the traditional sense; hence he is not alive—having died and been transformed into a vampire. What nourishment Dracula (Bela Lugosi) does partake of is antithetical to the concept of life itself, for when vampires drink the blood of the living, these victims fall under the shadow of death. This process could be interpreted as a form of resurrection, in that through death the vampire's victim itself becomes transformed into a vampire. Yet such a transformation is in opposition to the spiritual resurrection of Christianity, hence vampires are deemed to be unholy creatures.

Vampirism is even indirectly described as a sin in the Bible. In Leviticus 17:10, it is ordained that the consumption of blood is forbidden: "Any Israelite or any alien living among them who eats any blood—I will set my face against that person who eats blood and will cut him off from his people. . . . You must not eat the blood of any creature because the life of every creature is in the blood; anyone who eats it must be cut off." Vampires are cut off from society by the fact that they are nocturnal creatures, forced to keep inverse hours and walk by night while others sleep. This biblical passage also implies that those who consume blood are to be shunned not only by their peers but by God as well, which is also the case with vampires. Despite this exclusion from the divine, however, Dracula seems to be well acquainted with the Bible, or perhaps just one part in particular. In what has become one of the most famous lines from the 1931 film, Dracula tells the newly arrived Renfield (Dwight Frye), upon seeing a spider that awaits its prey, "The blood is the life, Mr. Renfield," a direct reference to the passage from Leviticus. That Dracula, briefly displaying a dry, macabre sense of humor, should invoke this passage is both ironic and somewhat blasphemous, which is entirely in keeping with the unholy nature of vampires.

On the surface, Dracula would seem to be the least monstrous of the classic Hollywood monsters. He may certainly be creepy, but he does not appear as immediately threatening as the Wolf Man or the Frankenstein monster, both of whom startle people with such distinctive traits as their size, fur, tattered clothing, and deathly skin tone. Dracula appears more like a wolf in sheep's clothing—or fine men's clothing, in this case. It should not be forgotten that Dracula is in fact a count, and is able to use this noble status to his advantage. He need not hide his physical being, but rather, at night steps out in a top hat, white tie and tails, be it to the theatre or simply strolling the London streets, both of which he does in the film.

Along with this gentleman status would naturally come a mastery of formal dining customs and etiquette. It is with food that Dracula is able to win Renfield's trust; however, it is also through the count's interaction with food that his deceptive nature should have been revealed to his victim. In the film, Renfield travels to Dracula's castle to complete the paperwork for some property the count wishes to own in London. In the interest of acquiring a legally binding contract, the count must be on his best behavior with his guest—at least until the paperwork is completed.

Upon meeting Dracula for the first time, Renfield is completely overwhelmed—his carriage driver has seemingly disappeared, he is concerned for his luggage, and he is more than a little put off by the castle's spooky atmosphere. "It's really . . . good to see you," Renfield says hesitantly, struggling to maintain diplomacy in the face of uncertainty. "What with all this, I . . . I thought I was in the wrong place!" he admits. "I bid you . . . welcome," Dracula graciously replies. Yet the count soon lets his taste for the macabre slip as he leads Renfield up a giant staircase, pausing at a spider's web to deliver the "blood is the life" line, along with the infamous words, "Listen to them . . . children of the night. What music they make!" at the prompt of a wolf's howl in the distance. Together, these two off-putting statements might prompt one to suspect something sinister beneath the count's strange demeanor, yet Renfield apparently chalks it up to eccentricity and continues to follow his sanguine host.

Dracula leads Renfield to a large guest room lit by many candles. "I'm sure you will find this part of the castle . . . more inviting," says Dracula. "Well, rather!" replies Renfield. "And the fire, it's so cheerful!" he adds. Dracula then beckons toward a dining table. "I didn't know. . . but that you might be hungry?" he says, spinning a web for his prey. Renfield thanks him, but expresses further concern for his luggage. When Dracula assures him that it has already been brought upstairs, Renfield becomes more comfortable and approaches the table. The camera pulls back to reveal a meal waiting there, complete with two candles to set the proper dining mood. Renfield sits down at the table and begins to observe the room, which is well kept and free of cobwebs and vermin. His initial hesitations now appear to have been overcome by Dracula's hospitality.

"And now, if you're not too fatigued" says Dracula, "I would like to discuss the lease on Carfax Abbey." When told all that remains is the signature, Dracula studies the lease closely. When Renfield cuts his finger on a paperclip and blood appears, Dracula becomes frenzied and draws nearer, but quickly turns away in disgust upon seeing the crucifix around Renfield's neck. Renfield sucks the blood from his finger while Dracula watches longingly—a gaze that startles his guest. To smooth over this awkwardness, Dracula again tries to placate Renfield through gentlemanly behavior at the table—reaching for a goblet and a bottle of wine. "This is very old wine. I hope you will like it," he says sinisterly. The connection between food and religion becomes overt here; wine becomes a substitute for the blood that Dracula has just been denied, as wine is substituted for the blood of Christ in the Eucharist. The fact that we are shown a crucifix between the appearance of the blood and that of the wine makes the religious metaphor even more palpable.

Dracula pours a glass of wine for his guest. Renfield looks at the lone goblet—"Aren't you drinking?" he inquires. "I never drink . . . wine" is Dracula's infamous reply. This refusal to engage in fellowship with his guest should have immediately made Renfield suspicious of his host. To muse philosophically about spiders, praise the musical qualities of howling wolves and be overly captivated by the sight of blood streaming down someone's finger is one thing, but when your host refuses to drink with you, it's time for you to leave. Dracula knows this, being well acquainted with dining etiquette, yet his taste for blood seems to have dulled his appreciation for vintage wines. There is also the symbolic aspect of drinking wine, as Dracula would not want to participate in any act with even the slightest religious overtones. Yet there is in fact a very simple, tactical reason why Dracula will not drink with his guest—the wine has been drugged. Renfield drinks the poisoned cup while his host stares at him with a predatory gaze. "It's delicious!" exclaims Renfield, who unbeknownst to him is participating in a sort of last supper of his own, in that he will soon lose his appetite for regular food, and turn toward insects as his preferred form of nourishment.

The religious imagery of this scene is even more pronounced in the Spanish version of *Dracula* from the same year. The modern practice of dubbing Hollywood movies into other languages for foreign markets was not yet widespread in the early 1930s, as studios often used foreign casts to shoot a version of the same film on the same sets after the English speaking production had gone home for the night. When the Spanish Renfield cuts his finger it is not on a paperclip, but rather with a knife while slicing a loaf of bread. With the bread, wine and blood all mixed together in the same scene, the religious symbolism is unmistakable. The scene actually plays better in the Spanish version, but the American producers likely thought that such an overt metaphor would not play well with audiences or the censors. Another difference between the two films is that in the American version, Dracula does not pour the wine and Renfield does not actually begin to eat his meal until after their business has been discussed. In the Spanish version, however, Dracula pours his guest a glass of wine as soon as he sits down at the table. Renfield cuts into his meat and begins eating as he and Dracula then start to talk business. This is symptomatic of the different attitudes between Latin and North American countries regarding time. Americans typically adhere to a monochronic notion of time, preferring to do individual tasks in succession—"first things first"; hence in the Hollywood version business is discussed before the pleasure of dining begins. A Spanish audience would instead adhere to a polychronic notion of time, in which multiple tasks are attempted at once—so it would be completely natural to discuss business at the same time as eating dinner. The two versions of *Dracula* provide a compelling case study, because while almost identical to one another in the overall narrative, they reveal many striking cultural differences when studied closely.

While Dracula's status as a nobleman affords him a privileged place in society, other monsters do not blend in so easily. Most are outcasts, living on the edges of society, like the characters in the 1932 film *Freaks*. This was director Tod Browning's follow-up to *Dracula*, adapted from a story titled "Spurs" by the English fantasy writer Tod Robbins. The film tells the story of a close-knit band of circus sideshow performers who take revenge on one who has wronged them, and stars an array of real-life midgets, a legless man, an armless woman, and other such "freaks." The uncomfortable sight of these human anomolies "so stunned some of the preview audience that several women ran screaming from the cinema, and the major distributors refused to handle it."[3] The film was little seen for decades, and was banned in Britain for more than thirty years until 1963.

Food plays an important role throughout the film, used for both thematic and dramatic purposes. In the original prose story, a midget named Jacques Courbe is greeted with ridicule by the circus crowd, who throw banana skins and orange peels at him. Yet when Jacques later proposes to a woman, the connection between fruit and pain does not stop him from telling her, "You will be as happy, mademoiselle, as a cherry tree in June."[4] This fruitful metaphor is a deliberate one, meant to invoke the symbolic connection between food and fertility, as a June cherry tree would be starting to produce fruit, hence overtly fertile. Later in the story, Jacques himself is compared to a piece of fruit on his wedding night: "His chin was just above the tablecloth, so that his head looked like a large orange that had rolled off the fruit dish."[5] The use of such imagery is used to underscore the deformed nature of these characters, the message of the film seeming to be that if the Lord tells us to "be fruitful and multiply," then this band of grotesques must be rotten fruit, spawned from bad seeds.

Throughout the film, food is used for its potential to horrify the audience. In one scene, two of the circus freaks sit eating dinner together, sharing gossip as they dine. Each is enjoying a beer with the meal, yet one of the women has no arms and is forced to lift the drink with her feet. Her toes curl around the glass as she raises it to her lips, smiling happily as she takes a long sip before putting it down. For many viewers, particularly those in the early 1930s, this would have been an unsettling sight, and director Browning shrewdly exploits the disturbing potential of this connection between food and the grotesque. Eating and drinking are two of the most natural human functions, yet when set in the context of these "unnatural" humans the ordinary can become horrific.

Eating is not the only natural activity deployed by Browning, for he also intertwines food with sex, this time in a scene featuring two of the film's non-freaks. Cleopatra the trapeze artist (Olga Baclanova) is trying to seduce Hercules the strongman (Henry Victor) in her wagon, inviting him in for a drink. "Feel like eating something?" she asks. "Always!" replies Hercules. Cleopatra holds up an egg and asks "How many?" "Oh, I'm not very hungry . . . about six!" he answers, and they soon embrace and kiss. With the egg being a symbol of female fertility, their culinary foreplay becomes an appropriate metaphor for the offscreen sex that will soon occur. That she offers to cook him eggs also serves as dramatic foreshadowing of the film's shocking conclusion, in which Cleopatra's legs are cut off by the vengeful circus freaks, transforming her into a "chicken lady" who lives in a box and speaks only in squawks. This climax is further foreshadowed by the fact that when she and Hercules kiss, they are overseen through the wagon's open door by one of the freaks, the half-man/half-woman. Hercules quickly chases him/her away, yet the sexual confusion that this character embodies will haunt Cleopatra when she is made into half a woman at the film's end, when, so to speak, the chickens come home to roost.

The combination of food, freaks, fear, and foreshadowing comes to a full boil in the legendary banquet sequence, for which the film is best remembered. The midget Hans (changed from Jacques in the original story) has fallen in love with Cleopatra, so she and Hercules devise a plan for her to marry Hans (Harry Earles) for his money and then poison him. Once married, a wedding feast is thrown for the newlyweds, where the alcohol flows freely, as does the bride's contempt for her new husband. The more Cleopatra has to drink, the more belligerent she becomes, mocking Hans and laughing in his face when he tells her how happy she has made him. Some of the more mentally challenged freaks even laugh along with her, adding a further sadness to the proceedings.

Soon the freaks begin to sing a song, one that we gather is used traditionally to welcome new members into their fold. "We'll make her one of us!" says one of the midgets, standing on the table. "A loving cup, a loving cup!" he proclaims. The half-man/half-woman begins to sing, and the rest soon follow: "We accept her, one of us! We accept her, one of us! Gooble gobble, gooble gobble! We accept her, we accept her! Gooble gobble, one of us!" The singing continues as Hercules laughs, and jeeringly says to Cleopatra, "They're going to make you one of them, my peacock!" This line adds further ironic foreshadowing, as the freaks do indeed literally make her one of them in the end, turning her into a fowl monstrosity.

Hercules' statement causes Cleopatra to stop laughing, and she looks aghast as the singing continues. The midget has now begun walking around the table, offering an oversized goblet full of alcohol for everyone to share. Cleopatra slowly rises from her chair as the cup continues around the table. She begins to back away as the cup is brought down for her to partake of the drink, and more importantly to participate in this unifying ritual. The midget stops in front of Cleopatra with the cup, takes a sip himself, and then passes it to her, as Hercules repeats, "They're going to make you one of them, my peacock!" She stares at the cup in disgust as the song continues, and soon begins to yell over the singing: "You . . . dirty . . . slimy . . . FREAKS!" The singing abruptly stops, and she again yells "Freaks! Freaks! Get out of here! Now!" Hercules starts to laugh as the freaks rise and begin to leave the table. "You filth! Make me one of you, will you?" Cleopatra screams to the departing crowd. She then begins to yell at Hans, berating him in front of Hercules. He soon picks up the midget groom and places him on Cleopatra's back, so that she gives her new husband a humiliating "'horseback ride" around the banquet table as the freaks file out. Hercules follows behind her, blowing a horn as the wedding reception quickly deteriorates into a mockery of the sacred tradition it is meant to be.

The "loving cup" that the freaks share functions on multiple levels. To drink from it is an expression of unity—an acceptance of one's status as an outsider from regular society and a celebration of one's inclusion in this band of merry outcasts. It is a simple gesture, but one through which the freaks can feel a sense of belonging and of being truly human. Cleopatra denies them this chance when she refuses to share in the ritual, declining their loving offer of community and ridiculing them for it. There is also an element of religious symbolism, in that the sharing of the "loving cup" is similar to that displayed in the ritual of accepting the sacrament. Each member of a church congregation takes a sip from the same cup to represent that they all share the blood of Christ, and in turn are themselves all spiritual brethren with the rest of the congregation. First Corinthians 10:17 states that in accepting the sacrament, "all of us, though many, are one body"—a body marked by deformity in the case of the freaks. Each one puts the cup to his or her lips, figuratively leaving a part of the self behind, and in turn sharing a part of that self with the other members. Food and drink often play a large role in a community's social traditions: "Stress is placed on the social function of food in bringing out sentiments that help to socialize an individual as a member of his [or her] community. The function is the maintenance of the system."[6] Cleopatra refuses to join their community and be "one of them,," and as such refuses to put the cup to her lips when it has been touched by those she regards as dirty, slimy freaks.

Cleopatra's betrayal of this community in rejecting the symbolic cup and attempting to poison one of their members, prompts the freaks to seek revenge. At the start of the film a carnival barker tells us that the freaks live by a certain code of conduct: "Their code is a law unto themselves. Offend one, and you offend them all." No doubt the rejected cup would have been deemed equally as offensive as the attempted poisoning, leading the freaks to take an eye for an eye, and a couple of limbs as well.

A group of freaks of a different kind appear in 1932's *Island of Lost Souls*, directed by Erle C. Kenton. The film was the first major adaptation of H. G. Wells's novel *The Island of Dr. Moreau,* in which the good doctor (Charles

Laughton) practices unnatural animal experiments. Just as some of the circus freaks looked half human (or, in the case of missing extremities, literally were), so too do the animals on Moreau's island appear to be mutated mixtures—half human, half beast. Similarly, just as the freaks lived according to a particular code, Moreau's creatures live in accordance with "the law," which is invoked several times in the film.

At the center of the law is food and the tension between human and animal appetites. The first time we encounter the law in the film, Dr. Moreau stands on a cliff before his creations, who are gathered below. Brandishing a whip, Moreau cracks it once demanding attention as he sternly asks, "What is the law?" His query is met by the group's spokesman, who goes by the moniker Sayer of the Law, played by an unrecognizable Bela Lugosi. The Sayer responds, "Not to run on all fours! That is the law! Are we not men?!" The rest of the group then echoes in unison: "Are we not men?" Moreau again asks, "What is the law?" and the sayer replies "Not to eat meat!" followed by "That is the law! Are we not men?" The creatures again repeat their response, and Moreau asks one final time what the law is. "Not to spill blood! That is the law! Are we not men?"

After the response is again repeated, the Sayer looks to Moreau and cries, "His is the hand that saves! His is the hand that heals! His is the house of pain!" The discourse inherent in Moreau's law is one that rewards civility and punishes carnal desire. Moreau believes he has made these beasts men, and wants them to believe it as well—hence their forced response of "Are we not men?" The man-beasts must deny their animal instincts to run on all fours, to eat meat, or to shed blood. That Moreau must even devise such a law, let alone violently enforce it, is evidence of the fact that his attempt to make men from beasts has not been entirely successful thus far.

During a dinner that Moreau hosts for his human guests, a comment is made about one of the circumstances of Moreau's law. "Doc, I see you're a vegetarian," says Captain Davies. "On account of the natives" replies Moreau, "They've never tasted meat." "No long pig?" asks the Captain. "Long pig?" inquires another guest. "He means human flesh," answers Moreau. The doctor is clearly aware of the tentative humanity of his creatures, in that any taste of meat might spark their animal bloodlust. In his essay "On the Civilizing of Appetite," Stephen Mennel states, "normal eating behavior involves a capacity for considerable self-control."[7] The animal appetite is contrasted against the human or "normal" appetite in that animals are not thought to have the same level of or capacity for self-control as humans, who are not motivated by bloodlust. Moreau sees to it that his creatures do not have the option of losing their self-control, having made sure their diet cannot instill carnivorous impulses.

Moreau's dietary law bears an interesting resemblance to a similar command in the Bible. The passage from first Corinthians 8:11 reads, "If what I eat causes my brother to fall into sin, I will never eat meat again, so that I will not cause him to fall." The fear is that if Moreau's beasts are allowed to eat meat and develop a taste for flesh, they will soon shed blood to get it, causing them to "fall into sin." The irony of this biblical passage's relevance to the film is that the command refers to the consumption of meat that has been sacrificed in the name of a false idol. In creating life by his own hand, Moreau is himself a false god of sorts, yet one who commands that no blood be spilled in his name. Moreau may even compare himself with Christ, in that the Sayer of the Law declares that Moreau's is the hand that saves and the hand that heals.

In the film's climax, after learning that Moreau had secretly ordered one of their brethren to kill Captain Davies (Stanley Fields), the creatures abandon the law and turn upon their master, killing Moreau in his own house of pain. Indeed, Moreau's fears prove correct, as one beast's act of killing is enough to drive the others to the same act. The creatures kill their master/god, and for most it is their first act of spilling blood. With the law no more, they are free to pursue a carnivorous appetite, destroying their false god in the process. As such, the act of eating meat does not cast them into sin, but instead redeems them from the tyrannous rule of the man they have been commanded to worship and obey; their sacrifice is made not in order to praise their god, but to bury him.

Kenton's film presents Moreau's attempt to refine the palate of his creations as ultimately one formed with his own self-preservation in mind, although Moreau supposedly intends his efforts as an attempt to civilize a savage race in the hopes of advancing the process of evolution. Just six years after the movie's appearance, the sociology of eating habits was analyzed by Norbert Elias in his seminal work, *The Civilizing Process*.[8] Elias presents the argument that there has been a largely continual refinement of manners over the past several centuries, with steady changes from the Middle Ages through modernity in terms of the common expectations for how people should behave. In turn, the process of internalization through which people adapt to these changing norms is also in a constant state of evolution, so that much of the behavior of the Middle Ages is now seen as distasteful, particularly with regard to food consumption, such as using one's hands to eat. Modern society has even gone so far as to remove most of the "animalness" from our food, and animal slaughter has been removed from the daily food preparation of most people. In contrast, a primal creature must hunt for its food, and either kill or starve. To become civilized is to deny this process, to cook and to dine rather than to butcher; civilized beings do not shed blood themselves. Even though most people are several steps removed from the process by the time they eat meat, animals have still been slaughtered and blood spilled.

Elias argues that the process of becoming civilized entails acquiring higher levels of repugnance, with a corresponding rise in shame and embarrassment over unacceptable behavior. It is this shame and repugnance that Moreau tries to forcibly instill in his creations. Their unified response of "Are we not men?" is evidence of this, especially given its terse, rhetorical nature. When one of their ranks actually does spill blood, he is chastised for it, with the act considered by all to be truly repugnant—until it is discovered that Moreau himself ordered the killing. With their sense of morality shaken to the core, their notions of what is distasteful changes rapidly, and they quickly lose any embarrassment they might have had over their beastly appetites. In his book *Keywords*, Raymond Williams writes that civilization "may be seen as capable of being lost as well as being gained"[9]; major dietary changes may be seen as one possible way in which a civil society might revert back to an acceptance of formerly distasteful behavior.

One character in *Island of Lost Souls* serves as a particularly interesting example with regards to the connection between the culinary and the civilized. While we are told in the film that the beasts are vegetarian, we never actually see them consume food. In the original novel, one of the creatures details the specifics of their diet: "Eat roots and herbs—it is His will."[10] Such a diet relies mainly on foraging—cooking skills would not be necessitated for such cuisine, nor would knowledge of formal dining customs. Yet one character stands in sharp contrast to the others in this respect: M'ling, Moreau's man-beast servant (Tetsu Komai).

Whether through formal training or natural ability, M'ling has apparently mastered many if not all of the dining customs that would be enacted in the home of an English gentleman such as Dr. Moreau. M'ling serves various kinds of alcohol throughout the film, along with the correct glasses customarily required for each variation. We assume that he sets the table (being the only visible servant), and it is implied that he cooks the meals as well, as Moreau informs him of how many will be dining with him, not mentioning any chef. During the meal, M'ling waits attentively while Moreau and his guests dine, holding a bottle of wine and topping up each glass when it gets low. M'ling is a busboy, waiter, and chef all rolled into one, and with such an extensive knowledge of dining etiquette, we would expect his eating habits to be more refined than those of the other creatures. Cultural theorist Claude Levi-Strauss sees the process of "transforming food from the raw to the cooked state . . . as marking the emergence of humanity."[11] With M'ling evidently preparing Moreau's meals, the servant seems to be more civilized than his peers because of these cooking skills.

Indeed, this knowledge positions M'ling as being more refined than the rest of his beastly brethren, which is also evidenced by the fact that while most of the creatures go shirtless or don well-worn clothing, M'ling wears a three-piece suit and bow tie. In fact, M'ling appears to be somewhat ostracized from the others, likely a result of the cultural refinement that has won him a privileged position on Moreau's island. When the beasts declare at the end of the film that the law is no more, M'ling merely watches as the revolt ensues. Through the composition of shots, director Kenton visually sets M'ling apart from the others. In cutting away from the mob to a close-up of M'ling looking down from the cliff above, Kenton creates a "reaction shot," emphasizing

M'ling's response to the revolt. This technical choice helps to underscore the thematic nature of this scene, as M'ling is not stirred to join in the action with his peers upon learning of the law's cessation, but instead reacts against them and runs off to warn Moreau.

Yet despite his civilized differences from the others, food does play a part in stirring M'ling's inherently animalistic nature elsewhere in the film. On a ship delivering animals to Moreau's island at the film's start, we find M'ling hard at work preparing food. However, his duties are not nearly as refined as those which he will carry out in Moreau's home. Instead we find M'ling—with no tie, his shirt slightly unbuttoned—hauling a heavy bucket across the ship's deck, a bucket which contains slops for the dogs. Fetching slops surely qualifies as perhaps the most thankless, unrewarding method of food preparation in existence, especially for someone with more sizable culinary talents. M'ling gets his face rubbed in this unsavory mess when he is struck by the ship's captain and hits the deck, lying face down in puddles of slop meant for the dogs from which he has long ago evolved. Not surprisingly, reduced to this situation, M'ling's animal nature emerges—he bares his fangs and lunges at the captain on all fours while emitting a fierce cry.

The lost souls of Moreau's island seek acceptance from their master, for to break his dietary laws would mean punishment in the house of pain. The freaks of the circus use food to seek acceptance through the ritualistic customs performed at the wedding banquet. Dracula uses food to gain Renfield's acceptance, creating a false comfort for a sinister purpose. Yet none have ever tried so hard to find acceptance as the most misunderstood monster of all—the Frankenstein monster. While the lost souls are motivated by fear, the freaks by a desire for respect, and Dracula by a need for control, the Frankenstein monster's primary motivation is to be loved. While he is denied romantic love by the mate promised to him in *Bride of Frankenstein*, the monster is able to find brotherly love when he shares a meal with another societal outcast.

The first culinary question that might be asked about the Frankenstein monster is a simple one—does he need to eat? No mention is made in the original 1931 film of the monster's bodily desires, nor do we see him consume anything.[12] Furthermore, the monster could not cook food even if he wanted to, as he is deathly afraid of fire. As such, he would have to consume any food in its raw state, which Levi-Strauss denotes as the mark of an uncivilized being. The monster (Boris Karloff) certainly dresses the part of a lower-class member, not being blessed with the fashion sense that Dracula, for one, possesses. While the count's aristocratic manner allows him to be impeccably dressed, the Frankenstein monster looks like a member of the proletariat in his torn sweater, soiled wool jacket, and heavy boots.

Yet while Dracula demonstrates the luxury of refusing to share a meal with his guest, the downtrodden Frankenstein monster actually hungers like a poor man in the 1935 sequel *Bride of Frankenstein*. Never turning down a chance to eat, the monster (Boris Karloff) in fact displays the signs of thirst and hunger that we do not see in the first film. Early in the sequel, we find the monster wandering through the woods eating some variety of root vegetable (raw of course, in conformance with the ideas of Levi-Strauss). The monster comes across a small brook and stops to take a drink. He takes another bite of root as he kneels down, and grunts thirstily as he scoops the water in his hand. As he drinks from the stream, he catches sight of his reflection in the water and splashes his hands at it angrily. This is an important moment in the monster's budding self-development, which will further progress once he moves from drinking water to wine. Later in the film, the monster will be asked, "Do you know who Henry Frankenstein is, and who you are?" It is a question that indicates his developing capacity for self-reflection.

The monster later encounters a family of gypsies camped in the woods, roasting meat on a small spit over a fire. The monster sniffs the air hungrily as he spots the family through the trees, and soon approaches them. He tries to communicate his hunger, grunting and waving his hands toward the meat and then toward the gypsies—appealing to them without hostility to offer him food in the spirit of friendship. When the gypsies scream and begin to flee, the monster reacts badly, pushing them aside as he tries to grab the meat. It falls into the fire as he fights off one of the gypsies, who is no doubt trying to protect his dinner just as much as he is his family. The monster reaches into the fire for the meat but burns his hand instead and screams as he retreats into the forest, unfulfilled.

As the monster makes his way through the woods, he eventually hears music playing in the distance. This makes him smile, and he heads toward a small cabin. Looking in through a window, he sees an old man playing the violin. This is not all he spies, however, as there is also a kettle of food hung over a roaring fire. The kettle is framed prominently in the center of multiple shots of the man as he plays, indicative of both the monster's hunger and the central role that food will continue to play in his development and refinement.

The monster enters the cabin with a growl. The man (O.P. Heggie) stops playing, welcomes the monster, and explains that he is blind. He soon realizes that the monster cannot talk and is hurt, and goes to bring him some food. He gets a bowl and dips it into the pot; the monster recoils at the sight of his new friend moving toward the fire, grunting and gesturing with his hands, afraid that the man will be burned as he was in his own attempt to get food from the gypsies. When the blind man successfully retrieves the bowl from the kettle, the monster becomes still, looking up at the man in curious awe, likely wondering how he has emerged unscathed. The monster is brought a bowl of soup and a piece of bread for his first supper, which has several religious overtones to it. The blind man is dressed in a long robe and has a long white beard, clearly meant to resemble one of the apostles. He clasps the bowl between upturned hands as he moves slowly toward the monster, as if performing a pious ceremony. "I have prayed many times for God to send me a friend," he says, pausing for a moment before handing the bowl to the monster. The film's music underscores the scene's religious significance, as we hear organ music playing softly in the background, which will soon turn into the familiar strains of "Ave Maria."

The monster smiles as he accepts the bowl with a grateful grunt, quickly taking it to his lips and slurping up the liquid. As expected, the monster's eating habits are not very refined. He takes a giant bite of bread, with the rest falling carelessly to the floor. He buries his face in the bowl, quickly gulping down his soup, and once finished wipes his mouth with his hand. The monster's development will make great strides as result of this meal, however. Once done eating, the blind man says a prayer of thanks for their newfound friendship, and the monster quietly sheds a tear, proving his inherent humanity.

The next scene shows the two friends seated at a table, enjoying a daytime meal of bread and cheese. While the blind man has a knife on his plate, utensils are noticeably absent from the monster's, being the unsophisticated eater that he is. It is unknown exactly how long the two have been living together at this point, but it is safe to assume that the two have shared each other's company for at least a few days. Once done eating, the blind man says "And now for our lesson. Remember? This is bread," he says, picking up a half-eaten loaf and handing it to the monster. This implies that there have been previous lessons, which the monster is asked to remember. As he takes the loaf, the monster draws on what he has learned, silently mouthing syllables before speaking the word "Bread!" Here the film replicates childhood growth patterns, in which food usually plays a critical role in the development of human speech (since words for foods often follow the "mama" and "dada" expressions of small children).

The monster smiles and takes a giant bite of the loaf after saying what is, to the audience anyway, his first word. "And this is wine, to drink" says the blind man, continuing the lesson. He pours a cup and hands it to the monster, who echoes the word "Drink!" They clink their mugs together, and the monster takes a long sip. "Good!" he says, copious amounts of wine sloppily spilling down his chin in the process. Perhaps unbeknownst to the monster, he is learning more than just how to say a few simple words; the blind man is teaching him about the Eucharist, a miniature version of which the monster has just enjoyed. The two then go on to proclaim their brotherly love for one another: "We are friends, you and I! Friends!" says the blind man, shaking hands with the monster.

After teaching the monster how to smoke, the blind man tells his friend "Before you came, I was all alone. It is bad to be alone." "Alone . . . bad" the monster says contemplatively. "Friend . . . good," he adds, his eyes starting to twinkle. He extends his hand proudly to the blind man, enthusiastically repeating "Friend good!" as they again shake hands and laugh. The monster here learns about societal behavior, which will culminate in his desire that a mate be created for him, fulfilling the traditional societal expectation that people ought to get married rather than stay single. The monster then continues his rapid progression by learning the basic principle of human morality. After the monster declares that fire is "no good!" the blind man states, "There is good, and there is bad." The monster looks pensive as he repeats this lesson: "Good. . . . Bad."

The monster's morality is quickly tested, however, as two wayward hunters soon enter the cabin in search of directions. It is fitting that the monster has just performed the Eucharist, because it will prove to be his last supper with the blind man. The hunters recognize the monster, and one prepares to fire his shotgun. The monster rushes at him, knocking the hunter on to the table, sending everything tumbling down to the floor. The bread and wine that were symbolic of the monster's progress toward becoming civilized—and of his possible salvation—now lie discarded as a result of the violence from which he cannot escape. Director James Whale presents the monster as a tragic figure, even going so far as having him tied to a pole in a Christ-like position when he is captured by a mob of torch-wielding villagers earlier in the film. (Oddly enough, the film was originally released on Good Friday of 1935.)

After the pious company of the blind man is denied him, the monster later finds himself enjoying the hospitality of the devilish Dr. Pretorius (Ernest Thesiger). Another "'mad" scientist who has succeeded in creating life, Pretorius wishes to make a female companion for the monster, with the help of Dr. Frankenstein (Colin Clive). After a long night of grave robbing, Pretorius enjoys a meal by himself in an underground burial tomb. He pours himself a glass of wine, and with a hearty laugh raises it toward a skull sitting on a coffin that has been transformed into a makeshift table, and toasts it: "I give you . . . the monster!" He takes a drink, slams the glass down, and continues laughing to himself, unaware that the subject of his toast in fact lurks behind him in the shadows. The monster approaches, and Pretorius invites him to share his company, as well as his dinner (which, as in *Dracula*, is offered with an ulterior motive rather than in the spirit of friendship). Picking up a piece of chicken from the table, the monster smiles and takes a bite, snapping the carcass in the process. Just as we think the monster's table manners might not be progressing, he then drinks an entire glass of wine in one go without spilling a single drop, a marked improvement over his prior sloppiness when drinking with the blind man.

Yet while his eating habits may show improvement, the monster still displays a certain ignorance as he shares a drink with Pretorius. Upon spying the bottle, he points to it, and turning to his host says "Drink . . . good!" repeating the ritual of the Eucharist that has been taught to him. The context in which the monster receives the sacramental wine is not a holy one, however; here a coffin is used in place of an altar. Pretorius has just finished toasting the monster, a man-made rather than a divine creation, and by joining him in a drink the monster shares in his host's blasphemous invocation. The Bible in fact warns against such misuse of the sacraments, stating in first Corinthians 11:28, "That if anyone eats the

Lord's bread or drinks from His cup in a way that dishonors Him, he is guilty of sin against the Lord's body and blood. . . . For if he does not recognize the meaning of the Lord's body when he eats the bread and drinks from the cup, he brings judgment on himself." The monster has learned to appreciate the physical act of drinking, but has not learned the spiritual element behind the ritual the blind man tried to teach him. As such, he allies himself with Dr. Pretorius in the creation of a female companion, an effort that will bring disastrous results for the monster—as if judgment had indeed been brought upon him.

As outcasts from society, the monsters in the horror films of the 1930s use food as a way of trying to become civilized, with the ultimate goal of being accepted by humanity, if not actually becoming human. Food plays a major role in the creation of identity, as the process of making sense of "the world, and the ordering of people and events, operate[s] through elementary everyday practices to which eating and drinking are utterly crucial."[13] As with the cinematic monsters, for most people our own knowledge of and interaction with other cultures is largely through the consumption of food. A love of a certain culture's food often leads us to a more rounded appreciation of that culture, just as we will likely not be made welcome if we do not enjoy another culture's food or fail to master the dining etiquette that is a reflection of the culture's larger moral attitudes. Food plays an important role in the social rituals that bring people of different cultures together, and in the rituals through which one's own culture is maintained. Food "is an ideal symbolic medium, not only because it is essential to life but because there is some recognition, either conscious or unconscious, that it is both dangerous and powerful."[14] Horror films rely heavily upon such symbolism, because they draw on primal human fears in order to frighten their audience. Food, and in particular food that carries religious overtones, figures prominently in these monster movies, because the symbolic potential of these elements creates a wealth of resonant imagery with which to inspire fear. At first glance the monsters may seem like they want to eat us, but most of the time they would rather join us at the dinner table. Creators of 1930s horror movies used food scenes in part for their power to show the monsters' potential for becoming civilized. At the same time, since eating is such a common activity, these same scenes, while showing monsters hoping to become accepted by humans, to become human even, could expose the hidden appetites within audience members and cause them to wonder if within their own civilized beings there lurked some share of monster-like appetites.

Notes

1. *Dracula*, directed by Tod Browning, 1931 (with Bela Lugosi, Dwight Frye, David Manners, Helen Chandler); *Freaks*, directed by Tod Browning, (based on Tod Robbins' "Spurs"), 1932 (with Wallace Ford, Leila Hyams, Olga Baclanova, Roscoe Ates); *Island of Lost Souls* (based on the novel *The Island of Dr. Moreau* by H.G. Wells), directed by Erle C. Kenton, 1933 (with Charles Laughton, Richard Arlen, Leila Hyams, Bela Lugosi); *Bride of Frankenstein*, directed by James Whale, 1935 (with Boris Karloff, Colin Clive, Valerie Hobson, Dwight Frye, Elsa Lanchester).
2. Susan Allport *The Primal Feast: Food, Sex, Foraging and Love* (New York: Harmony, 2000), 57.
3. Peter Haining, ed., *The Ghouls* (New York: Stein and Day, 1972), 134.
4. Ibid., 138.
5. Ibid., 139.
6. Jack Goody, *Cooking, Cuisine and Class: A Study in Comparative Sociology* (Cambridge: Cambridge University Press, 1982), 13.
7. Stephen Mennel, "On the Civilizing of Appetite," in *The Body: Social Process and Cultural Theory*, eds. Mike Featherstone, Mike Hepworth, and Bryan S. Turner (London: Sage Publications, 1991), 128.
8. Norbert Elias, *The Civilizing Process: The History of Manners*. 1939. Trans. Edmund Jephcott (New York: Urizen Books, 1978).
9. Raymond Williams, *Keywords: A Vocabulary of Culture and Society* (London: Fontana Press, 1976), 60.
10. H. G. Wells, *The Island of Dr. Moreau* (1896; reprint New York: Signet, 1988), 60.
11. Claude Levi-Strauss, quoted in Goody, *Cooking*, 18.
12. *Frankenstein*, directed by James Whale, 1931 (with Colin Clive, May Clarke, Boris Karloff, John Boles).
13. Peter Scholliers, "Meals, Food Narratives, and Sentiments of Belonging in Past and Present," in *Food, Drink and Identity: Cooking, Eating and Drinking in Europe Since the Middle Ages*, ed. Peter Scholliers (Oxford: Berg, 2001), 7.
14. Allport, *Primal Feast*, 131.

21

Engorged with Desire: The Films of Alfred Hitchcock and the Gendered Politics of Eating

DAVID GREVEN

Marion Crane (Janet Leigh), the seeming protagonist of Alfred Hitchcock's 1960 film *Psycho*, and Norman Bates (Anthony Perkins), proprietor of the motel in which Marion will be murdered, share a tense, quietly menacing meal: sandwiches, milk, and myriad morsels of intrigue. Actually, *share* is not the right word: Norman watches Marion eat the meal he has prepared for her, as if she were a newly captured rare and exotic creature. "You eat like a bird," Norman observes. "You'd know, of course," she responds, looking around at Norman's various stuffed birds, owls, and other birds of prey. But Marion is the real "bird"—British slang for woman, analogous to the American "chick," which continues the ornithological pattern—prey to Norman's murderous psychopathology. Marion's tentative, deliberate, only occasional bites of her sandwich signify ladylike decorum and finesse, but they more crucially signify her mounting unease and discomfort. The eating of the blandly homey all-American meal of sandwiches and milk—so redolent of comfort-food stability bordering on complacency—camouflages but also grotesquely parodies the simmering anxieties that will boil over during the scene. Food (meant to be satiating and pleasurable) and its ritualistic consumption (meant to signify intimacy) are denatured. Food becomes a symbol of what cannot be ingested by these characters: terrible truths, perceptions about others' behavior, self-knowledge, responsibility for one's actions. Rather than facilitating intimacy, eating signifies instead the growing emotional gulf between these memorably lonely, unhappy characters, a gulf that becomes unbridgeable. The meal that

297

lies between Marion and Norman signifies the gendered gulf between them as well.

The psychiatrist (Simon Oakland) in the film's infamously explanatory penultimate scene insists that Norman's murders of young women are "crimes of passion." He tells Marion's sister, Lila (Vera Miles), that Norman was "aroused" by Marion, that he "wanted" her. If the sandwiches and milk are viewed as symbolic of a kind of courtship offer, Marion's hesitant consumption of them represents her pointed lack of interest in Norman as a suitor. In his vigilant monitoring of her eating, he is like an anxious would-be lover, desperately checking for any flicker of interest from his desired object. If you take Norman as a queer figure (as I do), however, the meal he prepares for Marion, squishy and soft, nonphallic (unlike, say, the steak Marion and her more conventionally heterosexual boyfriend Sam discuss eating in their first scene together in a *different* hotel room, the site of actual if postcoital heterosexual eros), and her circumspect delicacy about ingesting it, underscore the unthinkability of Norman's sexual relationship with Marion or any other woman. Thus, it becomes clear that food and eating can be used to signify specifically gendered gulfs and anxieties between characters in Hitchcock films. Hitchcock's other films consistently reinforce these themes.

In this essay, I first establish the primacy and prevalence of eating (and drinking) throughout Hitchcock films.[1] While it would be tempting to offer examples from the English Hitchcock films, weighing the distinctions, I will keep my focus on the American ones. I then offer an analysis of the competing tensions that inform the depiction of eating in Hitchcock: national, cultural, sexual, cinematic tensions that give Hitchcock films their distinctive aftertaste.

Surreal Liverwurst: *Spellbound*

Let us begin with a Hitchcock film in which food is gloriously powerful as a source and a symbol of communion and intimacy: *Spellbound* (1945). Dr. Constance Petersen (Ingrid Bergman) anticipates, with her fellow psychiatrists at the mental asylum Green Manors, the arrival of Dr. Edwardes (Gregory Peck), the brilliant author of the acclaimed new psychoanalytic tome, *Labyrinth of the Guilt Complex*. Young, handsome Dr. Edwardes replaces the aging Dr. Murchison (Hitchcock stalwart Leo G. Carroll). Dr. Murchison, we are told, has suffered some bouts with depression, but it is Dr. Edwardes who seems addled. Constance eventually discovers that Dr. Edwardes is really an amnesiac named John Ballantine, a young man who was being treated by the *real* Dr. Edwardes for the guilt he has always felt for his younger brother's death. Dr. Murchison has killed Dr. Edwardes and used the temporary amnesia of Ballantine to his advantage. The movie follows Constance's attempts both to free Ballantine from his labyrinthine guilt for *two* deaths (one he only accidentally caused, the other he never did) and from charges that he murdered Edwardes. Ultimately, Murchison kills himself when Constance discovers his murderous secret; Constance and John are then free to marry.

Kitschy though it is, *Spellbound* is one of Hitchcock's most emotionally satisfying—and critically neglected—movies. One of its most distinctive features is its heroine's role as the hero's savior. Tireless in her efforts to heal John of his devouring guilt, prim, circumspect, bespectacled Constance transforms into an emotionally alive, spontaneous, and vital woman as she helps to restore John's sanity. Early in the film, the droll, acidic Dr. Fleurot pointlessly flirts with Constance, who is always unmoved by his charms. He embraces her rigid form and announces, matter-of-factly, "It's rather like embracing a telephone book." As archly played by John Emery, Dr. Fleurot, with his feminine name and theatrical air, seems more like a queer figure than a romantic pursuer of Constance. His queer *louche*ness only intensifies the sense that no heterosexual ardor infuses Constance's life. Held in yet deeply appealing, Bergman's Constance leads a tautly controlled life, gracious to her superiors (Murchison), wryly acerbic toward annoying suitors (Fleurot), and coolly yet sensitively analytical toward her patients. But as soon as she sees Edwardes/Ballantine (who will be referred to as Peck from now on, for simplicity's sake), she turns soft, warm, fleshy, tactile, erotically charged—her vision, evidently, improves too, since she stops wearing her glasses. Falling in love, which she appears to do instantaneously, transforms her into a lushly physical, feeling woman. These are, of course, floridly conventional modes of feminine behavior in the movies, and Constance is the archetypal repressed girl-with-glasses. But the film's emphasis on Constance's desperately vigilant attempt to restore Peck's sanity makes the film's sexual politics unusual. It is true that women are most often cast in the roles of either caregivers or vamps in 1940s films, but Constance is much more than a caregiver. She may get moony-eyed over Peck but she remains a professional doing her job, using her psychoanalytic acumen (with the help of an old psychoanalytical mentor) to free Peck from emotional and legal problems (she exonerates him of murder charges, after all) and also to decode the stratagems of the duplicitous (and quite frightening) Murchison. *Spellbound* is a gloriously silly romantic fantasy. Given the terrible costs of the pursuit of romantic love in most Hitchcock films, the achieved happiness of Constance and Peck is especially sweet.

Food serves as a sign of Constance's dissolving repression. In one early sequence shortly after Peck arrives at Green Manors, the rapidly progressing romantic couple take a stroll through mountainous vistas on their way to a picnic. Constance, sounding intoxicated with happiness, prattles on about the terrible harm done to humanity by romantic poets, as if we all fall in love to "Shakespearean sonnets." This outdoor walk between lovers is the locus classicus in Hitchcock of the early stages of romantic love. There are similar scenes in *Notorious* (1946) and *The Birds* (1963), but none as blissfully happy as the one in *Spellbound*, in which pragmatic words scurry in the opposite direction from the swooning romantic feelings being conveyed. Peck does not buy Constance's protestations. He asks her if she wants a ham or a liverwurst sandwich.

In a lyrical close-up in which she appears utterly rapt, Constance replies, exultantly, "liverwurst," sounding as if she were now basking in afterglow.

Confirming this sexual symbolism, in the next scene the huffy homosocial horde of psychiatrists all sitting together regard now-disheveled Constance with disdain. Queeny Dr. Fleurot plucks a rogue leaf from Constance's hair, all but announcing that she's been behaving like a shocking harlot. He acidly observes the trace of mustard on her chin and asks if she's eaten a ham sandwich. "Wrong as usual, Dr. Fleurot," she confidently reprimands him. "It was liverwurst!"

In the Production Code–dominated classic Hollywood, words and visual metaphors had an extra burden of suggesting what could not be explicitly represented. The liverwurst becomes a sign of Constance's newly remade romantic identity. If the previous scene signified sexual intercourse, the liverwurst, a spread, represents the supineness of lovers in sexual intercourse, spread out, in this case, on a flat field that studs them with leaves. The vaguely unseemly meatiness of the liverwurst suggests, as well, a grotesque concupiscence. The way Hitchcock makes use of the overrich connotation of liverwurst is like a statement of postcoital sexual disgust, both at the public exposure of sexual relations and at the postlapsarian associations of carnal excess with corrupt morality. The trace of mustard is like *The Human Stain* of Philip Roth's 2000 novel. In the novel, that stain is the trail of presidential semen on Monica Lewinsky's blue Gap dress, so human and so contested. The dried mustard signals the irremovable stain of sexual activity and sexual guilt, the "Yellow Letter," one could say. But Constance's bracingly unembarrassed response to florid Fleurot's insinuations suggests a modern-day Hester Prynne—Hester Prynne as sex and free love radical.

Spellbound also features a famous dream sequence designed by the great surrealist artist Salvador Dali. As Constance and her old mentor both decode Peck's dream, the Dali images represent the dream itself. (Hauntingly beautiful, this sequence is nevertheless much shorter than the filmmakers intended it to be, the studio having snipped it, much to Bergman's chagrin.) In one tableaux, a young barmaid (interpreted as Constance by Constance herself and her mentor) serves drinks to Peck within an atmosphere of homosocial bickering that represents the Murchison murder plot. The film's psychoanalytically feverish associations of Constance with this hootchy-kootchy libation bearer confirm that, at least in Peck's mind, Constance really *is* a whore. Constance may feel freed and sexually liberated, then, but Peck subliminally regards her as a provocateur, as damaged, lascivious goods. Even in an unabashedly romantic movie like *Spellbound*, Hitchcock still stings us with recognition of the impasses inevitably impeding intimacy. Vulnerable and feminized though Peck is in this film, the Ballantine character is still subconsciously misogynistic in that he views Constance as a carnal monster. The film leaves a residue of uncertainty on the presumably ardently romantic future of the couple.

Champagne, Chicken, Coffee, and Catharsis: *Notorious*

More than residual uncertainty marks the progress toward fulfilling romantic love in Hitchcock's great romantic thriller, *Notorious* (1946). Though the film ends on a seeming note of hopeful romance for American spy Devlin (Cary Grant) and the "notorious" Alicia Huberman (Ingrid Bergman), the majority of the film provides an unrelenting depiction of the sadistic potentialities of spoilt romance. Rather than whips and chains, food signals the increasingly sadomasochistic tensions between the characters. Like elements in a concoction from a futurist cookbook, the principle ingredients on *Notorious*'s menu—champagne, chicken, and coffee—cohere into a poisonous recipe for heterosexual enmity. These disparate ingredients suggest the untenability of achieving fulfilling romantic love in an increasingly inhuman world.

"Dev," as he's called, is an American spy who enlists Alicia, the daughter of a convicted Nazi war criminal, to work for the U.S. government on a job of routing out Nazis hiding in Rio de Janeiro, Brazil. Alicia's notoriety stems from her reputation for having slept around; having fallen in love with Dev, she begs him to believe "that I've changed, and I'll never change back." Dev refuses to tell her he loves her or to acknowledge explicitly that he believes she has, indeed, so changed. Alicia, wounded, prideful, and terribly infatuated with Dev, proceeds to taunt him with challenges that he doesn't love her, that, implicitly, he views her as a whore (*Notorious*'s depiction of Alicia's promiscuity is as explicit as classic Hollywood gets); Dev stays stoically clenched and steadfastly unresponsive.

In a famous scene, Alicia and Dev kiss for a long time while he answers a phone call from a government representative, who is asking him to come to headquarters and learn what assignment Alicia will be given. In between Dev's curt responses to the official he speaks to, Dev and Alicia kiss. The effect, at least to my mind, is not so much erotic as it is unsettling. Alicia's barely suppressed desperation and Dev's terror at being engulfed by Alicia's love permeate the scene equally. The overbearing intimacy with which Hitchcock's camera stays fixed on the anxious lovers produces an effect that is almost suffocating. As they kiss, Alicia seems eager to devour the unwilling meal of Dev, engorged with desire to consume her bad object-choice. The absence of food in this simulation of eating only reinforces the intense loneliness of both characters—the impossibility of ingesting and possessing the desired object.[2] (It would be many years before Hannibal Lecter made eating people a blasé phenomenon.)

Once at headquarters, Dev is informed—by another menacing homosocial horde, from which he is pointedly excluded—that Alicia's assignment will be to spy on rogue Nazi Alex Sebastian (Claude Rains): she is to have an affair with Alex in order to get secrets about his Nazi stronghold in Brazil. "I don't think she'll do it!" Dev protests. The government men, bemused by Dev's response, inform Dev that, from what they know of notorious Alicia, she's precisely the kind of woman who *will* do it. Dev leaves, leaving behind the bottle of champagne he had bought for his imminent lovely romantic evening with Alicia.

Notorious is, like Choderlos De Laclos's *Les Liasions Dangereuses,* an unflinching exploration of the cruelties lovers perpetrate on one another. Like the doomed love of classical tragedy, the love between Dev and Alicia seems to make their lives more hateful, more poisonous, before their extraordinarily cathartic reconciliation at the end. This movie asks what the charcter Charles Ryder asks in *Brideshead Revisited*: "Why does being in love make me hate the world? It's supposed to have the opposite effect."

Though Dev bitterly opposes the plan to use Alicia as Mata Hari, he just as adamantly refuses to let Alicia in on his secret love for her. He lets *her* decide what she wants to do. And because she perceives his grim silence on the matter as a tacit collusion with the government officials' view of her as a sexual monster, Alicia accepts the job to get back at Dev—to act the whore because she believes he sees her *as* a whore.

These contrapuntal motivations manifest themselves in the next scene, when Dev returns to the hotel, having to reveal her assignment to Alicia, as she valiantly prepares a chicken in the little hotel-room kitchen. In their previous scene, before Dev left for headquarters, the subject of the chicken Alicia would make them for dinner was suggestive of rapturous carnal delight between them. Noticing a lack of cutlery, Dev asks, "What will we eat the chicken with?" Intoxicated with love, much like *Spellbound*'s Constance, Alicia gaily responds, "We'll eat it with our fingers." Eating without utensils, unabashed tactile eating, ripping apart carnal flesh with carnal avidity, sharing food like animals in the wild, Alicia and Dev will be a new Eve and Adam, before sexual knowledge made life bad. But now, as Alicia strains to make the chicken, food's untrustworthy mysteriousness or absence signifies the chasm between Alicia and Dev: As Alicia struggles to cut up the chicken, she worries, "I hope it isn't done too much." Her inability to discern the chicken's doneness echoes her inability to gauge the fluctuating relationship Dev has with her. And the absent champagne bottle, prefiguring the deadly wine bottles filled with covertly acquired uranium ore in Alex Sebastian's wine cellar, complexly represents both the phantasmatic presence of Dev's endangered, contested phallic power and the evanescent bubbly happiness of their love, now pointedly absent, forgotten and left somewhere else. The champagne bottle also metonymically represents the generally addictive personality of Alicia, who takes to the bottle just as she takes to sundry sexual partners. It is little wonder that by the end of their terrible, hurtful conversation on the balcony, in which neither is able to make the right decision toward ensuring their romantic happiness, the controversial chicken remains hopelessly uneaten, having grown, like their passion, ugly and cold. The scene ends with Dev absently hunting around for that lost champagne bottle.

Married, finally, to Alex Sebastian, on whom she spies, Alicia takes Dev, in another famous sequence set during a luxurious party at Alex's estate, down to the wine cellar, where the uranium ore wine bottles are kept. It is interesting that Cary Grant's Dev crouches beneath the bottles, looking up at them, but not noticing one bottle in particular, which looks especially large as it looms above him, inexorably moving forward till it crashes to the floor, spilling shiny black dust. If these bottles are obvious phallic symbols, Dev's prostrate position beneath them suggests that he is in a humbled, subservient position of devotion to a phallic power with which he struggles—and to the phallic order of male dominion before which he kneels. The wine bottle also encapsulates the spirits of romantic love. The shattering of the wine bottle here represents the similar rupturing of Dev and Alicia's romantic bond—but its artificial content, its unnatural contents of uranium ore rather than wine, suggests that heretofore their romantic love has been filled with deadly, illusory contents. Now that these illusions have been violently shattered, the pair will have to reinvent the terms of a new relationship, find new bottles of wine filled with pleasure, not poison.

Alex and his mother, the formidably icy, evil Mrs. Sebastian (Leopoldine Konstantin), discover that Alicia is a spy and decide to kill her—but quietly, almost gently. They poison her, slipping noxious powder into her coffee. There's a deeply chilling scene in which they slip up, allowing Alicia to see their consternation when someone else (a kindly old Nazi doctor) reaches for her coffee cup. She rises as if to flee, but is blinded by nausea and pain. She sees the shadowy, swirling images of Alex and his mother, her murderers, looming above her, but is powerless to resist them. Just as Dev seemed in danger of being consumed by Alicia in the phone-kiss scene, now Alicia seems in danger of being consumed by Alex and his mother, absorbed into their shadowy evil. They have transmitted their evil to Alicia through the poisoned coffee, turned themselves into the liquid essence of evil force-fed to Alicia.

If Alicia is, as Tania Modleski writes, "the woman who was known too much,"[3] what she ingests and does not ingest is significant. And if Alicia is a whore redeemed through love by the end of the film, in the strictly heteronormative design of the film, food and her consumption of it reflect these qualities. She drinks to avoid pain, whereas it is drink that *symbolizes* her pain, as well as the promiscuous, desecrate-the-bodily-temple lifestyle that ostensibly torments her and stalls her romance with Dev. Drink stands-in for sexual fluids, the rampant exchanges of which brand Alicia as notorious. (I wish to point out that the film's depiction of Alicia, despite this resolutely misogynistic schema, is everywhere sympathetic and responsive to her.) She is not allowed to drink the champagne of mutually loving ardor with Dev, only the condemnatory coffee of the Sebastians' killing plans. Because of Dev's cowardly cruelty toward her, Alicia has imbibed death, not love, headed for Thanatos, not Eros. When Dev rescues her, he rescues himself, as well—from the hell of his own solipsistic terror at embracing love. There are few moments in cinema as piercingly exquisite as Dev's revelation to Alicia, on her death-bed, that he loves her. "Oh, you love me!" she responds. Like Eurydice finally in Orpheus's arms, Alicia submits to being saved even as she saves her beloved from nihilistic oblivion. Continuing the theme of emotional eating and succor, Alicia makes Dev repeat that he loves her. "It gives me strength," she says, as if feeding on his love, drinking it greedily the way a vampire drinks blood.

Notorious suggests that the most satisfying gustatory experience involves emotional rather than literal food. In fact, the eating of literal food comes to seem treacherous, even unnatural: far better to gorge on desire. This is truly a film in which, in the end, lovers live on love.

Lachrymose Lobster, Bruised Brandy: *Rear Window*

It seems appropriate to follow up two Ingrid Bergman romances with two featuring Grace Kelly: *Rear Window* (1954) and *To Catch a Thief* (1955). Grace Kelly is at her sleekest and most elegant as Lisa Freemont, the glamour-plate society girl who loves Jeff, the wheelchair-bound, leg-in-a-cast peeping tom-photographer-protagonist of *Rear Window*, one of Hitchcock's coldest and most popular films. Waking sleeping Jeff (James Stewart), Lisa enters like a wide-screen dream of heavenly sex. In looming, overwhelming close-up, we see her face before she plants a (uncharacteristic for Hitchcock) slow-motion kiss on Jeff's bemused mouth. In so extravagant a close-up, Lisa seems more sphinx than siren; the theme of the devoured male occurs again here, as Jeff (and we) disappear in the immensity of Lisa's shocking close-up gaze.

Lisa and Jeff are one of Hitchcock's most tortured couples, despite their randy, delightfully urbane banter. Like Dev and Alicia, they play sadomasochistic games, a pattern that culminates in Jeff's witnessing of Lisa's mortal danger in the apartment of the wife-murderer he's been spying on. The fellow residents of Jeff's New York City apartment complex—the initially amatory and then alienated young couple, the lonely musician, the lonely single woman ("Miss Lonelyhearts"), the blond good-time-girl contortionist who entertains hordes of male visitors, the childless couple on the fire escape so devastated by the loss of their pooch, the termagant busybody painting lady—form a funny and frightening variety show, nightmarish fantasies of what sadistic Jeff and pouty Lisa might become. Certainly the murdering Thorwald (Raymond Burr) and his unfortunate, unhappy, harpy wife grimly suggest married Jeff and Lisa in later years.

The chief source of explicit tension between Jeff and Lisa is the difference in their lifestyles. Jeff claims that his ragtag, hectic, living-at-wit's-end life as a gritty, globe-trotting photographer fatally clashes, in terms of long-term possibilities, with Lisa's fabulously fashionable East Side style. Again, very much like Dev and Alicia, Jeff and Lisa are an incompatible couple: Jeff, like Dev, aloof, emotionally ungiving, and scared; Lisa, like Alicia, desperate for a "little birdcall from her dream man." Putting up with the indifference of the men they helplessly love makes the women just as masochistic as their men are sadistic.

Food serves as a sign of Lisa's affluence, which Jeff both appreciates and rebukes, and of the curdled romance between them. After threatening to devour him through close-up, Lisa announces that she has brought the high-fashion restaurant "21" to Jeff. Waiting outside the apartment is a waiter from 21, armed with various pans of hyperelegant food. Jeff certainly does not hesitate to guzzle the fine wine Lisa has brought, all but wresting it from her grasp. This 21 meal is Lisa on a plate, fashionable fabulousness in food form. Once the lobster has been artfully arrayed on plates before them, Lisa, trying to keep the banter smooth, says that the meal, at least, produces no complaints. With deeply weary petulance, Jeff says, "Lisa . . . it's perfect." Lisa grimaces.

The shot of the ostensibly decadent lobster sums up all the simmering animosities and tensions of the scene. What should be—like the idealized love of Jeff and Lisa—a sumptuous feast looks instead, in close-up, like the jaundice-yellow remains of a botched autopsy. This lobster is much more fetid than it is frolicsome—you shudder at eating it, just as Jeff shudders at marrying Lisa.

Lisa learns that if she's to develop a relationship with Jeff, she must develop an appetite for murder. She becomes—or forces herself to become—convinced that Thorwald really *did* kill his wife. When Jeff's wryly unconvinced police detective friend comes over, to tell murder-hounds Jeff and Lisa that Thorwald couldn't possibly have killed his wife (which, of course, he *has*), Lisa presents him with a brandy snifter in which she swirls warmed-up brandy. As they all discourse on murder while sipping warm brandy, these three suggest the decadent appeal of 1950s affluence. Their shared brandy over murder talk makes them seem like swanky ghouls, sophisticates mulling over murder as they savor their luxuriant pleasures. But the undertow of sad irony here has its source in what has enabled the newly fortified bond between Lisa and Jeff: Lisa's self-willed conversion into an aficionado of murder. Only by becoming as obsessed with the murder as Jeff does Lisa find a way to become a part of his life. What should be a sign of the couple's cultured tastefulness—drinking brandy properly—becomes, instead, a symbol of their muddled morality. Their seeming good taste only thinly masks their morbid relish for the suffering of others.

Whole Chicken, Cut Up: *To Catch a Thief*

The 1955 *To Catch a Thief* is not nearly as complex or ingenious a film as *Rear Window*. Still, it's a more interesting film than it's generally given credit for—certainly a much darker one. Almost as if resuming a conversation briefly paused, Grace Kelly again plays an uptight woman of (new money) privilege who has surprisingly brazen designs on a former cat burglar accused of a spree of crimes (Cary Grant). Kelly's rich girl here has more confidence than Lisa Freemont. Taking Cary Grant on a terrifyingly breakneck-speed ride along the Riviera (strangely enough, the same conditions under which the later Princess Grace Kelly of Monaco died), Kelly is cool and contained; it is Grant who does the clenched freaking out. After this maniacal journey, the two stop off to have a picnic. Rummaging through and then offering contents from the picnic basket, holding out a chicken, Kelly matter-of-factly asks, "Would you like a leg or a breast?" Beyond the obvious sexual double entendre, this comment signals to us Kelly's casual comfort with her own body and sexuality—she doesn't care where Grant touches her, as long as he *does.*

Grant, for his part, doesn't appear particularly comfortable with Kelly's crisp display of coolly unself-conscious sexuality. Given his terror at her driving and his blank reaction to her lascivious offer of "food," Grant suggests a man who is either wearied of heterosexual presumption or a chauvinistic narcissist offended by this spectacle of 1950s girl-power. If the poultry leg or breast signify openly offered and available choice sexual offerings on Kelly's part, then it is disturbing that she views herself as components—views herself as the spectacle of woman in misogynistic culture, spatially regulated and distributed and presented. In this manner, she resembles the futuristic cow of one of the Douglas Adams's *Hitchhiker's Guide to the Galaxy* books, encouraging diners to sample her tenderest flesh. Kelly offers herself, then, *as* merely a leg or a breast, a synecdochic component of the phantasmatic female body.

The Loud Flamboyance of the Lambs: *Strangers on a Train*

An analysis of Hitchcock's 1951 thriller *Strangers on a Train* allows us to consider this director's use of food as metaphorical of homoerotic threat and queer issues. The first scenes between Guy Haines (Farley Granger), a tennis player trying to escape his shrewish first wife so that he can marry a senator's daughter, and Bruno Anthony (Robert Walker), a wealthy psychopath, comprise a banquet of fraught queer food issues. These early scenes are among the finest in the film, carefully textured and quietly terrifying. I will compare the American and the British versions of the film. The British version runs two minutes longer, and it has a different ending and "franker dialogue," as Leonard Maltin puts it in his handy *Movie and Video Guide,* in these opening scenes. This franker dialogue intensifies the gathering force of the film's homosexual themes, embodied by the loud flamboyance of the droll, murderous Bruno, played so hypnotically by Walker. Rightly sensing queer energies, the American censors cut out odd little moments between Guy and Bruno in their first scene; fascinatingly, tropes of food and eating dominate these cut moments.

Strangers on a Train, adapted from lesbian mystery writer Patricia Highsmith's novel, demonstrates the elasticity of Hitchcock's culinary symbology. Here, food mirrors and mimes homoerotic threat. Continuing the theme of the gulfs between characters represented by food, the items in the lunch shared by Guy and Bruno reflect their imminently disastrous relationship, predicated on their inability to communicate clearly or coherently, and, of course, on Bruno's insanity, and Guy's strange complicity in it.

As is well known, Bruno has a plan for the perfect murder: "You do my murder and I do yours: criss-cross!" Bruno will kill Guy's admittedly dislikable wife on the fairgrounds; he will then expect Guy to kill Bruno's father, whom he detests. As their conversation on the train comes to an end, Bruno believes that Guy has agreed to collaborate with him on his murder scheme. "We *do* speak the same language, don't we, Guy!" exclaims Bruno. Giving him the tolerant-of-crazy-people look that belies his odd indulgence of Bruno's behavior, the de-training Guy responds, "Sure, Bruno, we speak the same language." The gears of fate now lock into place; Guy has been hopelessly integrated into Bruno's psychotic world.

Speaking the same language becomes a shockingly clear metaphor for homosexual exchange, which is established right from the beginning of the film. We see shots of the two men's respective shoe-clad feet as they approach the train: Guy's sensible, dark, rather nondescript shoes, Bruno's flashy, two-toned shoes, a demented yin-and-yang black and white. Interestingly, these shoes greet each other before the men do. Pointedly, Guy's shoe brushes against Bruno's, which instigates their discussion. Given Guy's presumably horrified reaction to Bruno's relentless pursuit—of sorts—of him, the fact that it is Guy's shoe that brushes past Bruno's is crucial. They could be two men cruising each other in a restroom, playing the stall-invading, foot-tapping, shoe-scraping "tea-room" game.

Bruno orders "doubles" of scotch and water for himself and Guy. Guy initially says, "You'll have to drink both yourself," but when they arrive he helps himself to one, despite his protestations. An Alice in this queer wonderland, Guy drinks the drink Bruno has ordered for him; he imbibes Bruno's threatening but strangely mesmerizing homoerotic evil. Bruno then encourages Guy to have lunch with him in his "compartment." Having already begun drinking with Bruno, Guy might be expected to acquiesce to lunch. But he anxiously says no, asking the (rather overwhelmed waiter) if the dining car has a free table. Informed that there will be a twenty-minute wait, Guy looks worried. "There now, you see, you'll have to have lunch with me!" beams Bruno. In one of the minute but loaded moments cut from the American version, Bruno then encourages Guy to order lunch. We hear the ingredients of the lunch each man orders. Why would the American censors have cut out details as innocuous as what each man would order for lunch?

Bruno orders lamb, French fries, and chocolate ice cream. After he has ordered he urges Guy to order, as if encouraging him to glut himself on a Roman-orgy banquet-style repast. Guy orders a hamburger and coffee—a sensible, sturdy, "manly" meal, especially in comparison to Bruno's more lavish, decadent one. After their meal is over, their murderous compact established (unwittingly on Guy's part), Bruno complains that his lamb was "overdone."

Bruno's lamb signifies a European aesthetic sensibility, a precise, acculturated, finical "taste." Guy's all-American hamburger is plebian and standard—nothing sexually suspect informs the choice. That is precisely the point. Guy's vacillating interest in Bruno, his simultaneous indulgence in Bruno's personality ("I don't think you know what you want") and discomfited efforts to wrest himself free of it, altogether convey a sense of a man attempting to overmaster his willingness to be seduced by queer charms. Psychotic murd- erousness becomes a metaphor for Bruno's homosexuality, just as his tele- graphed homosexuality reinforces the sense that he is insane. Guy's frightened interest in Bruno's queer insanity visibly agitates him. His reluctant order of a regular guy's meal—hamburger—defends against any inclusion in Bruno's more polished, refined, decadent order. Guy certainly never says, "I'll have what he's having." Bruno's rich, luxuriant dessert seems especially so in the pointed absence of any in Guy's order. The longer British version also empha- sizes the inordinately taxed nature of the waiter's servitude. Carrying a large tray on his head, the overburdened waiter must repeatedly stop, turn around, answer questions, make his way back to the kitchen, and be yanked back to answer Bruno's incessant demanding questions. It is significant that the wealthy Bruno has no qualms about asking the waiter numerous questions, whereas the tennis pro but social climber Guy almost deferentially beams in appreciation when he places his order. It's not often that one considers race in the alabaster-white Hitchcock world, but it is significant, too, that the waiter is a man of color. In this feverish realm of queer intrigue and terrified complicity in it, the lower-class waiter of color caters to anxious white manhood, throw- ing meat into the ring of decadent sexual spectacle. Very subtly, the waiter's color and his stark separation from the entire spectacle of white privilege and gay panic reinforces the idea of homosexuality as a privileged white man's disease, just as Bruno's lunch does.

Murder Most Gustatory

Food functions as an important trope in innumerable American Hitchcock films. The uncannily glowing milk in *Suspicion* (1941), seeming evidence of ne'er-do-well husband Cary Grant's murderous guilt; the murder of a young man around which an excruciating dinner party literally swarms (*Rope*, 1948); the 1953 *Dial M for Murder*'s booze-laden discussions of murder plots; food as a symbol of oafish and arrogant ugly Americanness in *The Man Who Knew Too Much* (1956), especially in the scene in which Jimmy Stewart refuses to eat food "Arab" style while touring Morocco with his family;[4] dubious protagonist Scotty Ferguson seeing, for the first time, the fake Madeline and eating dinner with her all-too-human impersonator Judy Barton at Ernie's restaurant in *Vertigo* (1958), Hitchcock's masterpiece;[5] most plangently, the business with baking that symbolizes a mother-daughter rift in *Marnie* (1964): these scenes, images, and motifs all reinforce the freighted, gendered significance of food intake in Hitchcock's oeuvre. No film more unpleasantly confirms Hitchcock's own association of food with anxieties about the body and sexuality than his second-to-last, the 1972 *Frenzy*, made in his native England.[6] In this film, women are hideously murdered on camera, strangled by a serial killer who dumps their bodies into fruit bins. One of the detectives on the case is served indescribably grotesque and inedible meals by his wife. The relay in the film between women as food and women serving inedible meals indicates that food has become a trope of sadomasochistic exchange, as punishment, as suffering, as revenge, as atrophied connection. Frenzy most graphically highlights Hitchcock's use of food as a trope of the wounded and horrifyingly vulnerable body.[7] In his penultimate film, as in many of the earlier movies, eating symbolizes the wrenching struggles for gendered power that endow the films with a considerable amount of their enduring resonance.

Notes

1. Interestingly, Hitchcock biographer Donald Spoto quotes Hitchcock, "in a rare moment of self-disclosure," speaking about "his nearly lifelong celibate state, and of the psychology of food and sex that he did, after all, realize: 'As they get on, after five or six years, in most married couples, "that old feeling" begins to dissipate. Food oftentimes takes the place of sex in a relationship.' And with that he folded his hands across his enormous belly." See Spoto, *The Dark Side of Genius: The Life of Alfred Hitchcock* (Boston: Little, Brown, 1983), 519–20. In his book, Spoto notes several instances of the food-sex relationship in Hitchcock's work.

2. In a Freudian analysis, this obsession with ingesting the desired other squarely plants the lovers at an infantile oral stage, where "sexual activity has not yet been separated from the ingestion of food. . . . The *object* of both activities are the same: the sexual *aim* consists in the incorporation of the object"; this first sexual, oral phase "might be called" one of "cannibalistic pregenital sexual organization." See Sigmund Freud, *Three Essays on the Theory of Sexuality*, trans. James Strachey (New York: Basic, 1975), 64. (This work initially appeared in 1905; Freud tinkered with it repeatedly, and his last revised edition emerged in 1925 and has subsequently been regularly reprinted). But to avoid the pathologizing impulses in Freud and focus instead on his radical deconstruction of the "naturalness" of heterosexual eros, a point later only intensified by Lacan, Freud also discusses the enormous potential for disgust in oral exchanges between men and women, noting that the same young man who will passionately kiss a "pretty girl" will be repulsed by the thought of using her toothbrush. "The sexual instinct in its strength enjoys overriding this disgust" (*Three Essays*, 17–18). Notable in the Freudian context, then, is Dev's desire to break free from Alicia's ravenous and consuming kisses, which he successfully does: her sexual instinct's strength fails to overcome his apparent, if occluded, disgust.

3. Tania Modleski, *The Women Who Knew Too Much: Hitchcock and Feminist Theory* (New York: Routledge, 1988).

4. As Richard Allen points out, in his 1950s films, such as *Rear Window* and *The Man Who Knew Too Much*, it "is almost as if Hitchcock, in moving to America at the end of the 1930s, at once enacts and anticipates the 'feminization' of British culture in the postwar period, that involved, at once, an increased role for middle-class women in the public sphere and the embrace of American popular culture." See Allen, "Hitchcock, or the Pleasures of Metaskepticism," in *Alfred Hitchcock: Centenary Essays*, ed. Richard Allen and S. Ishii Gonzales (London: BFI, 1999), 229. If these 1950s films confront the dubious, anxious, defensive male protagonist with a newly independent transatlantic form of womanhood, food increasingly figures as a gendered battleground. Notice in *Man* the way Doris Day's wife character easily gets the hang of Middle Eastern dining dictates and attempts to tutor husband Jimmy Stewart, unsuccessfully, in her newfound skills.

5. "It is a striking feature of dining out that the restaurant, as an institution, offers all its patrons a sheltered anonymity . . . . This aspect of dining out, which invites the enunciation and performance of private fantasies, is a feature of the restaurant's appeal, which dates from its modern origins." See Joanne Finkelstein, "Dining Out: The Hyperreality of Appetite," in *Eating Culture*, ed. Ron Scapp and Brian Seitz (Albany: State University of New York Press, 1998), 205. What is so fascinating about Ernie's as a realm of private fantasy for Scotty is that, in introducing him to "Madeline" there, the villainous husband Gavin Elster displays Woman to the hero as if she were a cut of beef, like the steaks Scotty and Judy eat.

6. For an excellent discussion of food in *Frenzy*, see Donald Spoto's *The Art of Alfred Hitchcock: Fifty Years of His Motion Pictures* (New York: Doubleday Dolphin Books, 1976), 434–45. Spoto has revised this study numerous times, but I prefer his first edition. Overall, Hitchcock's finest critic remains Robin Wood, who has written numerous editions of his classic study *Hitchcock's Films*.

7. See Tania Modleski's essay on *Frenzy* in her powerful *The Women Who Knew Too Much*, especially pages 101–14, for a discussion of the association of women with defilement and filth in Hitchcock's work. I would argue that in Hitchcock, such associations are made to expose their general circulation in patriarchal culture. Food in Hitchcock becomes an appropriate trope for misogynistic men "gagging" on the indigestible meal of the powerful woman. Though I find myself often disagreeing with her, Modleski provides the sharpest and most powerful critique of Hitchcock's depiction of women in films like *Rebecca*, *Notorious*, *Vertigo*, and *Frenzy*.

22

What about the Popcorn? Food and the Film-Watching Experience

JAMES LYONS

The opening sequence of Wes Craven's horror film *Scream* (1996) depicts the terrorizing of teenage girl Casey (Drew Barrymore) by an unknown telephone caller. Alone in her family's house at night, Casey receives her threatening phone call as she prepares for an evening of watching horror videos. Presaging the onslaught of arch references and postmodern reflexivity in the rest of the film, *Scream* has its protagonist and her menacer briefly discuss the mores of film watching—in particular the question of combining home viewing with popcorn consumption. As Casey's pan of Jiffy Pop popcorn heats on the stove, the caller growls in her ear that "*I* only eat popcorn in the movies." Within the context of the film, Casey's transgressive act of domestic consumption serves as but one of a number of wrong choices that leads to her swift and bloody demise. Yet it is worth pausing to consider the wider implications of the sequence, and its enunciation of conventions pertaining to the intersection of food-eating and film-watching practices. However parodic and overblown the sequence might be, it nevertheless attests to the prevalence of the notion that food consumption is allied closely to the experience of film watching, and to the ways in which this intersection of practices is understood to be spatially embedded—mappable (and regulable) across a range of different sites.

I propose to examine the intersection of food and film-watching practices not as they have been depicted within particular motion pictures, but rather with reference to actual sites of film exhibition in the United Kingdom. One of the most exciting developments within cinema studies in recent years has been the growth of interest in the study of film exhibition.[1] Of particular interest here is the way in which scholars working on exhibition practices have sought to understand how specific audiences have experienced moviegoing at particular historical moments and in varied social contexts.[2] Such work has served to question a number of the assumptions inherent in many psychoanalytic accounts of spectatorship, which constructed largely ahistorical spectators.[3] The impact of cultural studies' ethnographic methodologies upon cinema studies has also helped to open up a space for considering the "relationship between movie-going and other social practices," an understanding predicated upon the notion that audiences as social subjects and cinemas as cultural institutions are imbricated in and mediated by a range of other competing and complementary spaces, practices, and discourses.[4]

This chapter wishes to make a contribution to this growing body of literature seeking to examine what Ina Rae Hark calls "the meaning of the moviegoing experience."[5] It considers the relationship between moviegoing and food consumption practices in the hope of developing a more sophisticated and nuanced account of "what audiences do with their experience of cinema."[6] As Kevin Corbett points out, this involves approaching "movie-watching as a social act," embedded within the patterns of activities and meaning-making experiences of peoples' everyday lives.[7] The consuming of food is one of the key ways in which audiences embellish and enhance the experience of film watching, and works to construct the meanings of moviegoing as a social practice. Yet scant attention has been paid by cinema studies to the myriad issues pertaining to the opportunities for food consumption that have long been an integral component of theatrical exhibition practices in the United States and abroad. Writers who have noted the role played by the technologies of cinematic food consumption, such as the theater concession stand, have tended to assign them a very minor role within larger narratives concerned primarily with other historical aspects of film exhibition.[8] However, it is clear that exhibitors themselves have long considered the opportunities for the selling of foodstuffs with high regard, and with good reason, since they have provided an essential additional source of profit. For example, the necessity for film exhibitors to share box-office revenues with distributors, with up to 90 percent of the box-office receipts sometimes going to distributors in the first weeks of a film's theatrical release, has placed the onus on theaters to find alternative sources of income, of which concessions are by far the most significant in terms of revenue.[9] Moreover, with current market research indicating that "89 percent of moviegoers head for the concession stand," food would appear to be an integral element of a large fraction of the audiences' visit to the cinema.[10]

In considering the implications of this high percentage of moviegoers' purchase and ingestion of foodstuffs, I take a cue from recent work undertaken into social practices of consumption within sociology and cultural studies. Within these fields the term *consumption* has been used not simply to denote the physical acts of eating and drinking, but has been appropriated from its origin with political economy and deployed in an endeavor to understand how people use a whole range of consumer goods and commodities, such as clothes, music, and television programs.[11] In this sense, consumption is seen as instrumental in the production of meaning, as individuals and groups use consumer goods and commodities "in the development and articulation of subjectivity."[12] As Stuart Hall points out, people "play the game of using things to signify who they are. . . . [Everybody] knows that today's 'goods' double up as social signs and produce meanings as well as energy."[13] One area that has met with extensive consideration within the writing on consumption is food. Already the subject of considerable scrutiny within anthropological and historical literature, contemporary studies of the role of food practices have examined their impact on the social production of meaning in relation to areas as diverse as "taste, status, class, gender identities, domestic power relations, tradition, migration, the civilizing process, new technologies, and commercial exploitation."[14] Crucial to many of these areas is a notion of place; as Deborah Lupton notes, practices and "discourses on food [are] articulated in a number of diverse sites."[15] Indeed, as David Bell and Gill Valentine argue in *Consuming Geographies*, "we are where we eat," explaining that "in a world in which self-identity and place identity are woven through webs of consumption, what we eat (and where, and why) signals, as the aphorism says, who we are."[16] This chapter takes up Bell and Valentine's suggestion in order to investigate the precise range of behaviors, practices, and institutional regimes in play if *where* we eat is considered specifically in relation to the activity of film watching.

As stated, my approach in this chapter is to consider the intersection of food-eating and film-watching practices as they exist within cinema exhibition sites. Clearly, this intersection of practices also exists in other places, most obviously in the home. As the opening sequence from *Scream* makes clear, the domestic environment is a convenient, and arguably by far the most frequent space for combining eating and film watching. Sitting down at home to watch a film on broadcast/pay television or on videotape/DVD, often with foodstuffs from the nearby kitchen or bought in from video stores, convenience stores, or fast-food restaurants is a recognizable element of domestic practice.[17] Indeed, it is one that manufacturers such as Jiffy Pop popcorn, or retailers such as Blockbuster Video have been eager to support and profit from, attempting unequivocally to replicate many of the foodstuffs currently available in cinema exhibition sites for domestic consumption. Much useful research could be undertaken into the many underexamined aspects of these domestic consumption practices and their attendant servicing industries.[18] Yet by restricting the scope of this chapter to a consideration of food consumption within the context of cinema exhibition sites, I am seeking to make a contribution to the growing body of literature concerned with issues of cultural power, meaning production, and audience behavior as they are patterned and articulated within public spaces—what Joanne Finkelstein, in her sociological study of the consumption of foodstuffs in the public domain, titled *Dining Out,* refers to as "the pursuit of pleasure in public."[19] As historians of urban space have shown, there is a symbiotic relationship between the emergence of cinema and the broader culture of modernity, whereby the legitimacy of the notion of pursuing pleasure in public was institutionalized, valorized for commercial profit, and also subject to a range of regulatory discourses and practices.[20] Film scholars have begun to generate fascinating accounts of how the activity of moviegoing, as the public pursuit of pleasure, has functioned at particular historical moments. For example, Jackie Stacy, in her influential study into the cinemagoing practices of female spectators in Britain during the 1940s and 1950s, demonstrates the significance of cinemagoing in terms of its ability to offer "escapist pleasures" in wartime and postwar Britain. Moreover, as Stacy points out, "what emerges from these repeated accounts of the pleasures of cinemagoing practices generally is the importance of moving beyond the pleasures of the text to include the pleasures of the ritualised event. . . . [and the] material pleasure of the cinema itself." The moviegoers Stacy interviewed stressed repeatedly the public nature of those pleasures—crowds of people queuing to get into the cinema, helping to engender the ephemeral but tangible "atmosphere" of the movie theater, and the "'shared intimacy' and 'heightened enjoyment' of collective consumption" in public.[21]

It could reasonably be argued that part of the pleasure of reading Stacy's own account lies in its ability to transport the reader back to the heyday of theatrical exhibition, to a period when cinemagoing was a preeminent form of leisure activity. The 1940s represents a moment before the long decline of movie audiences, a period when the public pursuit of moviegoing pleasure and its ritualized events, and the material gratifications of the cinema had an intensity and luminance seemingly far in excess of those offered by our own multiplex era's ethos of utilitarian design.[22] Yet the few accounts that have sought to consider the pleasures of contemporary moviegoing continue to verify the importance of "the pursuit of pleasure in public," albeit under quite different sociocultural circumstances. Martin Barker and Kate Brooks's research into the teenage audience of *Judge Dredd* (1995) examines the pleasures of cinemagoing for young people in the city of Bristol, England. In their conversations with this cohort of film viewers, what is clear is that the activities of cinemagoing and domestic video watching were consistently differentiated in terms of the range of meanings ascribed to their pursuance.[23] Video watching was most often connected to "having a laugh," which means "having an intensely group relationship in group-controlled space."[24] In contrast, cinemagoing was associated with being involved in the "mass participation" of an "event" which is frequently described as "special." Barker and Brooks stress the fact that for many of their interviewees, "being in the cinema is precisely important because it is a mass activity," and one that starts not with film watching itself, but rather is "an 'event' that begins in the foyer."[25]

Like Barker and Brooks, I, too, turn my attention to the cinematic experience as it begins in the foyer. In the next section I offer an overview of the history of food provision in cinema exhibition venues, drawing a comparative sketch of developments and practices in the United States and the United Kingdom, highlighting significant differences as well as key moments of influence and interaction between the two countries. This section also demonstrates the importance of issues such as taste, class, and questions of distinction to any understanding of the history of cinematic food consumption. I end the section with a consideration of the profound impact of the multiplex, which has reshaped the landscape of U.K. film exhibition over the last fifteen years and transformed the food concessions industry. As a means of access to the issues raised by food consumption and its relationship to moviegoing, the subsequent section offers a brief case study of food and film-watching practices as discernible through the opportunities for, and activities of, audiences in the city of Nottingham, England. What this case study suggests is that any consideration of the role of food consumption in enhancing and embellishing the moviegoing experience needs to pay close attention to how such activities are shaped by what Barker and Brooks term the "social geographies of cinema" and to the ways in which exhibition venues can be crucial to the 'maps of meaning' with which people make sense of their local environments.[26] This is made clear by the ways in which audience members negotiate with the range of opportunities for food consumption and moviegoing available in the city.

A Brief History of Food and Film Watching

I'm not putting people down . . . but not everybody has aesthetic taste. People in this city were still eating popcorn when people in other places were having coffee in street-front bistros.[27]

— Janice Williamson, "Notes from Storyville North"

In *Shared Pleasures: A History of Movie Presentation in the United States*, Douglas Gomery points out that it was the Great Depression that first compelled American movie exhibitors to start selling foodstuffs in their premises. As he notes, "moviegoing in the United States had always been accompanied by snack treats," but goods such as candy, popcorn, and soda would be purchased in nearby shops prior or subsequent to the show. Gomery states that during the 1920s, as theater owners sought to generate a "higher-class" tone for their new movie palaces, they refused to sell food, a practice that "had long been associated with carnivals, burlesque shows, and cheaper-class entertainment." However, the economic desperation brought by the Great Depression forced exhibitors to seek additional sources of income, and "throughout the 1930s concession stands opened in nearly every movie theater in the United States."[28] What is clear from this account is that right from inception, the controlling and regulating of food consumption was central to procedures employed by exhibitors in order to shape the meaning of moviegoing, organized around notions of taste and class, and demonstrating a keen awareness of food consumption as a thoroughly symbolic practice.

While a detailed historical survey of the place of foodstuffs within U.K. film exhibition at this time is yet to be written, theater programs from the period provide an interesting counterpoint to Gomery's account of U.S. practices. For example, a 1913 program for the New Gallery Kinema (1913–1952) in London's Regent Square, produced to accompany the screening of *Les Miserables*, boasted of the "first genuine imported lager beers on draught here" and informed patrons of "afternoon teas sold in the various tea rooms at popular prices" while "customers can also be served with light refreshments in the auditorium during the performance."[29] In addition, the program directed customers toward the New Gallery Brasserie and Grill Room, "opened by the proprietors of the Kinema [and which would] specially appeal to all our patrons."[30] In contrast to Gomery's account, what is evident here is the deployment of "sophisticated" foodstuffs in "genteel" surroundings used in order to generate a higher-class tone, and seeking to draw upon associations with continental Europe and the legitimate theater.[31] Indeed, the screening of films within London's legitimate theater venues brought moviegoers in contact with the extensive refreshment opportunities available in those locales. For example, a program advertising a film screening at the West End Theater in 1913 included a full-page photograph of the foyer and the Balcony Tea Lounge, and highlighted the availability of "special sandwiches; iced coffee; ginger beer [and] vanilla, strawberry and coffee ices."[32] This practice continued into the 1920s, with a program for the screening of Douglas Fairbanks's *The Thief of Baghdad* at the Theater Royal, Drury Lane in 1924 directing its patrons toward the "Refreshment Saloons" for "Soda Fountain Drinks and Ices."[33] What is clear is that on the London cinema exhibition circuit food and film were being brought together within the same venue for concurrent and allied consumption from the 1910s onward. In contrast to Gomery's account of the United States, a number of these exhibitors sought not to distance themselves from the selling of food, and thus from associations with carnivals and burlesque shows, but rather to embrace another lineage of live performance, namely legitimate theater, which had made the opportunity for sophisticated food consumption an integral feature of their patrons' visit.

As Mark Jancovich, Lucy Faire, and Sarah Stubbings point out, during the 1930s, cinema advertising in the United Kingdom regularly sought to foreground an exhibition venue's restaurants and cafes as a means of distinguishing it from competing picture houses.[34] This was particularly the case with cinemas aiming for an upmarket appeal, such as the Elite in Nottingham, the New Picture House in Edinburgh's Princes Street, or the Regal at London's Marble Arch. For example, the Regal's program to accompany the screening of *All Quiet on the Western Front* (1930) highlighted its tea room, lounge, and ballroom, while the June 1934 program for the New Picture House alerted patrons to its "Four-course lunch, Smoke room, and Wedgwood Dining Room."[35] The mobilizing of certain food-consumption opportunities as symbolic practices able to convey social status to exhibition venues, and thus to patrons seeking to partake in them, was crucial to the way in which exhibitors sought to generate indices of cultural capital in relation to their venues. Yet it is arguable that such venues were only nominally "exclusive," since all this luxury and grandeur could be purchased for the price of a theater ticket. In this sense, these sites could be understood more properly as "aspirational" places.[36]

In addition to these landmark venues, the 1930s saw new exhibition venues such as those opened by Oscar Deutsch's Odeon cinema chain, which included stylish modern cafés within their premises.[37] Modish concession stands in these cinemas also offered ice-cream, sweets, cigarettes and soft-drinks, items available at most city-center and neighborhood cinemas at this time. Indeed, it was only the impact of wartime food rationing in the United Kingdom from 1940 onward that halted the lucrative trade in cinema concessions, with sweet rationing in place until 1948. In the United States, the wartime rationing of sugar and chocolate also had a deleterious impact on cinema theater revenues, but many exhibitors found a solution in the shape of popcorn. While by no means a ubiquitous feature of the U.S. theater concession industry at this time—Andrew F. Smith points out that "many theaters in major cities had not sold much popcorn prior to the war"—it was well assimilated into the repertoire of foodstuffs comprising normative consumption practices within cinemas, in distinct contrast with the United Kingdom. As Smith states, popcorn was not rationed in the United States during the war, and "wherever possible, theaters introduced or expanded popcorn concessions." The war saw the highest yields of popcorn ever recorded, with theaters struggling to meet demand for a product that had few competitors at the concession stands.[38] Douglas Gomery notes that "by 1947, nearly 90 percent of U.S. movie houses sold popcorn," not surprising given that "even counting wage, overhead, and depreciation of equipment, the profit rate usually exceeded 100 percent.[39]"

There were, though, some notable exceptions to this general picture; the Loew's theater chain, for example, refused to sell popcorn in its New York cinemas until the 1950s. Indeed, Smith states that "some theaters even required 'that customers arriving with popcorn check it at the door,'" suggesting that consumption of the foodstuff continued to carry an association with "cheaper class entertainment" that a number of establishments wished to avoid.[40] Moreover, the significant art film theater exhibition business that emerged in the United States in the postwar period sought to offer patrons a film-watching experience distinct from that available at mainstream theaters, and one of the ways in which exhibitors sought to do this was through the range of foodstuffs on offer. As Barbara Wilinsky points out, many of these cinemas "featured cafes rather than concession stands. Instead of offering popcorn and lower priced candy . . . many art houses offered coffee and pastries." As she notes, the growth of art house theaters in cities and college towns during this period cannot be disassociated from key developments in the role of culture in U.S. society more generally. In particular, she points to the fact that "the belief that economic discrepancies were disappearing . . . led to a growing emphasis on taste and culture at that time."[41] Such a climate witnessed a proliferation of popular and academic discourses concerned with questions of taste and cultural distinction, which in turn impacted upon the film industry. For example, Wilinsky cites John Belton's work on the promotion of wide-screen cinema during the period, identified as an attempt "to offer people a way to differentiate themselves from others in the middle-class film audience."[42] What is clear is that cinema foodstuffs, recognized as symbolic consumption practices, were deployed strategically to assist in the mobilizing of such cultural distinctions, and that popcorn remained a peculiarly emblematic commodity in this regard.

With this in mind, it is interesting to trace the differing trajectory of the foodstuff within the history of U.K. film exhibition. Andrew Smith writes that popcorn arrived in the United Kingdom during World War II as one of the number of "luxury" items that traveled overseas with U.S. servicemen in order "to lend a homey touch to military life," adding that "servicemen introduced popcorn to civilian populations all over the world." He notes that after the war "several American popcorn promoters broke into European markets," including the United Kingdom. Yet he also points out that British consumers preferred a product sweeter than that most frequently sold in the United States, and cites the success of British popcorn promoters who produced caramel corn, such as the Bard Brothers, or House of Clark, manufacturers of Butterkist popcorn.[43] It is worth pausing to consider the context of this British response to an imported U.S. product in the postwar period. As Duncan Webster notes, a populist discourse of resistance to American influence on British society circulated in "'a number of printed and broadcast contexts' during the war and its aftermath," and he cites the impact of the GIs in providing a "startling and direct experience of American popular culture."[44] Webster quotes Dick Hebdige in pointing out that "Americanization became more and more common as a kind of shorthand: 'By the early 50s, the very mention of the word "America" could summon up a cluster of negative associations.'"[45] Yet Hebdige also argues that "positive images of America did persist throughout the period. . . operat[ing] out of sight of the discourse of Americanization" and had a particular appeal to young and working class people. Moreover, in contrast to fears that 'Americanization' would lead to a homogenizing of British culture, it is more accurate to note that "as American popular culture is exported, it is also transformed."[46] Such sentiment is echoed in Arjun Appadurai's recent writing on the global cultural economy; Appadurai counters the cultural homogenization thesis with the argument that "at least as rapidly as forces from various metropolises are brought into new societies they tend to become indigenized in one or another way."[47] The British response to U.S.

popcorn products at this time can be understood as evidence of this process of transformation and indigenization, catering for an audience that was predominantly working class in composition.[48]

The postwar history of U.K. cinema exhibition is one marked by a spectacular decline in attendance. Cinema admissions fell by over two thirds between 1945 and 1960, maintaining a relentless downward spiral into the 1980s, until reaching their nadir in 1984.[49] Commentators have offered a series of (sometimes conflicting) reasons for this state of affairs, but it is evident that this singular statistic requires analysis with the aid of multiple determinants, attentive to the contingent nature of causal factors at play at any moment of this dispiriting trajectory.[50] What is clear, as Jancovich, Faire, and Stubbings point out, is that the "new affluence" in British society from the mid-1950s onward "created a whole series of new leisure forms that competed with cinema for the population's leisure time, displacing cinema from the centre of people's leisure."[51] Moreover, the parlous state of the U.K. cinema exhibition business was echoed by the supine approach to theater concessions; reflecting on his origins in the U.K. cinema concessions business in the 1960s, Robert Callan, founder of the concessions firm TLC stated that "in the '60s and '70s practically the only products sold in the cinemas were ice creams, orange squash, and candy-coated popcorn. Nobody viewed the business differently until the advent of the American multiplex."[52]

Although Callan's inventory of concessions somewhat overstates the paucity of choice (sweets and chocolate were also staples of concession fare at this time) his comments do reflect accurately upon the profound impact of the multiplex on most aspects of the U.K. cinema exhibition business, including the sale of cinema foodstuffs. Beginning with the opening of the AMC (American Multi Cinemas) multiplex in Milton Keynes in 1985, the construction of multiplex cinemas in the United Kingdom has been marked almost ever since by exponential growth.[53] By 2002, there were over 200 multiplexes in the country, out of a total of around 650 cinemas. Crucially, in 2002, multiplex cinemas accounted for 54 percent of the United Kingdom's screens, the largest national concentration of screens in such venues in Western Europe, and nearly 90 percent of admissions. The period of multiplex expansion also witnessed a significant rise in the number of admissions, with 1999 seeing the highest attendance figures in over twenty years.[54] Yet for the concerns of this chapter, perhaps the most illuminating statistic of all is the impact of the multiplex revolution upon concessions revenue. In 1989, the average ticket price in the United Kingdom was £2.20, while cinema expenditure per capita was £3.38, indicating that an additional £1.18 was being spent on supplementary purchases, the overwhelming majority of which would be concessions. By 1998, the average ticket price in the United Kingdom was £3.71, but the cinema expenditure per capita was £8.48. Thus in this period the cinema ticket itself dropped from being 65 percent to only 43 percent of the total expenditure of the cinema visit.[55] Research conducted in 1995 estimated that concession revenue for major exhibition chains in the United Kingdom had more than doubled since 1989, rising from £37m ($57.5m) to £81.5m ($126.5m) in 1994. As a survey in *Screen International* pointed out, "territories with the greatest number of multiplexes have also notched up the greatest profits from concessions," and in Western Europe that has meant the United Kingdom and Germany. For example, the pan-European multiplex exhibitor UCI estimated in 1995 that "54% of net profit after costs [came] from food and drinks sales" in its U.K. theaters.[56] Moreover, current net profit percentages derived from concessions are almost certainly above the 1995 figure, due in part to the extensive investment in consumer market research, and concessions hardware by exhibitors throughout the 1990s, the concerted move toward concessions promotions (e.g., film tie-ins and "meal deals") as well as the consolidation of the concessions retail industry by pan-European and transnational exhibitors—what *Screen International* referred to in 1999 as the rise of the "global concessions industry."[57]

In considering the impact of concessions profits on contemporary moviegoing, Gary Egerton writes that "the shift in emphasis from merchandising feature films to selling concessions shows up in contemporary motion picture theater design . . . today the most progressive type of theater, and the most characteristic of its era, the multiplex, tells its occupants that it is time 'to buy.'"[58] Moreover, the most recent developments in exhibition practices have worked to augment the consumption opportunities of the multiplex. In particular, the construction of megaplex cinemas of twenty or more screens in the United Kingdom, such as the Warner Village Star City in Birmingham (with thirty screens, the biggest venue in Europe), has moved the architectural logic of the multiplex forward, taking the opportunity presented by the increase in scale to innovate concession-stand design with a view to boosting revenue accrued from the sale of foodstuffs. For example, the introduction of "pass-through" concession stands, separating service and sale points for foodstuffs, is one of a number of changes made possible by larger foyer areas.[59] U.K. venues have not as yet reached the levels of integration seen in a number of U.S. megaplexes, which have incorporated full-blown food courts into their foyer areas. However, the way in which U.K. megaplexes function similarly as anchors for purpose-built leisure sites offering a repertoire of niche entertainment and consumption opportunities has enabled lucrative on-site synergies between moviegoing and food consumption, with patrons able to combine visits to the cinema with those to an assortment of themed restaurants in the vicinity.[60]

This brief overview attests to the centrality of the provision of foodstuffs to the history of cinema exhibition. Ever a source of lucrative income, foodstuffs have also been instrumental in shaping the physical geographies of exhibition sites, as well as the social geographies of moviegoing, playing a crucial role in organizing the experiential meanings of the cinema. The capacity of foodstuffs to function as repositories of symbolic meaning and to be mobilized in the service of constructing specific clusters of associations with particular exhibition venues is something to which exhibitors have long been attentive. However, to judge the key role played by the consumption of foodstuffs in the mediation of the cinematic experience with reference to commercial strategies alone would be to accept unequivocally the notion that audiences slavishly abide by the industry's modus operandi. Recent work undertaken into social practices of consumption within sociology and cultural studies has stressed the extent to which individuals and groups actively negotiate with the "opportunities to consume" as provided by commodity culture in all its various guises. It is with this notion in mind that the next section looks closely at the provision of food and film-watching opportunities, and audience members' negotiations with them, as they take place in the city of Nottingham, England.

Food and Film Watching: A Case Study

In 2000, I carried out a series of interviews with filmgoers in the city of Nottingham, England. These interviews were conducted in and/or outside of two different cinemas: the Showcase multiplex theater and the Broadway Cinema and Media Centre, a regional independent cinema and the self-proclaimed "home of independent and world cinema in the East Midlands."[61] I conducted 48 interviews with individuals who were disposed to respond to questions regarding their food and film-watching practices. Of these 26 were female, 22 were male, and the majority were between 16 and 35 years of age. Six of the interviewees identified themselves as Asian, the rest as white. The sample was relatively small, and the respondents had self-selected by their willingness to discuss their opinions, attitudes, and habits regarding food and film watching.[62] This last point attests to the fact that there are, of course, a host of methodological issues pertaining to the conduct of empirical audience research, including the complexity of the relationship between interviewer and interviewee, the framing of questions, and the methods of interpretation. Central to these issues is also the question of *why* audience research is being conducted, and what the answers are being purported to reveal. Indeed, it is perhaps the concerns raised by such notions that have inclined many film scholars to remain ensconced in library stacks and screening rooms.

Despite my own initial misgivings, the nature of the subject soon convinced me about the essential role audience research would play in helping to comprehend how and why audience members made particular choices about food and film-watching practices; how they understood the choices they made; what they thought of the experiences and pleasures of the practices they engaged in (or not); and what their attitudes were toward the opportunities for food consumption provided by theatrical exhibition outlets. Nevertheless, the claims I make for the findings of my audience research are modest—I do not claim that they are representative of filmgoers in general, nor even of the particular exhibition sites in question. Yet as Kevin Corbett points out, if we are serious about developing a "deeper understanding of the cultural significance" of moviegoing, we need to listen carefully to what people tell us about their experiences, "but also for how those experiences reflect and/or resist the social structures with which they are intertwined."[63] This research offers a contribution to that larger project, and thus also seeks to move beyond the industry's own statistical analysis of generalized consumer preferences and per-capita net profit breakdowns, and toward a more nuanced and critically informed assessment of cinematic consumption practices.

Nottingham Showcase Cinema is located on the outskirts of the city center, beside a main arterial roadway, and designed primarily for access by car. Surrounded by American-themed franchises such as a Mega-bowl ten-pin bowling center, a deep-pan pizza parlor, and a Tex-Mex restaurant, Nottingham Showcase is sited in a "landscape of leisure and entertainment" similar in thematic and spatial constitution to those in other British cities.[64] For example, the site shares great affinity with Avonmeads Retail Park, a similar complex in Bristol known locally as "Little America." Indeed, as Jancovich, Faire, and Stubbings point out, the opening of the Showcase cinema in Nottingham was accompanied by extensive coverage in the local newspapers emphasising its U.S. "credentials." Owned by American National Amusements, the Showcase was referred to by the press as "the splendid American venture on the ring road," exemplifying an "'all American' outlook on life" best illustrated by its approach to aspects such as "quality customer service" and "concession stands."[65] Such coverage attests to the fact that within a globalized consumer culture, it is observable that, as Simon Frith points out, "America . . . has itself become the object of consumption, a symbol of pleasure."[66] Yet it is important to caution against a monolithic conceptualization of the "imaginary America" as discernible in the Showcase's landscape of leisure. For example, the contrasting site of moviegoing to be considered in this chapter is the aforementioned Broadway Cinema and Media Centre. As an art house cinema sited in a gentrified section of the city center known for its preponderance of fashionable bars, cafés, restaurants, nightclubs and boutique shops, the Broadway engenders an alternative set of U.S. cultural connotations, suggesting New York and an urban/urbane theatergoing public. Thus, while it might at first be tempting to propose the Showcase as part of a homogeneous "little America," it is necessary to understand the distinct ways in which an "imaginary America" can be signified, and how symbiotic those varying significations may be. Indeed, just as so-called independent filmmaking can be seen to function by employing a rhetorical mainstream Hollywood cinema to help construct its alternative identity, so do the cinemas used to exhibit these pictures signify with reference to a framework of distinction.

Returning to the Showcase, what is clearly observable as one walks through the foyer is that the cinema's construction is entirely in keeping with Gary Egerton's comments about the centrality of concessions to contemporary multiplex theater design. As he points out, the multiplex ushered in the transformation from the "traditional backbar freestanding counter" to the "centrally located concession stand" which is able to serve many more customers in a much shorter time.[67] The foyer of the Showcase is given over to the "Refreshment Centre"'; everything and everyone is located in relation to this structuring center, which ensures that queues for the cinema's two auditorium entrances are separated spatially—and also ensures that it is not possible to pass into the theaters without moving past one of its two identical sides, offering a symmetrical opportunity for consumption. In line with U.K. industry estimates that "40% of the audience arrives within 10 minutes of the film's start," such refreshment centers also place an emphasis on high visibility and consumer predictability, nowhere more obvious than in the massive glass and chrome containers of popcorn that comprise the bulk of the refreshment center's walls.[68] Here popcorn functions as the paradigmatic, prototypical foodstuff, a synecdoche for the multiplex's cinematic offerings, connoting the requisite abundance, excess, and indulgence. This "aesthetic of abundance" is also followed through in relation to the displays for the other foodstuffs on offer, namely candy, soft drinks, pick 'n' mix, ice creams, and more distinctly signified "American" foodstuffs such as nachos and hot dogs. Moreover, the multiplex reinforces this approach to foodstuffs through its signature attitude toward portion sizes—namely, regular, large, and supersize. "Small" is omitted in favor of a "child's" portion, which on the one hand makes clear that the Showcase is geared toward encouraging and satisfying children's desires (something underlined by the pick 'n' mix sweet center at the back of the foyer, with scoops and bowls at a child's height), but also works to promote adult appetites upward due to the stigma of ordering a child's portion.

Although such sizing strategies are obviously employed in the service of maximizing retail profit, the signifying of such abundance can also be understood with reference to sociologist Pierre Bourdieu's notion of cultural capital. As he points out, high cultural capital draws upon notions of "scarcity" in relation to consumption, implying that the products to be consumed are available only to the fortunate few, who know how to value such resources. Indeed, the Broadway Cinema's Café Bar overtly employs a strategy of scarcity through its practice of advertising some of its foodstuffs on a chalk board, highlighting daily specials which are limited in number—as supplies are exhausted, the names of the foods are wiped from the board. For a product to be exhausted signifies its value, even if the "exclusivity" of the Broadway's foodstuffs is performative rather than actual, since in terms of cost some are, in fact, less expensive than those on sale at the Showcase.

For those who arrive at the Showcase too late to browse the central refreshment center, the venue provides additional zones for foodstuff purchase. Beyond the glass doors that separate the foyer from the entrances to the movie theaters, a refreshment counter lines the wall of each of the two hallways. In terms of design, these counters are identical to the center in the foyer, only smaller, but offering the same product selection. These two counters clearly indicate where and when the Showcase expects and encourages the majority of its customers' foodstuffs will be consumed—namely, in the cinema itself. The glass doors serve to separate the foyer from the hallway where one enters the theatres—the refreshment counters offer a last chance to buy before one enters the theater, but also a proximate location for the purchase of foodstuffs during the screening. Thus the auxiliary refreshment counters reinforce the logic of the Showcase's design, which encourages the consumption of particular food-stuffs as an integral part of the movie-watching experience, and indeed seeks to frame this particular behavioral practice as both normative and desirable. This is also clearly evident in the distinct lack of seating in the Showcase's foyer area, designed to encourage a flow of customers into the theaters, and serves largely to engender simultaneous food consumption and film-watching activities.

Interviews conducted at the Showcase provide some interesting informa-tion concerning moviegoers' negotiations with the cinema's repertoire of food consumption opportunities. The Showcase's obvious zeal for encouraging cus-tomers to purchase its foodstuffs is aided and abetted by the cinema's location in an edge-of-city leisure complex, which makes it difficult for patrons to buy alternative portable foodstuffs in the vicinity. However, two pairs of inter-viewees declared that they often brought food purchased outside the Showcase to eat inside the movie theater, stating that the cinema sold its food at a price higher than they were willing to pay.[69] Interestingly, such behavior has been reported periodically by the U.S. news media in the 1990s, typically framed as lighthearted stories of patrons smuggling in food and drink as protests against rising concession prices.[70] Although the Nottingham Showcase doesn't display signs warning patrons against bringing their own food and drink, as is the case with many U.S. cinemas, interviewees stressed a reluctance to parade their own purchases, preferring to conceal them until ensconced in the darkened theater, suggesting that the venue has been able to establish a prohibitive cli-mate, albeit one only that is partially successful.

More intriguing were the categories of food brought by those who sought to smuggle items from elsewhere. What is striking is that interviewees stated that the type of food they brought in—namely, confectionery—was in keeping with the food sold in the Showcase; indeed, they often brought in exactly the same products as those sold at the cinema, M&Ms and Maltesers being two of the most common items. When interviewees were asked why they did not bring other types of food into the cinema, such as sandwiches or fruit, there was an overwhelming sense that such items would be not only inferior but in some senses also erroneous choices. It is possible to surmise that the long-standing practices of cinemas in encouraging food consumption in the the-ater, and suggesting specific categories of foodstuffs to be consumed, have naturalized the practice so successfully that deviations from or subversions of the food consumption opportunities that the cinema provides tend nevertheless to align themselves with the existing consumption paradigms.

It is arguable that there is also a sense in which eating such everyday foods as fruit or sandwiches in the Multiplex could be seen to evince an inability or reluctance to assimilate oneself fully with the sense of place identity that the Showcase wishes to generate. For example, five interviewees stated that going to see a movie at the Showcase represented the only time that they consumed confectionaries; for them, this formed an essential part of structuring their cinema visit as a "treat," as a space for its own site-specific, special consumption practices.[71] Indeed, it is quite clear that like other Multiplex outlets, the Nottingham Showcase works hard to encourage this type of behavior, in particular by offering "special" packets of confectionary in sizes and designs that are exclusive to the cinema. This logic is also in keeping with the "symbolism of sweetness" identified in the sociological literature on food. As Alan Beardsworth and Teresa Keil point out, "confectionary is regarded as both food and non-food" in the classificatory system of the Western diet. Never considered as part of a conventional meal, confectionary thus has a flexibility which allows it "to take on a wide variety of social meanings," according to Beardworth and Keil. One important example is the way confectionary is eaten on ritual occasions, such as Christmas, Easter, and St. Valentines Day. This ritual of confectionary eating is also enunciated in a number of interviewees' stated cinemagoing practices. However, as Beardsworth and Keil also note, there is a distinct ambivalence in contemporary Western attitudes toward sweetness, as "chocolate and confectionary can become associated with self-indulgence and guilt," and it is this contradiction that "is handled by socialized and ritualized consumption, which is more acceptable that individual, solitary use." It is the "clear social context and legitimization" of sharing a large bag of M&Ms at the cinema that helps to valorize the practice for consumer and confectioner alike.[72]

One notable consequence of legitimizing synchronous food and filmwatching in the cinema is the potential for discomfort on the part of those members of the audience who do not engage in such activity. Indeed, it is worth highlighting the fact that the majority of the foodstuffs sold by the multiplex are quite noisy to consume—popcorn, packets of sweets, nachos, and the like. At first it might seem counterproductive to sell products that could interfere with enjoyment of the movie, but "noisy" foodstuffs can be seen to serve a number of strategic functions. For example, a number of interviewees stated that they could not sit in the movie theater without any food or drink because the sound of others eating and drinking made them feel they were "missing out."[73] One interviewee expressed this most forthrightly with the sentiment that if the sound of crunching popcorn was going to be heard, he wished not to be the passive "victim," but instead the "perpetrator"—a sense of "if you can't beat them, join them."[74] What this suggests is that in the darkened theater, where the spectacle of the movie has replaced the spectacle of food on display in the foyer, the noise of food is vital to signalling its own existence and availability, and quite possibly increasing the likelihood of its consumption.

What such a notion of "missing out" also intimates is the idea, however transient, of community. Eating in the Showcase cinema is a ritualized community practice; to eat is therefore in a sense to integrate yourself within this ephemeral community, by doing what other people are doing. On one level, eating is, as one interviewee stated, a way of "sharing the cinema experience."[75] Indeed, large packets of popcorn and sweets facilitate this sharing activity in an environment where more direct forms of interaction such as talking and eye contact are made difficult and inappropriate. This conception of community practice also has implications for the fashioning and expression of identity; to eat, and to enjoy eating in the cinema is in a sense to accept a community identity—to be happy to be the type of person who eats in the cinema, and more specifically, someone who eats the particular foodstuffs the Showcase sells. Here we return to the notion of cultural capital—foodstuffs such as popcorn, sweets, coke, ice lollies, all packed with sugar, salt, and/or fat, are generally classified in terms of gastronomic hierarchies as rather "low culture." They are therefore in keeping with the arena of popular cinema in which they are consumed—a popular aesthetic that places the emphasis on function over form, something underlined by the fact that eaten in the cinema, foodstuffs cannot even be seen. Interestingly, a number of people interviewed about their food and moviegoing practices stated that they were not comfortable with eating in the Showcase, and on the rare occasions when they visited the cinema preferred to move quickly through the foyer and directly into the theater.[76] Expressing displeasure at those who ate, and ate "too noisily," these individuals clearly did not enjoy the food and film-watching practices available at the Showcase. Indeed, for these interviewees, fellow moviegoers were very markedly signified as "other" with explicit reference to their incongruent attitudes toward food consumption in the cinema.

The majority of interviewees who expressed displeasure with synchronous food and film-watching practices preferred to watch their films at the Broadway cinema. Unlike the Showcase, a venue designed around the centrality of concessions provision, the Broadway works in important ways to separate food and film-watching practices. In place of the Showcase's glass doors ushering the customer past refreshment counters and into the theater, the Broadway uses glass doors to structure the separateness of food consumption in its café from film watching in the cinema. In this way, the cinema may be visited without entering the café, and the café may prompt a visit without the intention of watching a film. This is also a reflection of the cinema's location within Hockley, an area of restaurants and cafés; a community identity helping to structure the Broadway's own internal consumption spaces and opportunities. Several interviewees stressed the Broadway's usefulness as a meeting place—helping to gather individuals for leisure activities in the surrounding community.[77] Thus the Broadway structures the separation of food and film watching as a selling point—enabling it to generate business which would otherwise go to surrounding cafés and bars.

It is fair to say that the Broadway is designed to make *not eating* in the cinema a viable community practice. In the Broadway cinema, the opportunity *not to eat* is a key component of signifying what moviegoing means; separating food consumption and film watching reflects a set of cultural values about the proper seriousness of engaging in both activities—namely, that film as art and food as aesthetic object each require a "pure" appreciation. It is worth noting that a number of interviewees who frequented the Broadway stated that they were disposed to visiting the cinema without companions, whereas none of those interviewed about their outings to the Showcase declared such behavior.[78] Also indicating displeasure at those who ate in the cinema, the former interviewees embraced the Broadway's capacity to create a space that made normative a "detached" mode of spectatorship that eschewed the bodily pleasures of food consumption and the noisy social rituals of popcorn sharing.

It is worth pointing out that, unlike a number of art house venues, the Broadway does offer some concessions provision. However, this is very low key—in fact, the antithesis of the Showcase's spectacle of consumables. Moreover, the selection is largely limited to small tubs of "gourmet" ice cream and regular sized chocolates, in keeping with the way in which histories of art house exhibition suggest such venues have long used sophisticated or up market foodstuffs to help foreground the distinction between the moviegoing experience they offer and that of the major exhibitors. Particularly apparent in the Broadway is the absence of popcorn, the sine qua non of multiplex foodstuffs, as well as the accompanying repertoire of U.S.-signified products such as nachos and hot dogs, gastronomic staples of the Showcase. The absence of popcorn is particularly telling, given that the phrase "popcorn movie" has of late become a common feature of industry and media parlance, used to refer to summer blockbusters and high-concept films, and to those marketed as action-adventure, children's films, teen comedies, and romantic comedies (with concessions suppliers keeping multiplex managers informed of how particular films perform in terms of accompanying food sales).[79] These are, of course, the categories of films against which the art house program has traditionally defined itself. In addition, a recent article in the London *Evening Standard* denounced the trend for Hollywood movie stars to take to the capital's West End theater stages, terming this too as "popcorn theater."[80] What is clear is how animate popcorn remains as a symbolic foodstuff, mobilized in discourses serving to enunciate notions of taste, and here also inflected by an articulation of national cultural provision, used to denigrate the insidious, "dumbing-down" influence of U.S. popular culture.

Conclusion

In their study of cinemagoing in Bristol, Martin Barker and Kate Brooks point out that "for many people, certain cinemas are associated with particular kinds of audience."[81] What is clear from the examples of the Nottingham Showcase and Broadway cinema is the extent to which negotiations with the venues' contrasting opportunities for food consumption, and the ways in which foodstuff provision functions to structure meanings and behavioral practices is crucial to audience members generating what Bourdieu calls a "sense of one's place" within these exhibition sites.[82] Bourdieu's suggestion that "taste classifies, and it classifies the classifier" can be seen to function both in how the interviewees negotiated the different cinemas' environments, and also in how they vocalized that negotiation in interviews—by asserting comfort or discomfort, they were also asserting a sense of identity.[83] As Stacey Warren notes, "popular culture, though laden with commodities, is primarily about the circulation of meanings," and this is clearly enunciated through the contrasting ways in which these exhibition sites embed food consumption provision and rituals in order to help shape the meaning of moviegoing.[84]

While the work of Bourdieu provides a useful framework for describing the relationship between social practices of consumption and the articulation of identity, its application to the subject of food and film watching does not fit neatly with class-based typologies of consumption. As Claire Monk argues, data compiled for the annual Cinema and Video Industry Audience Research (CAVIAR) surveys attests to the fact that many assumptions about the demographic profile of the cinema audience in the United Kingdom are obsolete, harking back to the long lost period of the mass cinema audience in Britain.[85] As she notes, industry research overwhelmingly points to the fact that "the UK cinema audience as a whole is predominantly middle-class, a finding which does not reflect the composition of the UK population as a whole."[86]

The notion that U.K. cinemagoing is primarily a middle-class activity underlines the fact that the types of distinctions generated by the differing approaches to foodstuffs taken by the Showcase and the Broadway operate with recourse to a performative, nominal notion of "exclusivity." Thus, the Broadway is seeking to cater to a notion of self its customers pursue, in the sense that its approach to foodstuffs serves to generate distinction based not on income per se, but on the symbolism of consumption, where the real value of foodstuffs lies in the social production of meaning, specifically in the generation of "cultural capital." This is not to say that such practices do not generate real effects; on the contrary, a number of interviewees who frequented the Showcase suggested that they did not feel comfortable in the space of the Broadway, one typical response being that it was a place for "trendies and intellectuals."[87]

Clearly, the choice to consume—and indeed, the choice *not* to consume—the repertoire of foodstuffs made available in cinema exhibition venues is tied intimately to the "the pleasures of the ritualized event" of moviegoing. The Showcase valorizes certain synchronous food and film-watching practices as normative and desirable for obvious commercial gain, but many audience members participate willingly for the payoff of experiencing the "'shared intimacy' and 'heightened enjoyment' of collective consumption" in public.[88] Recognizing cinema foodstuffs as symbolic goods allows for an assessment of their strategic deployment in mobilizing cultural distinctions between exhibition venues. The Broadway Cinema makes nonconsumption of foodstuffs a normative viewing practice, eschewing the bodily pleasures and noisy social rituals of food consumption in favor of a "detached" mode of spectatorship apposite for the cineaste's experience of art house fare. The Broadway's legitimation of the spatial and temporal bifurcation of food consumption and film-watching does not mean it has no interest in the conjunction of the two practices. On the contrary, its café bar provides a convenient site for pre and postviewing conversation, offering itself as the locus for a contemplative, reflective mode of response to the cinematic event, in contrast to the Showcase's privileging of the cinematic experience as constituted through the synchronous and the immediate. In this way food and film-watching practices can be seen as crucial in shaping not only the meanings of moviegoing but the epistemology of cinema itself.

Notes

1. For accounts of early cinema exhibition, see Richard C. Allen, "Motion Picture Exhibition in Manhattan, 1906–1912: Beyond the Nickelodeon," *Cinema Journal* 19, no. 2 (1979): 2–15; Miriam Hansen, *Babel and Babylon: Spectatorship in American Silent Film* (Cambridge, Mass: Harvard University Press, 1991); Thomas Elsaesser, ed., *Early Cinema: Space, Frame, Narrative* (London: British Film Institute, 1991); Gregory A. Waller, *Main Street Amusements: Movies and Commercial Entertainment in a Southern City, 1896–1930* (Washington, D.C.: Smithsonian Institution Press, 1995); and Melvyn Stokes and Richard Maltby, eds., *American Movie Audiences: From the Turn of the Century to the Early Sound Era* (London: British Film Institute, 1999). For work that takes in the classical period, see Douglas Gomery, *Shared Pleasures: A History of Movie Presentation in the United States* (Madison: University of Wisconsin Press, 1992); John Belton, *Widescreen Cinema* (Cambridge, Mass: Harvard University Press, 1992); Tino Balio, ed., *Hollywood in the Age of Television* (Cambridge, Mass: Unwin Hayman, 1990).
2. See William Uricchio and Roberta E. Pearson, *Reframing Culture: The Case of the Vitagraph Quality Films* (Princeton, N.J.: Princeton University Press, 1993).
3. See Janet Staiger, *Interpreting Films: Studies in the Historical Reception of American Cinema* (Princeton, N.J.: Princeton University Press, 1992). Feminist scholars undertaking ethnographic research into cinema audiences have challenged many of the assumptions held by psychoanalytic film theory about female spectators. For example, see Jacqueline Bobo, "*The Color Purple:* Black Women as Cultural Readers," in *Female Spectators: Looking at Film and Television,* ed. Deirdre Pribram (London: Verso, 1988); Helen Taylor, *Scarlett's Women: "Gone With the Wind" and its Female Fans* (London: Virago, 1989); Jackie Stacey, *Star Gazing: Hollywood Cinema and Female Spectatorship* (London: Routledge, 1994); Sue Harper and Vincent Porter, "Moved to Tears: Weeping in the Cinema in Postwar Britain," *Screen* 37, no. 2 (1996): 152–73.
4. Robert C. Allen, "From Exhibition to Reception: Reflections on the Audience in Film History," *Screen* 38, no. 4 (1990): 347-56.
5. Ina Rae Hark, "General Introduction", in *Exhibition: The Film Reader,* ed. Ina Rae Hark (London: Routledge, 2001), 1.
6. Richard Maltby, "Introduction," in *Identifying Hollywood's Audiences: Cultural Identity and the Movies,* ed. Melvyn Stokes and Richard Maltby (London: British Film Institute, 1999), 4.
7. Kevin J. Corbett, "Empty Seats: The Missing History of Movie-Watching," *Journal of Film and Video* 50, no. 4 (1998–99): 34.
8. For example, Douglas Gomery in *Shared Pleasures,* devotes a mere four pages of a three hundred–page account to the subject of exhibition.
9. Thomas Guback, "The Evolution of the Motion Picture Theater Business in the 1980s," *Journal of Communication* 37, no. 2 (1987): 63; Michael D. Sorkin, "'Smugglers' Are Eating Our Profits, Say Theater Owners,'" *St. Louis Post-Dispatch,* 31 May 2002.
10. Sandra Yin, "Film Buffers," *American Demographics,* September 2001, 12.

11. For theoretical work on the consumption of culture see Mike Featherstone, "Perspectives on consumer culture," *Sociology* 24, no. 1(1990): 5–22; Mike Featherstone, *Consumer Culture and Postmodernism* (London: Sage, 1991); and John Storey, *Cultural Consumption and Everyday Life* (London: Arnold, 1999).

12. Deborah Lupton, *Food, the Body and the Self* (London: Sage, 1998), 23.

13. Stuart Hall, "The Meaning of New Times," in *New Times: The Changing Face of Politics in the 1990s*, ed. Stuart Hall and Martin Jacques (London: Verso, 1990), 131.

14. Alan Warde, *Consumption, Food and Taste* (London: Sage, 1997), 22–23. For anthropological work on food, see Claude Levi-Strauss, *The Raw and the Cooked* (London: Jonathon Cape, 1970) and Mary Douglas, *Food in the Social Order: Studies of Food and Festivities in Three American Communities* (New York: Russell Sage Foundation, 1984). For seminal work on the sociology of food, see Roland Barthes, *Mythologies*, trans. Annette Lavers (London: Jonathan Cape, 1972) and Pierre Bourdieu, *Distinction: A Social Critique of the Judgment of Taste*, trans. Richard Nice (Cambridge, Mass.: Harvard University Press, 1984). For an excellent overview of the sociological literature on food, see Alan Beardsworth and Teresa Keil, *Sociology on the Menu* (London: Routledge, 1999).

15. Lupton, *Food, the Body and the Self*, 13.

16. David Bell and Gill Valentine, *Consuming Geographies* (London: Routledge, 1997), 3.

17. For more information on the way in which domestic technologies function to organize household activities, see Stevi Jackson and Shaun Moores, eds., *The Politics of Domestic Consumption* (London: Prentice-Hall, 1995).

18. The other key area for inquiry that cannot be approached here is the relationship between multinational food retailers and Hollywood studios, manifested most obviously in the realms of product placement and food/movie "tie-ins," such as that between Burger King and Warner Bros for the *Batman* franchise, or the McDonalds/Disney multiple-film cross-promotional deal. For more on these corporate synergies see Janet Wasko, *Hollywood in the Information Age* (London: Polity Press, 1994); and Janet Wasko, *Understanding Disney* (London: Polity Press, 2001).

19. Joanne Finkelstein, *Dining Out: A Sociology of Modern Manners* (Oxford: Polity Press, 1989), 22. I should point out that my approach is quite different from that of Finkelstein, who adopts a determinist view of public pleasure, with consumers viewed as conformist "dupes" unwittingly positioned by commercial interests. What I want to retain from her study is the notion of the growing importance of the pursuit of pleasure in public throughout the twentieth century, and its implications for formations of subjectivity and sociality.

20. See Leo Charney and Vanessa R. Schwartz, eds., *Cinema and the Invention of Modern Life* (Berkeley and Los Angeles: University of California Press, 1996). For a concise overview of developments in commercial public leisure from the 1930s onward, see Bruce A. Austin, "Movies and Leisure," in *Immediate Seating: A Look at Movie Audiences* (California: Wadsworth, 1989).

21. Jackie Stacy, *Star Gazing: Hollywood Cinema and Female Spectatorship* (London: Routledge, 1994), 94, 101.

22. For more on the architectural style of British cinemas at this time see Allen Eyles, *The Granada Theaters* (London: British Film Institute, 1998); Allen Eyles, *Odeon Cinemas* (London: British Film Institute, 2002); Richard Gray, *Cinemas in Britain* (London: Lund Humphries, 1996).

23. Similarly, David Docherty, David Morrison, and Michael Tracey's study of film-watching practices for *Sight and Sound* noted the distinction between home movie watching and cinemagoing, arguing that "a night 'in' is not a 'night out' spent at home." See Docherty, Morrison, and Tracey, "Who Goes to the Cinema?" *Sight and Sound*, Spring 1986, 85.

24. Martin Barker and Kate Brooks, *Knowing Audiences: Judge Dredd, Its Friends, Fans, and Foes* (Luton, XXXX: University of Luton Press, 1998), 55.

25. Ibid., 61–63; 79.

26. Barker and Brooks, *Knowing Audiences*, 61.

27. Janice Williamson, 'Notes from Storyville North' in Rob Shields (ed.) *Lifestyle Shopping: The subject of Consumption*, (London: Routledge, 1992), 217.

28. Gomery, *Shared Pleasures*, 79, 80.

29. *New Gallery Kinema* (London: n.p., 1913). For an overview of cinema exhibition in the United Kingdom during this period see Nicholas Hiley, "Nothing More than a 'Craze': Cinema Building in Britain from 1909 to 1914," in *Young and Innocent?* ed. Andrew Higson (Exeter, England: University of Exeter Press, 1999): 111–26.

30. *New Gallery Kinema*.

31. The history of the New Gallery Kinema deserves a further note. The cinema was the original venue for the Film Society, founded in 1925, intended to nurture a view of cinema as an art form rather than mere entertainment. It included among its members George Bernard Shaw, H. G. Wells, Maynard Keynes, Julian Huxley, John Gielgud, and Ivor Novello. Jamie Sexton argues that "the society has been seen as an important landmark in British Cinema for the way in which it both established a tradition of independent exhibition and influenced British intellectual film culture in general." See Sexton, "The Film Society and the Creation of an Alternative Film Culture in Britain in the 1920s," in *The Cinema in Britain 1896–1930*, ed. Andrew Higson (Exeter, England: University of Exeter Press, 2002).

32. *West End Cinema, "Forthcoming Attractions"* (London: n.p., 1913).

33. *The Thief of Badgad* (program; London: Theater Royal, 1924).

34. Mark Jancovich, Lucy Faire, and Sarah Stubbings, *The Place of the Audience: The Cultural Geographies of Film Consumption* (London: British Film Institute, 2003), 164.

35. *The Regal* "All Quiet on the Western Front" (London, n.p., 1930); *The New Picture House,* "Program for June, 1934" (Edinburgh: n.p., 1934).

36. As Jancovich, Faire, and Stubbings, *Place of the Audience*, points out, "many cinemas associated themselves with a life of leisured luxury, but they also presented themselves as places where all could, at least for a time, enjoy such a life" (172).

37. Barry Doyle, "Return of the Super Cinema in the United Kingdom," *History Today*, February 1998; Allen Eyles, *Odeon Cinemas* (London: British Film Institute, 2002).

38. Andrew F. Smith, *Popped Culture: A Social History of Popcorn in America* (Washington, DC: Smithsonian Institution Press, 2001), 110, 111.

39. Douglas Gomery, "The Economics of U.S Film Exhibition Policy and Practice", *Cine-tracts* 3, no.4 (1981): 38.

40. Smith, *Popped Culture,* 117.

41. Barbara Wilinsky, *Sure Seaters: The Emergence of Art House Cinema* (Minneapolis: University of Minnesota Press, 2001), 113, 2.

42. Ibid., 3. John Belton, *Widescreen Cinema* (Cambridge, Mass.: Harvard University Press, 1992).

43. Smith, *Popped Culture,* 117.

44. Duncan Webster, *Looka Yonder!* (London: Routledge, 1988), 183.

45. Ibid., 184., citing Dick Hebdige, "Towards a Cartography of Taste 1935–1962," *Popular Culture: Past and Present*, eds. Bernard Waites, Tony Bennett and Graham Martin (London: Routledge, 1982). 194–218.

46. Webster, *Looka Yonder!* 185.

47. Arjun Appadurai, "Disjuncture and Difference in the Global Economy," *Theory, Culture and Society*, no.7 (1990): 295.

48. As Sue Harper and Vincent Porter point out, by 1954 the working class accounted for 82 percent of the adult audience. See Harper and Porter, "Cinema Audience Tastes in 1950s Britain," *Journal of Popular British Cinema*, no. 2 (1999): 67.

49. Ibid., 67; David Docherty, David Morrison and Michael Tracey, 'Who Goes to the Cinema?" *Sight and Sound*, Spring 1986, 81–85. The Cinema Advertising Association report in 2000 stated that the postwar highpoint came in 1946, with 1,635 million admissions, and the low point in 1984 with just 54 million. Cinema Advertising Association (CAA), *Cinema and Video Industry Audience Research*, no. 17 (London: CAA, 2000).

50. The main bone of contention here is over the direct influence of suburbanization and television upon U.K. cinema audiences in the postwar period. Jancovich, Faire, and Stubbings, *The Place of the Audience*, asserts that the decline of cinema audiences in the 1950s has more to do with the impact of the Entertainment Tax levied at exhibitors, together with other financial burdens such as the British Film Production Levy and the Sunday Levy in raising ticket prices, than the impact of television (188–91). They also cite the deterioration in the condition of many cinemas, wedded to the postwar ban on inessential building as crippling many ageing suburban cinemas. Moreover, the claims for the direct impact of suburbanization don't account for the fact that is was suburban theaters, rather than city-center establishments, that bore the brunt of the closures; see Barker and Brooks, *Knowing Audiences*, 189.

51. Jancovich, Faire, and Stubbings, *The Place of the Audience*, 211.

52. Robert Callan, quoted in Tim Dowling, "True Concessions," *Screen International*, 26 July 1991, 12.

53. While the trade press has viewed the range of profit-oriented developments in exhibition practices with understandable zeal, it is important to note that the multiplex/megaplex revolution has by no means been accompanied by unequivocal paeans to its ability to catalyse the resurgence in U.K. moviegoing. Multiplexes have been accused of introducing a grinding homogeneity by ways of their architectural design and their rosters of programming, and have also been charged with having a deleterious impact upon the city centers they have left behind. Indeed, underlying the recent trend to site U.K. multiplex/megaplex venues in the center of cities has been "a concern for the vitality and viability of town centres without a cinema." See John Robertson, "Coming Soon: The Town Centre Multiplex," *Planning*, 28 November 1997, 22–23.

54. Paola Bensi, "Western Europe: The Advance of the Multiplex," *European Cinema Journal*, no. 2 (2002): 2–3.

55. Media Salles, *European Cinema Yearbook*, 8th ed. (Milan, Italy: Media Salles, 1999), 287.

56. Celia Duncan, "The Sweet Smell of Success," *Screen International*, 22 September 1995, 18.

57. Pamela Cuthbert, "Popcorn, Pop, and Escalating Profits," *Screen International*, 6 August 1999, 22.

58. Gary Edgerton, "The Multiplex: The Modern American Motion Picture Theater as Message," in Hark, ed., *Exhibition*, 155.

59. See Francesca Dinglasan, "How Sweet It Is: Leading Concessionaires and Circuit Buyers on How the Present is Shaping the Future of Cinematic Candyland", *Box Office*, May 2000; online at http://www.boxoff.com/issues/may00/concessions.html.

60. Jancovich, Faire, and Stubbings, *The Place of the Audience*, 336, points out that the geographic pattern of megaplex development in the United Kingdom has tended to be in contrast to the precedent set by the emergence of such "landscapes of leisure and entertainment" in the United States. While U.S. development has tended to be concomitant with suburbanization and conurbation, U.K. megaplexes have tended to be inner-city developments, as illustrated by their sobriquet as "urban entertainment centers."

61. *Broadway Cinema and Media Centre*, homepage, online at http://www.broadway.org.uk/.

62. See Stacy, *Star Gazing*, or Barker and Brooks, *Knowing Audiences*, for insightful discussions regarding the difficulties involved in interviewing cinema audiences.

63. Corbett, "Empty Seats," 45–46.

64. For an astute account of such "landscapes of leisure" see Stacy Warren, "'This Heaven Gives Me Migraines': The Problems and Promise of Landscapes of Leisure," in *Place/Culture/Representation*, ed. James Duncan and David Ley (London: Routledge, 1993), 174.

65. Jancovich, Faire, and Stubbings, *The Place of the Audience*, 335, quotes from the *Nottingham Evening Post*, 15 October 1987.

66. Simon Frith, quoted in Webster, *Looka Yonder!* 200.

67. Edgerton, "The Multiplex," 157.

68. Ralf Ludemann, "Spending Power," *Screen International*, 26 July 1996, 38.

69. John, 36 (insurance sales), Diane, 34 (receptionist); Andy, 28 (warehouse manager), Sara, 27 (retail sales executive).

70. See, for example, Phyllis C. Richman, "At the Movies, Carrying On over Carry-In; Rising Concession Stand Prices Lead to a Brown Bag Revolt," *Washington Post*, 18 April 1990; Sorkin, "'Smugglers.'"

71. Callum, 21 (bartender); Meera 23 (law student); Ashley, 38 (housewife); Mark, 39 (car sales).

72. Beardsworth and Keil, *Sociology*, 249, 251.

73. Benedict, 19 (student); Asram, 17 (school pupil); Ellie, 23 (estate agent); Tom, 26 (financial services); Stewart, 22 (insurance).

74. Asram, 17.

75. Emily, 24 (trainee journalist).

76. Martin, 45 (lecturer); Anthony, 38 (teacher); Alice, 34 (social worker); Pritti, 27 (accounts clerk); Simon, 24 (graduate student).

77. Martin, 45; Alice, 34; Tom, 24 (musician); Jules, 22 (nurse); Emma, 21 (student); Kelly, 20 (administrator).

78. Martin, 45; Tom, 24; Alice, 34; Kieran, 22 (graduate student).

79. For an indicative example of the use of the term see Jeff Jensen, "Killer Instinct," *Entertainment Weekly*, 19 July 2002, 24; and Dowling, "True Concessions," 12.

80. Matt Wolf, "Stars Stud London's West End," *AP Online*, 7 December 2000; <http://www.ap.org>

81. Barker and Brooks, *Knowing Audiences*, 61.

82. Bourdieu, *Distinctions*, 466.

83. Ibid., 6.

84. Warren, "'This Heaven Gives Me Migraines,'" 80.

85. Claire Monk, "Heritage Films and the British Cinema Audience in the 1990s," *Journal of Popular British Cinema*, no. 2 (1999): 23.

86. Monk, "Heritage Films," cites "the impact of low incomes and related access problems on cinemagoing habits among the less affluent and skilled social grades. Among these groups, shiftwork, multiple jobs, zero-hours contracts and other insecure forms of employment may all reduce cinemagoing opportunities; so may lack of car ownership, particularly if the nearest cinema is a multiplex." (26)

87. Caroline, 33 (dental nurse). As Jancovich, Faire, and Stubbings, *The Place of the Audience*, points out, the Broadway Media Centre made a concerted effort in the 1990s to throw off its "elitist" image and project itself as an accessible and diverse place. However, as they note, "the supposed diversity of the cinema's audience is also specifically set up against the supposedly homogenous and undifferentiated nature of mass culture and its audiences" (303).

88. Stacy, *Star Gazing*, 101.

Notes on Contributors

Nathan Abrams teaches modern U.S. history at the University of Southampton. He is coeditor (with Julie Hughes) of *Containing Culture: Cultural Production and Consumption in Fifties America* (Birmingham University Press, 2000) and coauthor, (with Ian Bell and Jan Udris) of *Studying Film* (Arnold, 2001). His forthcoming book is about the rise and fall of neoconservatism.

Raymond Armstrong teaches film studies at Queen's University, Belfast. From 1992 to 2001, he worked as a lecturer in humanities at the University of Ulster, Jordanstown, where he taught literature, drama, and film studies. He is the author of *Kafka and Pinter: Shadow-Boxing* (Macmillan/St. Martin's Press, 1999).

Michael Ashkenazi is TRESA Project Manager at Bonn International Center for Conversion, Germany. He is the coauthor, with Jeanne Jacob, of *The Essence of Japanese Cuisine* (University of Pennsylvania Press, 2000), and author of numerous scholarly publications about Japanese food, religion, and business.

Robin Balthrope is a lawyer who also holds a Ph.D. in American Constitutional History from Ohio State University. An independent scholar, she has taught at California State University–San Bernadino, State University of New York–Plattsburgh, and Indiana University–Purdue University in Indianapolis.

Timothy P. Barnard is currently an assistant professor in the Department of History at the National University of Singapore. His research interests focus on the history of Malay identity and the use of Malay film as a historical resource. His publications include "Vampires, Heroes and Jesters: A History of Cathay Keris," in *The Cathay Story*, ed. Wong Ain-ling (Hong Kong Film Archive, 2002); and *Multiple Centres of Authority: Society and Environment in Siak and Eastern Sumatra* (KITLV, 2003).

335

Anne L. Bower teaches American literature and composition at Ohio State University–Marion. Her scholarship includes editing and writing an introduction for a reprint edition of *The Historical Cookbook of the American Negro* (Beacon Press, 2000); editing and writing an essay for *Recipes for Reading: Community Cookbooks, Stories, Histories* (University of Massachusetts Press, 1997); and authoring *Epistolary Responses: The Letter in Twentieth-Century American Fiction and Criticism* (University of Alabama Press, 1997). She is currently working on an essay collection about African American foodways.

Debnita Chakravarti is a lecturer in English literature in Kolkat (Calcutta). At present she is completing her Ph.D. at the University of Reading; she has structured and taught courses on Indian cinema and Indian writings in English there. She writes for *Scope* (the online refereed film journal of Nottingham University) and has freelanced for a leading English daily, a monthly magazine in India, and various websites, covering women's issues, film, literature, and environmental themes.

Kyri Watson Claflin is a doctoral candidate in Modern European history at Boston University. She is currently finishing her dissertation, titled, "The Fat and the Lean: Food in Paris During Two World Wars."

Carole M. Counihan is professor of Anthropology and former director for women's studies at Millersville University. She is the author of *Around the Tuscan Table: Food, Family, and Gender in Twentieth Century Florence* (Routledge, 2004) and *The Anthropology of Food and Body: Gender, Meaning, and Power* (Routledge, 1999). She is the editor of *Food in the USA: A Reader* (Routledge, 2002), and coeditor, with Penny Van Esterik, of *Food and Culture: A Reader* (Routledge, 1997). She has published many articles and book reviews on food and culture in scholarly journals and encyclopedias and is coeditor of the scholarly journal *Food and Foodways*. Counihan's next project is a book based on the food-centered life histories she has been collecting since 1996 in a Latino community in the San Luis Valley of Colorado.

Margaret Coyle is a doctoral candidate in theater history and criticism at the University of Maryland; her dissertation concerns Carlo Goldoni and the material culture of eighteenth-century Venetian theatre. She is coauthor of the play, *Finally Heard: Heroines of the Uncivil War*.

Blair Davis is a Ph.D. candidate in the Department of Communication Studies at McGill University in Montreal. He was an instructor in film history and aesthetics for the School of Contemporary Arts at Simon Fraser University in 2003, and has an essay entitled "Horror Meets Noir: The Evolution of Cinematic Style, 1931–1958" in the forthcoming anthology *Horror Film: Creating and Marketing Fear*, ed. Steffen Hantke (University of Mississippi Press). He is also the coeditor, with Robert Anderson and Jan Walls, of a forthcoming book on director Akira Kurosawa.

Rebecca L. Epstein is completing her Ph.D. in Critical Studies at the University of California–Los Angeles Department of Film, Television, and Digital Media. Her dissertation focuses on the role of food in Hollywood gangster films. She has published several articles in the academic and popular press on food, fashion, and other topics concerning twentieth-century American popular culture. She currently lives and works in Los Angeles, where she is a writer and editor for *Los Angeles CityBeat*, an alternative weekly.

Laurel Forster is a lecturer in film, literature, and cultural studies at the Arts Institute at Bournemouth, in Dorset, United Kingdom. She is coeditor, with Janet Floyd, of *The Recipe Reader: Narratives-Contexts-Traditions* (Ashgate, 2003), a collection that explores the textual and narrative contexts of recipes.

Ellen J. Fried's writing has appeared in *James Beard House* magazine and the monthly James Beard Foundation calendar. She coauthored, with Dr. Marion Nestle, "The Growing Political Movement against Soft Drinks in Schools," the *Medical Student Journal of the American Medical Association*. An attorney, Fried stays on top of legal issues by teaching food law as an adjunct clinical assistant professor at New York University and as a guest lecturer at culinary schools.

David Greven is assistant professor of English at Connecticut College. His work has appeared in *Genders, Cineaste, Cineaction, Nathaniel Hawthorne Review, American Quarterly*, and elsewhere. Greven is a specialist in issues of gender and sexuality in nineteenth-century American literature, film, and television, and his book, *Men Beyond Desire*, which examines the construction of manhood in the antebellum United States, has been accepted for publication by Palgrave Macmillan.

Yogini Joglekar formerly taught German literature and film at St. Mary's College of Maryland, and is currently Academic Director of the Mountbatten Programme affiliated with the University of Cambridge. She is working on a book-length study of German detective cinema.

Miriam López-Rodríguez teaches in the Department of English at the University of Málaga, Spain. She is part of a research group working on American theater there and was coorganizer (along with Barbara Ozieblo and others) of the International Conference on American Theater held in May 2000 and May 2004. Her doctoral dissertation on Louisa May Alcott was published by the University of Málaga. She recently held a Fulbright Fellowship to study the Sophie Treadwell Papers at the University of Arizona, Tucson, and is currently co-editing (with Jerry Dickey) a selection of Treadwell's writings, to be published soon by Routledge. She is the coeditor, with Barbara Ozieblo, of *Staging a Cultural Paradigm: The Political and the Personal in American Drama* (PIE/ Peter Lang, 2002).

James Lyons is Lecturer in Film at the University of Exeter. His publications include *Selling Seattle: Representing Contemporary Urban America* (WallFlower Press, 2004) and *Quality Popular Television: Cult TV, the Industry and Fans* (BFI, 2003), coedited with Mark Jancovich. He is a founding member of the film journal *Scope*, and associate director of the Bill Douglas Centre for the History of Cinema and Popular Culture at the University of Exeter. He is currently researching product placement in American cinema.

Margaret McFadden teaches women's studies and women's history at Appalachian State University, where she founded the women's studies program in 1976. A specialist in feminist film, food studies, feminist theory, and comparative women's history, she was editor of the *National Women's Studies Association Journal* from 1997 to 2003, and has just completed the special issue, "Gender and Modernism Between the Wars, 1918–1939." She was Distinguished Fulbright Chair of Gender Studies at the Institute of Gender Studies, University of Klagenfurt, Austria, in 2004, and is the author of *Golden Cables of Sympathy: The Transatlantic Sources of Nineteenth-Century Feminism* (University Press of Kentucky, 1999).

Gretchen Papazian was awarded a postdoctoral fellowship at the Georgia Institute of Technology, and has taught at Agnes Scott College and Central Michigan University. Her scholarship focuses primarily on the ways women use food (and other elements and activities traditionally defined as "domestic") as a form of emotional expression. Her life, ideas, ambitions, and possibilities are also shaped by two children (Nicholas and Alice), Milo the dog, and Matthew the life partner.

Eric Reinholtz is an independent scholar who has taught both graduate and undergraduate courses at Florida Atlantic University, State University of New York–Fashion Institute of Technology, and Pace University; he now teaches at the Marlborough School in Los Angeles. In addition to recent publications on the films of Buster Keaton (*Interdisciplinary Humanities* and *Paradoxa*), his research has also examined the works of Rubén Darío and Federico García Lorca in the context of Spanish modernism (*Monographic Review*, *HiperFeira*, and *Journal of the Association for Interdisciplinary Study in the Arts*).

Marlisa Santos is an assistant professor in the Division of Humanities in the Farquhar College of Arts and Sciences at Nova Southeastern University in Fort Lauderdale, Florida. She also serves as assistant director of the Division and teaches writing, literature, film, and humanities courses. Her main areas of interest include film noir, mythology and fairy tale, Romanticism, and creative writing. She has published poems and creative nonfiction in such places as *Poetry Forum* and *Marjorie Kinnan Rawlings Journal of Florida Literature*, and has presented numerous conference papers on film, German and English Romanticism, and composition pedagogy.

Index

Index of authors, directors, film titles, and selected concepts